THE DIARY AND JOURNAL OF
RICHARD CLOUGH ANDERSON, *Jr.*

THE DIARY AND JOURNAL OF
RICHARD CLOUGH ANDERSON, *Jr*.

1814-1826

Edited by

ALFRED TISCHENDORF

Department of History

Duke University

and

E. TAYLOR PARKS

Historical Office

Department of State

DUKE UNIVERSITY PRESS

Durham, North Carolina

1964

PREFACE

Richard Clough Anderson, Jr., was a Kentucky legislator, member of the United States House of Representatives, first Minister of the United States formally received by an independent Latin American state, delegate-designate to the ill-fated Panama Congress of 1826, and author of a published article on the Constitution of Colombia. Anderson did not give a title to the writings included in this volume. The title adopted by the editors represents a composite of two headings used by members of his family—"The Diary of Richard C. Anderson, Jr., 1814-1825,"[1] placed on the backing of the bound volume that contains Anderson's work—and "The Diary and Journal of Hon. Richard Clough Anderson, junr.," which was written above the diarist's first entry in another hand.

Anderson kept his diary and journal on sheets of paper that varied in size from 6¾" x 8" to 3¾" x 6". After his death the section of the diary that he wrote while in Colombia was brought back to the United States, joined with the Kentucky portion of the diary, and bound, probably by his brother, Robert Anderson, in a light brown leather volume 12½" x 11½" x 4". The title was then placed on the back strip in gold design. The volume contained blank sheets of heavy paper, the centers of which were cut out and the pages of the diary and journal inserted to fit the openings. They were then secured in place by strips of glued paper, allowing the reader to see both sides of the page.

On May 17, 1814, at the age of twenty-six, Richard C. Anderson made his first entry in a journal that was kept until two weeks before his death in Cartagena, Colombia, on July 24, 1826. Anderson was not, however, a consistently industrious penman. His sixty-two entries in 1814 seldom contained more than fifty

---

1. The editors have used the date 1826 since Anderson's entries continue to July of that year. The date 1825 on the leather volume suggests that only that portion of Anderson's diary from 1814 to 1825 was originally placed in the book. The last portion of his diary is in an envelope at the back of the volume.

words each, but in 1815, when he made 141 entries, Anderson sometimes wrote more than one hundred words on a single day. In May of that year he wrote in his diary on all but one day, a record he never equaled in any month during the remainder of his life. Anderson faltered in 1816, made more than one hundred entries in 1817, and neglected his diary almost entirely between 1818 and 1822, managing to make only thirty-two entries during this five-year period. The result of this spasmodic neglect was that in 1822 his journal contained only about one-third of the total words that were recorded by the time of his death in 1826.

On April 5, 1823, when Anderson was notified of his appointment as Minister to Colombia, he sealed his diary after making an entry which asked that it be delivered to his son if he never returned from South America. He apparently left this portion of the diary with a relative in Kentucky and began his account of the Colombian phase of his career on June 15, 1823.

Although Anderson managed to make a few notes and comments during the remainder of 1823, it was not until 1824 that he began to write at length about his official duties and his private life as a diplomat in Colombia, and, even then, he was not a tireless scribe. Many days passed with no entries being made, followed by attempts to catch up with the activities that he had failed to record. It is only fair to note, however, that Anderson was improving as a diarist during the months just prior to his death. From January 1 to July 12, 1826, he made 127 entries, almost as many as were written during 1815, his most prolific year.

The sporadic quality of Anderson's writing requires explanation. He realized that he was not a consistent penman and occasionally chided himself for his lack of literary regularity. As early as April 12, 1815, he left sections blank in the journal with the promise that he would return to his desk and discuss the previous winter. He never did. In September, 1816, he expressed his intention to resume regular writing in the diary, but a few months later he was lamenting his procrastination. On September 12, 1817, he asked himself why his diary was comparatively barren. "I know not the reason. Things pass from my memory before I can record them." He never again approached the question directly, but the editors have reached certain conclusions regarding the problem.

Anderson at times was simply lazy. It is interesting to discover, however, that many of the gaps in the diary came when his financial problems were most pressing, when he or his family were suffering from the many illnesses that seemed to have plagued them, when he was engaged in long and arduous trips, or during long family reunions.

Anderson's failure to write steadily in his diary has not been as frustrating to the editors as one might imagine. Some of his best and most informative writing came when he brought together recollections of recent events under a single entry. It appears, in fact, that he sometimes enjoyed keeping the journal in this fashion and that this method was probably suited to his personality.

The editors decided to print the diary and journal as written by Richard C. Anderson, Jr., including an introduction covering the early years of his life, and some recollections—evidently based on notes taken by him each year—of Fourths of July from 1805 to 1822. Portions of the diary did not seem particularly illuminating to the editors, but they felt it was presumptuous to delete any material that might be of interest to professional or amateur historians. However, some routine remarks about the weather—fair, rainy, etc.—were omitted. Even here longer comments such as those on the late frost in Louisville were retained. The editors believe that judgments by readers regarding the character and personality of the Kentuckian should be based on an examination of the entire journal.

Certain letters from Anderson to members of his family, the official letter of Instruction sent him by Secretary of State John Quincy Adams as he set forth for Colombia, and a report by Consul Macpherson on Anderson's death are inserted in their proper chronological places. The Appendix contains (1) a copy of the first treaty negotiated by Anderson in 1824 and (2) a list of names with identifications of persons mentioned in the diary.

The editors have been careful, of course, to alert the reader at the points where the inserted materials appear. The few marginal comments in the journal made by Anderson's family and some of his descendants have not been included in this volume. Almost without exception they are merely condensations of Anderson's own words.

The editors have reproduced the diary as accurately as Richard C. Anderson's handwriting would allow. They have also attempted, using the standards established by some of the excellent editors of this century, to make the volume as readable as possible.

Anderson had considerable family pride. He wished to leave some of his thoughts and descriptions of the world in which he lived to his family. He was also anxious to advise his son, Arthur, to avoid some of the mistakes he had made. Although Anderson was aware that he had a position of some importance in the early history of the United States, there is no evidence that he contemplated the diary's later publication. This fact may help to explain the rather haphazard fashion in which it was sometimes kept. The dashes used to end most of Anderson's sentences have been changed to periods in the interest of fluent reading, and whenever necessary, capital letters have been placed at the beginning of sentences for the same reason. In other instances the editors have followed Anderson's form of capitalization. Dashes or solid lines used by Anderson to separate his entries have been omitted, but the editors have been careful never to omit his underlining of words in the text. His abbreviations have usually been retained when they were simple words, but the missing letters have been supplied in brackets when their omission seemed likely to make the reading of the diary more difficult. Brackets have also been used in sections where Anderson's writing is illegible.

The editors have attempted in most cases to supply what seemed to them to be Anderson's intention in the sentence, but at all times the reader may decide for himself whether or not he approves of the editors' interpretation. His spelling errors are usually allowed to stand uncorrected, but in cases where readers might be misled by the misspelling of places or names, the correct letters are given in brackets. Anderson employed various methods to introduce the entries in his diary, including the annoying one of inserting only the dates for periods of many weeks or even months. The editors have decided to give the month, date, and year for each entry throughout the diary, a technique which, in fact, Anderson used at various times in the original.

The principle followed by the editors in preparing this diary for publication was to identify every person or place mentioned in the document and explain events and situations that are not generally known. Although comments on prominent men may seem superfluous to many readers, the editors felt that the line between prominence and obscurity was somewhat thin in certain cases, and ended by including presidents, generals,

liberators, and famous congressmen and senators in their explanatory notes. The first names of persons mentioned by the
author have been given in brackets, but to avoid needless repeti-
tion when the name appears regularly in the diary this practice
is discontinued for a number of pages and then repeated only
sporadically as a reminder to the reader.

Certain modifications in the original plan have nevertheless
been made. The Anderson family has been discussed in the
Introduction, and, accordingly, the remarks later used to identify
these persons are short. The editors have also found it necessary
to omit from their identifications names of persons who are so
obscure that they have disappeared from written record. Details
of certain legal cases handled by Anderson in his capacity as
a lawyer have likewise been omitted from the volume. There is,
unfortunately, a lack of information concerning many of the
places that Anderson stayed overnight on his travels in Kentucky
and from Louisville to Washington during his terms in Congress.
Anderson apparently bypassed most of the famous taverns and
inns of the time and instead took bed and breakfast at the
homes of acquaintances or with people recommended to him by
some of his Kentucky friends. Footnotes at the bottom of each
page contain information on the events and places that need
explanation or identification. Cross references will, when necessary, guide the reader back to the original note. An asterisk
has been placed beside each name to be identified and these
names have been placed in alphabetical order at the end of the
volume.

Many debts have been incurred in the editing of this diary.
Permission to film the diary and journal was given to the
Library of Congress by Mrs. Edward L. Hicks, Jr., of Winnetka,
Illinois. Mrs. Hicks and her son, Edward L. Hicks III, of
Greenwich, Connecticut, the present owner of the diary and a
great-great-grandson of Richard C. Anderson, courteously and
carefully answered many questions concerning the diary and its
author. Mrs. Dorothy Thomas Cullen, the Curator of the Filson
Club Library in Louisville, Kentucky, helped to identify many
of the names in the diary and also directed the editors to the
Anderson home, Soldiers' Retreat, outside Louisville on Hurst-
bourne Lane. The staff of the Library of Congress, especially
those in the Genealogical Room, deserve the special thanks of
the editors for their help. Mr. Charles Gauld of the Inter-Amer-
ican University in San Germán, Puerto Rico, and Mrs. Anita

Strother of Louisville, Kentucky, descendants of Richard C. Anderson, helped to clear up many points about the life and family of their kinsman. Mr. Alexander Anderson of Sarasota, Florida, and Bumpass, Virginia, not only supplied the silhouette of Richard C. Anderson, but also provided information concerning the career of the notable Kentuckian.

During the final stage of the preparation of the manuscript for the press, Dr. Tischendorf died in Buenos Aires, Argentina. As his collaborator, I am deeply appreciative of his tireless energy and scholarly efforts expended in editorial work on the diary and in the identification of Richard C. Anderson's family, friends, colleagues, and acquaintances mentioned in it.

Arlington, Virginia   E. T. Parks

CONTENTS

MAPS

ILLUSTRATIONS

The silhouette of Richard Clough Anderson, Jr., which appears as a frontispiece is reproduced through the courtesy of Mr. Alexander F. Anderson.

The manuscript diary pages preceding the first text page of the present edition and facing page 166 are reproduced through the courtesy of Mr. Edward L. Hicks III.

INTRODUCTION

On August 4, 1788, Colonel Richard Clough Anderson, late of the Continental Line and one of Louisville, Kentucky's prominent citizens, announced the birth of a son, Richard Clough, Junior. This infant, doomed to die at the age of 38, was for a time the latest addition to a family whose history in America dated back to the seventeenth century.

The Colonel's grandfather, Robert Anderson, was born in 1644 in New Kent County, Virginia, shortly after the Andersons arrived from England.[1] He married, took up a land grant, became a vestryman at St. Peters' Church, and left two sons when he died in 1718. The oldest, Robert (1712-1792), later moved with his wife to a farm at Gold Mine in Hanover County, Virginia, where Richard Clough Anderson, the father of Richard Clough, Junior, was born on January 12, 1750.

The elder Richard left home at the age of 16 and went to work in a counting house belonging to Patrick Coots in Richmond.[2] Impressed with Anderson's abilities, Coots soon appointed him as supercargo on one of the company ships that made frequent voyages to Martinique, Barbados, and England. Their association was terminated by a heated argument concerning the relations of Great Britain and her colonies, and by

---

1. There is a division of opinion in the family as to whether the Andersons are of English or Scottish descent. Thomas M. Anderson, *A Monograph of the Anderson, Clark, Marshall, and McArthur Connection* (no place or date of publication.), p. 5, believes that Anderson lived on both sides of the Tweed River. This author notes that the name Anderson is Scandinavian and that the family's remote ancestors "came with the Danes, who, for a time, held the Eastern coasts of Scotland and England from Pentland Firth to the Humber." Readers interested in the Anderson genealogy should consult the volume above and W. P. Anderson, *Anderson Family Records* (Cincinnati, 1936).

2. The editors have examined the papers of Richard C. Anderson, Sr., at the Filson Club in Louisville, as well as the material contained in Rogers' Index at the same club. Most of Colonel Anderson's papers, containing material outside the scope of this volume, are at the University of Illinois. His life is also examined in Kitty Anderson's unpublished manuscript "A Historical House and Its Famous People," presented to the editors by Alexander F. Anderson.

the Revolutionary War in which Anderson rose from the rank of Captain to Lieutenant Colonel and served with distinction at Brandywine, Germantown, Monmouth, Savannah—where he was wounded—Charleston—where he was captured and then exchanged after nine months—and at the battle of Yorktown.

At the end of the war Colonel Anderson's military record, his association with important Revolutionary leaders, and his membership in the exclusive secret Society of Cincinnati, led to his appointment in 1783 as Surveyor of the Virginia Land District in Louisville, a job that entailed dividing the land reserved by Virginia in the West for Continental troops.[3]

The frontier community of Louisville bore little resemblance to hilly Richmond; it was, in fact, nothing more than a village of four or five hundred people in the early 1780's. Its population multiplied slowly, but changes in the town came swiftly in the last years of the eighteenth century. In 1782 a flatboat made an unprecedented voyage to New Orleans with furs, flour, salt, cordage, and medicinal herbs destined for the lower Mississippi Valley and Europe. Tailor shops, a blacksmith, and a carpenter's hut appeared on Main Street, and the owners attempted to work out a currency system in a town where coins from England, France, Spain, Holland, Arabia, and Austria competed with tobacco as a medium of exchange. In 1787 Louisville's first newspaper, the *Kentucky Gazette,* was founded; in 1788 the first brick house was built; and a year later the first church was erected. Work soon began on the Louisville-Bardstown and Louisville-Lexington roads, and, in 1800, a year marked by the appearance of the town's first bank, an ocean-going sailship came up the Mississippi for the first time and docked at the port.

Colonel Anderson's interests extended beyond his office in Louisville to the buying of land in the downtown district and to the building of a schooner, the *Caroline,* that was wrecked in the Bahama Islands after only one trip from New Orleans to Europe. He became the first president of the Lexington Lodge, the oldest organization of its kind west of the Alleghenies, at-

---

3. During the American Revolution the Continental Congress passed a military bounty land act to encourage the development of a regular army. Land warrants payable at the end of the war were given to those who enlisted. Privates could receive 100 acres and Major-Generals, for example, 1,100 acres. Virginia planned to meet her obligations by using the Kentucky country. She had not, however, made a systematic survey of the area when Anderson went to Louisville.

tended a convention in Danville that heralded the beginning of Kentucky's struggle for autonomy which ended with her admission to the union in 1792, and served as a presidential elector in 1792.

In August, 1787, Anderson had married Elizabeth Clark, daughter of John and Ann Clark, and the sister of the famed Indian fighter, George Rogers Clark, and moved to a home near the present corner of Chestnut and Clay streets. Two years later the Andersons and their year-old son, Richard Jr., left Louisville for a home ten miles east of the growing town on Beargrass Creek. Soldiers' Retreat, where Richard Jr. spent most of the next decade, lay at the end of a broad avenue, bordered by oak trees, that led from the highway to the farm.[4] The overseers' office and the servants' quarters—Colonel Anderson at one time owned twenty slaves—were to the rear of the main dwelling and formed a court around the garden above the spring house. The Colonel was a genial host and to Soldiers' Retreat eventually came such celebrities as Henry Clay, Andrew Jackson, Aaron Burr, James Monroe (a wartime friend of the Colonel), and George Rogers Clark, by then an embittered man living with his sister, Mrs. William Croghan. To this country home also came George Croghan, later the hero of Sandusky in the War of 1812, and Zachary Taylor, four years older than Richard Clough, Jr., to play with the Anderson children.

Young Anderson's education began at Soldiers' Retreat when his father hired a tutor to instruct him and his sisters. In 1800 he was sent to Albemarle and King William, Virginia, to private school, and later he went to Williamsburg where he entered William and Mary College in 1802. After graduating in a class that included Winfield Scott, he returned to Kentucky in 1806 to spend almost a year at Frankfort preparing for the law. He concluded his legal training at William and Mary in 1809. A year later he married Elizabeth Gwathmey of Louisville, and, somewhat reluctantly since his profession did not provide him with enough money to speculate in land, began the practice of law.

---

4. The farm is now part of the Highbaugh Farms on the Louisville-Shelbyville road. Portions of the original buildings and the family graveyard where Richard C. Anderson, Jr., and his father are buried, can still be seen at the farm. Only the writing on Colonel Anderson's twenty-foot-high monument is still visible. Librarians at the Filson Club will provide directions for those wishing to visit the farm.

From 1812 to 1823 Richard C. Anderson participated in the political life of his state and the nation, serving in the Kentucky House of Representatives during the 1812-1813, 1814-1815, and 1815-1816 sessions, as a Representative in the Fifteenth and Sixteenth Congresses of the United States, and again as a member of the Kentucky legislature in 1821-1822, serving as speaker of the lower house in 1822-1823.

Kentucky Republicanism was at floodtide during these years. In 1800, angered by the Jay Treaty, the excise tax on distilled spirits, and the Alien and Sedition Acts, and hopeful that Thomas Jefferson would permanently remove the barrier to western commerce on the Mississippi River, Kentucky voters had elected a Republican[5] governor and supported Jefferson and Burr in the national election. In 1804 another Republican governor had been sent to Frankfort, but in the middle of his term many of Kentucky's leaders were accused of complicity in Aaron Burr's western conspiracy, an accusation largely responsible for the election of a Federalist as governor in 1808. But from then until 1824 there was actually no two-party rivalry in Kentucky. The candidates for office were all Republicans and the various campaigns, at least until the passage of the so-called relief laws in the early 1820's, centered on personalities rather than real issues. Although Anderson was a Republican, his father was a Federalist, and that caused Richard Jr. some embarrassment during at least one election.

By 1821-1823 Anderson's enthusiasm for the law, lukewarm at best, and for his seat in the Kentucky legislature, was completely overshadowed by the hope that he would be given some sort of political appointment by President James Monroe. The diary explains why Anderson wanted the appointment but it does not explain why the diarist, who had no previous record of interest in South America, was chosen minister to *La Gran Colombia,* the name given to Simón Bolívar's short-lived union of Ecuador, Venezuela, and New Granada (Colombia) in the 1820's. Anderson family legend suggests that he was shunted off to Colombia because Henry Clay feared Anderson's political ambitions and wanted him out of the country, but the Clay papers and other available documents reveal no such sinister

---

5. The Republican party of 1800 was the forerunner of the National-Republican and Democratic-Republican groups or factions. The latter became the Democratic party under President Jackson.

intrigue.[6] During Monroe's search for men to send to various Latin American posts, he informed John Quincy Adams that loyalty to the administration would be considered in making the appointments, and that he wished "to distribute them to citizens of different parts of the union." In discussing the appointment to Mexico, Monroe further indicated that his concept of an ideal minister was a man of "respectable talents, handsome person, polished manners, and elegant deportment." Anderson fulfilled these requirements, and, furthermore, the Andersons and the President were good friends. It is also possible that Secretary of State Adams, who in 1825 referred in his diary to the "old and uninterrupted confidential relationship between him [Anderson] and myself," was instrumental in obtaining the appointment.[7]

On April 5, 1823, just before leaving for Colombia, Anderson sat in the home of a Louisville friend and closed a section of his diary. Although he wrote of what his fate might have been under different circumstances, he seemed rather confident that he was acting prudently in going to Colombia, hopeful of the future, and yet apprehensive of what was to come in a country of whose language, history, or conditions he knew little.

Anderson sailed with his family and servants for La Guayra on June 17, 1823. Three weeks later the ship arrived at the port, and after a short delay, the Anderson party began an overland trip that brought them to Bogotá in December, 1823. Colombia then stretched from beyond Guayaquil in the west to Guiana, south of the Orinoco River in the east, an area that embraced more than one million square miles. It was a nation of geographical contrasts—grassy plains, great forests, impenetrable swamps, and jungles—and a stifling climate, except in the higher altitudes, that too often bred insects, disease, and death. The two to three million inhabitants of this land included the whites, who made up less than one-fourth of the total and who lived in the larger settlements; more than 100,000 Negro slaves, most of them living in the coastal area but also in the Cauca Valley, the mining centers, and the great plains; and the

---

6. James P. Hopkins, University of Kentucky, to Professor Charles A. Gauld, Dec. 31, 1955.
7. For a discussion of the events leading to the appointment of ministers to Latin America see Charles Francis Adams (ed.), *Memoirs of John Quincy Adams Comprising Portions of His Diary from 1795 to 1848* (Philadelphia, 1875), VI, 111, 121-123. See also VII, 17-19, for an account of Adams' conversation with Anderson.

Indians, mestizos, mulattoes, and free Africans who made up the bulk of the population. With Bogotá as the capital, *La Gran Colombia* was divided into twelve departments and thirty provinces governed by a fundamental law that proclaimed all the freedoms except that of religious cults. Dominated by the figure of General Simón Bolívar, the most versatile of the warrior-politicians who directed the new nation in the 1820's, the country was already feeling the results of the Liberator's erratic rule and his preoccupation with other regions when Anderson presented his credentials in Bogotá.

The Kentuckian remained in Colombia as minister for more than two and one-half years, returning once to the United States for a short visit in 1825 after the death of his wife. During this visit Anderson was informed by President John Quincy Adams that he was the chief executive's choice to represent the United States at the Panama Congress which was to meet the following year. The President's friendship with Anderson, the minister's experience in Colombia, and the proximity of the Bogotá post to Panama, made him a natural choice for the job. Anderson accepted and explained his decision in his diary on February 28, 1826. Adams later decided to send another delegate with Anderson. The message nominating Anderson and John Sergeant of Philadelphia for the Panama meeting was delivered to Congress on December 26, 1825.[8] But Anderson had left on the return trip to his Colombian post before Adams transmitted this recommendation and arrived there in January, 1826, to wait impatiently for word that his nomination had been confirmed by the Senate.

The debates on the Panama Congress are not important here except as they relate to Richard C. Anderson. It is, of course, possible that some of the senators privately objected to Anderson for reasons of a personal nature or on the grounds that he did not have the requisite qualifications for the job. Perhaps Edward Thornton Tayloe, the private secretary to the United States Minister in Mexico, expressed the opinion of some when he wrote:

> Talents they [Anderson and Sergeant] undoubtedly possess, and enjoy merited reputation; but to conduct themselves at Panama, as representatives of the head of

---

8. James D. Richardson, *A Compilation of the Messages and Papers of the Presidents, 1789-1897* (Washington, D. C., 1896), II, 318-320.

the American System, requires a knowledge of that language which alone will be the medium of intercourse, the Spanish—a perfect knowledge of the character, the feelings, the views of those who represent the new American Republics —and that deportment, that high reputation, that sincere interest for the welfare of all America which can conciliate a clashing interest—which can dispel jealousies, and which can suggest opinions, whose honesty must be undoubted. I apprehend that as neither of those nominated is so gifted, that their influence will be weakly felt—the United States will acquire no additional importance as it might in fit hands—in fact, that the country will be disappointed in the Mission—"[9]

These sentiments are not, however, echoed in the Senate documents, nor do they explain why the debates dragged on through January, February, and part of March, or why the vote confirming Anderson as Envoy Extraordinary and Minister Plenipotentiary to the Panama Congress was 27 to 17.

The United States, reported the *National Journal* of Washington, was expected to take part at Panama in discussions relating to the frustration of any European plans to return the colonies to Spanish rule, the establishment of principles of maritime law governing neutrals and belligerents, the recognition of Haiti, and the abolition of the African slave trade. President Adams explained the role of the United States in somewhat different and more general terms, but the report of the *National Journal* was an accurate description of the agenda as it was understood by the Latin American nations that were to be represented at Panama.

The opposition to the mission centered around the opportunity it afforded for the coalescing Calhoun and Jackson factions to launch an attack on the Adams administration. The debate also contained overtones of the North-South struggle over slavery, and was further complicated by the hesitancy of many senators to involve the United States in what they believed to be a dangerous entangling alliance.[10] Senator Robert Hayne

---

9. C. Harvey Gardiner (ed.), *Mexico, 1825-1828: The Journal and Correspondence of Edward Thornton Tayloe* (Chapel Hill, 1959), pp. 118-119.
10. The debates are summarized in Samuel Flagg Bemis, *John Quincy Adams and the Foundations of American Foreign Policy* (New York, 1949), pp. 552-555; see also *The Register of Debates in Congress*, 1825-1826 (Washington, D.C., 1826), II, Pt. I, 147-343, particularly 151, 166, 177, 183-218, 295-298, 306-307, and 332.

of South Carolina, who voted "no" on Anderson's appointment, praised the minister to Colombia as an "honest and respectable man," but balked at United States participation in discussions that might lead to our recognition of Haiti, a country governed by Negroes. He also agreed with Senator Hugh White of Tennessee, who argued that the discussion of slave problems in other countries would unnecessarily disturb the United States. Thomas Hart Benton of Missouri, the only senator who split his vote— "yes" for Anderson and "no" for Sergeant—objected to the nominee from Pennsylvania because he had spoken against the admission of Missouri as a slave state. Benton said he had been informed that Anderson was going to Panama to plead the cause of the slaveholders. Why send Sergeant, a man who would hinder rather than help the envoy from Kentucky?

The nominations were confirmed on March 14, 1826. Anderson and Sergeant were ordered to proceed to Porto Bello where they would meet and go together to Panama. Sergeant correctly appraised the dangers of going to Panama in the sickly tropical season and tendered his resignation, a wise decision writes Samuel Flagg Bemis, "if he valued his life more than service to his country."[11] Anderson left Bogotá for Cartagena on June 12, 1826, and after an arduous journey arrived at Turbaco, a jungle village near Cartagena, where he was advised to stay away from the fever-ridden port. But Anderson's final entry on July 12, 1826, found him planning to go on toward Panama. Shortly thereafter an obituary notice appeared in *El Cometa Mercantile* of Cartagena:

> Died at this place, on July 25 [24], 1826, the Honorable R. C. Anderson, Jr., Minister Plenipotentiary from the United States to our Government. A violent fever arrested his career in life, and Death consigned his remains to dissolution. The ground that contains the ashes of our fathers is also intrusted with his. Thither they were followed by his brothers [Larz and Robert], his friends, and our entire people, spontaneously evincing their respect. We hope that a monument will be erected to remind the generations as they pass that slumbering there were the ashes of him who was the first link of political union between Colombia and the Republic of the North.[12]

11. Bemis, *op. cit.*, p. 557.
12. Quoted in Thomas M. Anderson, *op. cit.*, pp. 11-12. Anderson's body was later returned to the United States for burial at Soldiers' Retreat. In late 1826 the Panama Congress adjourned to meet later at Tacubaya,

Certain aspects of Anderson's diary are worthy of comment. The final days of his life have the quality of classic tragedy which, in fact, pervades much of the diary, affording a sometimes poignant view of a man whose journey to Colombia in 1832 was, for example, undertaken mainly to relieve his family from the debts that he had incurred in Kentucky. The diary is often a very personal document. In those sections where Anderson lectures his son on future conduct, discusses the attributes of a gentleman and the qualities of a wife, comments on the vanities of human nature, grapples with the problems of educating his daughter, searches for remedies to check the illnesses he did not understand, reflects on what he considers to be the good life, feels the inadequacy of his preparation in languages, or injects touches of humor—in all these and other passages the reader is given an intimate glimpse of a serious and conscientious man.

The diary also illumines the political, social, and economic history of Kentucky and especially of Louisville from 1814 to 1826. The names of some of Kentucky's foremost families— Breckenridge, Bullitt, Churchill, Clark, Clay, Crittenden, Madison, Rowan, and Slaughter—appear frequently as Anderson discusses the candidates, issues, and campaign tactics in various state elections. Although he had political ambition, Anderson generally viewed his career in politics with the eye of a man who participated in that activity because he was expected to by reason of birth and position. He maintained that the political arena was governed by a code of ethics. His criticism of those who deviated from his standard extended even to the office of the President. Although Anderson was suspicious of most politicians, he had little more confidence in the "sovereign people," whose right to vote he did not openly question, but of whose ability to vote sensibly he had serious doubt. To curry favor with the masses in order to hold a seat was unthinkable.

Anderson's honesty and rigorous standard of conduct extended to his practice of the law, a profession he found economically necessary but generally uninteresting. His speeches in Congress bear the stamp of his training at William and Mary

Mexico. New arrangements were made in Washington for sending delegates to the congress, but since the meetings never took place at Tacubaya, President Adams "sang a graceful requiem over the lost project." See E. Taylor Parks, *Colombia and the United States, 1765-1934* (Durham, N. C., 1935), p. 143.

College. Of more interest to modern readers, however, is a suggestion of the variety of tasks that were performed by a Kentucky attorney in the early 1800's.

It is not difficult to discover the major theme that permeates
the Kentucky portion of Anderson's diary. He lived at a time
when health problems, the development of highway and steamboat traffic, and Negro slavery—toward which he showed an
ambivalent attitude—constituted important facets of American
life. He found time to comment on these and likewise on national developments, such as the National Bank, when they
affected his fortunes or those of Kentucky. But his primary concern with the speculative mania (marketing he called it),
a prime factor in Kentucky history during his lifetime, is
obvious. In the diary is recorded something of the scope of
these speculative operations, of the opportunities for profit,
and of the risks inherent in such activities. Anderson's interest
in speculation reveals him in a variety of moods. Although he
was critical of friends who became a burden on their families
through unwise investments, he never questioned his duty as
a son to rescue his father from financial ruin brought on by
speculative maneuvers. His own dealings brought him deep
mental anguish and an admonition to his son, Arthur, to avoid
the pitfalls; but Anderson could seldom resist the lure of a
promising speculation and would have become involved in
Colombian finances had money been available. He viewed such
financial ventures as the normal occupation of a man who had
money and who wished to have more, and his optimism and
belief in the advantages of speculation never left him.

Readers concerned mainly with national affairs will find the
diary informative and interesting. Legislative procedures are
described through the eyes of a young representative, but his
best entries are those which chronicle the customs, behavior,
and qualities of the congressmen who lived with him at Dowson's
in Washington, or those which consist of comments on men such
as Henry Clay, whom he viewed with a mixture of respect and
distrust, William Henry Harrison, whom he heartily disliked,
John Adams, whom he saw once in Massachusetts, and John
Quincy Adams, John C. Calhoun, William Harris Crawford,
James Monroe, Timothy Pickering, and a number of other less
important figures in national political life.

Anderson made the transition from Kentucky to life in Washington with little difficulty, but much of what he wrote while in

Colombia was clearly the work of a man out of his element, a man whose existence was colored by personal tragedy and by situations that he found alien to his background. The diary also shows that Anderson did not feel he had enough to do in his official capacity in Colombia. Once the task of preparing treaties and adjusting old claims was completed—and even before these duties were accomplished—he missed the comforts of his home in Kentucky and his association with persons whose interests, education, and language were similar to his own. Anderson usually attempted to appraise sympathetically the experiences he was having in Colombia, tried to study Spanish, learned to tolerate many of the things that at first nearly drove him to distraction, and even came to appreciate what he called the sagacity of the Colombian people. He admitted at one point, however, that a trip to the United States would be "a return to the world."

Anderson's descriptions of Colombia and the journeys he took while in that country often repeat the work of other men who published volumes describing their adventures there. But the Kentuckian sometimes mentions places that they did not visit, gives a more personal and subjective account, and at times—as in the case of his trip on the Magdalena River in December and January, 1825-1826—reaches a vividness and grandeur in description that was not attained by any of the others.[13]

The diary also reminds readers of the Anglo-American rivalry in South America during the 1820's as Anderson vents his anglophobia on the British commissioners and the consul general who were in Bogotá to seek commercial and political preferment for their country. His comments are not, however, limited to the Britons in Colombia. Members of the United States consular staff, travelers and merchants in the Republic, and Colombian officials and social leaders were frequent companions of the envoy and his impressions of them are recorded in the diary.

Anderson never met Simón Bolívar, but his comments on the Liberator's character, his position in history, and the comparisons of Bolívar with Washington, Wellington, and Napoleon,

---

13. The reference is to books such as Charles Stuart Cochrane, *Journal of a Residence and Travels in Colombia During the Years 1823 and 1824* (2 vols.; London, 1825); William Duane, *A Visit to Colombia in the Years 1822 and 1823* (Philadelphia, 1826); J. P. Hamilton, *Travels Through the Interior Provinces of Colombia* (2 vols.; London, 1827); and R. Bache, *Notes on Colombia Taken in the Years 1822-23* (Philadelphia, 1827).

illustrate another facet of Anderson's life. The intellectual interests of the first United States minister to Latin America and
his familiarity with works of literature and history are impressive.
Swift, Plutarch, Sully, Middleton's *Cicero,* Las Cases' *Le Mémorial de Sainte Hélène,* and other authors and works are clearly
mentioned by a man not attempting to impress his readers, but
using them to explain or to enlighten further some situation
encountered by the diarist.

So much for the man and his diary. It remains only to
identify his family and other relatives. Colonel Anderson and
his first wife, Elizabeth Clark, had three children in addition to
Richard Clough, Jr. These included Ann (1790-1863), who
married John Logan; Cecilia (1792-1863), who never married;
and Elizabeth (1794-1870), who appears in the diary as Mrs.
Isaac Gwathmey. In 1795 Anderson's mother died and in 1797
his father married Sarah Marshall (1779-1954), second cousin of
Chief Justice John Marshall. She gave birth to twelve children,
but only two of them have important places in the diary. These
were Larz Anderson (April 9, 1803-February 27, 1878) who
graduated from Harvard, went to Colombia while Richard Jr.
was minister, and later was twice married, the second time to
Catherine Longworth of Cincinnati; and Robert Anderson
(June 14, 1805-October 25, 1871), who graduated from West
Point in 1825, informed Secretary of State Henry Clay of his
brother's death in Cartagena, served with Winfield Scott in the
Mexican War, and was in command of Fort Sumter when the
Civil War began.[14]

Richard Anderson's wife, Elizabeth Gwathmey, was the
daughter of Owen and Ann Clark Gwathmey, who came to
Kentucky soon after the close of the American Revolution.
She was also Anderson's first cousin since both Owen Gwathmey
and Colonel Richard Anderson married Clark sisters. Richard
Clough and Elizabeth had eight children. Three (Arthur, Annita
Nancy and Elizabeth) survived their father and lived with the
Gwathmey family after 1826. The present owner of the diary,
Edward Hicks III, is a descendant of Elizabeth, the oldest
daughter, and her husband, Lafayette Flournoy.

The close relationship existing between the Anderson and

---

14. Letters written by Sarah Marshall Anderson and Larz Anderson
may be viewed in the Anderson Papers, Filson Club, Louisville. The
papers of Robert Anderson, which include letters from Colombia in 1825
and 1826, are in the Library of Congress.

Gwathmey families, and the continual appearance of the Gwathmey clan in the diary, requires that some attention be given to
that family's genealogy. Richard Anderson's wife, Elizabeth, was
one of the twelve children of Owen and Ann Clark Gwathmey,
most of them mentioned in the diary, although seldom more
than once. The oldest was John, who built Gwathmey's Indian
Queen Hotel in Louisville, helped to draw plans for the first
courthouse in that city, and died in New Orleans in 1824. The
others were Isaac R., who married Anderson's sister, Elizabeth
or Betsy; Temple, whose son Brooke is also mentioned in
the diary; Ann, who became the wife of Mr. William Boothe
and died in childbirth; Samuel, who married Mary Boothe in
1807; George, who married Sophia Garard in 1814; Lucy (Mrs,
Peter Priest) ; Frances (Mrs. Paul Skidmore) ; and Catherine or
Kitty, who became the wife of George Woolfolk in 1817. Diana
Moore, the oldest daughter, married Thomas Bullitt of the
Louisville Bullitts of Oxmoor farm; and it was their son,
Ferdinand, who died in Colombia while serving as Anderson's
private secretary. A daughter, Eloise, accompanied Anderson's
daughter Elizabeth to school near Bardstown, Kentucky, in
1825. A detailed genealogy of the Bullitt family is, however,
outside the scope of this volume.

THE DIARY AND JOURNAL OF
RICHARD CLOUGH ANDERSON, *Jr.*

The writing of this, occupies pleasantly
notwithstanding you may think it foolish,
point of an evening—I should have thanked
my father even for such a scrawl of his
life as this I would have forgiven the
Egotism—

  I was born on the 4th August 1788
in the Stone house back of lot No. 1 in Louis
-ville, which was built by my father & is
now owned by Cuthbert Bullitt—My
father moved to his present situation in Beargrass
a year or two after my birth—The recollec
tion of incidents which occurred before my
fifth year is too slight to enable me to
state their time or manner with correctness
& I remember that I was with my F &
Mother at Doctor Warfields (the place
now owned by Miss Dickenson) and to
a question from Mrs W. to my mother, she
replied that I would be 6 years old

PART I: THE EARLY YEARS[1]

The writing of this, occupies pleasantly [,] notwithstanding you may think foolishly, part of an Evening.[2] I should have thanked my father even for such a scrawl of his life as this & would have forgiven the Egotism.

I was born on the 4th August 1788 in the Stone house back of lot No. 1 in Louisville,[3] which was built by my father & is now owned by Cuthbert Bullitt.* My father moved to his present situation on Beargrass [Creek] a year or two after my birth.[4] The recollection of incidents which occurred before my sixth year is too slight to enable me to state their time or manner with correctness.

I remember that I was with my f. & Mother at Doctor [Elisha] Warfields* (the place now owned by Miss Dickinson) and to a question from Mrs. W[arfield] to my mother, she replied that "he would be 6 years old tomorrow." This was on Sunday—& from calculation I now know it must have been in 1794. In the fall of that year my f. went in company with Majr. [William] Croghan* &c to Virginia & returned on the night of the 8th Decr. My sister Betsy [sic for Elizabeth]* was born on the 7th the day before. My m. was never well afterwards, she died on thursday 15 Jany. 1795, aged 27 & some months.[5] I had been taken to my Grandfathers Several days before but ret[urned]d with Mrs. [Denis] Fitzhugh,* then [Mrs. James] Ofallon [sic for O'Fallon]* on the day of her death. I lived generally with

---

1. This title, and those for Parts II and III, have been supplied by the editors.

2. This section of the diary was written in 1815 and 1822.

3. The house was on the northeast corner of 6th and Main streets. Main Street, like Market and Jefferson, ran nearly east and west and was ninety feet wide. Sixth Street was sixty feet wide. An interesting description of Louisville during this period is found in H. McMurtrie, *Sketches of Louisville and its Environs*, (Louisville, 1819).

4. See above, Introduction, for a description of Soldiers' Retreat.

5. See Introduction.

my G. father [John] Clark* until the fall. Occasionally however I staid a week or two at home with my father. In the fall he went to Virginia & I remained at my G. f's until the Spring following when he returned in Company with Charles Anderson* and Wm. Dabney.* Soon afterwards C[harles] A[nderson]* became our schoolmaster in my fathers house & continued to teach there my sister [Ann Anderson],* [John] Logan* and myself till the Summer when he established a school on the land then owned by Genl. [Samuel] Wells* in a house on the South side of the Branch once occupied by Genl. W[ells].*[6]

C[uthbert] Bullitt* son of Colo.[nel] B. [,] George & Sam[ue]l Wells [Junior] & Nat[haniel] Pope,* McKennedy[?] & N. Earickson was among my school fellows. I went to school at that place for two years. In the meantime (17th Sept. 1797) my father was again married.[7] During this time my progress was tolerably good until I undertook the latin language—in that the Teacher was deficient.

C[harles] A[nderson]* taught in my father's house from the summer 1798 until Nov. 1800. At that time [I] went to V[irgini]a with Mr. T. L. Elliott in company with Ro[bert] Gaines. This trip was undertaken at the solicitation & persuasion of T. E[lliott] for the purpose of becoming a pupil of the Revd. Mr. Maury* of Albemarle.[8] However after a delay of two or three months in King W[illia]m it was determined that I should remain as a scholar with Mr. E[lliot]. With him I lived from March 1801 till October 1802. He was a good teacher. The neighborhood was most kind polite & hospitable—hospitable beyond any I have ever known. I remember it gratefully and affectionately. I here became acquainted with Lucy Hill Walker* and became as much attached to her as a boy could be to a fine and handsome & good girl. In the fall 1802 by the invitation of my Uncle Matthew Anderson* of Gloucester [Virginia] I went to his house, tho only to prepare for becoming a pupil of W[illia]m & Mary [College].[9] I had visited this Uncle in the Spring preceding. My Uncle tho eccentric, was most kind & affectionate to me for more than four years during which time I was under his Control and management. I will revere his memory as long

6. Well's land is located on Map 1, p. 5.
7. See Introduction.
8. See Map 2, p. 67, for the location of Albemarle County, Virginia.
9. Founded in 1693 and located in Williamsburg, Virginia. See Map 2, p. 67.

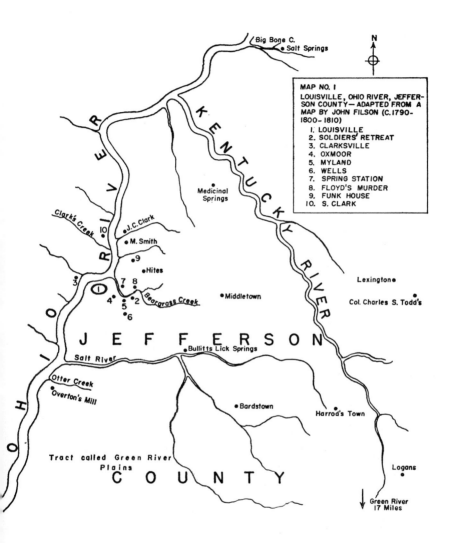

MAP NO. I
LOUISVILLE, OHIO RIVER, JEFFER-
SON COUNTY— ADAPTED FROM A
MAP BY JOHN FILSON (C.1790-
1800- 1810)
I. LOUISVILLE
2. SOLDIERS' RETREAT
3. CLARKSVILLE
4. OXMOOR
5. MYLAND
6. WELLS
7. SPRING STATION
8. FLOYD'S MURDER
9. FUNK HOUSE
10. S. CLARK

as I can remember that he lived. He was a proud, independent & most honest man.

About the middle of Nov. 1802 I went to W[illia]msburg and became a Grammar boy & boarded in the house of Parson Brackers[?]. Anthony Lawson since dead & J. Page grand s. of Gov. [John] Page* were also boarders. I boarded with him during the whole "four courses" which I spent there. Rt. Revd. Bishop [James] Madison* presided in the University during my time there. Ro[bert] Andrews* [was] prof. of Mathematics[10] during a part of the time; he was succeeded by Geo. Blackburn,* [Henry] St. Geo. Tucker* was prof. of law during the first year— Judge Wm. Nelson* afterwards—J[ohn] Bracken* of dead languages & L. H. Gerardin* of living languages. On the 11th July 1806 I left Wmsburg & arrived at my fathers on the 1st Sept. None of the family knew me. In October I visited in company with E[dmund] Clark* & Saml. Rose that part of the Ohio R. land opposite the mouth of the Wabash.[11] I remained at my fathers until the last of Feb. & then went to Frankfort & became nominally a student of John Allen & a boarder of Will. Trigg. I remained at Frankfort, except during occasional visits to Jefferson, about a year, at which time I returned to my fathers house. On the 4th July of 1808 by request I delivered an oration in Bullitts yard. In Sept. G[eorge] Croghan* & myself set out for Wm & Mary where I remained as a student of law until the 25 of Feb. [1809]. I came by way of Washington (where I witnessed the inauguration of Presdt. [James] Madison* 4th March 1809) & Pittsburgh to Louisville. I remained in Frankfort until October 1809 when I moved to Louisville & commenced the practice of the law. On the 1st Dec. 1810 I was married & staid by invitation at the house of J[ohn] Gwathmey* until March. I then moved to the house owned by W[alter] Pearson [*sic* for Pierson]* on Walnut Street. My prospect of practice was good but hardly furnished me with money for the necessary marketing.[12] On the 24th of Dec. 1811 my daughter E[lizabeth] C[lough] A[nderson]* was born. In the Spring 1812 I became a candidate for the [Kentucky] legislature & in August received a greater vote than any man had ever gotten in the

---

10. The William and Mary College records list the Reverend Robert Andrews as Professor of Moral and Intellectual Philosophy. He was appointed in 1777.

11. Anderson was then near Uniontown, Kentucky.

12. The phrase "necessary marketing" refers to Anderson's interest in land speculation.

County. The question of the right of legislative instruction to a Senator in Congress was most warmly agitated before the Election between N[orborne] B. Beall* & myself.[13] I declined becoming a candidate at the next election & turned my attention to my profession, from which however it was in some degree withdrawn from an inclination to engage in the lot speculation which prevailed. In March 1813 I purchased the house on Market Street owned by Doctor [I. N.?] Hughes.*[14] From this period altho my income was very small, my attention was devoted more to the prudent appropriation of the money I had than to its acquisition by my practice. In 1814 I again became a candidate & was elected to the K[entucky] H[ouse] [of] R[epresentatives]. Until the present time politics & speculation have engaged more of my time & attention than the law—1815.

Fourth of July[15]

July 4, 1803. I was in Wmsburg. Saml. B. Archer, Marm. [*sic* for Mann] P. Lomax & Wm. O. Allen delivered orations in the Church, against the order of the professors for which they were suspended. Wm. P. Edington's [*sic* for Edrington] oration was rejected. H[enry] A. Dearborn's* was rec[eive]d. I think he did not speak.

July 4, 1804. In Williamsburg. Wm. Newson [Nevison], John Y[elverton] Tabb, John Hayes, Francis T. Maury, delivered orations in the Church. Peter Mayo and John Jones wrote "for the fourth" and their orations were received but they did not speak.

---

13. Anderson was referring to the "instructions" sent by the Kentucky legislature to Senators Henry Clay and Richard Mentor Johnson regarding the course of action they were to follow in the discussions preceding the War of 1812.

14. The principal streets in Louisville were then Water, Main, Market, Jefferson, Green, Walnut, and South. These were intersected by twelve other streets in 1819—First, Second, etc. Market Street was ninety feet wide.

15. Most of this section which Anderson called "Fourth of July" was written in 1822, but the prodigious feat of memory which one of Anderson's descendants attributed to the author is a myth. Anderson kept a "memo book" in which he made notes and these notes were later transferred to the diary.

July 4, 1805. In Williamsburg. Edw. [*sic* for William O.] Goodwin [*sic* for Goodwyn], Charles H. Smith, Peter Smith delivered orations in the Church.

July 4, 1806. In Williamsburg. R. C. Anderson jr,. Wm. S. Archer,* George Blow, Linn Banks,* John [*sic* for Joseph] F. Mayo and Wm. Waller delivered orations in the Church. A few students dined at the Raleigh. I was at a Ball at night which was one or two doors below the Raleigh.

July 4, 1807. In Frankfort—at a barbacue near Leestown. Spent the Evening and night at a drinking frolic at Taylors[16] in company with J. J. Marshall,* R[ichard] A. Maupin,* P[resley] N. O'Bannon,* Jno. Williams, E. Rector, R[ichar]d. Taylor.*

July 4, 1808. I delivered an oration in Bullitt's lot & dined with the company there—at a Ball in the Even'g & danced with E[lizabeth] C[lark] G[wathmey].[17]

July 4, 1809. In Frankfort—At a Barbacue in South Frankfort near R[ichar]d Taylors* house. At a dance in the Evening.

July 4, 1810. J. H. Woolfolk[18] del'd an oration. Dined at Mr. [Owen] Gwathmeys* on Harrods Creek.[19] There was a public dinner in Hunters yard, Louisville to which my father went.

July 4, 1811. I was at a dinner in the Bottom near the Mouth of Beargrass [Creek] to which Genl. G[eorge] R[ogers] Clark* was escorted from Maj. [William] Croghans* by the cavalry & a great number of Gentlemen.[20]

---

16. The Taylor home was built in 1785 by Colonel Richard Taylor, the father of Zachary Taylor, and was located three miles from Soldiers' Retreat.
17. The Gwathmey family genealogy is discussed in the Introduction.
18. Members of the Woolfolk family are identified in the Appendix, List of Names, but an exact identification of this man cannot be made.
19. See Map, 1, p. 5. Harrods Creek in 1810 was forty yards wide where it emptied into the Ohio River above Louisville.
20. Clark, then 59 years old, was the victim of a stroke and had had his right leg amputated. He lived at Locust Grove, near Louisville, with his sister Lucy and her husband, Major William Croghan.

July 4, 1812. I dined in Middletown in Evans back yard with a few Gentlemen on an Electioneering expedition.

July 4, 1813. Sunday. We dined at S[amuel] Gwathmey's* in Jeffersonville. On Monday I[saac] R. Gwathmey* spoke in the court house and a balloon ascended in the Evening in presence of a very large company.

July 4, 1814. I dined at a Barbacue at the Schoolhouse near Shively.[21] There was an exhibition and dance—a rainy day.

July 4, 1815. I went to a Barbacue in Middletown. It was one of the most pleasant and handsome I ever saw. All my fathers family were there—B[rooke] Hill,* W[illiam] C[hristian] Bullitt,* Doctor [William Brown] Wallace,* A. H. Wallace, J[ohn] Gaines,* W[illiam] Tompkins, and other young men.[22]

July 4, 1816. A fine clear day. I went to Louisville in the Early part of the day & returned & went to a Barbacue in Middletown to which Betsy had gone before me. There were not many persons.

July 4, 1817. A fine clear day. My family & myself were at Mr. [Owen] Gwathmeys* on Harrods Creek. I went on that day to Michael Smith's to have an apple mill made.[23] The day was passed in the usual family way. Mrs. [Frances Gwathmey] Skidmore* was there.

July 4, 1818. I was in Louisville in the morning, having gone down the day before. I came home to dinner and went to Middletown to a ball which commenced about 4 o'Clock in the evening—staid until sunset & returned. A fine clear day.

---

21. A few miles southwest of Louisville.
22. Anderson's sentence structure is misleading. All the men mentioned were not relatives.
23. The home of Michael Smith, who made the cider mill, may be located on Map 1, p. 5.

July 4, 1819. A fine clear day—Sunday. Mr. B[rooke] Hill* & lady & Miss Patsy Hill dined with us at Myland.[24]

July 4, 1820. I & my family were at Mr. [Owen] Gwathmey's* on Harrods Creek. A fine day in the Early part—a shower in the evening.

July 4, 1821. A day of incessant rains. My family & myself were at home in the brick house at the upper end of Market Street.

July 4, 1822. The early part of the day clear—the latter part very rainy. My daughter Elizabeth* and Sister [Mary] Louisa*—both sick at my house.

---

24. An extensive search for the exact location of Myland has been fruitless. It was probably on a corner of his father's farm or somewhere between that farm and the Bullitt's Oxmoor farm, located on the modern Louisville-Shelbyville road.

PART II: FROM KENTUCKY TO WASHINGTON, 1814-1823

Louisville Feb 4 - 1814

Dear Father[1]

For some time past I have seriously contemplated a chance of my residence for one in the country. Indeed my first wish to settle in town resulted entirely from its supposed convenience with regard to my business. My feelings have ever desired the peacefulness of the country. I have of late determined to leave town provided I could procure a seat which pleased me. In putting the plan into execution I should be governed by my future feeling as to my professional pursuits whether I should continue the practice without interruption or retire for a few years from it and return to it in the Superior Courts. This plan I have occasionally thought of but have never matured it and should be influenced in my course of duty weighing the relative pleasure or agriculture and the bar. The indisposition which I have at intervals for several months had, though not serious (I believe) but yet troublesome and vexatious, has not a little contributed to influence my wishes. This last reason I hope however will be of temporary existence. Some years ago you made to me the offer of Watt's place provided I deemed it a proper situation for residence, but I would now very gladly make it the seat of my permanent abode if you have not since made any arrangement which would be broken by it. My own opinion always has been that if it could be enlarged

---

1. This letter did not appear in the original diary. It has been inserted in its correct chronological position by the editors. The letter may be found in W. P. Anderson, *op. cit.*, p. 125.

by the purchase of some adjoining land on the East (I believe it belongs to Laurence) it would be one of the most desirable seats I ever saw. In its cultivation I should delight.

If you have made any arrangements inconsistent with this you know me too well to suppose I could wish it violated. I am aware of the incumbrances of the tenant and If I could indulge my feelings entirely I should wish to retire to the Country immediately[,] but I apprehend I could not conveniently arrange my business so as to leave town finally much before that incumbrance would expire. This idea of removal I have not mentioned, as it may never happen[,] and if it should agreeably to my wishes[,] I should not make it known before the period arrived[.] It might have effect on my situation in town. Betsy is well and I am doing by business.

I am affectionately

R. C. Anderson jr.

May 17, 1814.[2] Riding in company with Genl. Sam[ue]l Wells* on this day about a mile beyond [John] Floyds* fork on the road from Louisville to Shelbyville on the ridge where two hollows one on each side nearly reach the road, he informed me that *there* was the spot of "Floyds defeat."[3] The old road then (14 Sept 1781) ran ten or fifteen yards to the right of the present road; behind a poplar immediately on the left of the (now) road stood a man of F's party during the action. He was found tomahawked in the same spot next day without any appearance of having been shot. In a sink hole 10 or 15 yds to the right of that tree are buried Genl. Well's father & others. Near a hollow on the present road towards the fork Wells gave F[loyd] his horse.

2. This is Richard C. Anderson's first entry in his diary. The previous sections, as explained before, were written in 1815 and 1822.

3. Floyd's Fork may be located on Map 1, p. 5. A prominent leader in early Kentucky, Indian fighter, delegate to the first legislative assembly in May, 1775, and among the first members of the first county court in the Louisville area, John Floyd was killed when riding from Spring Station to his home on Beargrass Creek. The staff at the Filson Club will direct visitors to the Floyd Monument.

Offered for the legislature, no other candidate offering.[4]

May 18, 1814. Judge [Stephen] Ormsby* told me that he dined last summer with Mrs. Montgomery widow of Genl [Richard] Montgomery* killed at Quebec.[5]

May 31, 1814. My little daughter Elizabeth C. died.[6]

June 20, 1814. The prevailing fever, which has slain a great number, seems to subside. Still there are a few severe cases.

July 4, 1814. A very rainy day. The only rainy 4th of July I ever remember. Went down & di[n]ed at Cathills school house. The prospect of support at the election, pretty good.

July 5, 1814. Published a short address to the People & re-published my speech of 1808.

July 6, 1814. Visited the South part of the County vis. [namely] [Hugh] Coopers,* I. G. Moores, Stephens, [John] Withers,* [David] Standiford,* Stephen Richardson, [Philip] Boyers,* & Martin. Appearance favorable to my Election.

July 7, 1814. Lyle a gambler exposed for cheating T[homas] D. Carneal.* T. D. C. accused by G[eorge] R. C. Floyd* of combining with L[yle] to cheat. Hand bills printed by both. Public opinion rather v[ersu]s Carneal.

July 11, 1814. Circuit court commenced & each days business finished on the fixed day.

July 14, 1814. I was told Judge [Fortunatus] Cosby* would resign his jud-seat. It is probable I will be solicited to accept the succession. It is probable I may accept & hold a year or two.

---

4. James Hunter later appeared to contest Anderson.
5. Late in 1775 the Continental Congress authorized two expeditions to Canada. The one under Benedict Arnold proceeded through Maine toward Quebec. The second under General Richard Montgomery captured Montreal, then proceeded to Quebec, where the young officer was killed in the assault.
6. His daughter, the first Elizabeth, was two years and five months old when she died.

July 17, 1814. Mrs. [Richard C.] A[nderson]* with S. T. F. [and] C[uthbert] & T[homas] Bullitts* family set off for the springs.[7]

July 28, 1814. Visited Genl. Y[elverton] P. Wells* by request to ascertain the strength of Netherland's right to his land, which the Marshalls[8] sold on that day. Bought [George and Thomas] Pomeroy's* land by request. Thompson Taylor* present & *drunk,* drew a knife on C[harles] Quincy [*sic* for Querry].*

Prospect of election exhibited the[re] too fair to leave any doubt of my success.

July 31, 1814. Heard that G. R. C. Sullivan had bought J[ohn] G[wathmey]s* right to [lot] No. 11—a good deal alarmed and disposed to compromise.[9]

August 1, 1814. Election came on. Goes favorably. My father votes for [Henry] M[assie]* v[ersu]s [Judge Stephen] Ormsby* which is circulated in papers to hurt my election.[10]

August 3, 1814. Election closed. Anderson 1045. [James] Hunter* 1004 T[hompson] T[aylor]* 33. [James D.] Breck-[enridge]* 210. S[amuel] Churchill* has probably succeeded for the [Kentucky] Senate tho R[ichard] Barbour* is 100 before him in the County.

August 4, 1814. My birthday.[11] Mr. O[wen] G[wathmey]* & wife dine with me.

7. Might be the Salt Springs or the Medicinal Springs, northeast of Louisville, or Bullitt's Lick; see Map 1, p. 5.
8. The family of Sarah Marshall Anderson, Colonel Anderson's second wife.
9. John Gwathmey was already too deeply involved in property speculation and was selling some of his acquisitions to pay his debts.
10. See Introduction for mention of the political differences of father and son. Ormsby had come out for Anderson Jr. in the 1814 campaign. There was no difficulty in ascertaining Colonel Anderson's vote since it was given, like the rest, orally.
11. Twenty-six years old.

August 5, 1814. Betsy & myself go to Jeffersonville[12] & spend the day & night with Major E[dmund] Taylor.*

The news of the attack on Praire de chien & of the boats ascending the Miss[issippi]—reached Town. It is supposed that the British at P. de chien came from Michel Makinak [*sic* for Michilimackinac].[13]

August 6, 1814. Every day more convinced that C[raven] P. L[uckett]* is a meddling officious fellow & wishes for an opportunity of mortifying me or defeating my views.

August 7, 1814. Spent the whole day at home—Betsy being very unwell.

August 8, 1814. Be[ing] pestered with the County Court. L. Hoke told me that he came in the Court house to vote for me but was prevented by Majr. [John] Hughes* telling him that I was a Federalist.

August 9, 1814. Spent the Even'g by invitation at [William Brown] Wallaces* to hear *three fiddles*.[14]

August 12, 1814. Procured a deed from Trustees to lot No. 11. Allen C. Bullitt & T[homas] Prather* voting for it— J[ames] T. Gray* & Sutton against it.

August 15, 1814. Went with Betsy to the Springs. She remained with Major [Edmund] Taylor* for several days. She is benefited by the Waters.

August 17, 1814. Went to Middletown & heard Mrs. Brown's story of [John] Roach's attempt on her virtue.

---

12. Unless otherwise indicated, Anderson is referring to his wife Elizabeth when he mentions "Betsy." Jeffersonville, their destination, was located on a high bank of the Ohio nearly opposite Louisville. Jeffersonville was laid out in 1802, and its population in 1814 was about 400 persons.

13. In June, 1814, an American force took the Indian post at Prairie du Chien on the Mississippi River nearly five hundred miles from Mackinac. Lt. Colonel McDougall, the British commander, sent 150 soldiers and 500 Indians to take the fort. They reached Prairie du Chien on July 17 and after a short skirmish the fort surrendered.

14. Anderson's father may have been part of the trio. He owned an expensive violin and was an accomplished musician.

August 20, 1814. My father & his wife came down.[15] They gave me a deed for Wells.[16] I have a great inclination to buy up the interests of Genl. [Jonathan or George Rogers] Clarks* heirs to two fractions in Indiana.

The militia met for a draft. A company of Volunteers is raised by Capt. [John] Hughes* & [Captain Thomas] Joyes.* The subscription to equip is about $4000.[17]

September 1, 1814. The volunteer company is set aside by the Gov. [Isaac Shelby].* A mob attacks Capt. Hoke for petitioning the Gov. to that effect. Several harsh observations made of me for writing the petition. I shall expect it will be urged at the next election.

September 6, 1814. A great deal of rain & hot weather for several days. Clears up hot.

The report of the Enemy's taking Washington confirmed. A considerable excitement among the people. [John] Armstrong* execrated without any body's knowing his conduct.

A public dinner given to George Madison* at which Genl. B[reckinri]dge[18] & N[orborne] B. B[eall]* presided. R. C. A. jr. present.

September 8, 1814. Sold five acre lot to [Walter] Pearson [*sic* for Pierson].* Not much pleased with the sale.

For several days have had a serious idea of moving to Indiana at some period—viz in a year or two.

---

15. Sarah Marshall Anderson, see Introduction.
16. The land referred to in Anderson's letters to his father, above, pp. 11 and 12.
17. Many volunteer companies were formed in Kentucky during the war, particularly after the River Raisin battle in January, 1813. Considerable fervor attended the raising of these groups and many individuals unfit for military service did their part by subscribing funds for equipment. Governor Shelby's refusal to allow the formation of Hughes's company may have had a political basis.
18. General John Breckinridge died in Lexington, Kentucky, in 1806. His brother, James Breckinridge (1763-1833), was brigadier general during the War of 1812, but lived near Fincastle, Virginia. John Breckinridge's son, Joseph C. (b. 1788), a major in the War of 1812, was a resident of Fayette County in 1814. Also, there was a James Douglas Breckinridge (d. 1849) practicing law in Louisville in 1814. See *Biographical Directory of the American Congress* (Washington, D.C., 1950), p. 884.

Besty has been at her fathers for two weeks.

It is said that George G[wathmey]* is to marry S[ophia] W. Gerrand [*sic* for Garard]*—which is very much disliked by his family.

September 15, 1814. People throughout the County un-healthy—ague & fevers.

September 18, 1814. Dine with Mr. [Benjamin] Tompkins.* Turn the conversation on farming designedly to procure some insight.

September 19, 1814. Dine with Isaac Dabney.*

September 20, 1814. Came to Louisville. A rainy eveng. Betsy remained at P[eter] Funk's* (with whom she dined) all night.[19]

September 21, 1814. T[homas] D. Carneal* as agent of W. Lytle entered into a Contract with my father relating to the Copy of his books.[20] I fear the misunderstanding will not be closed by the contract. Rainy day.

September 25, 1814. Betsy & myself with Temple G[wath-mey]* his wife & children came home. Overtook [William] Littell* on the road who told (the eveng before) his gig[21] had been turned bottom up & he bruised to a mummy.

September 26, 1814. A fair and fine day.

September 27, 1814. Same. Attended S. P. Brooks sale at the request of G[eorge] C. G[wathmey].* B's farm is apparently a fine grazing farm—60 stacks of hay I counted. Old Jo[hn] B[rooks]* told me that he purchased 10 or 12 claims to the land he lives on.[22]

---

19. See Map 1, p. 5, for location of the Funk home.
20. The books were those kept by Colonel Anderson in his capacity of surveyor in Louisville. They are now in the University of Illinois library.
21. A light, two-wheeled, one-horse carriage.
22. This reflects the tangled condition of Kentucky's land system. Virginia was not able, for a number of reasons, to handle the distribution of her western lands until 1766. By then the claims of squatters, French and

September 28, 1814. Visited the circus & disappointed in the performance. Am seeking money among debtors to meet a creditor tomorrow & receive one more proof that Man is not to be relied on—and that proof *my* creditor will receive to-morrow!

September 29, 1814. A foggy morning. Am writing a gentle dun to [Paul] Skidmore*—from whom if I do not get the money, I am sure to get what a debtor ought always to give when he does not give the money, fair words. I got at first fair words & *then* the money.

Dr. [I.] Hughes* (true to the charge) comes for his money— pay about 2[s]3[d].[23]

September 30, 1814. J. Wilsons negro man fell in the well & killed. Supposed that he was attempting to catch the bucket or chain when the windlass broke & was drawn down.

News of [Thomas] M[a]cDonoughs* victory on Lake Champlain (11th inst) came to town.[24]

October 2, 1814. Betsy & myself remained at home till evening talking of Oxmoor.[25] G[eorge] G[wathmey]* married about sunset & 5 of Cuthbert B[ullitt]'s* children christened.

Musquetoes have been troublesome for several nights. I am told this is the 1st summer since 1802 in which they have been so.

Indian War veterans, and others had produced confused and overlapping claims. It is not surprising that Brooks found difficulty in obtaining a clear title to his land. See Thomas D. Clark, *A History of Kentucky* (New York, 1937), pp. 87-90.

23. There was no uniform American currency in the West and coins of many countries were used.

24. The British attack aimed at Lake Champlain in September, 1814, was designed to cut New England off from the rest of the country. Sir George Prevost, commanding the British fleet, cornered a small American flotilla under Commodore Macdonough in Plattsburg Bay. Macdonough was the victor and the British land forces, which were waiting for Prevost to control the lake, went back to Canada.

25. Anderson and his wife had probably been to Oxmoor for the christening of the Bullitt children. Oxmoor was built by Alexander Scott Bullitt, a nephew of Captain Thomas Bullitt, the surveyor who laid out Louisville in 1773. It was located nine miles from Louisville on a thousand-acre tract bordering Beargrass Creek. It is still the Bullitt family home.

The Weather still *dry* & very warm.[26]

October 3, 1814. Still warm & clear. The river has been unusually high this summer, so high as to prevent the pavers from getting stone.[27] The River has been high—the summer very wet & warm—the town & Country sickly.

E[dward] Tyler* applied to borrow money—when I was seeking $30 to pay a creditor. I *think* if I can so manage my property as to make it produce $1000 pr. annum I will retire to the Country contented.

October 10, 1814. County Court day. A majority present & all insulted by [James or Richard] Ferguson.* [Achilles] Sneed's* Jacob who is accused of Burglary bailed *quero.*[28]

October 12, 1814. On Wednesday evening after supper I left Mr. [William] Booth[e]s,* Mrs. [Ann Gwathmey] B[oothe]* expected to be delivered of a child in a short time.

E[lizabeth] C. A[nderson]* remained. Between 12 & 1 oC. a servant informed me that his Mrs. was dead.

October 13, 1814. Great distress prevails among the relations of Mrs. B[oothe]. I received several suggestions from A[lexander] Pope* of the approaching pressure for money.

October 20, 1814. The Banks curtail their discounts.[29]

October 23, 1814. Went to Shelbyville to procure money of J. Masterson—disappointed. J[ohn] Logan* sick. Understand

---

26. A general statement of the health of Louisville may be found in McMurtrie, *op. cit.,* pp. 146-152.

27. Limestone was supplied from the rock in the bed of the river and in *ibid.,* p. 117, it is claimed that it was obtained with a simple crow bar. "Marble of various colors," McMurtrie wrote, "is to be procured in plenty from the banks of the Kentucky river and its tributary branches." The stones were probably being used to build a road to Shippingport, then two miles below Louisville.

28. *Quero,* a legal term—now so obscure as to be unidentifiable—of the early 1800's.

29. Making it more difficult to borrow money. Kentucky's meager banking facilities were not keeping pace with the demand for money in a growing state. The state lacked enough banking institutions in 1812-1814, but, as Anderson's diary later indicates, it was beset with too many banks by 1819-1820.

that the tavern keepers in Frankfort mean to charge $7 pr. week for board.

October 24, 1814. Ride in the rain the whole day from J. Fords to Mrs. S. Clarks.[30] Betsy had gone to town before I arrived.

I am fearful of a call on my paper. I see no means of preventing a protest, but the sale of Hardyman.[31]

October 31, 1814. Relieved for the present—no call in Bank. The pressure for money increasing.

An idea begins to prevail that the collection of money will be postponed.

Much conversation about an increase of banking capital. [I am] favorable to it.[32]

November 1, 1814. The fall has been good for some time. The wheat however is injured by the want of rain.

It is said that there are very few hogs in the Country—that pork will probably be $4.

November 3, 1814. Applied to [Aaron] Applegate* for possession of Oxmoor. I have some prospect of getting the Circuit Judgeship & giving up my business to I[saac] R. G[wathmey]* to close.

November 6, 1814. It has been rainy for several days.

November 7, 1814. Have been endeavouring to collect a little money. I have to borrow money to buy wood & to go to Market.

November 8, 1814. Dined with T[emple] Gwathmey.*

November 9, 1814. Early part of the day very fine. I this day

---

30. See Map 1, p. 5.
31. Hardyman was located one mile from Soldiers' Retreat on Beargrass Creek.
32. Anderson and other speculators who hoped to profit from a rise in land values obtained loans, placed a down payment on the lands of their choice and hoped to sell at a profit before the last payments were due. New banks would mean that loans might be obtained more easily.

again heard of the prevailing idea prejudicial to me—that I wrote to the Gov. [Isaac Shelby]* to break up the Vol[unteer] —company. I expect this is held till the next Election, by some to blow me up. In the evening [Carver] Mercer* & myself went in the ponds to hunt. We saw ducks geese & deer but killed none.

November 10, 1814. The militia consisting of [Gabriel] Slaughter's* and parts of [James] Grays* reg[imen]ts assemble—a very noisy set.[33] The day is fine & warm. It is said now that Kitty G[wathmey]* is to marry G[eorge] W[oolfolk].*

I have a great hunting fever.

C[raven] P. Luckett* has at last wriggled himself into [an] ap[pointmen]t [as] Adj[utan]t Gen[era]l.

November 11, 1814. Rainy morning.

November 12, 1814. A very fine day—very warm for the season.

November 13, 1814. Warm. Went to my fathers who was unwell. Staid all night—rainy.

November 14, 1814. Came to town—cloudy. No court on account of the indisposition of [Judge Fortunatus] Coxby [*sic* for Cosby]* & absence of [Denis] Fitzhugh.*

November 15, 1814. Fine day—warm. Court opened to try a criminal. Criminal permitted to enlist. No other business done. Militia still here. No tents nor arms for them.

November 16, 1814. Court opened again. Heard a few motions. Warm—it rained nearly all last night but fair & warm in the day.

November 17, 1814. Court opened. D[enis] Fitzhugh* arrived last night. Day warm. Troops still here. Doubtful whether they can get arms. Rainy all the Evening.

---

33. Regiments were also raised by Senator Richard M. Johnson and John Adair, Governor of Kentucky, 1828-1832.

November 18, 1814. Clear morning, cool. D. Fitzhugh* tells me that he has bought [Brunfilds ?] lot for $75. *Another* instance of *others* benefit arising from *my* information.

Some time in *this* month Betsy & myself went to the Country for the purpose of staying during the Winter.[34]

November [20,] 1814. Set off for Frankfort.[35] Oders charged $7 per week for board. I board with R[ichard] Taylor at $4.50.[36]

December 23, 1814. I left F[rankfort] for Mrs. [Owen] G[wathmey]'s where I find Betsy well on the 24. Remain there until [December] 29—& return. Spend pleasant Xmas. T[homas] Bullitt &c with several gentlemen were there.

My character somewhat increased during this Session of the legislature.

Not having my memo book with me I must omit many interesting events which I intended to record.[37]

The Winter is very cold during great part of January— but fine & clear.

February [15,] 1815. The legislature adjourned this day & on the next I went to Mr. [Owen] Gwathmey's.* All well. The C[ounty] Court is now sitting. [I am] unprepared for business.

Betsy remains at her fathers.

March 15, 1815. A daughter born called Elizabeth Cl[ark].* All well.

April 1, 1815. Still remain at Mr. [Owen] G[wathmeys].* I go to Louisville twice a week.

---

34. Anderson and his wife spent the winter at the home of her father, Mr. Owen Gwathmey.

35. See Map 2, p. 67.

36. This was approximately one-third of the amount paid by Anderson at Dowsons in Washington when he served in the Fifteenth Congress in 1817-1818.

37. This was the memo book used by Anderson when he wrote the section, Fourth of July, see above, pp. 7-10.

April 3, 1815. The River is now higher than it has been since
'93—certainly. Some say higher that it was then.

I paid 12½ cents for *ferrying* at Keigers mill.

Took depons. [*sic* for deposition] for [George R. C.]
Floyd* vs [Henry] Massie.*

April 10. 1815. A great deal of rain has fallen. The river very
high yet. Much property destroyed at Shippingport.

I hear that the people at Flatrock [*sic* for Flat Rock] are
dissatisfied with me for voting against their precinct.[38]
S[amuel] Churchill* I apprehend is very inimical to me.

I shall offer for the legislature.

April 11, 1815. Go up to Mr. [Owen] G[wathmeys]* with
Miss Fanny G[wathmey].* All well. E[lizabeth] C. [Ander-
son]* cried very much with the bellyache.

April 12, 1815. Came home. Betsy did not come according to
appointment as her mother is very unwell.

I shall leave the next pages for remarks of Events happened during the last winter, which may occur to me from time
to time and on the next leaf go on from this time. April 12,
1815.[39]

April 12, 1815. Supped with T[homas] Bullitt* & played at
the widow[40] with him[,] Doctor [?] & Colo[nel] [John or
George] Croghan* for nine pences till Eleven. A fine day.

April 13, 1815. A fine morning. I understand that ground
very near my No. 11 has sold for $80 pr. foot. This ensures
$3000 on the purchase [I made] from D[enis] Fitzhugh.*[41]

---

38. Flat Rock was located eight miles east of Paris in Bourbon County,
Kentucky. The petition asked that a voting place be established in that
area, and Anderson was on the committee that considered the petition.

39. Nothing more was ever written on the page.

40. In various games the widow is any extra hand or part of a hand,
as one that is dealt to the table.

41. Lot. No. 11 was between the present site of 8th and 9th streets at
Chestnut and Walnut streets. Land values in Louisville rose in spectacular
fashion during this period. Anderson was pleased with his $80 per foot
sale; in 1817 the price was $300 a foot.

April 14, 1815. A fine day. Leave town, go by my fathers to Mr. [Owen] G[wathmey]'s* & come down with B[etsy] & Mr. G. on the [15th].

April 15, 1815. An unfavorable morng. but fine day. Resolution of abandoning the law becomes stronger. The idea is pretty general that I shall be a candidate for Congress. Have never hinted such a thing myself.

My imagination has for 12 mos. formed the kind of life most pleasing to me—a small farm, excellent orchards, vineyards, meadow &c., butter, cheese, &c. in abundance—everything all ways prepared for a friend.

I have rented the house & lot on M[ain] Street to N[icholas] Clarke.* Very much pressed for money.

April 16, 1815. Sunday—very warm. Unwell from a cold in the head.

On Thursday Chambers hinted the prop[r]iety of my straightening the road through my Oxmoor land & said that if ever I should do it from choice or necessity he would give a good price for the land on the N. side. No doubt he has a plan for changing the road to effect that end.

April 17, 1815. Court day. S[amuel] Churchill* assures me he did never say what is ascribed to [him] by report, of me concerning the Election precinct. No court this day.

April 18, 1815. Court met. A fine day.

April 19, 1815. A fine day. Very unwell.

April 22, 1815. The Court has not gone through the 1st days business. Very cool. I defend [James R.] Hinley* for larceny. Acquitted without argument. Between 8 & 9 oClock P. M. G[eorge] R. C. Floyd* shot Cassius Garrard [*sic* for Garard] in the hand.

April 23, 1815. Sunday very unwell—full of bile.

Mrs. [William] Macconnel [*sic* for MacConnel]* dines here. She came gallanted by [William] Littell.*

The child [Elizabeth C. Anderson]* very ill. Send for Doctor [Richard] Ferguson* in the night.

April 24, 1815. A fine day. Child still ill. Myself too unwell to go to Court.

G[eorge] C. Gwathmey* is determined to prosecute G[eorge] R. C. Floyd*—which I regret.[42]

April 25, 1815. [James] Hinley* paid me a watch &c in discharge of the balance of my fee.

I have become a candidate for the legislature. The prospect fair of my Election.

April 27, 1815. I have been more pressed for money since I returned from Frankfort than ever. I have been dunned for small accounts three or four weeks ago & still they are unpaid.

April 29, 1815. Jacob Hinkle* expressed a great wish that I should offer for Congress at the next Election. I have understood that it is becoming daily more the Subject of Conversation.

B[enjamin] Hardin* Att[orne]y for this district & member of Congress, will neither attend at this Court nor resign.[43]

On this day[,] after a contest since Wednesday[,] the Ejectment[44] of [Samuel] Oglesby [*sic* for Ogelsby]* vs Preston's heirs for a part of the poplar level is decided by a verdict of the Jury for the defendants—[John] Rowan* & [Frederick W. S.] Grayson* for pl[ainti]ff [and] [James D. ?] Breckenridge* & myself for def[endan]ts. Rowan more chagrined than I ever saw him, it is said that he had a contingent fee[45] of half the land, worth about or more than $5000.

---

42. Floyd was a close friend of Colonel Richard Anderson.
43. See Appendix, List of Names. Hardin was in Indiana and Washington, D. C., during this time and Anderson evidently did not feel he was performing his duties in Kentucky satisfactorily.
44. In law, an action for the recovery of possession of real property, plus damages and costs.
45. John Rowan was, in other words, to get a portion of the land if he won the case.

My present plan is not to build on No. 11—which will make itself & will be in market without aid[46]—but to build as soon as I have funds on the upper corner of No. 108 which will very much aid the balance nearer the Centre of the Town.

April 30, 1815. Sunday. Colo[nel] Ga[briel] I. Johnston* died on this day. He survived nearly all his friends. The world said he was a bad man.

Wayne a Gambler for whom [William] Littell* became (Yesterday) bail ($700) eloped this morning.

May 2, 1815. In Mr. T[homas] Todd's funeral sermon yesterday at Colo[nel] Johnston's* he desired [*sic* for asked] his audience if they saw anything in his life, which could induce them to attack his sincerity to his declarations, to believe him when he pledged his veracity that if they would strive, they would believe & never regret that they had attended to their bible. This with me is a strong argument. He is a man of truth & a mind to discern, if then he has striven, and does believe, why may I not strive believe & be happy.

Nimrod H. Moore horse whipped [John] Welch [*sic* for Welsh]* in the Street yesterday.

Indictments found vs G[eorge] R. C. Floyd* for shooting C[assius] Garrard [*sic* for Garard]*[47] & N[imrod] H. Moore for assaulting [John] Welch [*sic* for Welsh.]*

W. T. Quincy told me that his offering for the legislature depends on T[hompson] Taylor.* If Taylor does, he will not. I do not as yet apprehend any danger.[48] No matter from which I *apprehended any danger* has been yet stirred.[49]

May 3, 1815. A cool morning & indifferent market. This day the cases of [Henry] Massie* vs [Benjamin] Sebastian* &c. &

---

46. It will bring a good price without any building being placed on it.
47. The tone of Anderson's diary suggests that Floyd and Garard may have fought a duel.
48. Thompson Taylor did not run for the legislature in August, 1815.
49. This probably refers to Anderson's fear "of a call on my paper," which never occurred.

[George R. C.] Floyd* vs [Henry] Massie* were taken up in preference to common law cases on the 4th day—those having been set at the Feb[ruar]y term for the 15th day. This produces great inconvenience & hardship to litigants whose cases are on the 4th, 5th, &c. & are waiting with their witnesses.

D. P. Rankin again has told me that W[illiam] L. Thompson speaks of me in a manner that indicated he is not friendly. I know not the cause either personal or political.

The Miss Todds[50] dine with us.

May 6, 1815. The Court has closed. The four last days have been occupied with the cases of [Henry] Massie* vs [Benjamin] Sebastian* &c & [George R. C.] Floyd* vs [Henry] Massie.*

Unusually cold for the Season.

For several days I have been solicited to be a Justice of the peace.

T. Elliot is with us. He talks too much for his own good. Meany buys a negro man from a Spaniard for $100. They come here[,] the Spaniard is drunk, I wrote a bill of sale but would not attest it. However I apprehend the Span[iar]d is a *knave* & the negro not his own. I am sure Meany is [making a mistake.]

May 7, 1815. Mrs. T[emple] Gwathmey* & Mr. O[wen] Gwathmey* dine with us. Betsy gave O[wen] G[wathmey] the gold key belonging to the Watch I got of [from] [James R.] Hinley.*[51]

May 8, 1815. County Court. A very cool & chilly fog. A severe frost in the Country and a *little* in the back parts of the Town.

Robt. Shaw* is adjudged by the County Court the father of Magdalena Baker's illegitimate child. The Court adjudge

---

50. The Todds could have been the sisters of Charles S. Todd. See Appendix, List of Names.

51. See above, April 25, 1815.

that he shall pay $300 in six annual payments for the maintenance of the child. I think the bond is void as it is made payable to the mother. It is however difficult to get redress as the County Court would not listen to the objection.

This circumstance reminds me of the case at the last March term, when a single [woman] swore that John Lightfoot was the father of her child. He proved by two persons that they had seen her go to bed with her brother-in-law & Lightfoots brother swore that he had frequent connection with the woman. The Court adjudge Lightfoot the father.

May 9, 1815. Much to my joy the County Court decided this day the motions of W[illia]ms [and] [A]d[a]ms vs [Alexander] Pope* &c. which had been on the docket near two years and about which Dubberly my client had bedogged & beteazed me almost past endurance. Now the fee is pleasant.[52]

May 10, 1815. A Battalion muster day.[53] Mr. B[rooke] Hill* & F. Gaines[54] dine with me.

May 11, 1815. The first pleasant day for more than a week—fine & clear—till the Even'g (late). There is a muster at Bannerstown, to which I go & return.

May 12, 1815. It rained all night. I attend the place for mustering near my fathers. The whole battalion is drenched in rain. We retire to Middletown. A man whose name is Woods in conversation very much disposed to insinuate that I told a falsehood in denying that I had promised the Flatrock people to vote for their precinct.[55] My election seems as certain as any uncertain thing. If H[enry] Churchill* should offer[,] [James] Hunter* or myself (probably) must yield. I think it would be Hunter.[56]

---

52. Anderson's handwriting in this section is difficult to decipher, but it is clear that he considered this case of major importance.

53. Like other politicians, Anderson found these musters—and the frequent barbecues as well—to be convenient places to campaign for elections.

54. Identification not certain but probably a relative of John Gaines, see Appendix, List of Names.

55. See above, April 10, 1815.

56. Churchill did not run and Hunter was Anderson's opponent in August, 1815.

May 13, 1815. It rained all last night. I staid at Lawes in Middletown with [James] Hunter,* R[ichar]d Barbour,* &c. Breakfast with J. [Fine?]. His wife tells me that she makes all her table salt from the brine left after taking her meat out.

Go to Reuben Taylors* to Bat[talion] Muster [.] All favorable to my Election.

I return home by Colo[nel] [Richard] Taylors,* Thompsons, E. [Spillsbee] Colemans,* &c.

May 14, 1815. Whit Sunday. Mr. S[am] Gwathmey* & family dine with us. A cool day. They tell us of the Circumstance of Maj. E[dmund] H[aines] Taylors* negro woman giving arsenic to her Mistress. She made several attempts. Succeeded in one. She was detected & has confessed. Mrs. T[aylor] is living but it is feared will not never [*sic* for ever] be well. What is the punishment for administering poison where death does not ensue? I apprehend it is neither punishable by Common law or statute.

Upon examining the code I find it is punished by death under a law of 1811—where the person administering is a *slave.*

The astonishing intelligence of Napoleon having again ascended & without blood or a contest the Throne of France is confirmed.[57] The world however at this day does not want evidences of the instability of human fortune.

I deem Buonapartes return more surprising than his dethronement—not however because I supposed the French really inimical to his government, for in truth he had raised their mil[itary]-character so high, rewarded his officers in so princely a manner & cherished the arts & sciences with such imperial munificence, that the French feel their national pride connected with his existence & consider his reign a

---

57. Napoleon escaped from Elba and on March 1, 1815, landed on the Mediterranean coast of France. For a hundred days, from March 20, 1815, when he re-entered Paris, the French Empire was reborn. On June 18, 1815, Napoleon was defeated at Waterloo.

revival of the times of "the grand Monarque."[58] I had supposed that the British would have taken means to render his return physically impossible, if not by death by a watch too strict to elude.

May 15, 1815. Easter [*sic* for Whit] Monday. I attend a Cockfight at [Jacob] Hinkles* near town. H[enry] Churchill* says he will not be a candidate. I rather distrust his sincerity. I dine with Capt. Sam[ue]l Camp* on my way.

May 16, 1815. A very rainy day. A great quantity has fallen & still continues. The spring is wet almost without parallel.

May 17, 1815. Cloudy, but warm & raining moderately[.]

May 18, 1815. Cloudy, warm & raining moderately[.]

I hear that Federalism is again buzzed as a charge against me. I do not apprehend any serious imputation of that kind.

A thought has this day occurred to me that John Logan* may probably be a candidate for Congress at the next Election—if he should be elected to the Legislature the present year. I think his prospect would be very good.

If it were not for an inclination to leave the law, to get rid of County electioneering, & the vanity of now[59] being a Member of Congress I know it would be better for me, my ambition & for my domestic case & comfort to continue in the State legislature & seek an opportunity some time hence of going to the Senate US.

May 19, 1815. Very cool.

May 20, 1815. Saturday, A severe frost. I have asked several old men if a frost as late in the season has been recollected by them. They all except one say they have not & I somewhat doubt the recollection of the gentleman who says he remembers a severe [frost] in Virginia on the 22nd of May. I think

---

58. Louis XIV (1643-1715).
59. Anderson's syntax is unfortunate. He meant that he *wished* to have the honor of serving in Congress "now" i.e., at an important period in the nation's early development.

I have more than once seen frosts about [the] 8 or 9th of May.

May 21, 1815. A slight frost. My mother who came yesterday remains here. About 8 oC I set out for Overtons Mill on Otter [Creek][60] where the right of possession is about to be tried between him [Overton]* & J. S. Bates[.] Pass by N. Lewis—Dine at Mrs. Read[s] & sleep at Mr [Dittos?] [.] Here I first saw fringe around pillow cases.

May 22, 1815. A fine day. We meet at the mill and the Jury find[s] for Overton[.]* Otter is a beautiful stream affording fine mill seats but I think the County is too poor to produce wheat. Return & lodge at Mrs. Read[s].

May 23, 1815. J. S. Bates is now in the third day of his lying without cessation.[61] Arrive at home about 12. Betsy has crossed the [Ohio] falls[62] with other ladies invited by Colo-[nel] [William] Miller of the 17th Reg[imen]t.

May 24, 1815. A fine morning—warm showers.

I am impressed that I could make money by entering into Merchandizing with some safe hand. I prefer D[enis] Fitzhugh* to anyone I know. If I could raise the capital I would propose it. Although I dislike placing my property at hazard, so sanguine I am that money must be made if prudently managed that I entertain an intention that a year or two hence if I can get a partner perfectly safe I will convert a part of my property into a mercantile capital—& it is possible that a branch in the country near Oxmoor on the road might do well & increase the value of my land.

Money judiciously laid out in the purchase of land in the

---

60. These points may be located on Map 1, p. 5.
61. See above, May 21, 1815.
62. "The falls of the Ohio," wrote McMurtrie, *op. cit.,* p. 13, "are caused by a body of Limestone that stretches across its bed, operating like a dam upon the river above, which finding its course interrupted, continues to swell until rising superior to the obstruction it rushes down the declivity by a thousand different passages." The draught of the falls began above Jeffersonville. See Map 2, p. 67.

Indiana (new purchase)[63] would be very prudent & safe. The land in that country populated by poor persons (divided into small tracks [*sic* for tracts]) & worked by freemen instead of slaves, will be highly cultivated & become more valuable than any Country settled by Virginians held in large parcels & cultivated by Slaves.

Captain [James] Hunter* my colleague teas with me. He seems [to] have laid aside all trades for that of a candidate.

May 25, 1815. B[rooke] Hill* sups with us & Miss L. Booth[e]. The conversation turns on the propriety of preserving the newspapers we received in younger life, as affording amusement in old age. In age the sources of amusement are few & if we are mindful of the future we would carefully preserve everything that could add an additional one. The circumstance that we know the pleasure which we should receive by keeping those short lived histories of trifles & still fail to do it, is high evidence how much we care for present ease & how little we care for future comfort.

May 26, 1815. P[eter] Funk* & wife dine with us. I hear again that public conversation in Shelby speaks of me as a Candidate for Congress at the next Election (1816).

On Tuesday last (23d) I saw over the bottoms of the Ohio [River] a mile or two below the Mouth of the Salt River[64] the effect of a Huricane which passed thro that part of the Country in the Spring 1813 surpassing anything in its destruction of trees that I have ever witnessed. For about a quarter of a mile in width not a solitary tree has escaped unhurt. I do not mean that every tree is blown down but every one (literally I speak) is either blown down or stripped of its limbs and at this time no one on horseback without proper tools for cutting the road can pass through. This is my opinion from accurate observation.

---

63. For a brief sketch of events in Indiana, 1805-1816, see Dan Elbert Clark, *The West in American History* (New York, 1937), pp. 350-351.
64. See Map 1, p. 5.

May 27, 1815. A horse race below town in the Bottoms.

May 28, 1815. A very warm day. Betsy went with Mrs. T[emple] Gwathmey* to my fathers.

May 30, 1815. Still very warm. I have a disagreeable cold in my head produced by pulling off my flannel on Sunday— although I thought I was very careful.

T. Barbour[65] tells me that J[ames] Hunter* has expressed some fear of my not being elected. I cannot tell whether it be ignorance or perfidy. I think however he [Hunter] is true in his profession of friendship & has taken up that impression from the representation of others. He however has never disclosed any apprehension to me. I do not trust in any *real* friendship. My attention has always been more polite & more flattering than that which he usually receives. To this circumstance[,] connected with the idea that his political fate may be linked with mine, I ascribe his friendly course.

Eat Strawberries & milk with D[enis] Fi[t]zhugh[.]*

May 31, 1815. A warm day—a slight shower. [I am] still dis-ordered in the head[.]

June 1, 1815. Much cooler than yesterday. Betsy returns from my fathers.

June 3, 1815. Went to a muster at Shiveley.

W. T. Quincy & myself the only candidates on the ground.

June 9, 1815. Warm days since Sunday. Cool nights. Eat a squirrel dinner near Mrs. Clarks.[66]

June 10, 1815. A pleasant day. Go to a Muster at Flat Rock. Treated very civilly. Notwithstanding what I have heard and what indeed they have said I think a large majority will vote for me. They seem bent on the precinct.[67] I saw

65. A member of the Barbour family of Jefferson County, see Appendix, List of Names, Richard Barbour.
66. See Map 1, p. 5.
67. See above, April 10, 1815.

two of the Featheringales whipped. Lodged with Geo. [illegible]. Had several invitations.

June 11, 1815. Warm day. Was at Flat Rock Meeting house —a crowded audience. Passed by my fathers & came home. On this day I heard from W. T. Quincy that one man had been urging my writing a petition for [Captain] L. Hoke addressed to the Gov. [Isaac Shelby]* for the purpose of preventing his acceptance of the Volunteers, as a reason against my election.[68] This is the only time I have heard of a transaction from which I once anticipated great agitation & exertion against me. However it has not yet taken the course I expected.

   From my own observation & circumstances related to me, I am convinced that W. T. Quincy is an insincere man & "not to be relied on."

June 12, 1815. County Court. Bentons road established through T. Elliott's land.

   I have yet no doubt of my Election & of [James] Hunters.*

June 13, 1815. It rains all day. T. Elliott is with us.

June 14, 1815. Mr. [Leaven] Dorsey* tells me that he offered to L. Lawrence* $30 pr. acre cash for his land adjoining Oxmoor.[69] L[awrence]'s* price is $35.

June 20, 1815. A very hot day. At the solicitation of D[enis] Fitzhugh* I write to M[artin] D Hardin* & express a willingness to act as a director of the [Branch of the] Bank [of Kentucky] here.

   I deem the establishment of an independent Bank at this place as a circumstance wh[ich] would tend more to enhance the value of property than any single occurrence which could take place. Its immediate effect would I think be very great,—probably a part of the value it might attach

---

68. See above, September 1, 1814.
69. This is the Lawrence (Laurence) mentioned in Richard C. Anderson, Jr., to R. C. Anderson, Sr., February 4, 1814; see above, p. 12.

would be fictitious[.] Indeed that seems to me certain; altho the permanent utility would be great. I am not alluding to its effect on the Country in a commercial or political view but only to its effecting [*sic* for effect in] promoting the property of Louisville & its vicinity.[70]

June 24, 1815. At the request of R[ichar]d Winchester I attend a Jury assembled for the trial of the right of property in Middletown between R[ichard] W[inchester]'s children [as] claimants & J. Taylor on an execution. The property is declared to belong to the children. I think the case very doubtful. Mr. Cassidy [is the attorney] for Taylor (of Virginia).

I breakfasted with W[inchester], he is a well informed, observant man. He calculates on & make[s] 30 bushels of wheat per acre—estimating the wheat at 4/ [*sic*] he says the expense per acre is about 11 or 12 dollars leaving a net profit of 8 or 9 dol[lars].

In explanation of the reason that L. Lawrence's horses are *not* fat & James Brown's* always are—he said L. L[awrence]* always laid out more work than his hands & horses could conveniently & comfortably do. J[ames] B[rown] always something less than they could do. Brown's plan was certainly most neat & comfortable & he thought most profitable.

June 26, 1815. A very cool morning.

June 27, 1815. Old Mr. [Leonard] Harbolt* told me this day that he never promised, but he believed he must vote for me. He has been in very violent opposition to me heretofore. This affords another instance of the aptitude of most

---

70. The only source for currency at this time was the Bank of Kentucky and some independent wildcat banks. The Kentucky Bank was issuing a limited number of notes, but because its directors feared that such a procedure would ruin the institution, it was not redeeming its paper in gold or silver. Anderson and others believed the answer was to expand the currency. The results of this plan are explained in Thomas D. Clark, *op. cit.*, pp. 201-204, and in later sections of the Anderson diary.

men to fall in with the prevailing current. My election is now conceded by all. Such things ought to teach me that few men can be relied on in cases of difficulty or distress[.]

July 1, 1815. An excessively hot day.

July 3, 1815. I rode to [Jacob and Elizabeth] Hites* fulling mill & saw D[avid] L. Ward's* fields of wheat, which in extent exceeded any I have ever seen in K[entucky].

July 4, 1815. In company with B[rooke] Hill* [and] [Benjamin] Tompkins* I go to Middletown to a very pleasant barbacue. There was a select dinner party & ball at "Gwathmeys"[71] in Louisville.

July 10, 1815. The circuit court commences its session.

July 12, 1815. Hugh Cary is tried for exhibiting a gambling table & [is] defended by Hawley & myself. The charge was plainly proved. I rested the defense on the unconstitutionality of the law as inflicting "a cruel punishment[.]" The jury doubted and differed, but on the instruction of the Court for which they asked, found a verdict of guilty. This is the first verdict of guilty under the law I have ever heard of.

July 13, 1815. Timothy[72] was taken very ill & continues so. I ascribe the disease to the fatal sickliness of the place which must continue until the ponds are drained of the stagnant water, which by inattention is daily increasing.[73]

July 14, 1815. The judgment vs H[ugh] Cary is arrested. Judge [Fortunatus] Cosby* has not attended this term on account of indisposition.

July 17, 1815. There is no Court this day as Judges [Fortun-

---

71. John Gwathmey's Indian Queen Hotel, one of Louisville's two hotels.
72. One of twenty slaves belonging to Colonel R. C. Anderson, see above, Introduction. Richard C. Anderson, Jr., had slaves throughout his life. The heyday of Kentucky slavery was in 1820-1830, but Kentucky's field crops were not as adaptable to slave labor as was the cultivation of rice, sugar cane, and cotton further south. For this, and other reasons, slavery decreased rapidly after 1830 in Kentucky.
73. See McMurtrie, *op. cit.,* pp. 145-152.

atus] Cosby* & [Denis] Fitzhugh* are sick. I have nearly
made up my mind that I would be willing to accept the
Judgeship if Cosby should resign.

There is now an attempt in operation to induce F[red-
erick] W. S. Grayson* to become a candidate for the legislature, doubtless for the purpose of excluding [James]
Hunter* on account of his hostility to [Judge Stephen]
Ormsby.* The intention I reprobate altho He would *make
a very good member*. I think he has no chance.

July 18, 1815. The desire is plain to put down any one who
dares to investigate [Stephen] Ormsby's* votes.[74] His friends
are very sensitive and cannot bear that any one should even
speak in doubt of his qualification or success. It is reported
that he has interfered in the present County Election personally[.]

July 20, 1815. There has been [no] court since Saturday
[since] the Judges are still sick[.]

July 22, 1815. This day I attend a called muster at the X
roads [Stephen] Ormsby,* [James] Hunter,* [Samuel]
Churchill,* [illegible], & myself are there.

Betsy dined at Colo[nel] R[ichard] Taylor's* in company with Mrs. E[dmund] Taylor.*

July 23, 1815. It has been very warm during the whole of
the last week. The aspect of the ponds is dreadful.

July 25, 1815. Capt. F[rederick] W. S. Grayson* has declared
being a candidate for the legislature[.]

July 26, 1815. It has rained a great deal during the night &
this day till 12 oClock.

Altho the Spring was unpromising the corn is now fine
and the pro[s]pect of a good crop very great[.]

No news of the declaration of war by England[,] Russia[,]

---

74. Ormsby was re-elected to the United States Congress in the August,
1815, elections.

or Austria vs France has yet arrived[.][75] Prodigious preparations are making on both sides for human slaughter to
gratify the passions of a few.

Very little is yet said on the subject of the next president.
If [James] Monroe* was not a Virginian I have no doubt
of his Election. The N. York influence will want Governor
[Daniel D.] Tompkins.* I strongly believe that the P[resi-
dent] or V[ice] P[resident] may come from S. Carolina or
Georgia. For several years the members from S. C. have
been the most conspicious in the house on the rep[ublican]
side & the Geo[rgia] representation very respectable. [Lang-
don] Cheves[,]* [William] Lowndes,* & [John C.] Calhoun*
and [William W.] Bibb* [and William Harris] Crawford*
have given their states much political importance[.] H[enry]
Clay* will not permit himself to be overlooked. However,
I think he is hardly ripe yet.

Geo[rge] Madison,* R[ichard] M[entor] Johnson* &
Ga[briel] Slaughter* are spoken of as candidates for the
Gov.'s place. R. J. M. most probably will be.[76]

July 27, 1815. My kinsman B[illy] Anderson* of Virginia
visits me. He is a violent demo-republican[.][77]

I yesterday heard that an idea had been suggested by
some one that [Stephen] Ormsby* was instrumental in
bringing out [Frederick] Grayson* partially for the purpose
of introducing him this year, that he might succeed Ormsby
the next in Congress. Altho this must be conjecture, it
strikes me very forcibly as being correct.

July 29, 1815. I got to a Quarter race below Town. Two
boys were knocked down & materially injured by a horse.
Betsy went home with Mrs. [William] Croghan yesterday.
B. Mills was in town this day. He is one of the most in-

----

75. Anderson was discussing the possible action of these countries in
view of Napoleon's escape from Elba and his return to France.
76. Anderson was a poor prognosticator; George Madison was elected
in 1816.
77. The origins of the modern Democratic party go back to the Anti-
Federalist and Democratic-Republican parties.

dustrious indefatigable lawyers I ever knew. By his assiduity he is almost a great lawyer. He is a valuable counsel & a useful partisan on account of his unceasing perseverance.

July 30, 1815. Very warm. I went to Major [William] Croghans.*

Genl. G[eorge] R[ogers] Clark* told me that he never knew an Indian to have the toothache.

July 31, 1815. I was in Middletown & dined at my father's with one Maddocks.

August 2, 1815. Genl. G[eorge] R[ogers] Clark* informed me that [Thomas] Cresap* did not kill Logan's*[78] family as stated by [Thomas] Jefferson* in his notes. He [Clark] knew Logan & Cresap* and was with C[resap] at Wheeling when the murder was committed about 30 miles above. He says [J.] B[uckner] Thruston* applied to him several years ago for information & he believes at the instance of T[homas] J[efferson] which he gave, but no publication has ever been made of it. He was present at the treaty near Chillicothe[79] made by Lord Dunmore* & the Indians, where Logan said (as he thought) that Cresap had killed his family —but Cresap denied it with indignation. Genl. [George Rogers] C[lark] says that Cresap was a noted man at that time which accounts for the Indians supposing it was done by him.

August 4, 1815. I was at a barbacue near old Mr. [John] Welsh's* on Floyds fork. It was supposed there were fully 500 people present.

78. The frontier advance of the American settlers was checked in 1774 by Indian troubles that led to what is known as Dunmore's War. Lord Dunmore, seeing particular trouble developing in West Virginia, sent a force to represent the authority of Virginia at the forks of the Ohio. During quarrels there a number of friendly Indians, including the family of the Mingo chief, Logan, were killed. Also see Appendix, List of Names, Thomas Cresap.

79. In June, 1774, the Virginia militia was called out by Lord Dunmore to attack Indian tribes at Point Pleasant near the mouth of the Great Kanawha River. The Indian resistance was broken.

I see or think I see a question arising out of the applications for a precinct in this County, which will be very troublesome to manage. Unfortunate for the member's future popularity.

August 7, 1815. The Election came on 1st day. Anderson 599—Hunter—Q[u]incy—Barbour was 142—before Churchill —2d 151—3d 194. Final vote A[nderson]: 1472[,] [James H[unter]* 11!   27[?]. Several people have desired me to offer for Congress since the Election commenced.

August 9, 1815. [Henry] Churchill* elected by 8 votes. Election contested.

August 10, 1815. I set out for the Springs.[80] Colo[nel] [Alexander Scott] Bullitt* is very ill.

August 11, 1815. I dine at Shelbyville & lodge with J[ohn] Logan*.

August 12, 1815. Dine at Robinsons & lodge at McAfees[.]

August 13, 1815. Arrive at the Springs—Where I remained until the 19. The time was not very agreeable[.]

August 19, 1815. I left the Springs & lodged at Robinsons and next day arrive at Mr. [Owen] Gwathmeys[.]*

September 17, 1815. The last month has been spent at Mr. Gwathmeys. My family is still there. Every three or four days I come to town. Within this period the news of Buonapartes abdication has reached us—of [Stephen] Decaturs* victory over the Algerines & the peace with them.[81] I am again

---

80. See above, July 17, 1814.
81. In March, 1815, an act of Congress approved hostilities against the Dey of Algiers, who had been plundering American Mediterranean commerce. Captain Stephen Decatur sailed on May 10, captured two Algerian ships, and sailed into Algiers harbor. Decatur obtained a treaty whereby the Dey promised to stop molesting American commerce or demanding tribute, and agreed to release all United States prisoners without ransom. Decatur also received similar guarantees from Tunis and Tripoli. Trouble with the Barbary States was at an end.

endeavouring but I fear too modestly, to become a director.[82] C[raven] P. L[uckett]* is surely the prince of wrigglers.

September 18, 1815. At O[wen] Gwathmeys* there was a slight but plain frost this morning.

September 19, 1815. Very cool yesterday & this morning[.]

September 24, 1815. Betsy[,] myself[,] the child[,][83] &c with Mr. Gwathmey leave his house & go to my fathers.

September 25, 1815. I go to town. There is now & continues to be great & unusual unhealthiness in the town & country, particularly Country[.]

September 28, 1815. I was again in Town. T[homas] Prather* applies to know if I will serve as Director.[84]

I have endeavoured in vain to get possession of Oxmoor.[85] B[enjamin] Applegate says he cannot procure a place. If we cannot get possession—Betsy will go with me to Frankfort.[86]

September 30, 1815. We dine with Mrs. Edw. Miller.

October 1, 1815. We came home in Fredericks carriage. Cecilia [Anderson]* comes with us. The weather has been fine for the last week.

My father proposed to lend me several hundred dollars this day which he lately received & has no immediate use for.

October 4 and 5, 1815. Fine weather. The Musquetoes still continue. They have been here in greater numbers this season than ever were before.

October 6, 1815. It rained all day. I write a petition against the division of the County at the request of Major W. Edwards.[87]

---

82. Of the branch of the Bank of Kentucky in Louisville with a capital of $100,000. Thomas Prather was president.
83. Elizabeth. See Introduction.
84. Branch of Bank of Kentucky at Louisville.
85. See below, March [no date,] 1816.
86. To the 1815-1816 legislative session at the capital.
87. In 1780 Kentucky "County" was divided into Fayette, Lincoln, and

My sister Betsy came down for the purpose of procuring equipment to prepare her for a journey to Georgia with J[ohn] Logans,* who is advised that it is indispensable for his health that he should travel.

October 7, 1815. My Wife has been complaining several days of a pain in her breast. To day about 12 oC. it became very violent. Doctor [Richard] Ferguson* treated it as cholic & gave her some relief.

October 8, 1815. Sunday a gloomy dark day. Doctor F[erguson] this morning pronounced Betsy's complain[t] an e[n]-largement of the liver. If it be so she has been affected with it several months.

October 9, 1815. Betsy is still in considerable pain. This is County Court day & many persons are in town but I do not go to Court.

October 10, 1815. Betsy somewhat better.

October 11, 1815. Betsy still easier. On this day I qualified as a director of the Bank having received the notification of my appointment a few days past[.][88]

October 12, 1815. Betsy is not so well as yesterday. Mr. and Mrs. [Owen] Gwathmey* came to town yesterday.

I never have seen so great a prospect of improvement in this place & so many busy people.

I took my seat as a director of the Branch Bank. On this day John Gwathmey* applied to me with a conciliating pre-amble to aid him by a loan of my name in [the] Bank to the amount which a director can borrow; $5000—in other words for me to borrow the money for him.[89] He is a most friendly

---

Jefferson counties. Jefferson County, where Anderson lived, was divided in the east in 1784 to form Nelson County. The division alluded to here did not take place.

88. See above, September 17, 1815.

89. John Gwathmey's financial status cannot be determined exactly, but from 1816 to 1818 he sold much of his property in Louisville, including the Indian Queen Hotel.

and benevolent man and kind kinsman & few men will go so far to aid a friend or a stranger, but I know well his encumbered embarrassment (altho I do not know the whole extent of his debts) and I am so thoroughly convinced that not only all his property will be swallowed by his debts but that his friends who are assisting him must eventually be materially injured in the Shipwreck that I cannot agree to the request of the man who has hardly refused any man in his life.

October 13, 1815. Betsy passed a most painful & miserable night. It is the anniversary of Mrs. Booth[e]'s death.[90] Mr. and Mrs. G[wathmey]* are with us. This day she is somewhat easier at 1 oClock.

October 14, 1815. Fine weather. Betsy is much better.

October 15, 1815. Betsy is in considerable pain[.] This day was spent in taking down the substance of Jacob Sandusky's testimony relating to the surveying of the Town tract.[91]

Sandusky told me that he came to this place (the Rapids of Ohio) in May 1774 in company with John Floyd,* Ja[me]s Douglas,* Isaac Hite* & H. Taylor* &c[.] He was [James] Douglas' chain carrier in surveying in this County and as such [surveyed] the town tract. From this neighborhood they went on Beargrass [Creek]—Harrods Creek &c thence to Bullitts lick which they surveyed & then towards Elk horn.[92]

October 22, 1815. The weather has been very fine for a week. Betsy has become better very slowly.

November 1, 1815. There has been a town meeting on the subject of a Bank and all seem either very anxious or disposed to favour it.[93]

Like most other business here, persons are foremost in

90. Ann Gwathmey Boothe; see above, October 12, 1814.
91. James Sandusky, Jacob's father, is mentioned in discussions of early Kentucky surveys by Clark, *op. cit.*, pp. 48-57.
92. *Ibid.* These places are located on Map 1, p. 5.
93. For an earlier discussion of this matter, see above, June 20, 1815.

supporting it who neither by their wealth or influence can give weight to the measure.

Betsy is getting well slowly.

There is very great excitement among the people of the County produced by the enormous levy imposed for the building of the bridge over Beargrass [Creek]. It is certainly very essential to the *upper part* of town as in my opinion it will cause the usual landing to be immediately beyond the bridge instead of its present place, the mouth of Beargrass. To that part of the County lying above, on & near the [Ohio] river it is also important.[94]

November 3, 1815. In the evening I go to my fathers on my way to see [George] Woolfolk* in Shelby for the purpose of [buying] Nelson[,]* a negro man.

November 4, 1815. Netherton tells me that my offering for Con[gress] is frequently spoken of & wished in Shelby. [George] Woolfolk is [an] industrious, saving, & safe man.

The day like yesterday. I return home.

November 5, 1815. W[illiam] H[.] Booth[e]* is filled with the mania for buying lots. We have agreed to buy No. 93 & 107, if practicable.[95]

November 11, 1815. Last night it became cold. This morning clear & very cold. The streets are frozen & small ponds covered with ice.

November 13, 1815. Court day. A fine clear day but cool.

Bought Rose[,] a daughter of Daphne[,] belonging to the Estate of Ed[mund] M. Clark* [accepted] $291. High price.

A Mr. Hay addressed the grand jury. He speaks correctly —but with a very long song.

---

94. The bridge was finally completed in the summer of 1818, but in a few weeks the structure collapsed. This was a lesson, said McMurtrie, *op. cit.,* p. 10 n., "not to be so *economical,* and for the future instead of employing a carpenter or Stone Cutter, to have the advice and assistance of a professional Engineer, in all *public works* of this nature."

95. Anderson here admits to the same mania as his brother-in-law.

November 14, 1815. B[enjamin] Hardin* addressed me for the purpose of ascertaining my sentiments towards [John] Rowan* as Speaker.[96] On the same day I received a letter from J[ohn] J[ordan] Crittenden* stating his intention of being a candidate. I have advised him to offer. I think his prospect of success very fair.[97]

November 18, 1815. On this morning news was brought to town that a man named Landers who was a few days ago very much whipped by R. Marders[98] & Baxter on a suspicion of stealing Marders money had been found dead in a cave near Isaac Clarks Mill. Notwithstanding all the minute circumstances attending the findings were told apparently in the plainest manner, it turned out false in the whole. I went out with several others to ascertain the truth.

The manner in which the body lay, the place, time & person who found him were all stated in the report. Memo: Many of the reports[,] even those which seem best authenticated & where the scene of action is at the neighbour's door, become false on examination. We frequently take "facts as granted" for many years when by accident we find they are totally untrue.

[John] Rowan* told me he was a candidate for the Chair. In the same conversation he stated that the vote from Nelson [County], Washington [County] &c on the Louisville B[ank] question would no doubt depend on the aid they got in the bill for branching [*sic*] the Court of Appeals.[99] This observation was not only *too low* for the dignity of a legislator, but

---

96. Speaker of the Kentucky House of Representatives.

97. John Jordan Crittenden had served in the Kentucky legislature since 1811 and was now considering running for the United States Congress.

98. This may be the brother of Jefferson Marders, who owned a mercantile business in Middletown, Kentucky, but the relationship cannot be proved.

99. The establishment of a Louisville Bank was part of a plan to expand the currency. Kentucky's financial problems were not unique. By 1815 there were at least 208 wildcat banks in the United States, some of them issuing money with no more assets than a printing press. The Kentucky Bank (as indicated below, December 23, 1815) had no desire for competition in the form of other state-established banks.

approached corruption. The questions have no connection.

November 27, 1815. This has been the finest fall I ever knew. With the exception of two very cold days & some warm rains the weather has been fair & fine[.]

November 29, 1815. There has been a very heavy rain since last night. It is now raining.

This memo: has been discontinued from the day above until this day the 8th of Sept[ember] 1816. I will now supply the chasm with some of the occurences [*sic*] which are passed with as much accuracy as my recollection permits me.

I never date the period unless I am certainly accurate.

November 30, 1815. Fanny Gwathmey* was married to Paul Skidmore.* Betsy was at Mr. [Owen] Gwathmey's[.] I did not go on account of the Court[.]

December 2, 1815. I went to Mr. Gwathmey's on my way to Frankfort with Ben. Chambers* who was sent up by his brother [John Chambers]* to [see] Wm. Waller.

December 3, 1815. I went on to Frankfort—lodged at Sneeds. This is a very good house.

December 4, 1815. Arrived in Frankfort & take up boarding with [Daniel] Weiseger* in room No. 1.

J[ohn] J[ordan] Crittenden* who had become a candidate for the Speakers chair, had almost relinquished his pretensions, so artfully had [John] Rowan* (through others) appealed to his friendship & vanity. I soon removed all objections & he was elected.[100]

December 23, 1815. The Bank bill for Louisville was introduced during the early part of the Session, but suffered to lie on account of a proceeding at the board of directors of the K[entucky] Bank which produced very great excitement & was indeed a most extraordinary measure. In order to prevent

---

100. General Assembly, House of Representatives, *Journal* (Frankfort, 1815), shows that Anderson voted for Crittenden on December 4, 1815.

the passage of the bill then pending before the legislature Entitled a Bill to Establish the Farmers Bank of Kentucky[101] by detaching from its support all those who expected branches under the institution, the Board passed an ordinance establishing Branch Banks at Winchester, Shelbyville, Richmond, & Hopkinsville—places to which they had refused banks a few weeks before & at which by a letter addressed to the applicants they declared "it was inexpedient to Establish Banks." The proceeding produced great indignation & no one openly approved it. The design was avowed by some of the directors & not denied I believe by any. It had a partial effect. The whole representation from Madison [County] was changed by it & all from Christian [County] but B[enjamin] W. Patton.*

On this day I left Frankfort on my return home. I had previously heard that Mrs. A[nderson] had been ill with a complaint in the liver.

December 24, 1815. I arrived at Mr. T[emple] Gwathmey's* where B[etsy] remained during her illness.

December 25, 1815. A fine cold day—snow on the ground. W. Ferguson offered me $100 per foot for the lower half of No. 11—refused.[102]

December 31, 1815. Left Louisville for Frankfort. Lodged at my fathers.

January 1, 1816. Travelled from Middletown in company with a Mr. Slaughter to Sneeds.

January 2, 1816. Arrived in Frankfort.

February 3, 1816. The Legislature adjourned. The Bank bill passed the lower house & was lost by 15 to 16 in the Senate. A Second [bill] passed the lower house.[103]

---

101. See *ibid.* for Anderson's vote—not a surprising one—favoring the establishment of the Farmers' Bank.
102. See above, April 13, 1815.
103. Anderson was busy during this session. He brought in a bill to

There has been a great deal of very cold weather this winter. A deep snow fell in January.

February 4, 1816. Arrived at home in Louisville[.]

March [no date], 1816. During this month & April we moved our property & ourselves to Myland my present residence.[104]

April 20, 1816. Court commenced[.]

May 2, 1816. I became a Candiate for Congress.

This spring has been most unusually dry & the prospects of corn are very bad[.] I have planted about 30 acres of corn[.]

May 15, 1816. A frost. The last night I staid at [David] Standifords* on my return from Bullitt [County] where I addressed the people two days in succession[.]

May 17, 1816. I went to Shelbyville.

May 18, 1816. I was at Muster at 1.

May 19, 1816. Addressed a large assembly of people in Shelbyville[.]

June 10, 1816. Capt[ain Edward] George* one of my opponents for Congress returned with me from Louisville & staid all night.

July 1, 1816. I was at New Castle & addressed the people[.]

July 3, 1816. I returned home. It has rained every day for 3 or 4 days. I staid last night at Wm. Woolfolks.*

---

lower the penalties on insolvent debtors, a bill to compel the speedy adjustment of land claims, and a bill to incorporate the Louisville Library. He spoke during legislative discussions regarding the navigation of the Mississippi and Ohio rivers, and sat on a committee to consider the petition of certain Warren County citizens who wished to be excused from militia duty. He also served on a committee that considered the petition of Jefferson County citizens asking for the establishment of another election precinct. Anderson voted for increasing the salaries of judges on the county courts, but voted against a bill for increasing the number of justices of the peace in Allan and Adair counties. His vote on the salaries for county court judges became an issue in the congressional election of 1816; see below, August 5, 1816.

104. See above, September 28, 1815.

July 4, 1816. At a barbacue at Middletown[.][105]

For several weeks the People of Kentucky & indeed generally of the Union have been in a most wonderful ferment about the passage of a law called the *compensation bill.* It will certainly defeat [Stephen] Ormsby* but I am unwilling that my success should be ascribed to his vote on this Bill as I should in any event have been a candidate, with a full assurance that I would outpoll him[.][106]

August 3, 1816. I went to Drakes [boarding house] in Bullitt [County.]

August 4, 1816. To Shepherdsville[.]

August 5, 1816. In Shepherdsville at the Election[.] I returned home that night, a part of my way in company with F[rederick] W. S. Grayson.* Soon after my arrival W[alter] Spencer came from Shelbyville informing me of [Stephen] Ormsby's* unjustifiable & ungenerous attack on me & my vote for increasing the Judges salary[107] & the effect [of Ormsby's speech] in procuring many votes for [Captain Edward] George.*

August 6, 1816. I went in the morning to Shelbyville & made a Speech[.]

August 7, 1816. Made another Speech to the people[.]

Came to Middletown after the poll closed.

This election which has occupied much of my time & most of my thoughts for several weeks has now closed & eventuated in my Election by the following vote

---

105. Anderson's campaign stops may be traced on Map 2, p. 67.

106. During the first term of the Fourteenth Congress the legislators raised their own pay from $6.00 a day (about $900 a year) to $1500 a year, making the pay retroactive. Since Congress then usually sat about five months a year, feelings against this bill ran high. Clay found himself fighting hard for re-election in Kentucky because he supported the bill, and R. M. Johnson was also embarrassed by his vote. The law was repealed but the question soon came up again; see below, December 24, 1817.

107. See above, February 3, 1816, footnote.

	Anderson	George	Ormsby
Shelby [County]	914	520	27
Jefferson	1305	45	274
Henry	68	986	5
Bullitt	291	18	88
	2578	1569	394

The amount of Georges vote in Shelby was most unexpected.

August 30, 1816. A most horrid murder was committed this morning by Armstead Churchill* on Joseph Frederick about sunrise. There is prevailing great indignation against all the Churchill family. His sister Mrs. [Mary Churchill] Bullitt* is accused in conversation of false swearing before the Inquest[.]

September 1, 1816. It has since the rains in the beginning of July been extremely dry.

September 7, 1816. We have had rain this week. The crops have been very much shortened by the last drought.

By the purchase of some negroes, repairs & other unavoidable expenses, (including however some purchases of lots) I have been compelled to increase my loan in Bank to near $5000.

There is a prospect of great Bank [trouble] as the Sec[retar]y [of the] Treasury [Alexander J. Dallas*] is exerting himself to compel a resumption of Specie payment. Altho the Banks at Phila—N. Y. & Baltimore doubtless wish to postpone it—I think there will be a resumption during the next summer.[108]

---

108. A bill to create the Second Bank of the United States was passed in April, 1816, and branch banks were soon established in Lexington and Louisville. A bill introduced by Daniel Webster, adopted by Congress, and scheduled to go into effect on February 20, 1817, virtually compelled the resumption of specie payments by state banks and resulted in a contracted note issue. This, writes Thomas D. Clark, *op. cit.,* pp. 200-201, "created confusion and brought forth criticism [in Kentucky]. It was claimed that the United States Bank stifled the Kentucky Banks and that it attempted to convey all the gold and silver out of the State."

September 8, 1816. Sunday. At home with my family & here again resume this journal regularly.

June 4, 1817. From that incurable and almost universal spirit procrastination, I have failed to continue these notes as I intended.

The last fall (1816) was unusually fine. The weather continued good except three days of rain at Xmas until about the 10th of Jany. From that time it was the severest winter I ever felt. I remember days as cold, but never so many.

George Madison* Governor of this State died in October last. He was a most honest & virtuous man. He had of late become the most popular man in the state—but he was I think a weak man.

His death has occasioned a great agitation in the State. Lieut[enant] Gov. [Gabriel] Slaughter* has succeeded to the administration of the government. Can he constitutionally discharge the duties for the whole of Madison's term or must a new election intervene? is the question which agitates the State. A proposition was brought forward in the legislature to elect a Governor by J[oseph] C. Breckinridge* & supported by J[ohn] J[ordan] Crittenden* &c.[,] opposed by [Lee] White,* [John] Rowan* &c. & negatived by a large majority. This idea was surely wrong—but now that seems to be abandoned but [it] is vehemently & very extensively maintained that an election must take place for Gov. & Lt. Gov. by which a new era will commence. Of this opinion are many eminent men, [George] Bibb,* [Jessie] Bledsoe[.]*

It is more plausible than the other but I think not right. Very probably it may prevail. The people are fond of opportunities of displaying the "soverign [*sic*] power"— and listen favourably to a construction, which gives them power in preference to one which declares they have surrendered it.

C[harles] S. Todd* had been appointed Secretary [of State] by [Governor] Madison.* He wrote to [Gabriel] Slaughter* declaring that he would not be in the way of any other appointment, if he wished to make one. Slaughter[,] considering that a resignation[,] appointed J[ohn] Pope.* That excited great clamour but was approved by the Senate. This I believe has produced the clamour for a new election.[109]

A warm contest took place between J[ohn] Pope* & [Peter G.] Voorhies* in Jan[uar]y for a seat at the directory of the Bank.[110] The enemies of Pope strove to give it the character of a political contest, but he succeeded. I voted for him & took (tho not designedly) an active part. Circumstances suddenly occuring [sic] produced it. I have no doubt it was noticed & will be remembered.

I was at Frankfort in Jan[uar]y. I became acquainted with G[eorge] Robertson* & T[unstall] Quarles.*

I think they are but moderate men—particularly the latter.

May [no date], 1817. I rec[eive]d by my father a polite offer from H[enry] Clay* to assist me in procuring pleasant lodging in the City during the session of Congress. This agrees with my opinion of the man. He is too sensible not to be very polite. By such modes of politeness & courtesy, he draws to his support young men, who are flattered by his attention. Many before him have used this manner & he excels. These young [men] become his supporters & puffers. If he has ambitious designs, which he may very honorably have, he

---

109. Anderson's explanation generally follows the account presented by historians. The question was debated by legislators, newspapers, and, to use Anderson's phrase, "the people," who questioned candidates about their stand on the question prior to the legislative elections in August, 1817. The issue became more heated because of the actions of "Governor" Slaughter against men who were personally antagonistic to him. Those who stood for a new election chose a majority in the House of Representatives, and on August 18, 1817, this House voted to hold a new election for Governor. The more conservative Kentucky Senate then defeated the bill, thwarting, some observers maintained, the will of the people. Slaughter finished the term to 1820, but as a compromise his title was "Lieutenant and Acting Governor." The issue, as Anderson's diary later indicates, did not die. It exacerbated Kentucky factionalism and created a belief that the offices of the state were within the direct control of the electorate.

110. The Kentucky Bank, not the United States Bank.

knows too well the importance of securing all those who from present situation or *power* may have weight enough to aid him. Our acquaintance is very slender. [First words of sentence illegible] with a man less clear sighted or less polite to justify his message. I will write to him. He will think the bait is taken & that I am flattered by his attention & I will think that that very idea will make him friendly & may be of use to me.

At the Nov. term of the Jef[ferson] court Judge [Thomas ?] Metcalf[e]* granted a continuance of [Armstead] Churchills* [murder] trial on his affidavit that he could not have a fair trial in this County & that he wished on that account for an opportunity to apply to the legislature for a change of Venue. I think it an illegal and outrageous decision.

The law authorizing a turnpike has produced a little exertion in the County to take the stock [of the turnpike company.][111] I made a speech at Middletown in encouragement of the plan. I fear it will not be commenced very soon.

It seems not to be accounted for—but I believe the fact that the seasons are some degree changed—the Winter severer and the spring later. This spring has been unusually late. Now 6th June it is disagreeable in the Evening & morning without a fire.

R[ichard] Barbour,* J[ames] Hunter,* Wm. C[hristian] Bullitt,* A[lexander] Pope* & M. Denny are candidates for the legislature. The last 2 are opposed to the election of a Gov. until the term of 4 yrs. is expired. I think the first two will be elected.

W[illiam] C[hristian] Bullitts* course has produced an unfavourable impression on me. I suspect him solely devoted to *self*. His refusal to disclose his sentiments on the question

---

111. On February 4, 1817, the Kentucky legislature passed an act authorizing a private company "to build an artificial road" from Lexington through Frankfort to Louisville. When this was completed in 1820 the old Wilderness Road was henceforth known as the Lexington and Louisville Turnpike. The people of Middletown, where Anderson gave his speech favoring the building of the road, used the Pike to come to Louisville to shop.

of the election and his asking me "if it would be proper," induced me to *believe* that he was seeking to get the votes on both sides & to *suspect* that he was delaying, to take the stronger side. His conduct, I think, was not open & candid. His perseverance, & frugality will make him succeed in life. In Swifts history of the last year of Queen Anne's reign[112] he says; that Lord Oxford was of [the] opinion that it is not prudent for the Minister to have *too* great a majority in the house of Commons [because] they might become unruly for want of business. Swift thinks this was an unwise refinement of policy in Oxford[.]

It is certain that a party will keep more united & true to its ends, if a strong opposition gives full employment to it.

About the 20th of May this spring [1817] the locusts have appeared in considerable numbers. Their appearance was foretold by several writers in the newspapers—who said that they appeared in 1783, 1800 & would appear every 17 years. I have not as yet discovered any injury from them, nor do I know on what they subsist.

This winter 1816-17—is the first time I ever knew wheat to sell generally for 6[s]/5[d] bushels[.] The price is now one dollar at the barns.

For two or three years the Steamboats have been in operation on the Mississippi & Ohio—but from the disasters which have happened to them, or unskillfulness in their management or negligence, they have not been valuable until lately. In Apl. 1817 Capt. [H. M.] Shreve* of the "Washington" arrived at Shippingport in 25 days from N. Orleans and thereby gave the first practical demonstration of the great utility of Steam navigation[.]

June 7, 1817. I resume my journal.

This day I attended at Murphy's on N. Buckner's notice to take the deposition of J. McCawley relating to lot No. 11.

---

112. Jonathan Swift (1667-1745), *The History of the Four Last Years of the Queen* (London, 1758).

McCawley said he came to the Country in 1776 & was the first who brought the news of the declaration of independence.

The trial of [Armstead] Churchill* for murdering J[oseph] Frederick[113] came on at Shepherdsville this week. The Jury was divided on a case of the vilest murder I ever knew. The Court adjourned & left the Jury locked up who soon broke the door & went out.

Sunday rainy. At home. Eliza Skidmore—Sydney A. Gwathmey*—[Mary] Louisa Anderson,* Frances Tompkins, John Overton,* Rob[er]t Anderson* & John Anderson* dined with us.

June 9, 1817. Went to Louisville.

This day commenced the carrying of the US. mail in Stages on the route from Louisville to Wheeling.[114] This is a new evidence of the wondrous improvement of the Western Country & those who come after me will wonder as much at my admiration as I do at this unparalleled improvement which it has received in my memory.

June 10, 1817. A very cool disagreeable day.

A[ndrew] Brentlinger came to see me concerning the land he lives [on]. His father-in-law J[ohn] Funk* gave it to him verbally—& put him in possession more than 20 years ago. He has lately died without a will & the heirs claim a division[.]

June 11, 1817. A very hot day[.]

June 16, 1817. Monday. I went to Louisville. The Washington & Vesuvius Steamboats have arrived from N. Orleans in 28 days. The course of trade has already changed[.]

June 18, 1817. The [Doctor] Ro[bert] Miller,* was with us

---

113. See above, August 30, 1816. Churchill was granted his petition to have the trial moved from Jefferson County to Bullitt County.

114. A year later the United States mails were being carried between Wheeling and Washington on the National or Cumberland Road.

most of the day, & those who know him must know how irksome the time was when the rains prevented all relief from walking & politeness [and] also from reading.

Capt [Abraham] Chapline* & my father were here in the Evening.

June 19, 1817. I was in Middletown.

June 24, 1817. I was in Louisville[.] Colo[nel George] Croghan* & Lady from N York arrived at Majr. [William] Croghan's.*

From my own observation & that of others I am induced to believe that [William] Logan* wishes to get into more active life (ie) into Congress. If so, here is another evidence of the restlessness of man. He now holds an honourable & convenient office & one more elevated than his talents could have justified him in expecting. It is impossible he could ever distinguish himself in Congress but what is gotten is not valued. He is popular & would probably at this time succeed against any one in the district.

June 26, 1817. Went to Louisville.

June 27, 1817. The prospects of corn are now fine. Fair [weather].

June 28, 1817. I went to Louisville. There is in town a great alarm about the Small pox—which is said by all the physicians except Doctor [Jonathan] Burrell* to prevail there. One person has died. All who have seen it—declare it the S. pox.[115]

June 29, 1817. Went with the family to Mr. [Owen] Gwathmeys[.]*

---

115. "In 1817, the small pox ravaged the town, and although every endeavor to cut short its progress by vaccination and preventing all intercourse between the sick and the well was made by the faculty, yet, from the slothful negligence of the civil authorities, it was impossible to prevent its inoculating the place for each succeeding year." McMurtrie, *op. cit.,* p. 148.

July 1, 1817. Went to Louisville from Mr. G[wathmeys] by the mouth of Harrods Creek. The Ohio higher I think than I ever knew it at this Season. I ferried at [Craven P.] Luckett's* old Mill on H[arrods] Creek—& could not cross Beargrass [Creek] above [David L.] Ward's* tan[ning] yard[.]

July 2, 1817. Returned to Mr. G[wathmeys] by [my] home— rain[.]

July 4, 1817. Went with Mr. G[wathmey] to Michael Smiths to get an apple mill made.[116]

July 5, 1817. Came home. Dined at my fathers. Returned in the Evening.

July 7, 1817. Went to Louisville with Mr. [Paul?] Skidmore* by Transylvania.[117]

July 9, 1817. Left Louisville. Went by [my] home to Mr. G[wathmeys]. The Small pox is spreading—slowly I think[.]

The leaves on my apple trees are very yellow[.] More so than they were last year. I ascribe it to not cultivating the orchard.

July 10, 1817. I return to Myland with the family.

July 11, 1817. Went to Louisville. The Pike returned yesterday from St. Louis. She is the first steamboat that ever went there. The second death from the Small pox occurred this morning.

July 12, 1817. Rains in the neighborhood. The season for a few weeks has been fine for corn &c[.]

The agitation about a New Election of Governor continues through the State.[118] Seven or Eight members of the Convention have declared it was their intention at the formation of the Constitution that there sh[oul]d be no election

116. The Smith home is located on Map 1, p. 5.
117. Founded in 1780 at Lexington, Kentucky.
118. See above, June 4, 1817.

in a case like the present. One only Tho[mas?] Clay has stated that his intention was different.

July 14, 1817. Court day. The prevalence of the Small pox will probably prevent the Court from doing much business.

July 15, 1817. The Court adjourned for the term. I have heard this summer of rust in corn[.] It appears on the under leaves, turns them yellow & proceeds upwards.

J[ohn] Logan* & family came to my fathers today[.]

July 19, 1817. I went to Louisville. Mrs. Tunstall died this morning of the Small pox. There have been several heavy rains in the neighborhood. Mr. Sam Gwathmey* & family came to Myland.

July 20, 1817. The Season fine for corn[.]

In a conversation with Mr. Saml Gwathmey we both thought that a new party w[oul]d probably arise composed of a section of the democrats, who would form the opposition. [We thought] that the fed[eralist]-party w[oul]d fall in with & be merged in the admin[istration] party—that H[enry] Clay* might be one of the organizers of the new [party.] The New party would endeavor to retain the name of Dem-Rep—& stigmatize the other as federalists. The admin[istration] party w[oul]d support J[ohn] Q[uincy] Adams* for the next presidency.

July 22, 1817. Dined at my fathers.

July 23, 1817. Dined at Mr. [Isaac?] Dabneys*[.]

July 25, 1817. I went to a Sale of J.[ohn] Funks* estate. There were a good many people. [Senator] J[ohn] Pope's* letter to [Chilton] Allan* of Henry County has just come out & produces much conversation.[119] It shews the restlessness of Pope* very forcibly.

---

119. The letter reportedly referred to the quarrel between Charles Todd and Gabriel Slaughter, and was an attempt to keep the issue of a New Election alive.

July 26, 1817. I went to Louisville[.]

July 27, 1817. Saml. Gwathmey* & Ro[bert] Miller* dined here. My father & Mr. [William] Logan* came in the Even'g. A great rain this morning[.]

July 28, 1817. A clear hot day.

July 29, 8117. Went to Louisville[.]

August 3, 1817. I went to New Castle[.]

August 4, 1817. The Election day.[120] David White,* C[harles] H. Allen,* George Woolfolk,* Edw[ard] George* & Major Rice* [the] candidates. D[avid] White & A[llen] & R[ice] for a new election.[121] D[avid] W[hite] & [Charles] A[llen] ahead. I made a public annunciation that I would take charge of all C[laim]s vs the Gen[era]l Govt. & have them settled at the offices in Washington.[122] I went to Shelbyville in the Evening. J[ohn] Logan,* G[eorge] Knight,* B[erryman P.] Dupey,* [Bland W.] Ballard,* B Logan, Boyd, Thomas M[.] Hardin candidates—[on] the 3d. First ahead & against a N[ew] election[.]

The agitation thro[ugh] the State (except a few Counties) on the subject of a New Election of Gov: is very great. I think the Maj[ority] of the people is in favour of an Election—but it is not probable that it will succeed on account of the permanence of the Senate,[123] who were (nine tenths) against it last winter.

August 5, 1817. Remained in Shelbyville till after dinner. Came home in the Even[in]g. Found Betsy very sick with a sore throat & fever.

---

120. The election for the Kentucky legislature. Anderson was not, of course, a candidate, having been elected to the United States Congress in the previous election.

121. Anderson forgot to mention another candidate, Richard Barbour. The issue in 1817 was the status of Gabriel Slaughter and the question of a New Election.

122. The reference is to land claims.

123. Anderson was correct. Approximately one-fourth of the senators in 1817 were elected because they favored a New Election.

Frances Elliott had come on Sunday to stay during her fathers absence in Virginia[.]

August 6, 1817. I went to Middletown & voted for [James] Hunter* & [Richard] Barbour.* I understand there was much conversation on the vote. Some censure—more approbation.[124]

August 8, 1817. I rented the lower field to Chambers for wheat at 2% [of the yield] per acre[.]

August 11, 1817. Court day. I went to Louisville with D[enis] Fitzhugh.* I was informed there was much conversation & censure about my vote. This is unavoidable—tis foolish to be surprized or grieved[.]

I borrowed $150 of [from] A. Allen[.]

The Small pox still prevails. It is thought the disease is becoming more fatal.

August 13, 1817. W[illiam] Wallace has been with us several days making a cider press[.]

August 14, 1817. Went to Louisville with D[enis] Fitzhugh.* The director of the Bank sat for the 1st time in the New Bank.[125]

Pressed for money. I have borrowed of A. for a few day[s]—then of B to pay A then of C. to pay B.

Wheat is selling at 6/ & 6/9.

August 17, 1817. Tho. Elliott, I[saac] R. Gwathmey,* Mr. [Brooke] Hill* & Lady were at Myland[.] B[rooke] Hill has a great inclination to buy land & engage in Speculation. But I believe he has no money. He can only adventure on his credit. Th. Elliott has at length I believe disgusted every one by his trifling tatling & backbiting[.]

August 21, 1817. It has been very hot this week. Paid [W.] Wallace for Cider press—price $15.

---

124. Anderson voted against a New Election.
125. The directors of the Branch Bank of the United States in Louisville included, among others, John Gwathmey, John Clark, Henry Massie, and James D. Breckinridge; see Appendix, List of Names.

Went to Louisville[.] R[obert]* & T. Miller returned & staid all night with me[.]

August 22, 1817. Went to Louisville. Purchased C[arver] Mercers* house & 2/3 of his lot [at the] upper end of Market S[treet] for $4000.

Borrowed money of S[amuel] Arterburn[?]* at 15 pr. cent[.] The first time I ever gave usurous int[erest].

August 24, 1817. Betsy & myself at home during the day— it being Sunday.

August 25, 1817. Went to Louisville[.] Kitty Gwathmey* returned with me.

August 26, 1817. Mr. [Owen] Gwathmey* dined with us[.] Kitty went home.

The rage for emigration is now towards the Missouri (Boon's lick) & the Alabama.[126] The rich land in this territory will I think be more valuable than land of the same quality to the North. The Sugar or Cotton Country is more valuable than the Wheat[,] hemp or corn land.

August 30, 1817. I was in Louisville. Genls [Robert] Lytle* & [Richard] Taylor* were there[.]

August 31, 1817. Was at the Stone Meeting house with Elizabeth [Anderson]*—who cried & we came home during the Sermon.[127]

September 1, 1817. At Louisville[.]

September 2, 1817. Mr. & Mrs. [Brooke] Hill* visited us[.]

126. The great movement of population to the west which came after the War of 1812 reached a peak in 1818-1819 and was known as the Great Migration. Ohio received more people than any other region, but to the west settlers followed the Mississippi, both north and south, and pushed up the Wabash and Missouri. In the south, Alabama prior to 1820 had a few farms in the western half of the state, but the greatest concentration was in the region of the Great Bend of the Alabama River.

127. There were three churches in Louisville in 1817—Methodist, Catholic, and Presbyterian. Anderson's entry suggests a Quaker affiliation, but there is no record of such affiliation in the family records. Anderson's father was an Episcopalian.

September 4, 1817. Again at Louisville[.]

September 5, 1817. Remained all night in town.
    I[saac] R. G[wathmey]* came home with me. Mr. [Brooke] Hill & Mr. Boardman came in the Eveng. Mr. B[oardman] goes tomorrow to seek his fortune in Alabama[.][128]

September 6, 1817. My father & [Edward] Hough* of Chillicothe spend the Evening with me. H[ough] is an intelligent man[.]

September 11, 1817. It has rained very much lately.

September 12, 1817. Mr. [Brooke] Hill & Lady left Myland. Mrs. J[ohn] Gwathmey came here. Rain.

September 13, 1817. Constant raining.

September 14, 1817. J[ohn] Gwathmey came up at night[.]

September 15, 1817. Went to Louisville & stayed all night. G[eorge] C. Gwathmey* has lately returned from Missouri. He saw much fine land & thinks it is a fine country.[129] The want of water is an objection.

September [1]7, 1817. A Branch of the U. S. Bank has lately been established in Louisville. Success in this case gives another high proof of the effect of perseverance & high demands.
    For some time the great Sea Serpent seen by many near Boston has given matter for conversation & the newspapers. Hundreds have seen it. It is apparently about the size of a barrel & about 100 feet long. This is probably the best authenticated case of the existence of such monsters that has ever occurred.

September 20, 1817. Betsy & myself rode in the Eveng to see Mrs. [Robert] Miller* who is sick.

---

128. See above, August 26, 1817.
129. *Ibid.*

September 22, 1817. I went to Louisville—a little rain[.]

September 28, 1817. Betsy myself & the children went to Louisville.

October 10, 1817. We went to Jeffersonville. More land has been entered in that office within 3. mos. than ever was in the same time.

October 11, 1817. I entered a q[uarte]r section yesterday & sent money to Maj. [Zachary] Taylor*[130] to enter another. The Emigration is now great to Missouri & Indiana. The emigrants now take poor land within the Settlements which has been rejected for seven years. This is done by a greater number [in] preference to taking better land on the frontier[.]

I have determined, as far as the capriciousness of man & the uncertainty of things permit one to make a determination—to invest some money in public lands. I know not where.

Might not advantageous purchases be made in [the] Floridas— (they must I think soon belong to U. States[.]) In the Spanish dominions large concessions have been usually made to individuals. If they could now be bought they w[oul]d become much more valuable immediately on the cession[.][131]

October 12, 1817. We came home in the Stage—[132] M[ary] C.

130. The Washington *National Intelligencer* for October 31, 1812, announced that "the President has been pleased to confer the brevet rank of Major on Captain Zachary Taylor—the first brevet of any kind ever awarded by the government of the United States." The entering of claims— these were probably in the Michigan Territory where Taylor was stationed —was made through the General Land Office.

131. After the War of 1812 Florida became a center of smuggling, a haven for escaped slaves, and the origin of attack on Alabama and Georgia by English and Indians. Spain was clearly unable to control her territory and Anderson was, of course, correct in his long-range prediction.

132. A stage during this period was usually drawn by four horses that were changed about every twelve miles. The stage had three seats, the

Bullitt* & Sydney A. G[wathmey]* with us. The rain for the last two months has been unusually great.

October 20, 1817. Went to Louisville[.]

I think it strange that in times so interesting, so full of incident, in a country where improvement & prosperity so rapidly changes the face of things[,] that this journal is so barren. I know not the reason. Things pass from my memory before I can record them.

October 23, 1817. Great expectation is raised by the coming of the U. S. Branch B[ank.] I think it must enhance the value of property in Louisville & vicinity by the aid it will give to commerce.[133]

October 24, 1817. It is represented to me that a fine tract of Country is held in Indiana by the Delawares not more than 40 miles from the Ohio. If the Indian titles could be extinguished it would greatly increase the strength of that State—be an important acquisition to the Western Country—& be convenient to me if I desired to [in]vest money in public land. W[oul]d it not be well this winter to promote the idea of extinguishing it, to engage Gen. [William Henry] Harrison.*[134]

Geo[rge] Hite* on this day Wednesday applied to me to assist in getting an appointment. He prefers the Secretaryship of Alabama. I have no idea that he can succeed[.]

October 26, 1817. Sunday. An incessant rain [and] the branch higher than I ever knew it.

---

front seat facing the rear and the middle seat with a strap for its back. Each seat held three passengers.

133. Anderson, like most of his contemporaries in Kentucky, looked on the Bank with considerably less favor by 1819-1820.

134. Harrison, who was later to feel the sting of Anderson's acid pen, had been governor of Indiana Territory from 1801-1813, and was at this time a member of the House of Representatives from Ohio. The Delaware Indians were defeated by the Iroquois tribe and the Six Nations in 1720 and forced to move into Ohio. They sided with the French during the French and Indian War.

October 28, 1817. I went to Mrs. Bullitt's sale,[135] thence to Louisville.

October 29, 1817. The weather now as cold as I ever felt it in October.

Gen'l [Robert] Lytles* sale of lots in Portland[136] & along the avenue & bottom commenced yesterday. They sell very high. He has sold to the am[oun]t of $100,000. There have been this week sales of property in Louisville at a price we think enormous. It is still rising[.]

October 31, 1817. I went to Louisville.

November 1, 1817. Lytles sales again go on. I buy a lot of 5 acres at the extravagant price of $2000.[137] I think it prudent to invest some money where the public attention is so highly excited. Some contend that the town will go down stream & render the late purchase very valuable. I believe they may be valuable on account of their vicinity to Louisville but I do believe the town (the valuable part) will rather go up.

November 3, 1817. Go to Louisville & buy Holmes house & lot for $8000[.] I think I shall make money but it is not so great a speculation as many have lately made[.]

November 5, 1817. Great conversation about the presidency of the New Bank. Contest between T[homas] Bullitt* & [Stephen] Ormsby.* Much to my suprize it is thought O[rmsby]) will be elected. He is not qualified. He is not fit to be director. I am suprized that it is believed [Henry] Massie* will vote for O[rmsby.]

---

135. Her husband, Colonel Alexander Scott Bullitt, had died in 1816 and this sale was probably associated with that event.

136. Portland, near Louisville (and today a part of the city), was in 1817 divided into Portland Proper and the Enlargement of Portland. The former was laid out by Alexander Ralston in 1814, and the latter was surveyed in 1817 by Joel Wright. One-half acre lots in Portland sold for $200 in 1814; in 1817-1819 the price was $300.

137. See McMurtrie, *op. cit.,* pp. 115-116, for a description of the price rise.

November 7, 1817. I left home on my way to Washington[.] [A] bad rainy day[.]¹³⁸

Staid at J[ohn] Logans* in Shelbyville. Larz A[nderson]* goes in with me. 20 m[ile]s.¹³⁹

November 8, 1817. Came to Frankfort[.]

Rainy & muddy—20 [miles]

November 9, 1817. Breakfasted with Genl. [Richard] Taylor* at Doctor Wilkinson's. Arrived in Lexington 22 m[ile]s.

Went with J[ohn] J[ordan] C[rittenden]* & T[homas] T. C[rittenden] to Major Parker's.

November 10, 1817. Breakfasted & dined with Maj. Parker.

Supped with L[ewis] Sanders* in company with [John] Fowler,* [James] Morrison,* [William Taylor] Barry,* [John or Thomas] Crittenden, [Joseph H.] Hawkins.* [John] Fowler disapproves *all* [James] Monroes* conduct since his presidency.

November 11, 1817. Leave Lexington in company with J[ohn] J. Crittenden & T[homas] Speed.* Feed at Paris 18 m[ile]s. Meet J[ohn* or James*] Bate[s.] I go to Millersburg 8 miles. W[illiam] P. Fleming* accompanies us going to Washington, K[entucky].

November 12, 1817. Go to Licking (Evans) 13 m[ile]s to breakfast.

This is a very windy day & is becoming cool[.]

Passing Mays Lick we came to Washington [Kentucky] 20 miles put up at Stiths.

---

138. Anderson's trip to Washington may be traced on Map 2, p. 67. He took the old Wilderness Road from Louisville to Maysville, and the Maysville Pike—formerly Zane's Trace or Trail—to Wheeling. He then caught the National Road for the next portion of his journey. The trip to Washington took twenty-two days. The average fare on such a trip was 10 cents a mile.

139. By the 1820's the stagecoaches might reach a speed of twenty miles an hour, but this was not the case when Anderson made his trip. His journey was also probably slowed by the construction on the National Road, which opened the following year along the entire Washington-Wheeling route.

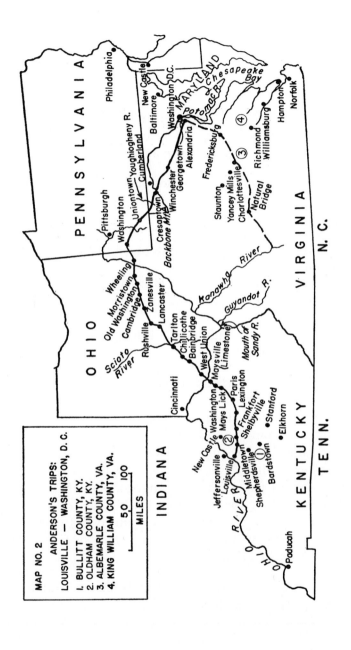

MAP NO. 2

ANDERSON'S TRIPS:
LOUISVILLE — WASHINGTON, D. C.

1. BULLITT COUNTY, KY.
2. OLDHAM COUNTY, KY.
3. ALBEMARLE COUNTY, VA.
4. KING WILLIAM COUNTY, VA.

50   100
MILES

November 13, 1817. Breakfasted at [John] Chambers* in Limestone[140] 4 m[ile]s.

Crossed the [Ohio] river & came to Senterey's [after] 26 miles[,] having passed West Union at 17 [miles] from Limestone[.]

November 14, 1817. Breakfasted at Kennons 8 miles. Mr. [Lawson] James joined us at Limestone. Lodged at Bainbridge 21 m[ile]s. A good house at Turner's[.]

November 15, 1817. Very muddy flat road to Basye's Chillicothe. 18 m[ile]s.

November 16, 1817. Passing a handsome bridge over the Scioto [River] we came to Tarylton 18 m[ile]s to breakfast at Lyhands[.]

Lodged at New Lancaster at Greens 16 m[ile]s.

N[ew] L.[ancaster] is on the Hockhocking [river.] Thriving & busy.

Here we fell in with Genl. P[hilemon] Beecher* who lives at this place.

November 17, 1817. Came to Hill's at Rushville to breakfast[.] 10 m[ile]s.

Came & lodged at Dugans in Zanesville[.] 26 m[ile]s.

This was a rainy muddy day.

The rapid improvement of this Country shews the good policy of excluding slaves & of the high benefits of dividing land into small parcels in the congress manner.

The land along the road from Chillicothe is very poor, it is thickly settled. The taverns are much better than the Country taverns in Ky. & the towns populous & populating beyond my expectations.

November 18, 1817. Came on to Cambridge 25 [miles] & put up at Stewarts [words illegible.]

---

140. Maysville.

November 19, 1817. We breakfasted at Beymers[141] in [Old] Washington[.] A very indifferent house & town. Thence we came to Spencers[,] an indifferent quaker house.

November 20, 1817. Breakfast at Eatons Morristown 5 m[ile]s[.] Thence to the Wheeling 21 m[ile]s[,] to Spriggs[,] a good house.

November 21, 1817. Breakfast at Bealls 10 m[ile]s. To Washington [Pennsylvania] 22 m[ile]s. Morrissons a good house[.]

November 22, 1817. Breakfast at Bolens 6 m[iles]. A miserable place[.]

To Brownsville 9 m[ile]s. Lodged at Brashear's[,] a good house[.]

November 23, 1817. Sunday[.] Breakfast at Union T[own] 12 m[ile]s.[142]

Fell in with Mr. [Benjamin] Ruggles.* We have passed since Wheeling a very hilly but thickly populated & well cultivated country[.][143] The land looks thin & the corn badly but it is said to be a fine wheat country[.]

Passing the Laurel Hills[144] from which Westward there is a most beautiful & sublime prospect of rills & mountains vallies & farms, we lodged at the Crossing of [the] Yohugamy [*sic* for Youghiogheny River], at Ockletrees (good house) 24 m[ile]s.

November 24, 1817. A cold morning. We breakfasted at

---

141. Built in 1802.

142. The National Road passed through Uniontown because of the influence of Albert Gallatin of Uniontown. Provision for the location of the Road was made by Congress on March 29, 1806. Construction was begun in Cumberland, Maryland, and Wheeling was selected as the western terminus. Stage fares on the road when Anderson traveled it were collected by hotel and tavern landlords who were agents for the stagecoach companies. The coaches generally ran three times a week from Wheeling to Washington, D. C.

143. For a description of travel on the National Road see Robert E. Riegel, *America Moves West* (New York, 1956), pp. 211-213.

144. See Map 2, p. 67.

Widow Jones 6 m[ile]s & came to [Jesse] Tomlinsons[,][145] a noted & very good house 14 m[ile]s.

This is the last stopping place on the Western Waters. I went to the Spring & drank of the waters I love[.]

Passing the back bone[146] We came to Mc[blank] a very good house 10 m[ile]s.

November 25, 1817. We breakfasted at Cresaps Town[.][147]

Having parted this morning with [General Philemon] Beecher* & [Benjamin] Ruggles* who took the Maryland road.[148]

We have travelled about 45 m[ile]s on the turnpike. It is a very fine road but I think unpleasant for horsemen[.]

Passing Frenchfort & Springfield two miserable villages we lodged at Higgins[,] a very good house 32 m[ile]s.

November 26, 1817. Breakfasted at Lexs 11 m[ile]s.

The weather has been good since we left Wheeling and for two or three days remarkably fine.

The landla[d]y has not yet shewn our breakfast but if I had not been long enough in the world to know that appearances are deceiving I should have woeful apprehensions of our meal[.]

Came on to Winchester 23 miles [and] put up at Mc-Gu[?] [.]

November 27, 1817. We went by the invitation of Mr. [James] Bate[s]* to his friend John Throckmorton's[.] We left Mr. B[ates]* & Larz [Anderson]* there, came on & lodged at Battletown[.]

November 28, 1817. Sent back the horses to Mr. B[ates] & took the stage. We were very much crowded. Colo[nel] J[ohn] Williams* of Tennessee, T[homas] H. Williams* of Miss[is-

---

145. One of the oldest inns in this section of the country. The original inn existed before the Cumberland-National Road was built.
146. Backbone Mountain, see Map 2, p. 67.
147. See Map 2, p. 67.
148. His companions went on to Cumberland while Anderson branched off to the south.

sippi], Colo[nel James] Pindall* of Va., Mr. [John W.] Campbell* of Ohio, Mr. [Levi] Barber* of Ohio were passengers. We arrived at Alexandria & on the 29. Came to the City in the Stage. We met the president on the way going to visit Fort Washington.

We arrived in the City. Mr. [John Jordan] Crittenden* & myself immediately waited on Mr [Henry] Clay* who introduced us to a Mess at Dowsons—[149] where we engaged boarding at $15 pr. week[.][150]

November 30, 1817. Sunday—a beautiful day. Mr. C[rittenden] & myself by invitation are still at Major D[avid] Trimbles* room at Davis[.][151]

It is said that Genl. [Samuel] Smith* will oppose Mr. Clay* for the chair. If it be true, he cannot succeed. It is surmised that before long Mr. Clay may break with the president. I know nothing to authorize—but I do think a new party will arise during the present or next session of Congress.

December 1, 1817. 11 o'clock. The fifteenth Congress will meet this day. It is a fine & most beautiful mor[nin]g. May the transactions of this Congress be as honourable to its Members & as glorious for their country, as the sun of this day is bright & splendid.

On this day Congress met—about 12 oClock[.]
Mr. Henry Clay* was elected Speaker

H Clay*   143
S. Smith*   6

Tho[mas] Dougherty* was elected unanimously Clerk & the other old officers appointed[.]

---

149. One of the more expensive boarding houses in Washington; it is mentioned by John Quincy Adams in his diary.

150. See above, November 20, 1814, for a comparison of prices in Frankfort, Kentucky.

151. Another boarding house.

December 2, 1817. The Presidents Message was delivered. It is a very good & interesting paper[.][152]

December 3, 1817. Mr. Clay moved that the Com[mittee] of [*sic* for on] Foreign Relations [Affairs] be directed to enquire what amendments are necessary to be made to the existing laws to secure to the S[outh] American patriots the observance of our Neutral obligations.[153]

In his speech he said altho our professions were neutral, that all our acts were against the patriots. From this & other observations the idea of a difference between the president & him is fostered.

I am boarding with Dowson on Capitol Hill. The Mess is composed of [Charles] Tait* (Georgia) [William] Smith* (SC), [Nathaniel] Macon* (N C) [Philip Pendleton] Barbour* (Va) [John Jordan] Crittenden* K[entucky,] Senators,[154] & [Thomas W.] Cobb,* [Stephen Decatur] Miller,* [James] Owen,* [Joel] Abbot,* [William] Terrell,* [Willard] Hall,* [Weldon Nathaniel] Edwards,* [Daniel M.] Forney* & Mrs. [William] Smith & Mrs. [Daniel M.] Forney & myself[.]

We pay $15 pr. week—& pay for own liquor. I fear it will be an expensive Mess. We have Madeira, Claret, Cider & porter every day—Champagne frequently. This is done I have no doubt against the wish of the majority. It may seem strange but I believe it a truth that it is submitted to from fear that an opposition might create a belief that the objection arose from poverty or [blank] and I am not sure that even the original proposer wishes it continued or likes the practice[.]

---

152. This was Monroe's first Annual Message. It was an optimistic message, particularly when he discussed the internal commercial expansion in the United States.

153. The question of whether or not to recognize the independence of the new Latin American states was argued in the affirmative by Henry Clay. His attitude reflected the anti-Spanish feeling of his section and also the Jeffersonian slant of his political apprenticeship. The search for a new issue of national and international dimensions also revealed his personal ambition.

154. Anderson was mistaken, since Smith and Barbour were not senators.

I have not yet discovered much talent in the Mess. Governor [Philip Pendleton] Barbour is pompous & florid in his language. [Nathaniel] Macon says some smart things but I cannot think (as yet) either of them great men. Macon must in a long public life & the excellent political school[155] through which he has passed have acquired a good deal of information but he is not more than an ordinary man. [Charles] Tait is an intelligent clever man—very pleasant & gentlemanly.

Of [William] Smith I cannot as yet form any satisfactory opinion—& indeed I may in three months change my opinion as to all.

Among the others I see nothing uncommon.

Several of the Mess especially [Charles] Tait & [Nathaniel] Macon have extended their views of the population & settlement of the W[estern] Country (even towards the pacific Ocean) very far—but they seem never to have supposed the possibility of the Seat of Gov[ernment] being removed or of any struggle or commotion arising on that subject. They seem to think that the W[estern] C[ountry]—will receive the requisite population to acquire the ascendancy and I can assure them that if the ability is ever possessed the power will be exercised[.]

Was it ever known that those who possessed power did not exercise it for their own convenience? & in this case the convenience of the *Majority* would be the good of the Nation.

December 6, 1817. I placed my brother Larz [Anderson]* at Mr. Ironsides.[156]

During this week & this day I have been introduced to Mr. [John] Forsyth,* [Thomas Bolling] Robertson* of S C [La.], Mr. [John Caldwell] Calhoun* S[ecretary of] War & others.

F[orsyth] & C[alhoun]—seem to be very pleasant agreeable

---

155. Macon was elected twelve successive times to the United States House of Representatives.
156. An English term for Harvard.

men. I have had not opportunity of forming any opinion of their Claim to high character[.]

On Wednesday last Mr. [John J.] Crittenden & myself were introduced by Genl. [William Henry] Harrison* to the president. Surely he [Harrison] is awkward & dull & I thought there was an awkward attempt at pomp & style in our mode of introduction.

December 11, 1817. We have had most beautiful weather for several days.

December 17, 1817. This day I made my first speech in Congress on the bill for commuting the Soldiers bounty land into money.[157]

December 24, 1817. I have made some further acquaintance with the Members. I begin to think there is not such a difference in men as I once thought.

Genl. [William Henry] Harrison* has talked himself very low here.[158]

[John] Forsyth* is a pleasant Speaker—[William] Lowndes* a very sensible one—but neither are orators, neither I think can be compared to [Henry] Clay* or [John] Rowan,* as mere speakers.

---

157. Anderson spoke on four occasions during this session of the Fifteenth Congress. Some congressmen belived that many ex-soldiers who held land warrants and who did not wish to pick up the bounty in land would sell the warrants to speculators. Henry Clay, among others, favored the government buying up these warrants at a probable cost of five million dollars, believing that it would cut the influence of the speculators. Anderson agreed with Clay and argued that such a bill "would exalt the government's reputation for justice and liberality." This particular bill was defeated.

158. Anderson's dislike for Harrison, expressed here and elsewhere in the diary, is not fully explained by the diarist. However, a glance at Harrison's actions at this time is illuminating. In 1816-1817 Harrison was being cleared of charges of misconduct in connection with the buying of supplies for the Northwest Territory when he was governor, and he may have offended Anderson by statements he made at that time. Harrison had also made derogatory remarks in private concerning the character of John Quincy Adams. He was angered further because he had not been given—or in fact even been offered—the job of Secretary of War. Harrison later annoyed some of the members of Congress by helping to prolong discussions on the motion for censuring Andrew Jackson in the Florida case. It must also be remembered that Harrison did not measure up to Anderson's concept of what constituted a gentleman.

On Saturday last the Compensation committee had a Meeting. I think we shall report at $9.[159]

Mr. [Uriel] Holmes* has certainly done nothing yet equal to the High character with which he came.

On the 20th I dined with Mr. Clay*—most of the Kentucky representation was with me[.] T[homas] B[olling] Robertson* has introduced a bill providing a mode for the A[verage] citizen to exercise the right of expatriation[.][160]

December 25, 1817. Xmas. This was a pleasant soft day. Engaged in writing letters.

December 26, 1817. Dined with [Thomas] Dougherty the Clerk. [Thomas Bolling] Robertson, [David] Trimble* & [John] Scott* of Miss[ouri] were along.

Yesterday for the first time I heard of the "confidential laws." I do not know what is the subject of them, but they were passed in 181[?] in secret session & although the injunction has long been taken off—The Predt. Madison has always withheld them from publication.[161]

December 27, 1817. A pleasant day. I was at the public library & the patent office.

159. See above, July 4, 1816; also below, January 10, 1818.
160. This bill was designed to secure the exercise of the right of expatriation. Those against the bill, which was defeated 67-40 in the House, argued mainly that the act of expatriation consisted merely of getting up locomotion to leave the country and taking up residence elsewhere. A person wishing to do so should, it was said, go into court and record his intention to renounce his citizenship.
161. The exact meaning of "confidential laws" is not clear. On December 31, 1817, Representative Richard M. Johnson (Kentucky) introduced a joint resolution to authorize the publication of the laws of the United States in the newspapers of the several states and territories. Through Congressional debates (January-April, 1818) runs the opinion that the laws should receive wider circulation. The Washington-Baltimore-Philadelphia press, however, did not echo any great concern. Actually, Congress approved three measures: (a) 3 Stat. 439, providing that the Secretary of State shall cause acts and resolutions of Congress to be published currently in not more than one newspaper in the District of Columbia and not more than three in each state and territory; (b) 3 Stat. 475, providing that a copy of the laws of the previous Congress be furnished each member of the current one; and (c) 3 Stat. 475, providing for the publication and indexing of all laws and resolutions at the close of the current and subsequent sessions.

December 31, 1817. Last night I suffered more with a cold in the head than I ever did before.

I have been for a day or two thinking on a subject which is soon to be presented to the House—& on which I intend to work. The question is, Is a man elected to Congress & who holds an office since the 4th March last, now eligible as a rep[resentative]? I think he is not. I am told the Committee will report in favour of his right. I think they will keep their seats. They are in truth too numerous to be turned out. One man, if he was not very conspicuous[,] would soon be disposed of.[162]

Mr. [William Harris] Crawford*, [John C.] Calhoun*, [William] Lowndes* & several S. C. members are now in our dining room—with the rest of our mess. This day Judge [Samuel] Smith* makes his birth day & these gent[lemen]—by invitation are regaling themselves with his champagne.

By a rule of the Mess each member's birth day must come on some day during the session & be celebrated with a dozen bottle[s] of Champagne[.]

January 1, 1818. A very fine day.

According to the Custom of the presidents on new years day, the rooms at the *palace* were thrown open. Five were soon filled. The company stood or walked through the rooms, each having first saluted Mr. & Mrs. Monroe. This moving about together with light conversation filled the time of an hour & two. Each one retired when he pleased. Wine & cake were handed through the Company. There was fine music.

January 10, 1818. We have generally had fine weather since new year. Unusually mild.

---

162. Samuel Herrick was elected to the House of Representatives but continued to hold a position as United States Attorney after the election. Herrick felt that he was not a member of the House until he took the oath, and that the provision that no person holding office under the United States shall be a member of the House did not apply in this case. Anderson argued that a person took on the responsibility of office on the day he was elected, not on the day he took the oath. Herrick resigned his seat after presenting his case.

The compensation bill has passed the H[ouse of] R[epresentatives] at $8 pr. diem.[163] I voted for $9.

I think Mr. [Uriel] Holmes* conduct in the Committee has disgraced him. He did refuse even to give his opinion in select committee—saying he was chairman & w[oul]d vote if there was a tie.

An idea extends that Clay is to head an opposition party.

Genl. [William Henry] Harrison is very low I think in the estimation of the house. He certainly is in mine. He is vain, little & intriguing.

For several days the HR. has been engaged with John Anderson[164]—who wrote a letter to a member—offering him a bribe of $500—to support his claims before the house. A warrant was immediately issued by the Speaker—& A[nderson]—was taken into Custody.

The questions debated are

1st Was the Warrant issued constitutionally without oath?

2 Have the [House] right to punish in any case where the contempt did not occur before [the House met?]

Can the House punish that which no previous law had declared an offense & to which no law had assigned a punishment.

The subject is still under debate. I made a short speech against the power on the last point. The whole subject involved was debated & every opinion expressed which could be entertained by man[.]

Capt. [Benjamin] OFallon [*sic* for O'Fallon]* has lately arrived in Town. He is an applicant for a Registership on the Missouri. Success doubtful[.]

---

163. See above, July 4, 1816; and December 24, 1817.

164. Colonel John Anderson, described by Richard M. Johnson as "a very gallant and a very brave man," who suffered heavy financial losses during the War of 1812, wrote a letter to Representative Lewis Williams (N.C.) offering him a fee of $500 for his services if he would assist in securing the settlement of claims for the losses sustained. (Anderson was a naturalized citizen, born in Scotland, migrated to the United States at age of 3.) After long debate over the House's power to punish for contempt, Anderson apologized for his action, and received a formal reprimand by the House. See *Daily National Intelligencer,* January, 1818, particularly January 17, 1818.

He thinks from a letter he saw from Clay to Genl [Thomas] Bodley* that Clay* would have been the next Gov[ernor] if a new Election had been ordered[.][165]

January 19, 1818. Altho I do not take an active part in anything which occurs here, still I see & hear so much that I do not attend to these memoranda.

Governor [William] Clark* came to Town on Friday.

H[enry] Clay may be an ambitious man, may be a bad man[,] but he is apparently the most frank politician I ever saw. He avows in all companies his views of the administration & of the course which he means to take as to the South Americans.

He intends to have the question tried in the House: ought we to recognize the Gov[ernment] of Buenos Ayres & probably some others?[166]

On the 14th I was at the Presidents drawing room.

Genl. P[eter] B[uel] Porter* seems to me to be very little like a great man.

I received an intimation that Judge [William] Logan* might offer for Congress.

Yesterday I dined with Mess No. 1 consisting of S[amuel] Smith,* [John] Gaillard,* T[homas] B[olling] Robertson,* H[enry] St. G[eorge] Tucker,* Genl. [Peter Buel] Porter, [Nathan] Sandford [*sic* for Sanford],* [Adam] Seybert,* [William] Irving* (NY), [Joseph] Bloomfield*[.]

January 24, 1818. The weather has been fine & mild for some time. On Wednesday last I dined with the President. Luxury is increasing in this Country as fast as our wealth or population. The same love of style, etiquette &c prevails here, which does among the aristocrats of Europe.

---

165. This is a further reference to the New Election issue which began with the death of Governor George Madison in 1816.

166. See above, December 3, 1817. On July 9, 1816, delegates from a few provinces in what is now Argentina, assembled with delegates from Upper Peru to declare the independence of the "United Provinces of South America," an area theoretically covering all of the Viceroyalty of La Plata.

No public & certain indication yet given of a new opposition party. Some of the administration [news] papers are attacking Clay.* There are several symptoms which are the usual precursors.

On yesterday I saw for the first time old Genl. Arthur St. Clair.* He seems very old.[167]

At my Request Mr. S. Sergeant has promised to ascertain where the contract entered into between Genl. [George Rogers] Clark* & H[umphrey] Marshall* now is.[168] I have thought it possible that some thing might be made by purchasing it.

January 26, 1818. N[athaniel] Pope* of Illinois dined with me.

January 27, 1818. This day Mr. [Jonathan] Mason* of Boston presented a resolution on the subject of the Massachusetts claim for Expenses of Militia called out during the War [of 1812] & not called for by the President.

February 8, 1818. Yesterday I for the first time heard the idea that high mileage would be the most effectual prevention against disunion arising from the great extent of country & the consequent remoteness of some sections from the seat of Government. It came I was told from Judge J[ohn] B. C. Lucas.*

On Friday the H[ouse of] Rep[resentatives] passed a bill giving a pension of $60 per month to Genl. [Arthur] St. Clair.* This is the highest pension ever given I believe in the U States.[169] I do not think it would have passed the house, but for the circumstance that he had an old claim against the Gov[ernment] which many members thought just & ought to have been allowed[.]

I have been in my room all day writing letters.

---

167. Nearly 84.
168. This contract related to the purchase of land northwest of Louisville.
169. Written in the margin at right angles to the text—"a great mistake R. C. A."

I was with Genl. [William] Clark* last night till ten at his lodgings at Davis. I am satisfied the Genl. is as sensible to popularity as most men—that he will be a candidate for the Government of the New State, when formed.[170]

This day I wrote to G[eorge] C. Gwathmey* to borrow for me $1500 with wh[ich] to buy Soldiers bounty land.[171]

I have no doubt that our Govt. is troubled with Amelia Island—that it knows not what to do with it.[172]

February 22, 1818. Sunday. The strange spirit of procrastination makes me omit for many days that wh[ich] I wish to do daily.

Since my last memo. I dined with W[illiam] H. Crawford* Secy. Treasury & staid with [John J.] Crittenden* at Crawfords request long after the company retired. From the interview that Even'g & some other very little things, I have taken up the idea that C[rawford]* had some hope of being the Pres[iden]t at the end of the present term—that we [*sic* for he] was not willing to wait for 8 years. He dropped some things which though not disrespectful towards the Pres[i]-d[ent] were not approbatory. This idea did not occur to me till within a few days. If he were to break off & could ally with Clay—it might be hard for the Presd. to keep his ground. May not however the number of those who wish to succeed him, be the safety of the Presdt.? I have no doubt N. York wishes [De Witt] Clinton* to be the successor.[173]

H[enry] Clay told me the other day that he wrote the little speech for the late V. President [George] Clinton*

---

170. The admission of Missouri as a state was under discussion in Congress. Law enacted in 1820.

171. Interesting as a follow-up to the speech given by Anderson in Congress, see above, December 17, 1817.

172. Trouble along the Florida border speedily reached a climax after the close of the War of 1812. Among the events that led to the United States government sending an expeditionary force to the area was the occupation of Amelia Island, at the mouth of the St. Mary's River, near the boundary of Georgia, by smugglers and bandits.

173. The rump congressional caucus that nominated William Harris Crawford for President on Feburary 24, 1824, was the last one to nominate a presidential candidate.

which he delivered when he gave his casting vote on the renewal of the Bank charter in 1811 & which gained him great applause.

I lately saw my old acquaintance John S. Smith of Baltimore.

A few days ago I rec[eive]d a letter from Charles Hill[.]

June 12, 1818. Myland. Three months have elapsed since I wrote one word in this diary. I mention this to show the indolence of Man, his ceaseless endeavour to postpone till tomorrow the trouble which ought to be encountered to day, & how prone he is to consider that trouble which requires the least exertion of mind or body. On the [blank] day of April 1818—I left Washington in company with Geo[rge] Robertson,* Wm. A. Burwell* & his son William for Baltimore in the Stage. Mr. B[urwell]* & his son stopped there. Mr. [George] R[obertson] & myself at 5 oC[lock] went in the Steam boat & arrived about day next morning at French town, were then conveyed with other passengers about 75 m[iles] in the Stages to New Castle [Delaware]. Immediately went in the Delaware Steam boat & arrived in Philadelphia about 12 oClock on Monday. The Steam boat is a most pleasant mode of travelling.

We staid in Phila. four days—visited the Museum, West's painting of Christ healing the sick—the Academy of fine arts, Hospital, [and] Alms house[.]

Gen'l John [William] Preston* of Va. & Doctor Rose were in the City at the same time, also Genl. [Philemon] Beecher,* Tho[mas] Claibourne* of Tennessee & Wilson Nesbit* [of South Carolina.]

I had a good opportunity of knowing [George] Robertson. I think he is a good man & clever—but I think he is in heart ostentatious, & that he wants decision. My acquaintance with him has not increased my opinion of his talents or usefulness of character.

We returned to Washington by the same mode of conveyance—having remained in Baltimore one night.

During my absence from the City the Navigation Bill passed.[174] I was sorry I was not present to vote for it. As it will probably be materially bad or good I was anxious that my opinion should appear.

Congress adjourned on the 20th Apr. I came to Georgetown that Evening & the next morning took the stage for Pittsburgh in company with [Joseph] Desha,* [Philemon] Beecher,* [Benjamin] Ruggles,* [Jeremiah] Morrow,* [Edward] Colston,* [Thomas] Patterson,* & [John R.] Drake.* [Joseph] Desha, [Thomas] Patterson & myself came on in the stage to Pittsburgh. The trip was not only the most unpleasant but the most fatiguing I ever underwent. I was wrong in saying I came in the Stage to Pittsburgh. Having met with Doctors [Benjamin] Tompkins* & Call on the way, the latter of whom had a horse, I exchanged my seat for him to P.[ittsburgh.]

I then descended the river in company with [Joseph] Desha, [George] Rennick* of Frankfort, Rooney, & [Major] Rice* of Bardstown to Limestone. I then came in another boat to Major [William] Croghan's* landing—borrowed a horse of him & got home on the 8 May—having been absent 6 mos & 1 day.

Of the late session of Congress I have nothing to say. If I was in any way disappointed, it was because I had made injudicious expectations. Every thing occurred as ought to have been expected & probably in the usual way. During the Session I purchased 15 soldiers patents in Illinois for which I gave an average of $96. I left Larz [Anderson] with Mr. Clay to go to Boston with his son Theodore.[175]

I made a slight acquaintance with Mr. [Horace] Holley*

---

174. 3 Stat. 432; April 18, 1818. This Act was the result of British action in closing the ports of the West Indies to American vessels, thus enabling her to carry the produce of the West Indies to the United States and goods from the United States to the West Indies in British ships. The Navigation Bill closed the ports of the United States to all British ships coming from ports that were closed to American shipping. If British ships did enter such ports in the United States, they were to be seized.

175. Theodore Clay was then 16 years old.

of Boston, who has lately been appointed President of Transylvania. I admire his talents, but cannot like him.

At home I found all well thank God. I did not expect it but am again a Candidate.

There is yet no opposition. I have the district very friendly[.] If there was opposition, I have no doubt but that my vote on the S[outh] American subject would be urged against, strongly in Shelby.[176]

But what occupies most of [my] thoughts now, is a desired speculation in the Missouri lands[.][177] The sale comes on in Sept. I fear I shall not be able to raise money to go[.]

June 12, 1818. I renew my journal.

June 20, 1818. On Sunday the 14th we had a good rain[.]

During the second week in this month [Nathan] Marders* commenced the turnpike road on Wingers land[.] I believe this is the first turnpike road ever attempted in Kentucky.

July 3, 1818. It has been fine growing weather for several days—good showers[.]

Within a few days we have partially determined to go to Washington this Winter—& take with us (the family)[,] my sister Betsy—& go by the way of New Orleans.

Town property is still rising in Louisville[.]

July 13, 1818. On Monday the 6th [July] I went to Shepherdsville. There were but few people at Court. There are new tavern keepers at the old stand—The Wiggintons. The land lady was very solicitous to assure me that "she did not associate with a single family in town." She said that she believed they were very good people but they were so low-bred.

---

176. Anderson did not follow the line set forth by Henry Clay.

177. Missouri's population by 1815 was over 60,000. Anderson may have been buying land there under the Land Law of 1800 for the legal minimum of $2.00 per acre. Purchasers could take up to four years to complete their payments.

July [*1*]5,[178] *1818*. From several different accounts it seems that large quantities of ice in the Northern seas, which have hitherto been Closed up by it, have lately disappeared and that expeditions are fitting out in England under the idea that the voyagers may be able to go much farther North than any navigator has heretofore gone. It is said that floating ice has been seen much farther South than it has heretofore been known.

Genl. [Andrew] Jackson* has lately taken Pensacola— I believe without particular orders. But if it is ascertained that the public sentiment will bear it he will be justified & the taking avowed. The Western people will approve anything which tends to scourge the Spaniards or aid the S[outh] A[merican] patriots.[179] Spain would surely go to War, if she had anything to war with—but she is miserably poor[.]

John Pope* has lately been in the County twice in a manner that convinces me the gen[era]l suspicion is correct —that he is endeavouring to ascertain the prospects of being elected to Congress from this district.

Mrs. T[emple] Gwathmey* came here with her children on thursday last.

July 17, 1818. We have had heavy rains four days successively. The spring was backward, cold & unfavorable. The season for a month has been very fine.

---

178. Anderson's lettering may have been obliterated, but the editors have supplied brackets on the supposition that he mistakenly wrote in the incorrect date.

179. On January 6, 1818, Jackson wrote President Monroe: "Let it be signified to me through any channel (say Mr. J. Rhea) that the possession of the Floridas would be desirable to the United States, and in sixty days it will be accomplished." John Spencer Bassett, *The Life of Andrew Jackson* (Garden City, N.Y., 1911), I, 246. Later, Jackson stated that en route he received (February 13, 1818) a letter from Representative Rhea communicating the President's approval of Jackson's suggestion to effect an unofficial authorized seizure of the Floridas. Monroe's story was quite different. Rhea could throw little light on the matter. For subsequent controversy regarding the letters, see *ibid.*, I, 246-249, and Marquis James, *Andrew Jackson: The Border Captain* (Indianapolis, 1938), pp. 827-829. In any case, Jackson marched into the Floridas and seized St. Marks and Pensacola before the end of May, 1818. He then appointed a civil and military governor, and returned to Tennessee.

By my advice I[saac] R. Gwathmey* has bought a lot of G[eorge] W[ood] Meriwether* for $7000. This is entirely speculation as he is not worth one tenth of the money for which he has bound himself.

I have taken 50 shares in the Comm[ercial] Bank of Louisville, not because I think it a judicious investment of money on account of the dividends—but merely to give me a fair opportunity of enjoying accommodations.[180]

It is now about 5 oClock. A dark rainy evening. Four of Mrs. T[emple] Gwathmey's children are here. They with mine are crying & quarreling.

July 31, 1818. From the 22d to 28 [July] We were at Mr. O[wen] Gwathmeys.* Mrs. Williamson & three sons were there.

Yesterday I saw Colo. R[ichard] M[entor] Johnson* at Louisville.

On Monday next the Election comes on.[181] This is the first time for seven years that I have not been able with confidence to say before the Election who would succeed. This now arises from the very general apathy on the subject. The Candidates are [Richard] Barbour,* [Alexander] Pope,* [James] Denny,* & N[orborne] B. Beall.*

If I were obliged to conjecture it would be that the two first would succeed.

August 12, 1818. The corn looks finely. I am told the new crop of wheat is selling at a dollar[.] Some has been selling all the season at about 3[s]/6[d]. It is very scarce. The demand is very great by persons living in Indiana[.]

The price of Louisville property still rises and has risen since the last fall to an extent truly astonishing. Ground on the Portland avenue[182] which Genl [Robert] Lytle* [sold]

---

180. Louisville then had three banking institutions: a branch of the State Bank of Kentucky; a branch of the United States Bank; and the Commercial Bank of Louisville, established in 1818 with a capital of one million dollars.

181. The Kentucky state election.

182. See above, October 29, 1817.

last fall for about $400 pr acre (then thought prodigious) has been lately sold by [Colonel] A. L. Campbell* for 4&5 thousand[.]

The Election has resulted in the return of [Richard] Barbour* & [Alexander] Pope* agreeably to my conjecture. But mine was only a conjecture for my expectation was not realized as to the relative state of the poll. The vote was

Barbour*	1002
Pope*	987
Beall*	911
Denny*	882

This is the greatest vote wh[ich] has ever been taken in this County.[183] I distinctly remember in the year 1800 that 800 was the no. of votes given at a very disputed election.

My dear wife Elizabeth has for some time spat blood. She is alarmed but I believe & hope it has no connection with any defect in the lungs[.]

August 21, 1818. H[enry] Massie* yesterday offered me twenty two hundred acres of land in Indiana for Myland and agreed to warrant (as far [as] Myland could support the warrant) that the land he let [me] have should be worth $40,000 at the expiration of 10 years. This is a great offer & nothing but a love of ease & an unwillingness to part with a farm when another could not easily be gotten prevents me from taking what is I think greatly more than it is worth.

From the late state Elections it appears that the friends of a New Election[184] have declined in number. The effect of a legislative body having the permanence of the State Senate has been eminently shown in the late struggle for a New Election. The last year nothing could have prevented one, if the members of each house had held their seats for *one* year only. But now the fervour has subsided and those

---

183. The vote reflected Kentucky's rapid population growth—73,000 in 1790; 200,000 in 1800, and 406,000 in 1810.
184. See above, June 4, 1817, July 12, 1817, and August 4, 1817, for previous discussions of this issue.

who were most unpopular for their opinions have been elected.

For many years my father has been amused with hobbies that have each for a time served to kill the weariness of old age, horses, cattle, marine sheep, hogs, hens have each had their day. Masonry now occupies all his time. Many ridicule these things but in old men surely they do not deserve ridicule. I think that it is very fortunate when avarice, ambition or other passions which rule man have ceased to act their part, that others can be found however trivial to give employment to the mind & to prevent the tediousness of doing nothing.

At the late election I have been returned to Congress without opposition. The circumstance does not delude me into the belief that it results from very great popularity. If there had been an opposing candidate I am sure that there would have been a strong vote for him. If I continue to offer I shall expect the storm.

September [*10 or 11*] *1818.* The rainy weather continued until about a week ago.

For three days it has been unusually cool.

I have been more severely pressed for money this fall than I ever was. I must sell some town property and am now endeavouring to effect [it]. It is for me to sell in time for the payments which I am to make the next year.

I am informed that I[saac] R. Gwathmey*—& my sister Betsy are to be married shortly[.]

The clamour against the US Banks is now much greater, than the prayer for their coming was.[185]

I am now agitated between two opposing inclinations. The one is to still live sparingly and devote myself & the money I can raise to the increase of my property by purchasing land—and the other is to live for myself by building

185. See above, September 17, 1817, for Anderson's comments on the coming of the United States Bank to Kentucky.

a good house, improving the farm & every way devoting my money for the comfort & pleasure of myself. My children, should they ever see this will wonder that I felt any doubt and will feel vexation that I did not lay out every thing for their benefit.

September 16, 1818. It began to rain last night about bed time. It is now near sun set & I do not think I ever knew more rain to fall in 24 hours. It is yet raining very hard.

My wife has been taking lessons at the singing school kept at my fathers by Metcalfe.[186]

On the last friday a jury met to assess the damages which Cuthbert Bullitt* would sustain by the Turnpike Company taking his stone, the parties met at B's spring below my land, he argued & his lawyer Blackwell argued till night. He was dissatisfied with the verdict & threatens to sue any who take stones. He objects to the constitutionality of the law[187] 1st— because it substitutes five men for a jury—2nd Because the law says that [in] estimating the damages you shall consider the benefits which the party will receive from the road. The Constitution says that no private property shall be taken for public uses, unless compensation be previously made.

J[ohn] Gwathmey* has sold his tavern to D[avid] L. Ward,* T[homas] Prather* & N[orborne] B. Beall* for 60,000 dollars—part of it on a long credit.[188] [The price is] thought cheap.

October 3, 1818. On the 3rd Monday in September I was at Shelby Court[.]

The weather has been fine of late. The nights cooler, than the season at this time of the fall usually. The rain

---

186. See Kitty Anderson, "A Historical House and Its Famous People" (mimeographed, n. d.), p. 2, for a statement of Colonel Anderson's musical interests.

187. See above, May [no date,] 1817.

188. See above, October 12, 1815, for an indication of Gwathmey's financial position.

of the 16th did great damage to the mills & bridges in the neighborhood. Beargrass [Creek] was higher than it was ever known to be & I believe Harrod's Creek & Floyds fork also were[.]

The Turnpike Co. has agreed to give me 9/ per rod (measured in length on the road) for the stone taken off my land[.]

The pressure for money generally is very great—on me is severe. I fear that I must sacrifice a part of my property. I have done what thousands have done before me & but few will fail to do after me, purchase *more* than I can conveniently *pay for*. If the sacrifice that I make is not very great, my property will still be very much enhanced by my adventures[.]

The people of Louisville are now very unhealthy.

Mrs. Clark widow of Genl. Jonathan Clark* died on Sunday last. She was a good woman and a most eminent housekeeper.

My little daughter Elizabeth is now sick with a fever & cold.

I have heard that it is in contemplation to carry the public mail on part of the Ohio & Mississippi in Steam boats. Surely no invention in any art or science is likely to produce such beneficial consequences to the Western Country as the invention of the new one of Steam—no nor all put together![189]

October 8, 1818. Great sickness & mortality in Louisville & the Country generally.

October 14, 1818. There is now certainly a disinclination to buy town property. The apprehension has arisen from the

---

189. Anderson was undoubtedly impressed by the voyage of the *New Orleans* from Pittsburgh to Louisville and on to New Orleans in 1811-1812. When the steamboat docked in Louisville a celebration took place and leading citizens were given rides in the vessel. Then in 1817 the *Enterprise* made a record run—twenty-five days, two hours, and four minutes—between New Orleans and Louisville.

pressure of the bank[.][190] This is the first damper it has ever received[.]

Mr. O[wen] Gwathmey* was with me on Saturday & Sunday. J[ohn] Gwathmey* has at last failed, that is his notes in Bank have been protested. It is not known whether his property will be sufficient, if it is not his friends & relations will be very much injured by him. He has sold property in the last 3 weeks for 110 thousand dollars and I know he has other property to the amount of $30 or 40 thousand. Still his solvency is doubtful[.]

Judge [Silas] Noel* has decided that the turnpike law is constitutional. The Banks are calling in & property here will not sell for cash. I shall endeavour very much to get some by the next winter for the purpose of purchasing soldiers lands in Missouri[.] This Spring [Fall?] has been unusually dry & cold[.]

December 25, 1818. Washington.

I left home on Sunday the 1st Nov[ember] & arrived in this place on the 18th. We came on the Kanawha route.[191] Mr. [John J.] Crittenden,* [John] McLean* of Illinois & Taliaferro of Union County Ky. in company. Left our horses in Fredericksb[ur]g [Virginia] & came in the Steam boat from Aquia Creek[.]

[The] autumn was very fine but the winter has set in with ususual severity. The whole country around has been bound in ice since the 15th inst.

190. Banks had been multiplying rapidly in Kentucky to meet the demands of borrowers. In 1818 the legislature chartered forty-six semi-independent branch banks, the largest in capital strength being located in Lexington and Louisville. The legislature then "solved" the currency problem by authorizing twenty-six institutions to issue $26 million in paper money.

The pressure alluded to by Anderson was probably the measures adopted by the United States Bank in 1818 to compel the state banks to redeem their notes in specie or close their doors. The Bank made a practice of gathering notes issued by state banks and then suddenly presenting them for payment, forcing the banks to call in their loans and often driving the borrowers into bankruptcy.

191. See Map 2, p. 67, for location of the Kanawha River. The route probably taken by Anderson may also be traced on the map, although the diarist was not precise in his description.

The finances of the country generally (I do not mean the government) were never in such a deranged & distressed state. The immense & improper issues from hundreds of Banks combined with the present great demand for specie to be exported to India have produced the embarrassment. The great premium offered for specie, causes the notes to be pushed on the Banks in great quantities & the Banks either call on their debtors or stop payment. Both modes have been adopted.

Real property & indeed all other I think must undergo a depression (temporary). I fear its effect on me will be troublesome. I have purchased property at a high price & I cannot now sell it. I have no fear (if I can meet the payment) of its ultimate value.

The time in Congress is dull[.] Public conversation is now all about Genl. [Andrew] Jackson & his execution of [Alexander] Arbuthnot & [Robert] Ambrister together with his general conduct in the management of the Seminoles, taking possession of Pensacola &c. The majority of the newspapers is I think against him. Certainly his conduct has been violent & unauthorized. I have no doubt the President thinks so & would be glad to get rid of him but fears that his [war] services have made him *too* popular to put down. The general impression is & I think it is correct that [illegible] hostility exists between Genl Jackson & [William Harris] Crawford* [,] secretary Treasury.[192]

My suspicions of last year that Crawford has some hope of becoming the President even at the next term have become stronger. His personal friends in this Mess are those who are more anxious to expose Jackson & in conversation

---

192. See above, July 15, 1818. During the Florida campaign Jackson captured, court-martialed, and executed two British traders, Arbuthnot and Ambrister, both of whom were accused of aiding the enemy. His actions produced repercussions in Washington. Cabinet members Calhoun and Crawford believed that Jackson needed disciplinary action, and both Houses of Congress made reports unfavorable to Jackson. President Monroe, influenced by popular approval of Jackson's Seminole campaign, did not punish him.

are most free with the character & conduct of the president in relation to his approval & support of Jackson.

The financial distress of the trading part of the people & Genl. Jackson are almost exclusively the subjects of conversation.

I board again at Dowson's No. 2 in my old room. Genl. [Montfort] Stokes,* [William] Davidson* of N. Carolina, Colo[nel William J.] Lewis* & lady of Va & Mrs [Samuel J.] Cabell,* [John] McLean* of Illinois have joined the Mess. Several have left it.

J[ames] D. Breckinridge* & [Thomas D.] Carneal* are in the City. B[reckenridge] has come on for the purpose of contracting to carry the mail from Louisville to New Orleans in steam boats.

This Evening I spent at [William H.] Crawfords playing whist.

I have several thousand dollars to pay during the next summer & I do not know where one thousand is to come from. I hear that my friend at home cannot sell my property. The next summer must be one of unpayment to me & I fear of some embarrassment.

The course of things is so precarious [and] circumstances may so materially change our conduct, that I have not much faith in resolutions made a year before they are to be executed, but I now think that unless my wife & children can come with me I shall not return the next winter. My personal wish is to come with them; I wish Betsy to see what might be seen in a visit to this Country.

January 3, 1819. This is Sunday. It has been snowing the whole day—& still snows[.]

The new year was a fine day. [At] 11 oClock—The Members [of Congress] attended the funeral of Mr. [George] Mumford* & at 12 oC the presidents levee.

February 14, 1819. Sunday Night[.]

This winter from about the middle of Dec. to the 11

of this month has been the mildest since 1805-6. On Friday 11th [February]—there was thunder & rain. On the next day & the next again there was a snow storm & sleet.

All my intelligence from home tells me of hard times. I fear I shall be very much embarrassed on account of my purchase in town property.

On Monday last the debate of 17 days closed on the subject of Genl. [Andrew] Jackson & the Seminole War.[193] I voted & spoke against the resolution of Censure.[194] This is the only prominent case in which [Henry] Clay & [Richard Mentor] Johnson* have ever differed. It is thought Johnson* will be the candidate for Governor of Kentucky[.]

B[enjamin] OFallon [sic for O'Fallon]* has been in the City for several days. He wants an Indian Agency. He has rather too much sail—but age may correct it.

The subject of the US Bank will soon come up in the House. I am perplexed to know what is right. These are propositions before us: 1st To repeal the charter by law[.]

2nd To issue a scire facias[.][195]

3rd To modify the charter with the assent of the stock-holders.

Then there are those members who are against doing anything. I think nothing will be done.[196]

[Thomas Bolling* or George*] Robertson & [Tunstall] Quarles* both wish to be governors of the Arkansas Terri-

---

193. See above, July 15, 1818, December 25, 1818.

194. Anderson delivered four speeches during this session of Congress (15th Congress, 2nd Session, November 16, 1818–March 3, 1819), one of them a spirited address justifying the execution of Arbuthnot and Ambrister. "Would you, Mr. Chairman, refuse the thanks of this nation to an officer who had won a brilliant victory, by a right movement, on unmilitary reasons? Would you reverse the vote which passed at a former session, giving the thanks of Congress to the victors of New Orleans, if it were now ascertained that the battle was won upon grounds which would be wholly disapproved by Steuben or Marshall Sax? Can you then, in this case, censure General Jackson for doing that for which he had authority and law, but for finding his reasons on the left instead of the right hand page of Vattel?"

195. A judicial writ, which in this case would ask the government to show cause why the act establishing the Bank should not be annulled.

196. Anderson was correct. Nicholas Biddle became president of the Bank in 1822 and served until the Bank closed its doors in 1836 after failing to secure a renewal of its charter.

tory. I care nothing—that is, very little about it—but if feeling or friendship should prevail I would give it to Q[uarles].*

I dined yesterday at Strothers with Colo[nel] P[hilip] P[endleton] Barbour.* I do not see now, how I can return next winter—unless I am more fortunate in raising money than I can expect. I do not see how it will be possible. I wish to come and bring all.

February 22, 1819. The debate on the right of a state to tax the US B[ank] Branches commenced this day by [Daniel] Webster* in the Supreme Court.[197] I think the Court will decide against the state right.

At the same time the debate is going on in the H[ouse of] R[epresentatives] on a motion to repeal the Charter of the Bank—& on another issue to issue a scire facias. I vote against both. It is probable that a great majority of my constituents are the other way & some will probably be wrathful—*but I care little enough about a seat here to do as I think right.*[198]

Washington May 8 1820[199]

Dear Father

I received a letter from Larz [Anderson]* on Saturday last; he was very well [but] he has declined the idea of leaving Cambridge [Massachusetts] at this time[.][200] I shall

---

197. *McCulloch* v. *Maryland.* The Maryland legislature, acting in the interests of the state banks, attempted to tax the branch of the United States Bank in Baltimore out of existence. McCulloch, representing the Bank, would not pay the taxes. Chief Justice John Marshall, delivering an opinion for a unanimous court, developed the theory of "implied powers" to declare that the state had no right to impede the National Bank by taxation. More importantly, he expounded on the origin and nature of the Federal Union.

198. The West, as Anderson indicated, hated what they felt was the "Eastern money power." Managers of the National Bank insisted that their policies were designed to create sound money practices, but westerners insisted that the Bank was merely ruining its competitors in an attempt to establish a monopoly position.

199. This letter was not in the original diary but has been added by the editors. It may be found in W. P. Anderson, *op. cit.*, p. 125.

200. His brother was then enrolled at Harvard.

write to him immediately and urge him to be more regular in his correspondence with the family.

I shall leave the city on Tuesday the 16th and expect to be home about the first day of June[.] We are in hourly expectation of receiving a Message from the President on the subject of Florida[.]

Remember me kindly to my mother and the family[.]²⁰¹

I am your aff: son

R. C. Anderson jr

*September 24, 1820.*²⁰² On this day with my family I removed to Louisville & occupy the brick house at the upper end of Market Street purchased of [Carver] Mercer.* The farm [Myland] I had rented last fall—with the view of coming to town to resume my profession. In Nov. [1819] I with Betsy & the two children, Elizabeth & Louis, left Myland for Virginia & Washington. We were accompanied by Miss Hill & by Ro[bert] Miller* as far as Stanford [Kentucky].²⁰³ There we met with Judge [William] Logan* who went on with us. I parted from the family at Albemarle [Virginia]. Betsy went to her relations in K[in]g Williams [Virginia] vicinity. We were accompanied in parts of our route by Colo[nel Tunstall] Quarles* & J[ohn] H[enry] Eaton* of Tennessee. We visited the Natural Bridge. On Xmas I left Washington to meet the family, coming to the City. I met them all [illegible] about ten miles South of Fredericksburg [Virginia]. Betsy & the children remained with me at Wash-

---

201. In the left hand corner of the letter Anderson wrote: "I have this day written to several persons in the district that I am not a candidate for Congress." During the first session of the Sixteenth Congress (December 6, 1819–May 15, 1820), Anderson served on the Public Lands Committee and delivered six speeches. The longest was on the question of the entrance of Missouri into the Union. Anderson spoke against a bill that would have prohibited the introduction of slaves into the territories of the United States west of the Mississippi. Congress, he argued, had no right to impose such a restriction on Missouri. It deprived Missouri of her sovereignty and would, among other things, open the way for all types of conditions to be placed on territories seeking admission.

202. The diary resumes at this point.

203. See Map 2, p. 67.

ington until the 10th of March when we went on a visit to
Baltimore, Philadelphia & New York.

We returned to Baltimore. Then Betsy & the children
with Obediah the driver took their departure for Pittsburgh.
Thence they descended in the Steam Boat Telegraph to
Louisville and arrived on the 7th Apl.

I returned from Baltimore to Washington & remained
till the Session closed on the 15th of May. This trip with my
family taken in all its parts was very pleasant. No material
accident occurred to mar its pleasure.

During the last summer [1820] we have remained at
my fathers, & at Mr. [Owen] Gwathmeys* & have now come
to town for the purpose of resuming my profession. This
has been produced solely by the depression in the price
of property. I have purchased much faster than I have paid.
I have partaken, as the preceding parts of these notes will
shew, largely of that spirit of speculation which was produced by the great & increasing prices of property, resulting
from prodigious issues of paper money. I purchased when
the circulating medium was .10 & must pay when it is 3!
My debts nearly equal $20,000. I have a good deal of
property as yet unincumbered but I cannot sell it. It takes
all my means to pay the interest[.][204]

204. This is a personal view of the so-called Panic of 1819. The new bank
notes issued by the state banks created an atmosphere "where private citizens
felt they were in disrepute unless they were financially involved in at least
one speculative venture. In the rapid distribution of new currency much
confusion resulted, for no one had worked out a basis of exchange. This
encouraged 'shavers' and brokers to practice nefarious trades. At first,
individuals were able to exchange their branch bank notes at a ten per cent
discount, but soon the rate rose to ninety-five per cent. By midsummer of
1819, the Kentuckians were thoroughly involved in a most unhappy financial
predicament. Business houses refused to accept the Kentucky bank currency
in payment for goods and services; branch banks of the United States would
not accept the Kentucky currency; and the 'wildcat' banks . . . refused notes
from one another." T. D. Clark, *op. cit.*, pp. 202-203. Kentucky seemed to
go bankrupt almost overnight. Land values sagged and real estate was worth
only one-sixth of its boom market price. Homes were mortgaged; business
was driven out of the state; and labor was loathe to come into the state. The
banks that were so easily chartered in 1817-1818 began to close their doors
and eventually had their charters repealed. As the banks pressed their debtors
for money and as land values declined, Anderson was in trouble.

A return to my profession is not my first view. I have an expectation of receiving some public employment, which will supercede the necessity of resuming the labours, which I look to with apprehension. I have declined a reelection to Congress & my successor is elected. My debts occupy my whole time & if I practise law, or obtain an appointment, it is with the object of liquidating them.

April 29, 1821. Last October I left home for Washington to serve the last session of my term. I went through Ohio in company with J. M. Luckett a young man lately of the Navy. I was sick at Redstone (at Evans) for two days. I then left my horse & went to the city in the stage[.] I boarded at Sawyers on the P[ennsylvani] (a) Avenue.[205]

According to my intention I took this session a pretty active part in the business of the house.[206] During the winter I had for two months a French teacher with me. It satisfied me that I shall never learn to speak French in America.[207] The opportunities of conversing in that language are not sufficiently numerous here to cause me to become familiar with it.

Some events occurred during this winter very interesting to me. They seem to indicate some good fortune, so far as good fortune is connected with political promotion. But nothing has yet come from appearances which at one moment seemed so flattering.

About the first of Feb[ruar]y [1821] an intimate of the president & his family told me that on the Evening before the Presdt. had told him that "he intended to appoint me minis-

---

205. Anderson spoke six times during the second session of the Sixteenth Congress that began deliberations on November 13, 1820.
206. Anderson is referring to his role on the Public Lands Committee, his speech on the reapportionment of representatives in Congress on the basis of the 1820 census, and his interest in the admission of Missouri to the Union.
207. Anderson's linguistic abilities were mentioned in a letter from Vicente Rocafuerte to Pedro Gual, Colombian Minister of Foreign Affairs, on February 15, 1823: "he does not know Spanish and according to what I have heard he speaks French with difficulty." (Letter, courtesy of Manuel Pérez Vila, Fundación John Boulton.)

ter to Rio Janeiro". In less than two days I learned that the intention was changed. The information which I rec'd was true. But the Presd. thought it was proper to postpone the Mission. Now it may never come. A thousand & more than a thousand things m[a]y prevent it.[208] So slight are the causes that produce elevation and depression—that there seems to be hardly the thickness of a wafer between a great man and a dog.

From other sources I recd. information, that the Presdts. intentions toward me are very favorable. I have, however, resumed my profession, not as my first object—but to give me employment for a time & may be for life.

I cannot avoid mentioning an incident which shows the fallibility, the weakness of men—even the best. The Presd. is a good man—popular—just reelected. Under these circumstances a few days before the close of the Session he wrote to me a letter headed "confidential" the sole object of which was to induce me to vote for & support a bill before the house making an appropriation for fortifications.[209] It was highly improper. He was the chief Executive officer & I was a member of Congress—but it manifested great weakness. The bill was comparatively unimportant yet so far were his feelings interested, that he risked his reputation & placed his fame on the prudence & honesty of a man, whom he considered as his friend, but of whose friendship he had never had the opportunity of receiving any remarkable proofs.

The next presidential election is the event that occupies the attention of all at Washington. [John Quincy] Adams & [William Harris] Crawford are the prominent candidates.

208. In February, 1821, the Portuguese royal family was in Brazil and John VI ruled the United Kingdom of Brazil, Portugal, and Algarves. In April John left for Portugal, fearful that a rebellion there that had ousted the Regency might lead to the end of the Braganza reign. He left his son, Dom Pedro, as regent in Brazil. Brazil's declaration of independence came on September 7, 1822, but the country was not secure until 1823. These events make the President's decision understandable.

209. "An Act Making Appropriations for the Military Services of the United States," approved March 31, 1821; 3 Stat. 633. Anderson voted "yea."

[Daniel D.] Tompkins & [De Witt] Clinton are spoken of—& [Henry] Clay also. Of the two first I would prefer Crawford —but I rather think that the prospects of the other best. Still in three years, so many events may happen, that no calculation can now be made with accuracy.

It seems to be understood that if [John Quincy] Adams be elected [John C.] Calhoun is to be the next Secretary of State.[210] Clay's course is certainly not yet taken. He cannot have much expectation of success himself but he will not come out for either of the others until that is ascertained.

I returned to Louisville in March [1821]; on horse back to Wheeling, thence down the river. I now reside in Town & practise my profession. The first Court is now sitting. I have appeared in one case.

At the last Court a verdict had been rendered for $500. I got a new trial & the jury now gave a verdict for $600. This is not without its mortification—that my first effort should be so unfortunate might well mortify.

I am very much solicited to offer for the [Kentucky] legislature—and as the *law* is not my *main* object probably I shall. If the expectations raised by the Pres[iden]t['s] conversations & positive declarations are not realized, I shall be injured,—seriously injured. I *cannot* devote my mind to my profession.

I am looking out eagerly for every opportunity to sell a part of my property to discharge my debts. It is important that it should be done. The Commonwealths Bank is just organized & I have some hope of the effect of the Institution on property.[211] My debts must be paid. My debts must be paid!

---

210. The appointment went, of course, to Henry Clay, amidst cries of bargain and corruption. For Anderson's view, see below, April 16, 1825.

211. By 1821 all banking charters in Kentucky except that of the Bank of Kentucky had been repealed. This Bank with its thirteen branches, and the two branches of the United States Bank, were the only ones left in Kentucky. On November 29, 1820, the Kentucky legislature chartered the Bank of the Commonwealth to "tide Kentucky over the depression." It was an institution without stockholders and was under officers elected by the

July 4, 1821. A great deal of rain has fallen lately. It is now raining very hard—and will I suppose prevent throughout the state the usual celebrations of this day. The Ohio has kept unusually full—& even now it is in good order for the Steam Boats & will probably be very high in a few days.

The New Bank has as yet no sensible effect on the price of real property—although specie is now at an advance of 55 [per cent] over the money of the Ky. Banks.[212]

To that uneasiness which my *own* debts give me there is added my father's unpleasant situation. In a few days executions to the amount of several thousand dollars will be issued against him & he has no provision to satisfy them. His course in life ought to give a valuable lesson to a son or any one who would observe it. I never knew within my recollection that he suffered the slightest inconvenience for the want of money, until lately. Now he is distressed. At the age of 70 he has become distressed by the consequences of an attempt to *increase* his fortune.

These memos. show that I have suffered some uneasiness about my pecuniary situation but I wish it distinctly understood that it has never arrived *at unhappiness.* I believe that I am as happy now, as when I thought myself worth more than treble my present property.

I can say almost without certainty that no loss of property (wh[ich] still leaves a certain subsistence) can distress me. I speak *knowingly,* that the knowledge, that I am worth $40,000 less than I thought myself to be worth three years

---

legislature and paid by the state. Its notes were assigned to the counties in proportion to the taxable property, and were to be loaned on mortgage securities to those who needed them to pay off debts or to "purchase products for exportation." Although the Bank boasted a capital of $2 million, its only real capital was an appropriation of $7,000 by the state legislature to buy the machinery to print notes. In short, the treasury of the state of Kentucky was being used as a kind of land bank to relieve debtors. This was also the purpose of the so-called Replevin Laws.

212. Anderson's apprehensions were justified, for within a year the Commonwealth Bank was in trouble. It issued $2,300,000 in notes and loaned $2,400,000 on mortgages. Its stocks fell to a fraction of their face value, and as debtors' property was seized by creditors the whole question of the financial operations of the state was headed for the courts.

ago has not diminished my happiness a cent's worth. It is the *first* information of a loss only that affects me. I have now perplexities in paying debts, raising money and saving from every way, than I had perplexities of a different kind but just as great.

I am a candidate for the [Kentucky] legislature. I think I shall be elected. [Craven P.] Luckett,* [James D.] Breckenridge,* Lee White,* S. Bray, R[ichard] Barbour,* G[eorge] R. C. Floyd* & J[ames] Brown* are candidates. My friends have been thinking of me as the next Speaker of the H[ouse of] Rep: & it is probable that I thought of myself long before they did. I see a difficulty which they do not yet. If the *old* speaker can be displaced, Judge [William] Logan* will wish to do it. This I think & Judge L[ogan] is my friend—& our friends will think that his claims are greater than mine.[213]

J[ohn] Rowan* came this Spring to reside in Louisville—professed to practice law—*but* I have no doubt to increase his chances of political preferment. Although, I think, that he has miscalculated, that is doubtless the object.

June 30, 1822. This is a Sunday of incessant rain. I am at home with the children. Mrs. [Denis] Fitzhugh* has been ill for several days & Betsy is now with her.

This spring & summer have been unusually hot & wet. Great alarm & just too, is raised in regard to the health of the town. My health has not been very good for several weeks. I believe (but am not sure) that mine is a case of dyspepsy. I was sick in Frankfort during the May session of the Legislature & immediately on my return home went with the family to the Big Bone lick.[214]

There has been great activity in business lately in town. There is a good deal of improvement in building going on & there is a prospect of better times.

Although the money character of the State abroad is very

---

213. Anderson was elected Speaker of the House.
214. See Map 1, p. 5.

bad—the Commonwealth's money is now passing two dollars for one. The laws which have been passed to *compel* Creditors to take this money have produced great excitement in the state.[215]

I was a Member of the last legislature. There were two Sessions. The second was called for the purpose of laying off the state into Congressional districts. During this session B[enjamin] W. Leigh* app[eare]d as the Com[missioner] of Va. to assert the claims of the holders of unlocated warrants to entry below the Tennessee.[216]

At this session an attempt was made (it is believed to be the first of the kind) to remove Judge Clarke [*sic* for James Clark]* from office, for giving an opinion that the endorsement or replevin laws are unconstitutional, by an address to the Gov[ernor John Adair.*] Some of the advocates of removal contended that the Jud[ge] had no right to pass on the constitutionality of the laws; others that although the Jud: had the right, that the legis: had the right to remove whenever they considered the decision vitally injurious to the interests of the State. The vote in the H. R. was 58 to 35. There not being 2/3ds for removal the motion failed. Unless the Court of Appls. shall declare the laws constitutional the excitement will continue & the subject will be prosecuted until the legislature finally prevails, I fear. I do not think that any conviction of political misrule, any public grievance will produce such wonderful irresistible torrent of feeling

---

215. These were the controversial Replevin Laws which were designed to alleviate Kentucky's financial distress and help the debtor. The law gave the debtor a delay of two years in paying his debts if the creditor refused to accept notes of the Bank of the Commonwealth of Kentucky as payment. Otherwise the debtor received an extension of one year. Further legislative action produced the Stay Laws, which declared that land could not be sold under execution to pay a debt unless it brought three-fourths of its value as appraised by a board of neighbors. The results of this stipulation were obvious, since these neighbors were usually also in debt and wished to support values.

216. In May, 1822, Leigh appeared before the legislature and, under the terms of a compact between Tennessee and Kentucky, asked for the appointment of commissioners to decide differences of opinions on boundary lines and on the matter mentioned in the diary.

among the people as these legislative acts, which regulate the rights of creditors & debtors. Whenever this relation is touched both sides lose reason & all regard for law & even the Constitution. Many of our most distinguished statesmen have taken a course on this subject well calculated to forfeit the confidence of every safe man in them. It is not to be understood that I doubt the motives of all. No indeed. I have had so many evidences of the fallibility of my own & all human judgement that a difference of opinion produces but little emotion in my mind. But the conduct of some of our dist[inguished] men is too inconsistent with their former course, not to be ascribed to some bad motive. Some seriously think they are right (God knows they may be) others are frantic from pecuniary embarrassment; others are corruptly taking advantage of the popular current to promote their views.[217]

At this session passed a law granting $10,000 to the institution of a Hospital at Louisville—also a law giving 2 pr. cent on all auction sales to the same purpose. These laws form the foundation of an institution that may last for ages!

This Session gave me an opp[ortunit]y of extending my acquaintance & consequence through the State. It was generally believed that I sh[oul]d be a candidate for the [US] Senate against Colo[nel Richard Mentor] Johnson.* This is not my present plan nor my first wish. Still circumstances may make me a candidate. At present I do not believe that any man in the State can succeed against [R. M.] Johnson. [John] Rowan* is avowedly most anxious to go to the U. S. Senate. I do not think that he has any chance although he is now doing every[thing] that a political desperado can do to

217. The Relief party that pushed through the Replevin Laws was in no mood to brook opposition from the judiciary. Judge James Clark presided over a case involving action to collect $219.67. He declared the Replevin Laws unconstitutional because it violated the national Constitution's right of contract, as well as impairing the right of contract clause in the state constitution. Clark was ultimately called before the Kentucky legislature to explain his decision. In 1823 the Court of Appeals upheld Clark's decision, and the members of the Relief party in the legislature retaliated by launching an attack on the Court of Appeals. This move, and the problems it created, provided an issue in Kentucky state politics for a number of years.

get there. He, C[raven] P. Luckett,* S. M. Brown, D. C. Terrell, W. Field & myself are candidates for the [Kentucky] legislature.

The last winter [1821-1822] produced a great change in the aspect of things as it regards the succession to the presidency. [John C.] Calhoun* is now (unexpectedly) the most prominent candidate & [John Quincy] Adams* seems a little in the background.

The Expectation which the conduct of the Presdt. has excited & which I expected w[oul]d have been realized before this time, has been defeated. That is, it is not realized. Still my belief is that it will be, & I shall suffer all the inconveniences of ex[press] disapptd. [*sic* for disappointment]—if I shd. finally be mistaken.[218] In the mean time I shall make use of all *fair* opportunities to increase my character & weight at home. The most open way now presented to me seems to be to go to the legisl. & to become the Speaker. This then is my present plan & I think the prospect of accomplishing it, is fair.

On the *29th Sept. 1822*—My daughter Elizabeth was taken sick at my fathers, where I had been with my family for some time. She became very ill. I had as little expectation of her recovery as I had that a dead child would rise from the Grave. But she did recover. The *6th day of October* [*1822*] was the day of the greatest unhappiness I ever felt. I have seen three of my children die but I have never suffered as much as I have with this one yet living. The difference in age & in apparent suffering accounts for the difference of feeling in me. Eight months have elapsed since that day and I can say now, with certainty, that it was the day of the greatest unhappiness I ever saw.

---

218. During this period, according to the John Quincy Adams Diary, VI, 23-24, the President and his cabinet were discussing possible appointments to South America. Calhoun was in no hurry, but Adams, noting that Colombia had sent a chargé d'affaires to Washington, suggested that the way was open to make an appointment to that country.

April 5, 1823. This day I expect to set out for Colombia in South America with my family.

Although some events have occurred which in the estimation of the world & probably in my own are well calculated to give pleasure, yet it has been a time of affliction to me & to all mine. The deaths of the last year among those who were dearest to me could not occur without striking my heart in a way never to be forgotten.

My dear son Louis died on the last day of July 1822. Elizabeth & her mother & my sister Louisa were all sick at my house in town: on the 17th July we went to the Country. Louis was quite well when we went to my fathers. On the friday following—I rode out. When I returned I found him lying on the floor with a fever. He never was well again. I believe the medicine never checked or touched his disorder; he died on the Wednesday week succeeding (31 July) about nine oclock at night. He was a most lovely child & I never think of him but with misery. He is buried at his grand father's[219] near his two sisters & a brother who have gone before him. In October [1822] Mrs. [Owen] Gwathmey*[,] mother of my Betsy[,] died after a distressing illness of many months. A better mother & a better woman never lived; she was about her 67th year & had been married 49 years. She was in perfect health until this unfortunate season.

In July [1822] Denis Fitzhugh* died; in September Major Wm. Croghan*—also in Sept. my brother in law Hezekiah Jones.* Mr. Saml. Gwathmey* lost two children— one a fine boy of 12 yrs. old. Isaac G[wathmey]* lost his only child—Mr. Tho[mas] Bullitt* one—Mr. G[eorge] Woolfolk* one.

These were deaths of our nearest relations. It was the most afflicting season that ever came over this Country.

Several of the most respectable heads of families fell—& hardly a family escaped the affliction of losing some member.

---

219. The reference is to Soldiers' Retreat.

The early part of the season was uncommonly wet & it now seems to be generally understood that a wet season produces great ill health.

It is not believed that any material effect is produced on the improvement or business of the town. Surely sickness & death are forgotten sooner than any thing in the world. It is probably however a wise dispensation of providence. If the afflictions produced by such mortality as prevailed last year were to last, the ordinary avocations of life would be abandoned, & indeed the design of Man's Existence defeated.

In October [1822] the legislature met—& I was elected the Speaker; Anderson 43, [John] Rowan* 33, D. Cosby 7. The session passed most harmoniously & happily for me, if any happiness can arise from giving very general (I believe universal) satisfaction. The legislature took the wise course of ordering a part of the Commonwealth's money to be cancelled & I began to think that the money issued would be redeemed & that we should again return to a sound currency, but from the indications lately given by the people I fear that the legislature will not be sustained & that new sacrifices will take place.

If they do, the paper will sink to four for one. However the situation of the people is greatly better within the last two years. A vast load of debt has been cancelled.

In January I recd. a letter from the President [Monroe] informing me that he designed to nominate me as Minister to the Republic Colombia.[220] In that month the nomination was made & ratified on the 27th. C[aesar] A. Rodney* was app[ointe]d Minister to Buenos Ayres—Genl. [Andrew] Jackson to Mexico & Heman Allen* of Vermont to Chili. Genl. J[ackson] does not accept.

This appointment is given to me under circumstances which made it not only agreeable but almost necessary. The Presd. having induced me for more than two years to expect

---

220. Monroe informed John Quincy Adams of his decision on January 12, 1823.

some such station, I had gotten out of business & the period had arrived when I could no longer be unengaged, without exciting notice. In a pecuniary point of view it was very convenient. This memo: shews that I am [in] debt & this mission shall pay these debts whatever may be the deprivations necessary to make it accomplish that end.

My wife, my daughter Elizabeth, my son Arthur & my daughter Nancy my only remaining children go with me. I am not without apprehension as to my health & that of the family—but I must go. My own health has been bad for several years. My stomach is very much deranged. Mr. Owen G[wathmey] goes with me to see his relations in Virginia. Ferdinand Bullitt* goes as my private secretary.

The thought of leaving friends, many of whom probably I shall never see again excites painful feelings. My father is old (about 73) & the idea of never again seeing a father, from whom since the hour of my birth I never recd. any thing but kindness & affection is afflicting. However comfort comes in the hope that he may possibly yet live several years.[221]

I hope that my son may have virtue enough to look at me with the feelings with which I now look at my father!

The United States is now under great excitement produced by the approaching presidential Election. [John Quincy] Adams, [William Harris] Crawford, [Henry] Clay, [John C.] Calhoun & [Andrew] Jackson have been considered as the candidates. The two latter I think will retire. Without having any strong feeling on the subject I have avowed my sentiments for Clay & wish that he may succeed[.] I think that in honesty & talents he is equal to his competitors & he is a Kentuckian. My own opinion is, that his prospect is not very bright.

During the last winter [1822-1823] & this Spring I see among my friends a manifest inclination that I should have offered for the next Governor's place. My ambition never

221. Colonel R. C. Anderson died in October, 1826, three months after the death of the diarist.

ran exactly in that way; and if I could have transferred the favour of my friends another way it is probable that I might have been a Candidate for the Senate US. if I had continued in Kentucky.

My stay in Colombia is wholly uncertain; it depends on the climate, our health, the expenses of living & many other things. If all these things are agreeable I shall certainly remain 3 or 4 years—perhaps longer.

Sometimes the notion comes across my mind of residing in Lexington when I return. It is a beautiful & healthy town. It is now assuming a scientific character. The schools there will enable me to educate my children at home—& in every way it seems to furnish as desirable a residence as any in the Western Country.

I have taken my passage in the Steam Boat Courier for Wheeling which promises to go this day.

Spencer & Reuben[222] are sent thro[ugh] Ohio with Mr. [Owen] Gwathmey's horses.

These papers I leave sealed up to be delivered to my son in the event that I never return or make no other disposition of them.

R. C. Anderson jr
April 5th 1823

at Mr. Tho[mas] Bullitts* in the front room up stairs.

---

222. Anderson's slaves. It was then common to send slaves ahead with horses or to transport family belongings to their destination.

PART III: RICHARD CLOUGH ANDERSON, Jr., ENVOY EXTRAORDINARY AND MINISTER PLENIPOTENTIARY TO LA GRAN COLOMBIA, 1823-1826

John Quincy Adams, Secretary of State, to Richard C. Anderson, United States Minister to Colombia, May 27, 1823.[1]

[extracts]

The revolution which has severed the colonies of Spanish America from European thraldom, and left them to form self-dependent Governments as members of the society of civilized nations, is among the most important events in modern history. As a general movement in human affairs it is perhaps no more than a development of principles first brought into action by the separation of these States from Great Britain, and by the practical illustration, given in the formation and establishment of our Union, to the doctrine that voluntary agreement is the only legitimate source of authority among men, and that all just Government is a compact. It was impossible that such a system as Spain had established over her colonies should stand before the progressive improvement of the understanding in this age, or that the light shed upon the whole earth by the results of our Revolution should leave in utter darkness the regions immediately adjoining upon ourselves. The independence of the Spanish colonies, however, has proceeded from other causes, and has been achieved upon principles in many respects

---

1. William R. Manning (ed.), *Diplomatic Correspondence of the United States Concerning the Independence of the Latin-American Nations* (New York, 1925), I, 192-208; Department of State, *9 Instructions, U. S. Ministers*, pp. 274-312.

different from ours. In our Revolution the principle of the social compact was, from the beginning, in immediate issue. It originated in a question of *right* between the Government in Europe and the subject in America. Our *independence* was declared in defence of our *liberties,* and the attempt to make the yoke a yoke of oppression was the cause and the justification for casting it off.

The revolution of the Spanish colonies was not caused by the oppression under which they had been held, however great it had been. Their independence was first forced upon them by the temporary subjugation of Spain herself to a foreign power. They were, by that event, cast upon themselves, and compelled to establish Governments of their own. Spain, through all the vicissitudes of her own revolutions, has clung to the desperate hope of retaining or reclaiming them to her own control, and has waged, to the extent of her power, a disastrous war to that intent. In the mind of every rational man it has been for years apparent that Spain can never succeed to recover her dominion where it has been abjured, nor is it probable that she can long retain the small remnant of her authority yet acknowledged in some spots of the South American continent, and in the islands of Cuba and Porto Rico.

The political course of the United States, from the first dawning of South American independence, has been such as was prescribed by their relative duties to all the parties. Being on terms of peace and amity with Spain through all the changes of her own Government, they have considered the struggles of the colonies for independence as a case of civil war, to which their national obligations prescribed to them to remain neutral. Their policy, their interest, and their feelings, all concurred to favor the cause of the colonies; and the principles upon which the right of independence has been maintained by the South American patriots have been approved, not only as identical with those upon which our own independence was asserted and achieved, but as involving the whole theory of Government on the emphatically American foundation of the sovereignty of the people and the unalienable rights of man. To a cause reposing upon this basis the people of this country never could be indifferent, and their sympathies have accordingly been, with great unanimity and constancy, enlisted in its favor. The sentiments of the Government of the United States have been in perfect harmony with those of their people, and while forbearing, as their duties of neutrality prescribed, from every measure which could justly be construed as hostile to Spain, they have exercised all the moral influence which they possessed to countenance and promote the cause of independence. So long as a contest of arms, with a rational or even remote prospect of eventual success, was maintained by Spain, the United States could not recognize the independence of the colonies as existing *de facto* without trespassing on their duties to Spain by assuming as decided that which was precisely the question of the war. In the history of South American independence there are two periods, clearly distinguishable from each other: the first, that of its origin, when it was rather a war of independence against France than against Spain; and the second, from the restoration of Ferdinand VII, in 1814. Since that period the territories now constituting the Republic of Colombia have been the only theatre upon which Spain has been able to maintain the conflict offensively, with even a probable color of ultimate success. But when, in 1815, she made her greatest effort, in the expedition from Cadiz, commanded by Morillo, Mexico, Peru, and Chile were yet under her authority; and had she succeeded in reducing the coast of Terra Firma and New Granada, the provinces of La Plata, divided among themselves, and weakened by the Portuguese occupation of Montevideo, would probably not have held out against her long. This, at least, was the calculation of her policy; and from the geographical position of those countries, which may be termed the heart of South America, the conclusion might well be drawn that if the power of Spain could not be firmly reseated there, it must be, on her part, a fruitless struggle to maintain her supremacy in any part of the American continent. The expedition of Morillo, on its first arrival, was attended with signal success. Carthagena was taken, the whole coast of Terra Firma was occupied, and New Granada was entirely subdued. A remnant of Patriots in Venezuela, with their leader, Bolívar, returning from expulsion, revived the cause of independence; and after the campaign of 1819, in which they reconquered the whole of New Granada, the demonstration became complete, that every effort of Spain to recover the South American continent must thenceforward be a desperate waste of her own resources, and that the truest friendship of other nations to her would consist in making her sensible that her own interest would be best consulted by the acknowledgment of that independence which she could no longer effectually dispute.

To this conclusion the Government of the United States had at an earlier period arrived. But from that emergency, the President has considered the question of recognition, both in a moral and political view, as merely a question of the proper *time*. While Spain could entertain a reasonable hope of maintaining the war and of recovering her authority, the acknowledgment of the colonies as independent States would have been a wrong to her; but she had no right, upon the strength of this principle, to maintain the pretension after she was manifestly disabled from maintaining the contest, and, by unreasonably withholding her acknowledgment, to deprive the Independents of their right to demand the acknowledgment of others. To fix upon the precise *time* when the duty to respect the prior sovereign right of Spain should cease, and that of yielding to the claim of acknowledgment would commence, was a subject of great delicacy, and, to the President, of constant and anxious solicitude. It naturally became, in the first instance, a proper subject of consultation with other powers having relations of interest to themselves with the newly opened countries as well as influence in the general affairs of Europe. In August, 1818, a formal proposal was made to the British Government for a concerted and contemporary recognition of the independence of Buenos Ayres, then the only one of the South American States which, having declared independence, had no *Spanish* force contending against it within its borders; and where it therefore most unequivocally existed *in fact*. The British Government declined accepting the proposal themselves, without, however, expressing any disapprobation of it; without discussing it as a question of principle, and without assigning any reason for the refusal, other than that it did not then suit with their policy. It became a subject of consideration at the deliberations of the Congress of Aix-la-Chapelle, in October, 1818. There is reason to believe that it disconcerted projects which were there entertained of engaging the European Alliance in actual operations against the South Americans, as it is well known that a plan for their joint mediation between Spain and her colonies, for restoring them to her authority, was actually matured and finally failed at that place, only by the refusal of Great Britain to accede to the condition of employing *force* eventually against the South Americans for its accomplishment. Some dissatisfaction was manifested by several members of the Congress at Aix-la-Chapelle at this avowal on the part of the United States of their readiness to recognize the independence of Buenos Ayres.

The reconquest, in the campaign of 1819, of New Granada to the Patriot cause was immediately followed by the formation of the Republic of Colombia, consisting of three great divisions of the preceding Spanish Government: Venezuela, Cundinamarca, and Quito. It was soon succeeded by the dissolution of the Spanish authority in Mexico; by the revolution in Spain itself; and by the military operations which resulted in the declaration of independence in Peru. In November, 1820, was concluded the armistice between the Generals Morillo and Bolivar, together with a subsequent treaty, stipulating that, in case of the renewal of the war, the parties would abstain from all hostilities and practices not consistent with the modern law of nations and the humane maxims of civilization. In February, 1821, the partial independence of Mexico was proclaimed at Yguala; and in August of the same year was recognized by the Spanish Viceroy and Captain General O'Donoju, at Cordova.

The formation of the Republic of Colombia, by the fundamental law of the 17th of December, 1819, was notified to this Government by its agent, the late Don Manuel Torres, on the 20th of February, 1821, with a request that it might be recognized by the Government of the United States, and a proposal for the negotiation of treaties of commerce and navigation, *founded upon the bases of reciprocal utility and perfect equality,* as the most efficacious means of strengthening and increasing the relations of amity between the two Republics.

The request and proposal were renewed in a letter from Mr. Torres, of the 30th of November, 1821, and again repeated on the 2d of January, 1822. In the interval since the first demand, the General Congress of the new Republic had assembled, and formed a constitution, founded upon the principles of popular representation, and divided into legislative, executive, and judicial authorities. The Government under this constitution had been organized and was in full operation; while, during the same period, the principal remnant of the Spanish force had been destroyed by the battle of Carabobo, and its last fragments were confined to the two places of Porto Cabello and Panama.

Under these circumstances, a resolution of the House of Representatives of the United States, on the 30th of January,

1822, requested of the President to lay before the House the communications from the agents of the United States with the Governments south of the United States which had declared their independence, and those from the agents of such Governments here with the Secretary of State, tending to show the political condition of their Governments and the state of the war between them and Spain. In transmitting to the House the papers called for by this resolution, the President, by his message of the 8th of March, 1822, declared his own persuasion that the time had arrived when, in strict conformity to the law of nations and in the fulfilment of the duties of equal and impartial justice to all parties, the acknowledgment of the independence declared by the Spanish American colonies could no longer be withheld. Both Houses of Congress having almost unanimously concurred with these views of the President, an appropriation was made by law (4th of May, 1822), for such missions to the independent nations on the American continent as the President should deem proper.

On the day after the President's message of the 8th of March, the Spanish minister, Anduaga, addressed to this Department a remonstrance against the measure which it recommended, and a solemn protest against the recognition of the Governments mentioned of the insurgent Spanish provinces of America. He was answered on the 6th of April, by a letter recapitulating the circumstances under which the Government of the United States had "yielded to an obligation of duty of the highest order, by recognizing as independent States nations which, after deliberately asserting their right to that character, had maintained and established it against all the resistance which had been or could be brought to oppose it." On the 24th of April he gave information that the Spanish Government had disavowed the treaty of the 24th of August, 1821, between the Captain General O'Donoju and Colonel Iturbide, and had denied the authority of the former to conclude it.

On the 12th of February, 1822, the Spanish Extraordinary Cortes adopted the report of a committee proposing the appointment of Commissioners to proceed to South America to negotiate with the revolutionary Patriots concerning the relations to be established thereafter in regard to their connexion with Spain. They declared, at the same time, all treaties made with them before that time by Spanish commanders, implying any acknowledgment of their independence, null and void, as not having been authorized by the Cortes; and on the next day they passed three resolutions, the first annulling expressly the treaty between O'Donoju and Iturbide.

The second, "That the Spanish Government, by a declaration to all others with which it has friendly relations, make known to them that the Spanish nation will regard, *at any epoch,* as a violation of the treaties, the recognition, either partial or absolute, of the independence of the Spanish provinces of Ultramer, so long as the dissensions which exist between some of them and the Metropolis *are not terminated,* with whatever else may serve to convince foreign Governments that Spain has not yet renounced any of the rights belonging to it in those countries."

The third resolution recommended to the Government to take all necessary measures, and to apply to the Cortes for the needed resources to preserve and recover the authority of Spain in the ultramarine provinces.

These measures of the Cortes were not known to the President of the United States when he sent to Congress his message of the 8th of March; but information of them was received while the bill making an appropriation for the missions was before Congress, and on the 25th of April a resolution of the Senate requested of the President any information he might have, proper to be disclosed, from our minister at Madrid, or from the Spanish minister resident in this country, concerning the views of Spain relative to the recognition of the independence of the South American colonies and of the dictamen of the Spanish Cortes. In answer to this resolution, the letter from Mr. Anduaga, protesting against the recognition, and one from Mr. Forsyth, inclosing a translation of the dictamen, were transmitted to the Senate, which, with all these documents before them, gave their concurrent sanction, with that of the House of Representatives, to the passage of the bill of appropriation.

This review of the proceedings of the Government of the United States in relation to the independence of Spanish America has been taken to show the consistency of the principles by which they were uniformly dictated, and that they have been always eminently friendly to the new Republics, and disinterested. While Spain maintained a doubtful contest with arms to recover her dominion it was regarded as a civil war. When that contest became so manifestly desperate that Spanish Viceroys, Governors, and Captain Generals themselves, concluded treaties with the insurgents, virtually acknowledging their independence, the United States frankly and unreservedly recognized the fact, without making their acknowledgment the price of any favor to themselves, and although at the hazard of incurring the displeasure of Spain. In this measure they have taken the lead of the whole civilized world; for although the Portuguese Brazilian Government had, a few months before, recognized the revolutionary Government of Buenos Ayres, it was at a moment when a projected declaration of their own independence made the question substantially their own cause, and it was presented as an equivalent for a reciprocal recognition of their own much more questionable right to the eastern shore of La Plata.

On the 17th day of June, 1822, Mr. Manuel Torres was received by the President of the United States as the chargé d'affaires from the Republic of Colombia, and the immediate consequence of our recognition was the admission of the vessels of the South American nations, under their own colors, into the ports of the principal maritime nations of Europe.

The European alliance of Emperors and Kings have assumed, as the foundation of human society, the doctrine of unalienable *allegiance*. Our doctrine is founded upon the principle of unalienable *right*. The European allies, therefore, have viewed the *cause* of the South Americans as rebellion against their lawful sovereign. We have considered it as the assertion of natural right. They have invariably shown their disapprobation of the revolution, and their wishes for the restoration of the Spanish power. We have as constantly favored the standard of independence and of America. In contrasting the principles and the motives of the European powers, as manifested in their policy towards South America, with those of the United States, it has not been my intention to boast of our superior purity, or to lay a claim of merit to any extraordinary favor from South America in return. Disinterestedness must be its own reward; but in the establishment of our future political and commercial intercourse with the new Republics it will be necessary to recur often to the principles in which it originated; they will serve to mark the boundaries of the rights which we may justly claim in our future relations with them, and to counteract the efforts which it cannot be doubted European negotiators will continue to make in the furtherance of their monarchical and monopolizing contemplations. . . .

Our commercial relations with the Colombian territory are

of so recent origin, and have depended so much upon the revolutionary condition of that country, under which they have arisen, that our knowledge of their state and character is very imperfect, although we are certain that they are altogether different from those which may be expected to arise from permanent interests, when the independence of the Republic shall be universally recognized, and a free trade shall be opened to its inhabitants with all parts of the world. The only important point now to be settled, as the radical principle of all our future commercial intercourse, is the basis proposed by Mr. Torres, of *reciprocal utility, and perfect equality.* As the necessary consequence of which, you will claim that, without waiting for the conclusion of a treaty, the commerce and navigation of the United States, in the ports of the Colombian Republic, should be received on the footing of equality with the most favored nation. . . .

The political systems of Europe are all founded upon partial rights and exclusive privileges. The colonial system had no other basis; and having no generous or liberal views of their own, it is not surprising that they should entertain and disseminate suspicions of the disinterestedness of others. The French Government sends an agent to Bogota, without daring to trust him with a credential or an avowed power; and he excuses his commission by misrepresenting our motives, upon *suspicions* which those to whom he makes the misrepresentation know to be unfounded, and by testifying to those who were benefitted by our recognition that we had made it by the sacrifice of some part of our influence in Europe. It must be admitted that the address of the agent in the performance of his trust was upon a level with the candor and frankness in which it originated. . . .

We are well aware that our recognition of South American independence was not palatable to the taste of any of the European Governments. But we felt that it was a subject upon which it became us to take the lead, and as we knew that the European Governments, sooner or later, must and would, whether with good or with bad grace, follow our example, we determined that both Europe and America should have the benefit of it. We hope, also, and this is the only return which we ask, and have a right to ask, from the South Americans for our forwardness in their favor, that Europe will be compelled to follow the whole of our example—that is, to recognize without condition and without equivalent. We claim no exclusive privilege for ourselves. We trust to the sense of justice, as well as to the interest of the South Americans, the denial of all exclusive privileges to others. The Colombian Government, at various times, have manifested a desire that the United States should take some further and active part in obtaining the recognition of their independence by the European Governments, and particularly by Great Britain. This has been done even before it was solicited. All the ministers of the United States in Europe have, for many years, been instructed to promote the cause, by any means consistent with propriety and adapted to their end, at the respective places of their residence. The formal proposal of a concerted recognition was made to Great Britain before the Congress of Aix-la-Chapelle. At the request of Mr. Torres, on his dying bed, and signified to us after his decease, Mr. Rush was instructed to give every aid in his power, without offence to the British Government, to obtain the admission of Mr. Ravenga; of which instruction we have recent assurances from Mr. Rush that he is constantly mindful. Our own recognition undoubtedly opened all the ports of Europe to the Colombian flag, and your mission to Colombia, as well as those to Buenos Ayres and Chile, cannot fail to stimulate the cabinets of maritime Europe, if not by the liberal motives which influenced us, at least by selfish impulses, to a direct, simple, and unconditional recognition. We shall pursue this policy steadily through all the changes to be foreseen of European affairs. There is every reason to believe that the preponderating tendency of the war in Spain will be to promote the universal recognition of all the South American Governments; and, at all events, our course will be to promote it by whatever influence we may possess. . . .

Our intercourse with the Republic of Colombia, and with the territories of which it is composed, is of recent origin, formed while their own condition was altogether revolutionary and continually changing its aspect. Our information concerning them is imperfect, and among the most important objects of your mission will be that of adding to its stores; of exploring the untrodden ground, and of collecting and transmitting to us the knowledge by which the friendly relations between the two countries may be extended and harmonized to promote the welfare of both, with due regard to the peace and good will of the whole family of civilized man. It is highly important that the first foundations of the permanent future

intercourse between the two countries should be laid in principles benevolent and liberal in themselves, congenial to the
spirit of our institutions, and consistent with the duties of
universal philanthropy.

In all your consultations with the Government to which you
will be accredited, bearing upon its political relations with
this Union, your unvarying standard will be the spirit of independence and of freedom, as *equality* of rights and favors
will be that of its commercial relations. The emancipation of
the South American continent opens to the whole race of man
prospects of futurity, in which this Union will be called, in the
discharge of its duties to itself and to unnumbered ages of
posterity, to take a conspicuous and leading part. It involves
all that is precious in hope, and all that is desirable in existence,
to the countless millions of our fellow creatures which, in the
progressive revolution of time, this hemisphere is destined to
rear and to maintain.

That the fabric of our social connexions with our southern
neighbors may rise, in the lapse of years, with a grandeur and
harmony of proportion corresponding with the magnificence of
the means placed by Providence in our power, and in that of
our descendants, its foundations must be laid in principles of
politics and of morals new and distasteful to the thrones and
dominations of the elder world, but co-extensive with the
surface of the globe, and lasting as the changes of time.

Up to the time of my departure for Colombia[2]

U. S. Ship John Adams

Commander James Renshaw Esqr.

1st Lieut. J. H. Lee
2d Lt. H. N. Page
3d Lt.   Wall
4th "   Varnum

Purser C. O. Handy

Master   John P. Tuttle

2. Anderson's writing resumes with this sentence.

Midshipmen

Williamson	Taylor
Thorburn	Morris
Shaw	Boutwell
	Green
	Blake
	Holt
	Leggett

Rec[eive]d passenger
Lt. Gardner of Marines

June 15, 1823. Sunday.

Soon after sunrise went from Taylors tavern at old point Comfort on board the U States Ship John Adams of 24 guns [—] James Renshaw Esqr. Commander. There being a head wind [we] did not leave Hampton Roads where the ship was lying.[3]

June 16, 1823. My old friend Charles Smith & his lady from Norfolk came & dined with us on the J[ohn] A[dams.] A head wind & [we] did not leave the roads.

June 17, 1823. About sunrise weighed anchor with a south (or side wind) & went to sea bound for Laguira.[4] A fair fine day. Mrs. A[nderson] sea sick.

June 18, 1823. A fair fine day. Wind the same.

June 20, 1823. Wind a little more favorable. Our course about S. E. Intending to touch at St. Thomas.[5] Fine day.

June 21, 1823. A fine clear day, wind the same. Saw many vessels but spoke none.

June 22, 1823. About sunrise spoke the brig "Margaret" from Martinico [*sic* for Martinique] to Boston.

---

3. Most of the trip to Colombia may be traced on Map 5, p. 205, and Map 3, p. 133.

4. Various spellings are given—La Guayra, Laguira, La Guaira—for this Venezuelan city, located on Map 3, p. 133, and Map 5, p. 205.

5. See Map 5, p. 205. Part of the Virgin Islands, an archipelago in the Caribbean Sea consisting of nine large islands and 75 islets.

My family on board consists of self, Mrs. A[nderson], Ferdinand B. Bullitt,* Elizabeth, Arthur, & Ann[,] children, Mary[,] Spencer [Hite] & Denis [Hite] servants.⁶ The weather has been so fine that there has been but little sea sickness in the family. Mrs. A[nderson], Ferdinand B[ullitt], & Denis have suffered most. I have felt nothing beyond a giddiness in the head.

Our company in the cabin is composed of my family, Captain [James] Renshaw, Mr. [C. O.] Handy, [and] Colo [Brooke] Young.*

One of the officers dines with us every day.

I devote a part of each day to Spanish. We have books & so far have had a pleasant voyage.

About 12 oC. spoke & boarded the Bengal from Buenos Ayres to N. York. We wrote to our friends in the U States. Dined with the officers of the wardroom this day.

June 29, 1823. The last week has not been so pleasant as the preceding one. The wind much stronger & not so fair. The sea [is] heavy & rolling—too much so for fresh-water men. Mrs. A[nderson] has been sick—& still is.

We find a remarkable irregularity in the trade winds. This was wholly unexpected & very unusual.

During this week we spoke the [blank] from Dominica for N. York. Got some pineapples & limes. The sea is so rolling that the officers suppose there has been a heavy blow somewhere to the Eastwd.

I read a little Spanish & sometimes Las Cases' St. Helena⁷ & play backgammon.

June 30, 1823. Still blowing with a chopping sea. This morning spoke & boarded the Visitor from [illegible] to

---

6. In a letter to the State Department in 1824 Anderson referred to the three slaves brought from the United States who were, "by the laws of Kentucky, slaves for life." They included Mary, "a light mulatto woman about 44—born in Kentucky"; Spencer Hite, who was 42 years old; and Denis Hite, a "dark mulatto" who was 16 years old.

7. Las Cases, Emmanuel Augustin Dieudonné, Count de (1766-1842), *Mémorial de Sainte-Hélène* (8 vols; 1821-1823).

N. York. Got some pineapples & oranges. We have every reason yet to be pleased with the Capt. & officers—& the voyage has not been unpleasant.

July 1, 1823. A more pleasant day than we have had lately. The Capt. has nearly given up his wish to visit St. Thomas, it being difficult to get so far to Windward.

July 2, 1823. A fine day. About 1 oClock the main topman cried out "lands." It was the Northern side of Porto Rico—a few miles to the East of St. Johns.[8] About [July] 3d we approached the town [of San Juan] with a pretty heavy sea. The pilot would not come out until we got near the harbour. We went in & anchored a little before sunset. The harbour is fine. The sheet of water is not large but it is deep & is well protected from the winds. It is said to be one of healthiest places in the W. Indies. The Capt., Lieuts: Page & Gardner went ashore & remained all night. They gave horrible accounts of their uncomfortable time.

July 3, 1823. About 1 oC. Mr. & Mrs. Simmons, Americans from Philadelphia came to wait on Mrs. A[nderson] & myself. We ret[urne]d with them to the town & spent some time viewing the town & its fortifications. It is the first Spanish town I ever saw—& its aspect to me is most forbidding. I will not describe it for those who have seen them do not require a description & those who have not would not believe one. I saw everything that looked like the want of snug comfort— everything that seemed to declare a state of intellectual night.[9]

But the appearance of the fortifications is that of terrible strength. I am told that it is very strong. To me who had no skill in that way it seemed so; both by sea & by land. There is however nothing about it which would declare that it was

8. San Juan, Puerto Rico, see Map 5, p. 205.
9. See Earl Parker Hanson, *Puerto Rico: Land of Wonders* (New York, 1960), pp. 287-288, for a description of the restoration of San Juan.

in a good state of preparation. There are about 6 or 700 soldiers in Garrison & nearly as many officers.

The circumstance of our going into a Spanish harbour & my going on shore excited some conversation among the officers & manifestly a little doubt as to its propriety.

I was a Minister dispatched to the Republic of Colombia,[10] which the Spanish contended was a rebellious & revolting colony & not a state—& was then at war with them. Although my presence might possibly produce a little mortification—the fact did not authorize any attempt to molest me. The circumstance of my being the Minister did not place me in a situation different from any other officer of the US. Govt. It was the act of recognition by my govt. alone that could give offence to them.

I do not know that the authorities in the town knew who I was. Colo[nel Brooke] Young* was also on board the Ship. He was an officer of the Colombian army. His situation too excited some conversation on the right of the Spaniards to take him from the ship when it came into their harbour. I have no doubt that the US. have violated their neutrality in giving him permission to go in the vessel. But I can hardly think that the S[paniards] have a right to come on board the ship to take him out. This would be direct war, as being in the ship he was *in* the U States. They have a just claim of complaint against the U States. No difficulty however occurred on this head. Young* did not go on shore very prudently; prudently as it would have been at once surrendering his shelter & he might properly have been considered as a spy. We procured some pine apples, cocoa nuts, bananas, mangoes, & musk melons—& sailed about 4 in the Evening.

July 4, 1823. A fine day. Passed the Mona passage near Zache Island. Went faster this morning than we have on the voyage —The trade winds being fair for running down Porto Rico.

---

10. For the boundaries of La Gran Colombia, see Parks, *op. cit.,* frontispiece.

The Sea was however too rough for all to dine together on the quarter deck as was contemplated.

July 7, 1823. In the evening saw the Rocas.[11] Stood off during the night.

July 8, 1823. In the evening saw the Mainland just before sun set & again stood off.

July 9, 1823. 11 oC. This morning we app[roache]d the shore & ascertained that we were to the leeward of Laguira. We are now beating up against the wind—& it is doubtful whether we shall get into port to day. The morning is very hot. Since we left Porto Rico we have had some very rough & unpleasant weather. Mrs. Anderson has been & still is very sick & exhausted.

July 10, 1823. This day we arrived at Laguayra. A clear & hot day. We were invited by Doctor [Samuel Douglas] Forsythe*[,] an American merchant who has been in this country several years[,] to go to his house in Maquitas [*sic* for Maiquetía,] a village near Laguayra.[12] We were received & treated by him with great politeness & indeed in very N. American style.

July 11, 1823. By invitation we & several officers of the John Adams dined with Colo[nel Francisco] Avendaño,* the Governor of L[a Guayra]. We had an excellent dinner—& many toasts complimentary to the U. S.

July 12, 1823. Dined with Mr. [Robert K.] Lowry* the American Consul.[13]

July 13, 1823. We remained at Dr. [Samuel Douglas] For-

---

11. Islas Los Roques, off the northern coast of Venezuela, see Map 5, p. 205.

12. See Map 3, p. 133. La Guayra's population was about 4,500.

13. In a letter sent to the Department of State on this date, Anderson commented on the military situation around Maracaybo and then noted that the rainy season in La Guayra made him doubtful about proceeding to Caracas. His next despatch to Secretary of State Adams was from Caracas on August 6, 1823.

sythes.* The weather is excessively hot from sun rise to about
9 oClock. The breeze then comes on & moderates the heat a
good deal. There is a constant swell & agitation in the harbour at L[a Guayra]. It is indeed an open roadste[a]d.[14]

July 14, 1823. We came riding on mules to Caracas. Elizabeth
[Anderson] & Arthur [Anderson][15] were in panniers[16] on a
Jack [ass]. The road is naturally very bad over a prodigious
mountain[17] but greater labour has been spent on it. It is now
a good mule road, cut in many places through the mountain
& paved whenever the descent is such to endanger it, by
washing. It is said to have been made by the native Indians
under the order of the Spanish Govt.[18]

We went immediately to the house of Doctor [Samuel]
F[orsythe]* by invitation—which we find spacious & convenient & furnished with every thing comfortable, even for
the largest family[.]

A large company dined with Doctor F[orsythe]* in com-
pliment to our arrival. Among the guests were Genl.
[Carlos] Soublette,* Intendant,[19] & his sisters—Genl. [Lino de]
Clemente* & family.

Madame Bolivar (a sister of the Presd.)[20] & family—
Doctor [Franklin] Litchfield,* Colo[nel Edward] Stopford*
(an English officer)—& lady & several others [were there].

Black hair, black eyes & black skin are almost universal.

---

14. The harbor provided, in other words, a protected place where ships
might ride at anchor. Anderson's description may be compared with that of
Bache, *op. cit.*, pp. 15-16; Duane, *op. cit.*, chap. II; and Cochrane, *op. cit.*, I,
7-8.

15. The sentence structure indicates that the Elizabeth referred to is his
daughter and not his wife.

16. A wicker basket that was carried on the back of the mule.

17. The highest point reached by the party as they went over the mountain De Avila was about 4,850 feet.

18. The journey usually took about five to seven hours. Although the road
was twelve feet wide in some places, one-way traffic prevailed. Certain days
were designated for going to La Guayra from Caracas and others from
Caracas to La Guayra. Coaches had once been tried on the road but this
practice was abandoned before the Anderson's made the trip.

19. The Intendant was in charge of administering justice, collecting taxes,
promoting business and trade, and organizing the militia in the Departments.

20. Bolívar had two sisters: Juana and María Antonia.

The Creoles have generally sparkling black [eyes] & much animation of look.

Soublette is a tall black, fine looking man, from his physiognomy I should judge that he was a man of much vigor & prudence. He has not the character of an able general & indeed his personal courage is doubted by some, but such a doubt would utterly [be] opposed by my judgement in faces.

My ignorance of the language makes me feel an insignificance I never felt before.[21]

July 17, 1823. We dined with Doctor [Franklin] Litchfield[,]* an American Gentleman who has been in the Country ten years & is married to a native. There we met again Spanish Company, to which we could look but not speak.

July 19, 1823. Genl. [Carlos] Soublette complimented me with a dinner at which there was a very large company of Gentlemen.

> Village of [Maiquetía] one mile
> East of Laguayra *July 12, 1823.*

Dear Father[22]

We arrived at Laguayra the day before yesterday, the 10th after a voyage of twenty four days from Norfolk. The latter part of the voyage was unpleasant. Although we had no severe blow, we had several days of bad weather, rough sea from continued squalls.

The family is now well. Betsy suffered a great deal from sea sickness. She had no relief from time, she suffered most during the last week. Her strength was exhausted & she lost much flesh. She will I think be quite restored in a few days. I was not sea sick at all.

We touched at Porto Rico & remained a part of two days at its port St. John's. This is a very fine Spanish Island, one of

---

21. See above, April 29, 1821, especially n. 208.
22. This letter was included in the original diary and was inserted at this point despite the July 12th date.

the richest in the W. Indies. It has a population of about 300,000. The harbour is very fine—the extent & apparent strength of the fortifications greatly beyond any thing I had ever seen. I was told that there were 1500 brass 32 pounders on the works & in the garrison. I saw most of the works & satisfied myself that it was very strong, had been erected at prodigious expense & that no care had been taken of it since its erection. It has a garrison of one regiment. The town is a most miserable looking place, truly Spanish with a population of 15,000. From St. Juan which is on [the] N. side of the Island we coasted along to the E. end & passed through the Mona passage between P[uerto] R[ico] & St. Domingo. Our original design was to go farther to the Windward & touch at St. Thomas but it was rendered impractical by the course of the Winds.

Laguayra is built at the foot of very high mountains that leave not room enough for a fourth of the town [on] level ground, the rest is built on the side of the mountains. Its population is 5 or 6000. Like all Spanish towns it is walled & forted. So far we have been peculiarly fortunate. Mr. [Samuel] Forsythe[,]* an American merchant who has been in the Country ten years[,] had his house in this suburb ready for us. We have been with him ever since our arrival[,] that is[,] in his house[,] for he is a rich bachelor who goes to town before we rise in the morning to his store & we see no more of him until 4 oClock. His house is very large having ten rooms (on the only floor) all with brick floor & with no window glass. Every thing is managed by his servants in American style & we are as comfortable as princes—& what is still better we are invited to go immediately into his house at Carraccas,[23] which he says has been ready for us for six weeks & which we are told is the finest in that place. He passes his time between his two places as his shopping or other business requires. If all this should be realized as the prospect

---

23. As in the case of La Guayra, various spellings were employed during this period.

seems to indicate we shall have been fortunate indeed, as the inns in this Country are most wretched. This little Village or Suburb [of Maiquetía] would be a more judicious situation for an exporting town than Laguayra. Neither has any thing like a harbour—but it [Maiquetía] has a better anchorage, had about 50 acres of level land to build on & is nearer Carracas, through which all the country produce comes & where all the capitalists live—this being merely the port. But the Spaniards selected Laguayra precisely because, from it, Carracas was least accessible; the object was not commerce but to protect themselves from the incursion of an enemy.

Yesterday we dined with Colo[nel Francisco] Avendaño* the Commandante of Laguayra & this day we shall dine with Mr. [Robert K.] Lowry* our consul. Tomorrow we go to Carracas about 15 miles hence over a tremendous mountain along which a wheel has *never* passed. The only conveyance is on Mules or Jacks. From the number of these that pass with loads I should suppose the commerce of this place [is] quite considerable. I am told that on some days 700 come down from Carraccas. I think 300 came yesterday loaded generally with Coffee & Cacao. We arrived to go up on Sunday to avoid the Mules as they do not pass on that day. I have arrived in this Country in the rainy season & fear that I shall not be able to proceed on my journey for some time; I shall not however decide before I to to Carraccas whether I shall run down the coast towards St. Martha [or Santa Marta] & ascend the Magdalena; or go by land to Bogota;[24] nor indeed will I yet determine when I shall proceed. I have not been here long enough to form any opinion on the political situation of the Country.

I wish you to write to me very frequently.

Give my love to my Mother & to all the children.

I am affectionately yours

R. C. Anderson jr

24. See Map 3, p. 133.

20th July Carraccas.²⁵ I have det[ermine]d to remain here for
some weeks. We cannot yet go by land. We have been very
politely recd. Like the towns through all this Country most
of the houses here are built of mud & sticks & covered with
tiles & floor [that] are of brick. Yesterday Genl. [Carlos]
Soublette*[,] gov. of Venezuela[,] gave us a Dinner & ball. He
is represented as a man of fine talents & great patriotism &
altho he retains his rank of Major Genl. in the army, as he
has been an unfortunate Genl.[,]²⁶ he will not be again called
to the field. His present station is a very important one as he
is Intendante with civil & military powers over this Department. Write soon & frequently.

Yours

R. C. A. jr

A ball²⁷ was designed [July 12 ?] but postponed for a
valid reason. About 7 oC. it was announced that Madame
[Soublette] was in the pains of labour—& in a few hours she
was delivered of a daughter.

The fashion of giving toasts is common, on the drinking
of which the Company rises & huzzas vociferously. This is
the practice at private houses. Indeed there is never what we
would call (in the US) a public dinner. Public rejoicings are
manifested by fire works, military & religious parades.

July 20, 1823. Sunday. We were invited to Genl. Soublettes
to celebrate the christening of his daughter (a week old)[.]
There was a splendid ball—at which Madame appeared. This
was the first occasion on which I had ever seen joy manifested by dancing on Sunday.

October 16, 1823. I have been detained at this place by the
season which is here called winter on account of the rain.²⁸ I

---

25. This section was added to the letter as a postscript.
26. In 1815 Soublette was the commander at La Popa, near Cartagena,
during one of the battles that preceded the reconquest of that port by
Spanish troops on December 6, 1815.
27. Anderson's diary resumes at this point.
28 It is interesting, in view of Anderson's financial problems, that he

expect to set off for Bogota on Saturday or Sunday on Mules with all my family. It is (I feel sensibly) a most arduous undertaking—& it will be a very expensive one. I long cherished the idea of going down the coast to Marycaibo [*sic* for Maracaibo] or to Carthagena[29] but I was deterred by the fear of fever—& have at length determined to undertake a journey which I believe has never been performed by a family—& which occupies the mail carriers forty five days.

My time here has been somewhat lonesome, although my family is around me & I have devoted much time to the language. Still, in my own country there are many objects of mental occupation which do not exist (for me) here—such as private business, conversation on public events & more than the interest which you take in every thing around you.

I have had very little association with the people. I do not therefore pronounce them or myself unsocial, but where there could be no conversation or none except thro an interpreter there could be but little pleasure in the association.

Doctor Forsythe* has treated my family & myself with unvarying politeness. He invited me to remain at his house while in Caracas. The invitation was accepted, under the agreement that all the additional expenses produced by my residence with him should be borne by me.

He is in his personal expenses & outfit one of the most extravagant & ostentatious men I ever saw. From his conversation & some litle incidents[,] hardly describable[,] I fear that his morals in commercial matters are a little lax. This quality is not however at all incompatible with what is generally denominated generosity. This last quality has so far been manifested towards us—but the day of *settlement* has not yet arrived—& the nature of the a/c. [*sic* for accounts] between us are such as admit of great extention on his part towards me

---

took advantage of the delay to write to the State Department asking for an advance on his first year's pay.

29. Usually spelled "Cartagena" in modern usage.

without it being in my power to *complain*. So true it is that if
you ever receive a favor from a man, you are in some sort his
Slave. I have determined to leave & sell my furniture.

October 19, 1823. The day of settlement has come & Doctor
Forsythe* has shewn himself to be a cold calculating *de-
ceiver*. There is in his account both enormity & meanness—
but it is paid. This day I set off for Bogota. The cavalcade
will consist of seven [or] eight saddle & five baggage mules.

November 21, 1823. Rosario de Cucuta. I arrived at this
place last evening having been traveling since the *19th Octo.*
with the exception of three days from Caraccas.[30] No material
incident has occurred on our journey. Such a journey in such
a country & along such roads with a family would always be
attended with many vexatious occurrences & we have had
many of them but none such as to produce distress. We have
had the good fortune to preserve our health.

Doctors Litchfield* & Forsythe* & Genl. Soublette* with
many other gentlemen attended us for several miles. Doctor
L. came with us to Valencia. The valley of Aragua is a rich
body of land, lying around the lake of Valencia. On the
fourth night we lay at the seat of the Marquis Del Toro—an
estate now valuable but one that might be rendered very
much so. I must abstain from any account of my journey or
what I have seen as an attempt of that kind would run into
an account of the aspect of the country & be but little short
of a history.

Capt. [Isidoro] Barrigas [*sic* for Barriga]* an officer of an
army & native of the neighborhood of Bogota attends us. His
services have been such as we could hardly dispense with.
He is guide. He procures us mules—*interprets* & indeed does
every thing. He cannot speak a word of English but he under-
stands my Spanish.

The vallies of Cucuta are celebrated for their fertility
& the fine coccao, which they produce. They are extensive.

---

30. The journey is traced on Map 3, p. 133.

This is the place at which the Congress sat & established the present Constitution of Colombia.

We remain here this day. I have been introduced to Genl. Fordo the Intendant of Boyaca.

This is the first town of Cundinamarca (or "The Kingdom" as it was once called.)

traveling from Venezuela

Bogota *Jan. 22 1824*

I arrived at this place on the 10th Dec. [1823] having left at the Village of Zipaquira[31] Betsy & the children. Colo[nel Charles S.] Todd* met me on the 9th beyond that village.[32] After announcing my arrival to Secy. [of Foreign Relations Pedro] Gual* & his appg. the 16th [December] for my public reception, I retd. to the village. I came down with my family on the 15 [December]. On the next day I presented my Credentials to the V[ice] P[resident Francisco de Paula Santander.][33] It was a public reception.

A few days afterwards Doctor Gual* expressed a desire to enter into a com[mercial] treaty—& said that he would present me a project. He has several times intimated that an alliance between all the republican govts. of America would be judicious & desireable to protect them against the designs of the alliance of Kings in Europe.[34]

Colo: Todd* has left this Country embittered to a most extra degree against almost every thing in it. He does not

---

31. See Map 3, p. 133.

32. Todd presented his credentials as "Confidential Agent to Venezuela and New Granada" in August, 1820. He returned to the United States in 1822 on leave, and was again dispatched to the area to advise the government officially of American recognition.

33. An account of the presentation ceremony and a text of Minister Anderson's speech on the occasion appeared in *Gaceta de Colombia* (Bogotá), December 21, 1823; reprinted in *Daily National Intelligencer* (Washington, D.C.), March 10, 1824.

34. Anderson's inability to speak Spanish did not hinder his relations with Gual, since the Foreign Minister had learned English during a stay in New York in the early 1800's.

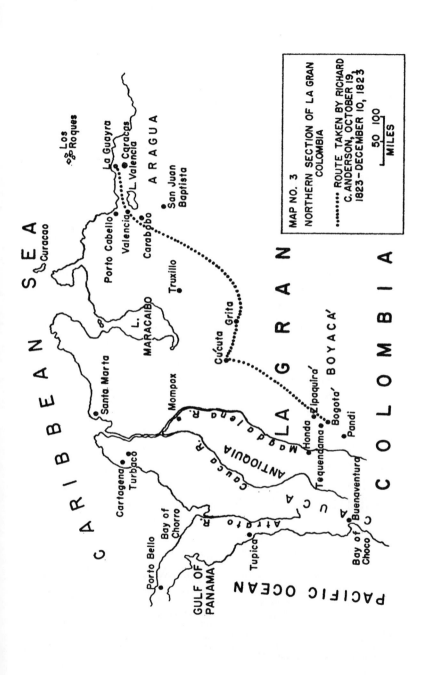

CARIBBEAN SEA

Curacao

Los Roques

La Guayra

Caracas

L. Valencia

ARAGUA

San Juan Baptista

Porto Cabello

Valencia

Carabobo

Truxillo

L. MARACAIBO

Santa Marta

Grita

Cúcuta

LA GRAN

Mompox

Magdalena R.

BOYACA'

Zipaquirá'

Bogotá

Pandi

Honda

ANTIOQUIA

Cauca R.

Tequendama

COLOMBIA

Cartagena

Turbaco

Bay of Chorro

Atrato R.

CAUCA

Buenaventura

Porto Bello

GULF OF PANAMA

Tupica

Bay of Choco

PACIFIC OCEAN

MAP NO. 3

NORTHERN SECTION OF LA GRAN
COLOMBIA

.... ROUTE TAKEN BY RICHARD
C. ANDERSON, OCTOBER 19,
1823 — DECEMBER 10, 1823

50   100

MILES

hesitate to ascribe forgery & every bad passion & bad action to the Secy. of Foreign Affairs. I do not know yet the character of the Chief men here, but I do know that Todd has as little common sense as any man whom I ever knew.[35]

The Bull fights, feasting & gambling occupied the whole town from the 24 to New Years day.

The congress sh[oul]d have met on the 2d [January] int. but there is not yet any probability of a quorum very soon.

The climate here is unpleasant. It is too cold to be without a fire. We have a house which is very large & convenient in its interior arrangement.

My present impression is that I shall remain until 1st Apl. 1825. In this I must be govd. by circumstances. I stay from the hope & the necessity of saving some money & I wish my children to acquire the Castilian language. Apart from these reasons I would not stay two months.

By remaining I have a prospect of saving a sum of money which I might have no other opp[ortunit]y of doing & I think it right to exile myself a little for that. In a few months (without some accident) I shall and I thank God, *be out of debt*. My son, Never permit yourself to be in debt. Your father, who has ever by the world been cons[idere]d a prudent man, has been rend[ered] uneasy for many years by that imprudence & had it not been for *good fortune* more than you shd. calculate on, many more years would have passed before he would have been extricated—perhaps never. At any rate [in] that part of his life in which he might most reasonably expect peace & tranquility he would have been harrassed in a way to mar its enjoyments.

That you will be honest, will I hope require no admonition from me—none would be of avail, if required. But it

---

35. Todd had already complained to Washington of Gual's "want of cordiality in his personal intercourse, [and] his notorious unfriendliness towards the United States," which Todd thought was due to the recollections of supposedly unkind treatment Gual had been accorded while in the United States. All official intercourse between the two men had ceased when Anderson arrived in Bogotá.

may be of service to beseech you to be *prudent*. *Do not go in debt*. It will make you unhappy. If it did not—it destroys your independence. Every debtor is the slave of his creditor.

January 22, 1824. Contd.

The day before yesterday Miralla* (a native of Buenos Ayres) & who left Louisville in the Steamboat with us in Apr. arrived from Caracas. He is a very sensible, talkative, man.

On yesterday [Isidoro] Barriga[,] * an officer of the Colombian Army, who escorted us by order of his Genl. & by his own inclination from Valencia to this place, left here for Lima. He is sent by the Gov: His attentions & services on the road were such as to make a lively impression on all of us. Without him our time would have been very unpleasant & embarrassing frequently. I gave him a letter to Bolivar* of recommendation—and another of compliment from myself. Betsy gave him a pearl breast pin, Elizabeth* a specimen of each of the coins of the US. & Arthur* a ring.

February 7, 1824. We are uneasy about the situation of Ferdinand Bullitt.* He was taken sick on the 6th Jany.—& although he has been both walking & riding since, he is now in bed & I fear dangerously sick.

The children are & have been all much indisposed with the bowel complaint. This is said to be a healthy place—the climate is certainly very unpleasant to me.[36]

February 8, 1824. At the request of Doctor Gual* we have had several conversations about a Commercial treaty. I have abandoned the expectation of concluding one [in] time enough to be acted on during this session of our Senate. Although it is not very easy to see with certainty the reason, still I am satisfied that he does not wish to conclude it immediately. Possibly he wishes this Gov[ernment] to keep its

---

36. Bogotá's average temperature is 57°. Anderson was then writing at the beginning of the rainy reason. A map of the city may be found in Bache, *op. cit.*, p. 223.

hands clear, that it may offer some exclusive privileges to Spain in consideration of "Independence acknowledged" or possibly he apprehends that England might feel some what offended by any marked preference for the US.

Some reason I am sure does operate to prevent a wish to have it concluded immediately.[37]

He has several times and anxiously referred to an "American Confederation" embracing all the free Govts. of America & designed to vindicate the principles of their Govts. against any association like the Holy Alliance.[38]

My present situation is as agreeable as it cannot [*sic* for can] be where almost all association is confined to my family. When the family is well, I cannot be unhappy. In their company & with my books the time passes well, but still there is [a] void which a more extended association or more active business alone can fill. I feel this & so does Betsy. And I already see that it will require some exertion to continue here as long as my finances require it. I live economically & can save some money. This is very necessary & it would be unpardonable neglect of myself & family if I did not. We talk of going home about the 1st Apl. 1825—either on leave of absence or finally. At that time I shall be *out of debt* (a most enviable & in this age a too rare situation) & have a small sum of money ready—but one greatly below that which would be required to make me easy. The conflict will then be between our inclination (very strong) to *return to the World,* or to continue here a year or two to increase that small sum.

We have been visited by & retd. the visits of Doctor Gual* & lady, Doctor [José Manuel] Restrepo*[39] & lady, Doctor

---

37. Gual stalled the negotiations because he hoped that the United States, in view of Monroe's speech in 1823, might be drawn into an alliance against any plan the European governments might develop to return the colonies to Spanish rule. Since the United States was evasive to the point of refusal on the subject of entering a Colombian confederacy, more interest eventually was shown in the negotiation of a commercial treaty.

38. There was advocacy of a general congress of the Americas in Colombian official circles as early as 1820.

39. The editors believe that Anderson was likely to be in contact with this

[José María Del] Castillo [y Rada]* & lady—Intendente [Carlos de] Umaña* & lady & some others. With many gentlemen of distinction I have formed slight acquaintances. The illness of Ferdinand [Bullitt]* has caused a cessation of all intercourse for a month.

There has been a manifest disposition among the persons in authority here & others to render me satisfied with the govt. & things generally.

In contemplating a return I cannot avoid looking ahead so far as to endeavour to ascertain in my mind what will be the most agreeable (practicable) situation. I shall not have wealth but barely [illegible.] A seat in Congress would in every way be agreeable & probably the most agreeable situation that could be offered to me. I have an inclination to go with my family to Europe. It is excited by a laudable & rational curiosity—to gratify myself—& wife & to gratify & improve my children. If I could afford it, I shall greatly prefer to go as a private man.

I very [much] wish that my children shd. be here long enough to acquire the faculty of speaking the Spanish language with facility. That consideration might keep me a year but apart from that & the money saving—wish I wd. not stay a month.

March 8, 1824. F[erdinand] B. Bullitt* died on the 18th Feby. about eight in the morning. Doctor [Henry George] Mayne [*sic* for Maine]* the Physician says his disease was a rapid decay of the liver. My feelings & those of the family are melancholy indeed. The distance from home & the absence of friends or immediate connections aggravate those feelings which at all times exist under such circumstances. The necessity of giving such distressing news to his father & mother is distressing too to me.

Immediately after his death we were invited by Doctor

Restrepo, who was a member of the cabinet. However, other possibilities may be examined in the Appendix, List of Names, under Restrepo.

Gual* to pass a few days at his Quinta.⁴⁰ He thought a change in residence for a short time wd. have a favorable effect on Betsys feelings & on the health of all. We went out on the 20th & remained until yesterday [March 7]. The place is agreeable & I think the health of the children is improved.

On the 1st [March] Colonels [John Potts] Hamilton* & [Patrick] Campbell* arrived—British Commissioners. H[amilton] is not a man of much talent, indeed he seems to be a weak man. C[ampbell]* I have not yet see[n] enough to judge. I dined with Doctor Mayne [Maine]* on the 5th [March.] Campbell was sick & I did not see him. Gual* is afraid that they have some commercial arrangements to ask, wh.[ich] it will be embarrassing to this Govt. to grant. He does not indeed like to enter on any treaty arrangement or even discuss it till the Gov[ernment] is formally recognized. But such is the imp[ortance] attached to the recog[nition] of GB. that probably matters of form will not be permitted to break up the present friendly appearance of things.⁴¹

The late sickness in the family has prevented any late step in the discussions with Gual, either on the treaty or the private claims.⁴² This I am sure is very agreeable to him for he wishes to know what the English want before he makes an arrangement with any one else.

March 15, 1824. Doctor Gual* lately had a conversation with me in which he intimated that he expected the British Gov: would soon make a proposition to this Gov: that she would guarantee the Indep: of this [country] & expect in return some commercial favours. His object seemed to me to impress me with a belief that there was danger that the US would not

---

40. His villa or country house.
41. Britain recognized Colombia on December 31, 1824, and signed a treaty of commerce with the Colombians on April 18, 1825.
42. These were claims of citizens of the United States against Colombia for injuries suffered during the period before Independence, and they involved the illegal seizure of ships and cargoes. Attempts to obtain a settlement of these claims through various agents were unsuccessful prior to Anderson's arrival in Colombia. In 1823 Gual told Anderson that he would examine the problem.

be placed on a footing of Equality unless we made similar offers. He seemed ashamed to acknowledge that the Gov: would grant to England any Exclusive privileges but he wished me to believe there was danger. He urged that the US should consider any attempt from Spain against this Country as an attempt on the part of the *Holy Alliance*; considering the inability of Spain[,] and therefore [thought] that the US. shd. in that event interfere. I endeav[ore]d to show that the US. could not interfere between this country & Spain without violating their own principles of the laws of Nations.

Gual* is a sensible, sagacious man, but he is not a liberal minded politician. He acts frequently right, but from narrow reasons. He does not feel the just importance of character to his Country—& does not mould his conduct with a view to her future policy & character. I fear he considers too much temporary Expedients.

The family is well. We have been urged by Mr. St. Maria [*sic* for Santamaría][43] to occupy his Quinta but we decline it. I have recd. $400 on account of my furniture sold by Doctor Forsythe* in Caracas. My present calculation is that I have money enough in this Country to sustain me until 1st May 1825 & to carry me home. In that event I shall have about $10,000 in cash & my property—as my Estate.

This is my daughter Elizabeths [ninth] birthday. She this day read the story of Bertrand in the Looking Glass. Arthur is now playing with a Black puppy Carlos in my office & Betsy is making a cover for the setee.
Yesterday I waited on the V. P. [Santander]* but he had gone to the Country.

I have been lately reading [Conyers] Middletons Cicero[44] in Spanish.

And am engaged a part of every day in examining a

---

43. See the Appendix, List of Names, under Santamaría.
44. Conyers Middleton, The Life of Marcus Tullius Cicero (3 vols; Boston, 1818).

project of a Com[mercial] treaty which Doctor Gual* has prepared, & making modifications to it. The treaty shows unceasing inclination to favour a War instead of a Neutral policy—& only because Austria now happens to be at War with France.⁴⁵ Doctor G. wishes to enlarge the catalogue of Contraband; not to admit that Free ships make free goods & the phrase in which many articles are expressed, shows the inclination of his mind. I am sorry to see it. Although he says he will yield these things, it is unfortunate that these new Republics shd. not be impressed with their true policy, the policy of fostering neutral instead of belligerent rights.

March 19, 1824. This day we received letters from the UStates to the 25 Nov. We rejoice once more at the health of our friends. Our previous advices had been only to the 28th October—our newspaper intelligence to the 14 Jany.

This day I dined with W[illiam] D[avis] Robinson,* in company [with] Colo[nel J. P.] Hamilton* & some Englishmen, Genl. [Rafael] Urdaneta* &c.

March 21, 1824. I waited on the V. President [Santander].*

The comments of the French Min[ister Viscount Chateaubriand and the French] Gazettes on the Message of the P[resident] of the UStates, was the subject of conversation.⁴⁶

---

45. Anderson was not accurate in his statement about Austria being at war with France in 1824. Gual told Anderson that too many European wars had developed because the countries concerned made no provision for arbitrating their differences. Gual wished to include in the treaty a stipulation that U. S.–Colombian arguments would be subject to arbitration, preferably by an outside nation. Anderson said that the principle of arbitration was a good one, but to write it into a treaty involved the "delicate" matter of United States sovereignty. See Harold Bierck, *Vida Publica de Don Pedro Gual* (Caracas, Venezuela, 1947), pp. 401-402.

46. The French Minister of Foreign Affairs stated to the British Ambassador that Monroe's declaration "ought to be resisted by all the powers possessing either territory or commercial interests in that hemisphere." The *Étoile* (January 4, 1824) editorialized: "Mr. Monroe, who is not a sovereign, has assumed in his message the tone of a powerful monarch . . . armed with the right of suzerainty over the entire New World." Quoted in Dexter Perkins, *The Monroe Doctrine, 1823-1826* (Cambridge, Mass., 1932), pp. 30-31.

It is manifest that the late message excites in Europe an attention superior to that which a like document has ever excited before.

Betsy is indisposed & has been a good deal so for two or three days.

The letters from K. Y. relate circumstances mortifying to every Kentuckian. The attempt to remove the Judges, to call a Convention for the purpose of rendering their tenure of office less permanent, the Governors Message of a most disorganizing kind, the doctrine of resistance of the dicisions of the Supreme Ct. openly arrived, connected with the sentiments & opinions of those who support their attempts in argument[,] are disgraceful indeed.[47]

I rejoice to hear of G[eorge] Robertsons* election as Speaker [of the Kentucky House of Representatives] because it was in opposition to the Chiefs of the disorganizing party.

J[ohn] Rowan* is the most abandoned disorganizer on Earth. For the purpose of gaining a seat in the UStates Senate next winter, he would support any position or doctrine that c[oul]d be propounded to him. I consider him the most shameful prostitute to his ambition & vanity, I ever knew. And unfortunately I have not confidence enough in the good sense of the Citizens of K[entucky] to believe that they will keep him out of the Senate.[48]

---

47. The background of this is found above, June 30, 1822. When the Court of Appeals in Kentucky in 1823 upheld the opinion of Judge Clark the whole program of relief for debtors set up by the legislature was threatened. Petitions from the voters in the state poured into the legislature demanding that the judges be rebuked. Governor John Adair did this, but his message that called for a reorganization of the court failed to receive the two-thirds majority necessary for passage. The court warned the people of the dangers of the course that was being pursued and continued to declare acts of the legislature unconstitutional. The Relief party continued to search for ways to break up the court's power. Its most radical members suggested that a convention be called to revise the constitution and to subject the court to legislative control. This project was dropped when the Anti-Relief party suggested that such a convention might lead to a freeing of Kentucky's slaves, the changing of the state capital, and the removal of Transylvania University from Lexington. The court fight had not, however, come to an end, see below, August 4, 1825, n. 166.

48. Rowan was elected at the next election.

March 22, 1824. A fine pleasant [day.]

Miralla* came to see me. This is a native of Buenos Ayres, who has lately been a resident of Havana. He is a man of talents, I think, he is very valuable & agreeable. His object in coming here I believe, is to urge this govt. to set on foot an expedition against Cuba—not with a view of colonizing it but emancipating it. I understand from him that the Govt. here is rather lukewarm—& well they may be—when they have some strong grounds for believing that all their strength will be req[uire]d at home.[49] They are fully able to defend themselves against any invasion Spain can make, but they have but feeble means to make an invasion into another country. They have indeed no means. They have no money. They can sustain an army here at home against an invading enemy without money, but they cannot get ships, naval stores of any kind or even provisions for a foreign effort without money.

March 23, 1824. Doctor [Henry] Mayne [*sic* for Maine]* Intendante Umaña* & lady visited us.

This day & the two last have been three of the pleasantest I have seen in Bogota.

On the 19th I wrote to Larz [Anderson]* intimating my wish that he wd. come to this Country, as probably I shd. have a treaty to send back in the fall. I also sent authority for him to receive $300.

I shd. never turn over a leaf without returning thanks to God for giving me an opportunity to relieve myself from debt. There are surely many blessings that demand greater thanks but to a man with a family, nothing scarcely can be a greater earthly curse than "debt" & its accompanying inquietudes. It prevents you from any of the enjoyments of

---

49. The strategic importance of Cuba had long been recognized by various powers, and by 1824 a rivalry had developed concerning its possession in the event that Spain could not exercise control over the area. Bolívar, Salazar, the Colombian minister in Washington, and others in Colombian official circles were among those who favored some sort of action to revolutionize Cuba and prevent its use as a Spanish base.

family & of this life, it destroys y[ou]r independence, it ruins your temper. It so fills all your thoughts as to prevent you from excelling in anything or exerting to any useful purpose your faculties. Then to receive a situation in which you are enabled to extricate yourself from these curses, does demand the highest gratitude.

Without accident or misfortune I will release myself from debt this summer [1824]. Few persons wd. regard a foreign mission as aff[ordin]g the means of paying debts—but *I have suffered under debt & I will use the economy necessary to effect my discharge.*

April 15, 1824. I have been in bed most of the time since the 25 ult. A dyspepsy or some disease of the stomach has tormented me for several years. I have taken various remedies; probably none with sufficient regularity or time to test them, but certainly all without any benefit. Under Doctor [Henry] Mayne [*sic* for Maine]* I am now using Calomel, in the form of the blue pill.[50] My family is harrassed with a vexatious bowel complaint—which has continued several weeks.

On the 9th March we recd. letters informing us of the death of my brother-in-law Thomas Bullitt.*

I cannot avoid feeling some little uneasiness on account of my responsibilities for my father. If I were at home there wd. be no danger but it may be set down as an universal truth; *that you can get no agent (however good) who does not think more of his own business than he will of yours.*

W[illiam] D. Robinson* & the English Gentlemen went on Saturday to the Salto of Tequendama;[51] R[obinson] has sent me a written account of the falls. It seems to have struck his imagination as a most wonderful work of nature[.]

The Congress of Colombia convened on the 5th [April] int [*sic* for inst.]. I am sorry to understand that the *illiberales,* that is those who are priest-ridden, & partake of all the igno-

---

50. Mercurous chloride, used often as a purgative.
51. For other descriptions of the Falls see Bache, *op. cit.,* p. 237, and Hamilton, *op. cit.,* I, 152-155. See also above, Map 3, p. 133.

rance which the Spanish despotism has [brought] prevail in the House of R.[52] Colo: [José María del] Real[,] a liberal gentleman[,] is Presd. of the Senate. Among the high officers of Govt.—there is much political liberality, indeed much information.

[Christian L.] Manhardt*[,] a naturalized citizen of the US & native of Germany[,] is here. I fear he is an envious dog. He does not speak absolutely ill of people, but seems to speak with more pleasure of their misfortunes or foibles, then of their good name.

It is understood that the English are not very well pleased with the V. P's message to Congress.[53] There is in truth, nothing in it to be displeased with, but the English have so long felt their power & are so inflated with the notions it inspires, that they do not think that equal treatment is fair treatment. I have not yet seen Mr. [James] Henderson[,]* the [British] Consul Genl. & family. [William D.] Robinson* says he is a man of some sense, full of vanity[.]

From a paragraph in a US. paper I understand that some conversation of mine in relation to a conversation with Mr. Calhoun,* has become public & even the subject of newspaper notice.[54] Now although my statement was perfectly true, still my indiscretion in holding such a conversation may have the effect of estranging the friendship of Mr. C[alhoun].* It shd. operate as a lesson to increase my prudence; I have a high opinion of Mr. C. Still I may have mortified him, or given him reason to think that I was not friendly, in a way that may have the effect of alienating him

---

52. More than one-third of the House were priests. A description of the conduct of the House may be found in Cochrane, *op. cit.,* II, 80-83.

53. A speech in which Santander urged that commercial treaties be made on the most-favored-nation basis.

54. A check of the files of the *National Journal* and the *Daily National Intelligencer* for the period of January to mid-March, 1824, reveals no account of the revelation. Calhoun's biographers (Capers and Wiltse—see Bibliography) make no mention of it. There seems to be no evidence that the revealing of the substance of Anderson's conversation wtih Calhoun was a factor in the gradual elimination of the latter from the presidential race in 1824.

& injuring me. I have nothing to do now but to profit in future by the effects of my indiscretion. My conversation must have been reported by Mr. [William H.] Crawford,* [Henry] Clay* or Genl. [Samuel] Smith.*

April 22, 1824. I have not been out of the house for a month. I gain strength.

No information has yet arr[ive]d giving me decisive knowledge as to the designs of the Continental powers regarding this Country.

The family is tolerably well.

I am now making an answer to Guals* project of a treaty. There is no difficulty in our concluding one, if he is anxious for it.

Old Mr. [Juan P.] Ayala⁵⁵ is one of our most frequent visitors—a most respectable & amiable old man. [He is the] Son in law of the Marquis St. Jorge.

Betsy & the children have extended their acquaintance & visiting among most of our very near neighbours. It is well not only as it furnishes the means of amusement to the children, but gives them the best opp[ortunit]y to acquire the language[.]

I have frequently thought of procuring & preserving facts with regard to the situation of this Country for the purpose of preparing & publishing "notes on Colombia" I know the danger of writing a book. But if I could vanquish my indolence I believe my vanity would vanquish the fear of failure. A very interesting & quite valuable book might be written by a man skilled in the ways of authorship.⁵⁶

Betsy is at this moment playing "Secretary" by copying some of my letters to the State Department & Elizabeth is

---

55. Consult Appendix, List of Names. The editors feel that the age of Juan P. Ayala, together with the military affiliations of the others (Anderson called him Mr.), indicates that this was the Ayala who was the frequent visitor.

56. See his "Constitution of Colombia," *North American Review*, XXIII (1826), 314-349. Anderson evidently made other notes and outlines for a longer work on Colombia, but these documents have not survived.

toasting some bread for me, while Arthur is calling for his bread & honey.

In payment for my furniture sold, Doctor Forsythe* sent me a bill on Colo. [Ferdinand] Sirakowsky* [or Sirakowski] for $1700. He [Sirakowski] paid $400 & I am a little uneasy about the balance—having released Forsythe,* who indeed was no better.

My good little Friend [Doctor Franklin] Litchfield* is appointed Consul at P[uerto] Cabello.[57] He is delighted & I am pleased, as it was solely on my recommendation.

April 23, 1824. Still employed in answ[erin]g Guals project of a treaty.

Recd. a note from Doctor [Félix de] Restrepo* & a present of a dozen of *Candles* made of the Laurel or vegetable wax, bleached in the Sun.

A fine morng. & cool day. It has not rained except a slight sprinkle for 3 weeks—The longest time I have ever known here without a hard rain[.]

April 26, 1824. Monday.

Yesterday the V. Presd. [Santander]* gave a dinner to the British Com[missione]rs. From indisposition I did not go. W[illiam] D Robinson* writes to me this morng. that it was a pleasant party & that his Toast was more applauded than any other—that [John P.] Hamilton* & [Patrick] Campbell* made neat speeches but that [James] Henderson* was wholly confounded & could say nothing.

April 28, 1824. I rode out this day for the first time for many weeks.

April 30, 1824. Betsy & the children walked to Bolívars* Quinta under the mountain. I rode & brought back Arthur on horseback. The conveniences of the Houses here are very great. Fountains of water are introduced in all. Most of the

---

57. For a list of the United States consuls appointed between 1822 and 1826, see Parks, *op. cit.,* p. 116.

good houses have from 15 to 20 rooms & the arrangements are such as to meet almost every want of a family.[58]

May 5, 1824. Doctor Gual,* W[illiam] D Robinson,* Doctor [Henry] Mayne [*sic* for Maine],* Messrs. [Christian L.] Manhardt,* Miralla,* St. Maris [*sic* for Santamaría]* [illegible], [Lino de] Clemente,* & Silva* dined with us. All well pleased I believe[.]

May 6, 1824. [William D.] Robinson,*[59] [León] Galindo,* an Englishman of Spanish parents[,] & [Carlton] Avery[,]* a Yankee[,] dined with me.

May 8, 1824. I rode out & waited on Mr. [James] Henderson.* I find him fully as agreeable a man as either of the other Com[missione]rs. I think however he has a dash of the Coxcomb—& I do not think highly of his judgment either as politician or in his domestic arrangements. His being without money on the river & purchasing a house here, while he is poor without family declare his want of good sense.

I infer from the Kings [George IV]* speech & the debates in parliament that the republics of S[outh] A[merica] are not to be immediately recognized by GBritain; unless something should produce a rupture with Spain.[60]

It is manifest that England sedulously (& rightly too) avoids a war, although she will engage rather than prevent the subjugation of this Country by the aid of Continental powers, which wd. at once throw into their lap all the benefits of the Commerce of this Country[.]

I dined at Doctor Guals* in company with the B[ritish] Com[missione]rs & others. No lady but Mrs. [James T.] English*—& no conversation but on the lightest subject. Indeed I have never heard the Com[missioners]s attempt a con-

---

58. See also Bache, *op. cit.,* p. 231. Bolívar's villa is still a tourist attraction in Bogotá.

59. A biography of William D. Robinson is being prepared by Professor Harold Bierck of the University of North Carolina, Chapel Hill.

60. See *Hansard's Parliamentary Debates,* Vols. IX-X (London, 1824). They indicate little discussion on the matter.

versation on any other subject—[James] Henderson* is very fond of writing & has written one book (a history of Brazil) and several pamphlets.

May 9, 1824. Sunday. Betsy & myself waited on Mr. & Mrs. [José Manuel] Restrepo.* Mr. R. is one of those who has been most polite to me. We also visited Colo: [Pedro] Brizeño Méndez* the brother in law of the V. P. [Santander].* Then we saw the V. P. & almost a dozen others, half of them Priests.

Their looks & the looks of the House (in a most dirty & wretched state) declared that they had been gambling & drinking all night. I am told that most of the officers of Govt. & others of distinction here, gamble at a most extravagant rate almost every night—and that [William D.] Robinson* has been fleeced by them[.]

May 10, 1824. The family is now in pretty good health, thank God.

May 13, 1824. The weather since the first of March has been most unusually dry for this place. The good weather however seemed to cease three days ago, it has been raining nearly ever since.

This day I rode out. The family [is] in tolerable health. A laxity of the bowels seems to remain with Arthur a most vexatious time.

Robinson* has entered into another contract with this Gov: for the delivery of arms & naval stores to the amount of 3 or 400,000 dollars.

He is a bold, wild, extravagant adventurer. Every one speaks of the goodness & kindness of his heart. He is certainly an enemy to himself & possibly others—certainly if they confide in his calculations.

I am now reading [Conyers] "Middleton's Cicero in Spanish, the second time—not for the history but for the Spanish.

My son Arthur has just come into the room & said "Oh papa dont write all the time." "I want to see the Wolf-book" —meaning a Book representing Romulus & Remus sucking the wolf.

May 16, 1824. A rainy, cold, disagreeable day. I have been writing to the UStates under the expectation of sending the letters to Carthagena by W[illiam] D Robinson*—who says he will go in 3 or 4 days—& will go soon in the Colon Ship Venezuela to the US.[,] having contracts with this Govt. for the delivery of arms & naval stores to the amt. of 3 or 400,000 dollars.

On Friday we dined at the Quinta of Mr. Santa Maria [*sic* for Santamaría]* on the invitation of [Christian L.] Manhardt,*[61] who lives with St. M.[,] Doctor Gual,* his family & eight or ten others dined there—& in spite of my good determination I ate too much & became sick.

Manhardt* gave us evidence how ridiculous an Entertainer can make himself by railing at his servants, complaining of his fare & making apologies. It is rarely or never done by any one who is much used to entertaining genteel company[.]

Yesterday I recd. a letter from Doctor G[ual]* desiring to know if I had the requisite powers for forming a treaty &c. He expressed his readiness to proceed with the negotiation. However in a lukewarm manner.

My son [Arthur] is still unwell. A weak stomach & continual laxity of the bowels make me uneasy.

May 24, 1824. Monday I rode out, but it rained at intervals, so as to prevent me from going farther than Mr. St. Maria's [*sic* for Santamaría's] quinta[.]

---

61. Manhardt's interest in placing a steamboat on Lake Maracaibo reflected Colombian interest in this comparatively new technological development. The first river steamboat, one of the first commercial steamers of any kind to reach South America, was the Fidelidad, which arrived at the mouth of the Magdalena River in 1824. Manhardt may have wished to operate on this river, but a two-year monopoly had already been obtained by Johann B. Elbers, see Appendix, List of Names.

On Wednesday the 19—[William D] Robinson,* [Henry George] Mayne [*sic* for Maine],* [Carlton] Avery* & [Christian L.] Manhardt* dined with me. Robinson & Avery went off on Saturday & Mayne [*sic* for Maine]* goes tomorrow.

My impressions of R[obinson] are much more favorable than those I had recd. from report.

Agreeably to app[ointmen]t Gual is to come tomorrow for the purpose of holding the first conference on a Commercial Treaty. I have been for several days engaged in reading the N[ews]papers from the UStates. On yesterday I recd. the first intelligence through a Baltimore paper that my arrival had reached the UStates. The passage of the New Tariff seems yet doubtful in Congress.[62]

Calhoun* is abandoned by his friends as a Candidate for the presidency & Genl. Jackson* seems to increase in popularity most astonishingly. I still think [John Quincy] Adams* will be the president[.]

On yesterday Betsy & myself paid a morning visit to Mrs. [José María Del] Castillo [y Rada],* Mrs. [James T.] English* & Mr. [Juan P.] Ayala.* This last is represented to be & seems to be a most amiable family.

For the sake of Arthur's health, the pleasure of exercise & all the pleasures connected with the Country, I am inclined to get a Quinta in the neighborhood of the city. I can think of but one disadvantage—that is the little opp[ortunit]y the children will have of learning the Spanish language—Whereas now from the number of their acquaintances among the neighboring children they improve very fast.

May 28, 1824. A dark morning—cool & unpleasant. We are to take a family dinner with Mr. [James] Henderson* this day— Who with his lady waited on us a few days ago.

---

62. The Tariff of 1824 was strongly opposed by the northern merchant and the southern planter. It was, however, supported by the hemp growers of Kentucky, the Pennsylvania iron interests, and the wool interests of Ohio and tariffs of 1816 and 1818. Woolen goods, glass, iron, and lead rates were increased, and a 25 per cent rate applied to hemp.

We have been invited by Mr. Santa Maria [*sic* for Santamaría]* to occupy his quinta for a few months. We shall probably accept it.

On Tuesday Doctor Gual* presented to me in due form his proje[c]t of a commercial treaty; after we had exchanged powers.[63] He still presents his article declaring that "Free Ships do not make free goods."[64] It is, I believe, intended to abandon this article in the Negotiation. But I have an apprehension that another subject (that of putting the US. on the footing of the most friendly nation) [may] make [or] create a difficulty, as he acknowledged that he was anxious to make some little reserve which might be hereafter offered to Spain in consideration of her recognition. He said that he thought the US wd. not object, inasmuch as Spain had so little commerce, that a concession to her would only be nominal & in truth of but little advantage to her & of no injury to us. Of course I can sign no such treaty—Although I believe *he* might safely sign a treaty placing the US. on the most fav[ore]d grounds & rely on her generosity hereafter to permit Colombia to grant to Spain some little commercial privilege.

I am now preparing a counter project for Gual & a letter vindicating the principle that "Free Ships make free Goods" & urging him to adopt it. Betsy is my Secretary.

June 11, 1824. A dark rainy Morng. about 7 oClock.

On the 28 ulto. [*sic* for *ult.*] We dined with Mr. [James]

---

63. Authorization from their respective governments to carry on the negotiations.

64. The value of Colombia's trade for the long run was probably exaggerated by both England and the United States at this time as they attempted to secure the best possible agreements with the new government. The English commissioners, and particularly Patrick Campbell, were disturbed by the possibility of a U. S.–Colombian treaty of navigation and commerce, and particularly by the principle "free flags shall make free cargoes" that might be included in the treaty. This principle, if generally adopted in agreements between the United States and the Latin American nations, would have aimed a potential blow at English sea power, for it would have meant that the neutral states of America could take over the carrying trade of Britain's enemies during a war and thus greatly diminish the effectiveness of British blockades.

Henderson* & family. They may be good people—but never did people manifest less decent fashion & more inclination to be fashionable. We dined with them in a company of fifteen or 16 again on the succeeding Thursday when the same inclination to be genteel & meanness which forbid it was displayed.

The season is now comm[encin]g which they tell us is remarkable [for its] winds & showers—what they call Paramours.

In a few days we shall go to the Hacienda of Mr. St. Maria [*sic* for Santamaría],* who has been preparing it for us with great care.

There are his brothers of that name who are apparently most generous & hospitable gentlemen. Each has offered his quinta gratis. One is certainly too much a man of pleasure to be estimated for every quality.

We have a neighbour whom I am sorry to leave. [She is] Señora Petronita Calvo with whom Betsy has become quite intimate. She is a sensible, cheerful woman, who takes great pains to teach the language & to make herself agreeable to us. The greatest loss I apprehend in going to the country is that which the children will sustain in losing the opp[ortunit]y of speaking in Castilian frequently. Colonel [Ferdinand] Sirakowski* is not forthcoming with the money yet.[65]

June 13, 1824. A Sunday. Arthur [Anderson] has several times of late been afflicted with the headache. This is unusual with a child of his age & makes his Mother uneasy, who has apprehensions of the dropsy in the brain, of which many children die in the UStates.[66]

Betsy & myself walked to Mr. Santa Marias [*sic* for Santamaría's] quinta. On our way we saw Messrs [John P.] Hamilton,* [Patrick] Campbell* & [James] Henderson*

---

65. See above, April 22, 1824.
66. Dropsy used by a layman of the 1820's in this context probably was a form of encephalitis or sleeping sickness.

riding out. Each [was] attended by his white servant in livery.

I waited on the VPresident. All well.

June 14, 1824. A pleasant day.

June 16, 1824. Doctors Gual,* [Félix de] Restrepo* & [José María Del] Castillo [y Rada]* Colos: Hamilton & Campbell & Mr. Henderson, Cade,* A[ntonio] Santa Maria [*sic* for Santamaría]* [Christian L.] Manhardt,* [Leandro] Miranda,* Umaña & [Captain Charles] Wilthew* dined with me. A pleasant party.

June 17, 1824. There was a great "fiesta" & procession, the "Corpus Christi" of the Catholics. We went to the house of the Mother of Mrs. Gaul on "Calle Real" to see the procession. Every home on the street was decorated by having the windows & balconies hung with the richest red silk.

June 20, 1824. Sunday. I rode out[.]

Yesterday I dined with Colo: Hamilton in company with about twenty persons. The V. P. and other dignitaries formed the company. Neither of the British Com[missione]rs ever attempted any political or literary conversation. I believe they neither have the ability nor inclination—but I cannot yet pronounce decisively on Campbell.[67] During most of the time at dinner we were entertained by Miralla*—who makes verses on any words given to him at dinner, extempore. Some of his rhymes show great readiness & some wit. But the company was exceedingly fatigued with him as I left them at 10 oC. & he gave no indication of ceasing, but still called on the Co. for *words*.

We have been anxiously looking for the mail since yesterday morng. Altho: I have no particular reason to expect

---

67. Campbell, for his part, was suspicious of Anderson because he then represented the commercial and maritime ambitions of the United States and later because he was the agent of what Campbell believed was an attempt of the United States to form an American Federation. See J. Fred Rippy, *Rivalry of the United States and Great Britain Over Latin America* (Baltimore, 1929), pp. 178-181.

important intelligence. He only who lives far from his country & at a place at which the mail arrives thrice a month, can estimate the anxiety which its expected arrival creates.

The VPresd. announced at dinner that information had arrived that the *Libertador* (Bolívar) had marched from Truxillo [*sic* for Trujillo] against the Enemy & that important news might soon be expected[.][68]

I do think that if Bolívar* resigns his dictatorship, leaves the Country in tranquility & returns to Colombia & becomes a private citizen he will be one of the most renowned men in modern history—and justly be deemed one of the greatest benefactors of the human race. And of this nothing depends on fortune but vanquishing the Enemy, and of this there is the greatest probability, even immediately or in a year or two.[69] All the rest depends on himself.

Buonaparte & Washington being dead Bolivar will be the most renowned man living. I am very sensible that [the Duke of] Wellington* & others have the advantage of living in a nation of poets & historians—but this can only give them temporary advantage. These same historians will write for Bolivar as well as for Wellington.

Mr. [Félix de* or José Manuel*] Restrepo & lady visited us.

Messrs. [Juan P.] Ayala,* Silva,* and [blank] a young man, a native of Carthagena dined with us.

June 21, 1824. A pleasant morng. Betsy, myself, & Elizabeth paid a visit to Mr. A[ntonio] St. Maria [*sic* for Santamaría].* I was sorry to see that every thing in the house bore evidence

---

68. Headquarters for Bolívar and Sucre in Peru was at Trujillo. After leaving this point in the middle of 1824 they marched for weeks along mountain trails and finally encountered the royalists at Junín, near Cerro de Pasco, on August 6, 1824. The battle was fought mostly with sabers and lances. The royalist losses were heavy, but the Spanish commander, General Canterac, managed to save most of the army by a speedy retreat.

69. Victory at the Battle of Ayacucho on December 8, 1824, resulted in an agreement by General Canterac and Viceroy José de la Cerna that all Spanish troops would be withdrawn from Peru and Charcas (Bolivia). The last of the Spanish soldiers departed from Callao, Peru, in January, 1826, and Spanish America was independent.

of very bad *housewifery*. I pity the man, the woman & all the family, where there is a Mother who has no skill in domestic management. It is really a domestic misfortune, much greater than it is generally deemed. It produces mortification to the Husband & to the Wife and too often breeds unhappiness. It is of evil example to the children & generally produces expense.

And that young man who thinks that a talent for managing the economy of a house with neatness is to be entirely disregarded in selecting a wife is under a mistake, which may be hereafter corrected by mortifying & unhappy experience.

June 22, 1824. A rainy morng—but becomes a pleasant day.

[Colonel León] Galindo* tells me that [Ferdinand] Sirakowski* is deemed a shuffling & shabby debtor. This is not pleasant news to a Creditor to the tune of $900.

June 24, 1824. A great feast day. We viewed the procession from the Balcony of the V. President. Like other Catholic Ceremonies, it was gaudy in the extreme & certainly looked as much like anything as a Religious Ceremony. It had the usual accompaniment of fire works & great shouting among the boys & vagabonds.

There was a Ball in the Evening in honour of the anniversary of the Battle of Carabobo.[70]

June 25, 1824. Colo: Campbell* & Mrs. English* waited on us. He soon goes to England[.]

June 27, 1824. Since Wednesday the weather has been very cool & unpleasant. There is a constant cold wind. The Thermomenter [*sic*] declares it 3 or 4° colder than it has been since my arrival in Bogota. It is now Sunday morng. & a very disagreeable & windy one.

---

70. The Battle of Carabobo, near Lake Valencia, was fought on June 24, 1821. It was decided in favor of the Colombian army by a magnificent cavalry charge led by José Antonio Páez and by the boldness of the British battalion serving with the Colombians.

We have been prevented from going to the quinta for the last 3 days by the indisposition of Mary the nurse[.]

No intelligence from K. Y. [Kentucky] since the 10th Feb:

June 29, 1824. This day the family went to the [Santamaría]* Quinta. All well.

June 30, 1824. A[ntonio] St. Maria [*sic* for Santamaría]* & Miss Johnson visit us[.] Recd. letters from K. Y. Thank God, our friends are yet well[.]

July 4, 1824. The Com[ande]r of the Guards with his music visit us & do compliment us & the day with a few tunes. Doctor Gual* & [Christian L.] Manhardt* take a family dinner. In the Eveng Miralla* & his wife, A[ntonio] St. Maria [*sic* for Santamaría],* nephew & Miss Johnson wait on us.

The weather has been tolerably pleasant for four or five days. We have had some warm rain, which is much pleasanter than the cold wind.

Manuel St. Maria [*sic* for Santamaría]* has generally eaten with us since our coming down.

I have recd. from Doctor G[ual]* a letter vindicating the principle that F[ree] ships shall not make F[ree] goods.[71] It is manifest to me that he does not wish to conclude a treaty soon, but it is equally manifest that he does not wish me to think so.

July 5, 1824. Colo: Hamilton* & Mr. Cade* visit us.

July 6, 1824. Colo: Campbell* leaves town for Engl. It is supposed that he carries back the joint rept of the Com[missione]rs. I send by him a letter [to] J. M. M. [acpherson] cont[ainin]g others for the US.

July 8, 1824. This day I send a letter to Doctor G[ual] vindicating the principles of "F[ree] Ships make f[ree] goods." It

71. See above, May 28, 1824.

does not go into the Enquiry of what *is* the rule, but what it *ought* to be among commercial & pacific nations.

[Manuel] St. Maria [*sic* for Santamaría]* generally eats with us & I believe is very much inclined to continue to do so.

For the last four or five days, it has rained frequently but slightly. I am told this is unusual in July.

July 10, 1824. This day twelve months [ago] we landed at Laguayra.

July 11, 1824. Sunday. A little windy. We have had several most bright & beautiful nights. I am not sure that I have ever seen the whole firmament clear in this Country, I am sure that it rarely occurs.

July 16, 1824. Now a cold disagreeable day. It has rained a part of every day for the last week or more[.]

Yesterday old Mr. Salazar* visited me with a young daughter & gd. daughter.

Old Don Sebastian Lopez walks to see us almost every day.

I am to meet Gual this day on the subject of the treaty[.]

July 18, 1824. I met Doctor G. on the treaty subjt. My suspicions are conf[irmed] that protraction & not the formation of a treaty immed[iatel]y is desired by the Govt.

Yesterday he came here on the subject of the claims for spoilations.[72] If he complies with his promises there will be but little difference between us. I understand him as admitting one or two cases in wh. the Evidence is very weak. His lady came with him & brought Elizabeth a partridge. In the Eveng. I killed a hare in the Garden—the first I have seen in this Country. It resembled the common North A hare or rabbit except that it had more hair or wool for the protection of his feet;—& less tail than our hare. It was hardly to be seen at all & without the white underneath it.

---

72. See above, March 8, 1824, n. 42.

July 21, 1824. This day I add[resse]d two letters to Doctor Gual, one on the subject of the regulations of this Country which deny to any but Citizens the right of accepting consignments & transacting the ordinary business of Merchants & also requiring that the Registers of all ships shd. *be delivd. to & kept by the custom house officers,* instead of the Consuls of the Nations to which the Ships belong.

The letter urged a change of the practice.

The other letter states the case of the Hibernia—a vessel having a clearance for S[an]t[o] Domingo, but actually coming direct to S[an]t[a] Martha.[73] My letter claimed for the Cargo the benefit of the law relating to direct importations from the UStates.

July 22, 1824. Betsy & myself took a long ride on the road towards the Salto.[74]

Yesterday Eveng. Mr. & Mrs. [James] Henderson* & their family took coffee with us on their own invitation. Doctor Gual also took his coffee here.

July 23, 1824. Doctor G. told me that the appl[icati]on in my late letters would all, he thought, be conceded in a few days.

July 24, 1824. Betsy has suffered very much last night with the toothache.

John Stucley & John Kennedy, two citizens of the US from N. Y. came to see me on the introduction of [Christian L.] Manhardt.* They are concerned in the SteamBoat.[75]

July 28, 1824. Betsy has been unwell for several days with the toothache & disordered stomach. This morning she does not get up.

M[anuel] Santa Maria [*sic* for Santamaría]* yesterday Evening retd. from an Excursion he made with the Vice P. to the country seat of the VP. St. M. gives wonderful

---

73. See Map 3, p. 133, and Map 5, p. 205.
74. Toward the Falls of Tequendama.
75. See above, May 16, 1824, n. 61.

accounts of the number of cattle & of the value of the Estate. I understand that it was one of the confiscated estates, which St. Ander [*sic* for Santander]* has had the address to get hold of, in payment of his arrears from the Govt.

Yesterday a Mr. [Augustus] Leland* of Boston, who has been merchandizing some time in S[an]t[a] Martha, came to see us. He has brought goods to this place[.]

July 30, 1824. A rainy morning.

I have been busy for several days copying my letters to Gual & to the Secretary [of State]—to be preserved in the office or to be sent to the Department [of State].

No news yet of the coming of Mr. [Beaufort T.] Watts[.]* the Secy of legation.

Although the family has been pretty well of late, with the Exception of Betsy's slight indisposition & we are eligibly & pleasantly situated, still time drags on heavily. I wish to be back with my friends, with those with whom I may communicate freely; to where all the little incidents around in some way interest or have connection with you. Maybe after all it is only the desire of change, the uneasiness under present things, which all mankind feel whether happily or unhappily I do not know.

July 31, 1824. It rained much last night. This morng. it is windy[.]

Last night I was at a "bagre de lujo y ambigu"[76] at Colo: Hamilton.* Betsy was too unwell to go. I feel this morning as badly as a man of regular habits, who has sat up till 3 oC. may expect to feel[.]

A report has arrived that the English Cabinet has determined to recognize the S. A. states—And also that [Agustín] Iturbide* has sailed from England for Mexico.[77]

---

76. Anderson's excursion into the Spanish language probably means that he ate a fish dinner at Colonel Hamilton's home.

77. On March 19, 1823, Iturbide, the Mexican emperor, presented his resignation to a "rump" parliament and went into exile in Italy. A year later, gambling on rumors that certain European powers planned to assist

A suspicion exists that he has had some understanding with the Holy Alliance. I hardly credit it. Although the dissentions in Mexico seem to invite foreign interference, I do not believe that Spain would entrust any enterprise of moment to that man.

August 1, 1824. A clear cool morning.

August 4, 1824. My birthday. All those who have arrived at their *36 year,* know too well the different sensations which the occurrence of a birthday produces at 18 & 36. It no longer produces joy of course, joy & gladness. It is now certainly a day of seriousness, perhaps of some melancholy. The mind and body have worked at the utmost strength[.] Whatever change the body may sustain must be for the worse. Many flattering illusions have gone—& if any still remain they are such only as are necessary to make life comfortable. The anticipation of great bliss & happiness in this life is gone.

There are not many who at my age have more cause to be contented. My children are intelligent & now in good health & free from vice. I feel no unhappiness from debt. With these things (with a proper mind) I ought to be as happy as any one. In my past life I have suffered much (I think) from the death of my children. I have suffered (not more I hope than a reasonable man ought) from debt. Although I have [been] through many petty vexations, which have for the time produced suffering, still *these* are the only two causes which I can acknowledge without shame. All other unhappiness has been without adequate cause & much as implies ingratitude to my Creator.

Yesterday my daughter & I went to see Mrs. English,* who returned with us & sat an hour. Colo: Hamilton* waited on me. Betsy & myself walked to see Mr. and Mrs. A[ntonio] Santa Maria [*sic* for Santamaría.]

Spain in the reconquest of Latin America, he returned to Mexico, landing at Tampico and advancing into the interior. He was captured and shot a few days later on July 19, 1824.

August 7, 1824. This is the anniversary of the battle of Boyaca[78] & there is great rejoicing & singing & parading in the Cathedral & out of it—& preparations for its celebrations this evening by a Ball at the V. P. & by eating, parading, & dancing tomorrow (Sunday) in the fields & farther by a masked ball on Monday Evening.

Yesterday I recd. a note from Genl. [Pedro] Brizeño [Méndez],* from which I infer that I shall get the money from [Ferdinand] Sirawkowski [*sic* for Sirakowski]*[79]

August 9, 1824. On Saturday Evg. Betsy & myself went to the VP's ball in honour of the day. There was a large collection of ladies & gentlemen, who danced late[.]

Yesterday we dined with Messrs. [Juan Manuel] Arrublas* & [Luis] Montoya* at a "Comida del Campo." However it was in a large house—a large company of gentlemen & a few ladies—dancing &c. The celebration I understand is to be continued tomorrow.

Betsy is this day in bed sick[.]

I recd. a letter from [Harris E.] Fudger* in wh. he asks leave of absence for 3 mos. No doubt he is in low spirits, for a man to come to S[an]t[a] Martha to live on the perquisites of a Consulship is wild indeed.

August 10, 1824. Yesterday Mrs. Silva,* son & daughter Carmalita came to see us. A very respectable & kind family.

A cool disagreeable morng. Betsy is still in bed[.]

August 12, 1824. Betsy is a little better. We have had two pleasant days.

Yesterday Evening Mrs. English* visited us escorted by Doctor Gual whom she had met on the way. She is a gay, sensible, agreeable woman about whom there have been

78. The Battle of Boyacá, fought on the plains near Bogotá on August 7, 1819, was decisive. The Spanish fled from Bogotá, and Bolívar occupied the city on August 10.

79. For an explanation of Anderson's constant reference to Sirakowski, see above, April 22, 1824.

many sad reports. She is recd. here by the most respectable people, Colombian & English.

This evening I have made out for Doctor G. an extract from my instructions relating to the proposed Confederation of American States. The design is to show the view wh. our Govt. takes of it, as far as they can understand it. It seems to be a great object here to produce a meeting of the Spanish A[merican] states at Panama. Whether the US. will be invited is doubtful & whether the meeting will be on principles wh. will admit her to join may be more doubtful.[80]

If the principle of an alliance of a defensive [nature] is to be s[uggeste]d to her, I apprehend she would not [commission] her representative. That would imply an engagement wh. she wd. probably not enter into with any power.

August 16, 1824. Betsy is better. Yesterday [Augustus] Leland* visited us with a Mr. [Carlton] Avery* who says that he was born in N. York—but who I apprehend has none of the feelings or interests of a citizen of the U States.

On Saturday Elizabeth, myself & Arthur *breakfasted* with Mr. [Johann B.] Elbers* at Bolivar's quinta. We sat down to table at 3 oC. The invitation declared it a breakfast. It however had the following constituents of a dinner—3 oC. wine, boiled and roasted meats, toasts, vegetables in abundance & every thing indeed to make a fine dinner, not omitting the dessert. The V. P. was in fine spirits. There was much dancing & Elizabeth waltzed for the first time.

I am invited by Colo: Hamilton* to dine with him on Saturday. By way of inducement he told me that he should have Colo. Penonego. Now Colo. P.[,] though a Senator &c.[,] is a black negro.

August 19, 1824. We recd. letters from K[entucky] but not so late as former dates[.]

On Monday Betsy & myself dined with Mrs. English.*

---

80. See above, Introduction, for a discussion of the Congress. See also, Parks, *op. cit.,* pp. 137-138.

Sec[retar]ys Gual[,]* [José María del] Castillo [y Rada]* & ladies were there with many others[.]

Yesterday Mr. Ellenworth [Illingworth] an Englishman & a Colo. Desmenard* a Frenchman visited us—with an invitation to go *duck shooting* on Tuesday.

August 20, 1824. Arthur [Anderson]* is very unwell with a head ache[.]

By the mail of yesterday I heard of the privateer Genl. Santander taking three US. vessels with Spanish goods on board. I fear very much that the troublesome question "do free Ships make Spanish goods free" will arise in my *admon* [-ishment]. I do not believe that the gov*t* will admit it. I do not believe they should [deny it.]

August 22, 1824. Sunday. Yesterday I was indisposed from loss of sleep, Arthur having been sick the night before. He is now better. I could not dine with Colo[nel] H[amilton]* & the *negro* senator.

Last Eveng. Mrs. Gual & her mother passed two hours with us.

The papers of the UStates give no certain indications of the result of the Pres. Election. I *think* that Adams* will be elected.

John Kennedy[,] a North A[merican] youth[,] has been with us all day.

August 26, 1824. Yesterday was one of the finest days I have seen lately.

The day before I went *duck shooting* about five miles [away]. I was nothing but a "gentleman Amateur[.]" However several gentlemen were very skilful and successful in killing ducks.

We dined same day (or night) with Mr. Ellenworth [Illingworth] an Englishman & Colo[nel] Desmenard [d'Esmenard] a Frencham [*sic* for Frenchman], two of the principal duck shooters[.]

Lately I have recd. a letter from Doctor Gual inviting a continuance of our negotiations. I so far distrust the inclination of this Govt. *to conclude* a treaty, that I have no sanguine hope of concluding one soon[.] He is more tardy too than I anticipated in answering my private note on the subject of the claims.[81]

For three days most assiduously engaged in copying letters for the department of State.

Day before yesterday I had a conference with Gual,* it wd. seem that the treaty wd. soon be completed. He seems anxious to introduce provisions declaring the slave trade piracy—must [*sic* for more] anxious I believe than he is to conclude it on some other points[.]

August 30, 1824. Monday morng. Visited by Colo. [Charles] Wilthew.* St. Rosa's days. The family well. The mail due yesterday has not arrived[.]

August 31, 1824. Yesterday we dined (in family way) with Doctor Gual—it being his birthday—that is her[?] Saints day. St. Rosa's day.

Elizabeth has been complaining for a few days.

This evening Doctor G. & myself are to have a Conference on the treaty.

September 7, 1824. On Saturday I recd. a letter from Larz [Anderson]* from which I expect to see him in a few days[.] Thank God—the family is well.

On [the] 5th I dined with Colo: Hamilton* in co: with [the James] Hendersons,* [José María del] Castillo [y Rada]* & [José Manuel] Restrepos* family, Mrs. English* &c.

I have had several Conferences with Gual.* I think I shall conclude a treaty with him—but I am not confident[.]

Doctor [Henry George] Mayne [*sic* for Maine]* here today[.]

September [?] 1824. The family is now tolerably well[.] On

---

81. See above, March 8, 1824, n. 42.

Friday a conference with Gual. Spanish tardiness. On Saturday Gual, Colo: Hamilton, Henderson & wife, Mrs. English,
Messrs. [Johann B.] Elbers,* Ellenworth [Illingworth], [Doc-
tor R. N.] Chayne [sic for Cheyne]*, Cade,* & St. Maria [sic
for Santamaría]* dined with us[.]

I am satisfied that the conversation of English Gentlemen
& ladies (even if the best company) is not as delicate in
language or in its subjects, as that of the N. Americans. Al-
lusions are frequently made & without exciting any particular noti[ce], which with us would be wholly intolerable.

September 15, 1824. I have two very sore toes. It will doubtless be thought very unimportant 20 years hence, but it is
not quite unimportant to me now, as they are very painful.

Yesterday I was composing a letter to the Secy. [of State
John Quincy Adams] giving to him a history of the negotiation, predicated on the idea that the treaty was concluded, as
there seems now every indication of it being done soon. I
wish to give him information before the session of Congress
but probably Spanish tardiness will prevent it.

September 20, 1824. A fine day. No news from Kentucky
since 10 June. We are suprized at not hearing from Larz
[Anderson].*

I have seen in a US paper a piece well ridiculing the idea
that Colombia is bound by the treaty of Spain & the UStates
made when she was a part of the Spanish Monarchy. I shall
dislike much indeed to be obliged to support any such pre-
posterous notion—though *my instructions direct it.*[82]

Indications are yet favourable to an early completion of
the treaty.

I am also to conclude a convention on the subject of the
slave trade.[83] I think it wd. have a very favourable effect on

---

82. A reading of the Instructions does not make clear how Anderson
arrived at such an impression.
83. The treaty was signed on December 10, 1824, in Bogotá, but the
United States Senate would not accept it. See below, December 10, 1824,
n. 110

the character of both Countries—& of course some effect on the reputation of the negotiators.

September 24, 1824. A cold unpleasant morning. There has been a rare season of dry weather.

[Christian L.] Manhardt* was here yesterday. He has just retd. from an excursion to the Country, during which he saw the bridge of Pandi. His representation is essentially different from that of [Alexander Von] Humboldt in several respects.

Doctor Gual* & his lady here last Evening.

It seems the British Ministerial paper says that Colo: Hamilton was not authorized to say *what he did* to the V. President. I did never have any doubt, as Gual & myself expressed to each other, that it was not intended that he shd. say what he did in public.[84]

September 30, 1824. For the last week I have written more assiduously than I ever did before for one week—to prepare the treaty which we have agreed to sign & the correspondence necessary on it. It was to have been signed yesterday—but it seems the V. P. through vanity wishes it signed on 3d. October—the anniversary of the day on wh. he swore to the Constitution[.]

Yesterday I recd. letters from K. Y. [Kentucky] to the 6th July. Thank God—all were well to that time. One also from Larz [Anderson]* at Carthagena who from his account must have had a terrible time. However all young travellers think that they have suffered more than ever was suffered before and [know] perfectly that every man after his adventures are over, is glad that they were perilous & strange. It increases his importance. He has seen & felt more than ordinary men have seen.

---

84. The reference is to *The Times* (London) which, according to H. R. Box Bourne, *English Newspapers* (London, 1887), p. 16, "was violently ministerial" during this period when factions and parties had their official spokesmen and organs. Hamilton's statement had implied the British government's dismay at the power of the Church in Colombian affairs.

made out of this Govt or its fund
or its Contracts in some way — altho I
do not exactly know in what way —
I will watch the course of things —

October 3 — Sunday —!

I have this day signed with
Doctor Gual Commissioner for Colombia
a Treaty of Amity, Commerce and
Navigation between the United States
of America and the Republic of
Colombia — It cannot fail to
excite some emotion in me — It is
the first Treaty between the UStates
& any Republic — It is with a State
now free, which for 300 Years was
an oppressed Colony of Spain — that

Elizabeth has just come into the room & has asked "what book is that? What do you write there?"

Arthur has not been well for some days.

October 1, 1824. A fine day. It has been quite dry for two months. The rainy season has been expected for some time. Yesterday I walked to the city—the first time for three weeks.

A few days ago Capt. Quartel* a commissioner from the Governor of Curacoa waited on me. He is a fine looking man [and] speaks English well. This day Mr. Bing [Byng]* a merchant of Curacao⁸⁵ was introduced to me by [Christian L.] Manhardt.* He has come to settle the claims of Adml. [Luís] Brion* on this Govt.

The late victory in Peru⁸⁶ seems now not to be so important as was first reported—but the situation of the armies gives good hopes of more decided advantages soon.

For some time past the idea has taken hold of me that something might be made out of this Govt. or its funds or its contracts in some way—altho I do not exactly know in what way. I will watch the course of things.

October 3, 1824. Sunday!

I have *this* day signed with Doctor Gual Commissioner for Colombia a Treaty of Amity, Commerce & Navigation between the United States of America and the Republic of Colombia. It cannot fail to excite some *emotion in me.* It is the first Treaty between the UStates & ANY Republic. It is with a State now *free,* which for 300 Years was an oppressed colony of Spain. That I shd. be the person who signed that treaty cannot fail to produce a strong emotion. In proportion to the importance of the Transaction is the apprehension I feel, apprehension not produced by judgement but by the possibility that it may not receive the approbation of the Authorities of my Country. I have certainly considered every

85. See Map 3, p. 133.
86. At Junín, see above, June 20, 1824, n. 68.

step most cautiously; I cannot think that there is any thing in it which can cause disapprobation.[87]

We are invited to dine by Doctor G[ual] in company with Colo. Quartel* the Dutch Comm[issione]r this day.

Junca* a French merchant was to see me to day.

October 5, 1824. The rainy weather seems setting in.

Arthur still frequently complains of a vicious head ache. His bowels have been disordered for many months[.]

Bogota *October 8, 1824*

My dear father[88]

Ten days ago that is by the last mail from Carthagena I received your letter sent by Larz [Anderson.]* By the same mail I received a letter from Larz, in which he informed me of his arrival at that place after extraordinary and most vexatious delays, both on his voyage and at Jamaica[.] However no doubt he has informed you of all the incidents of his voyage[.] From his letter to me I expect to see him in a few days and I intend to keep this letter open until the morning when the mail again arrives and I shall hear from him or the consul on what day he left Carthagena[.][89]

I am happy to hear from your letter and that of Mr. [Owen] Gwathmey* of the 4th July that you and your family are well. The season has now arrived to make us very anxious to hear how our friends in Louisville and its neighborhood passed the fall months. My family is tolerably well. Arthur very frequently complains of a head ache, which sometimes makes us uneasy, but he is now running about[.] Elizabeth & Ann are well[.] A disease of the bowels is a very common complaint in this country; particularly with all who have

87. The treaty was approved by the United States Senate on March 3, 1825, and proclaimed on May 31. The British secured a more favorable treaty in April, 1825, but the same advantages were quickly extended to American commerce.

88. This letter was not in the original diary but has been inserted by the editors. See W. P. Anderson, *op. cit.,* p. 126, for a copy of the letter.

89. Anderson noted on the left margin that "the mail comes from Carthagena in 20 days, but it will take Larz 30 or more."

to pass through the hot lands of the coast. However I have seen nothing to make me believe that this is a sickly country[.] The indisposition of my family as such might have occurred anywhere, with the exception of Ferdinand Bullitt's* case. That I believe was produced by the tropical sun and an unsound liver.

We have no important news here. We have been for some time in anxious expectation of hearing something interesting from Bolivar and the Peruvians. The last news gave an account of a successful engagement between two detachments of the armies and of the retreat of [José] Canterac the Royalist General.[90] In the Republic of Colombia everything is as tranquil as in the U States and more so than in Kentucky when the relief laws are under discussion[.][91]

However in many things, the people here are a long way behind those in the U States. Another generation will probably be necessary before they can come to the full enjoyment of all the blessings of a free Government. Larz will be able to give you a better account of it than I can write[.] However everybody who comes here and stays a short time, having seen but little more than the bad roads and bad accomodations goes away with a bad account. We shall of course detain Larz with us as long as possible[.] However he cannot remain long, as I shall wish him to be in Washington in the month of January. Betsy and the children send their love to you, My mother[,] Cecilia [Anderson],* Louisa [Anderson]* and all the children[.] Arthur very often dreams about being at his gran papas[.]

I wish you to write to me frequently
With love to Mother and all, I am,

affectionately yours
R. C. Anderson jr

October 9. I have detained the letter until the last minute but the mail has not yet arrived[.]

---

90. See above, June 20, 1824, n. 68.
91. See above, June 30, 1822, n. 215.

October 9, 1824.[92] By the mail of this day I send to the Secretary of State [John Quincy Adams] a copy of the Treaty & two letters explanatory of it & the negotiation which led to it.

Recd. a letter from Larx [*sic* for Larz] who is still in Carthagena. By the papers [I see] that [La] Fayette* has arrived in the UStates[93]—that [Joseph] Desha* is Gov: & [Robert P.] McAfee* Lt. Gov: of Kentucky & [Joseph] *Lecompte** a member of Congress. As old mother Patterson said "God help that *poor Kentucky* of a place where they make our 'Jammie' a Colonel."

October 10, 1824. Betsy was very sick last night. Waited on the V. P.

October 11, 1824. Betsy still quite unwell. Rains every day.

On Saturday I recd. a letter from W[illiam] D[avis] Robinson* at New York. He does not seem inclined to leave it soon. There is too much good eating & drinking there.

October 12, 1824. Rain [Manuel] St. Maris [*sic* for Santamaría]* who has not been here for several days, breakfasted with us this morning. He tells Betsy that he has procured for her some large dishes of old silver.

[James] Henderson* with several of his family & [Doctor Mariano de] Rivero* called without getting down.

October 13, 1824. Betsy is better. Last Evening the two brothers [B] Alcazar* came to see us.

Arthur & myself rode out, with Elizabeth on Mr. [Christian] Manhardt's mule.

Mrs. English* called on us—and Doctor [R. N.] Chayne [*sic* for Cheyne]* to see Arthur.*

---

92. The diary resumes with this entry.
93. The party at Colonel Richard Anderson's honoring the Marquis is described by Kitty Anderson, *op. cit.,* p. 2, but the story that the Colonel locked his liquor cabinet after the party because of the behavior of some of the guests may be family legend.

October 14, 1824. Rain—dark cold morning.

Colo: Grenier[,] an old Frenchman who has been an officer in the service of this Republic & who says that he came to the US with Count d'Estaing, came to me to get some letters which I had promised to give him for the US whither he is going. He is an old talking French man—said to be respectable enough.

Doctor Chayne [*sic* for Cheyne]* came to see Arthur[.]*

October 15, 1824. It does not rain but is raw & cloudy—pleasant in the Eveng. I dined with Mr. [James] Henderson.*

October 16, 1824. A pleasant morning. A little rain about 9 oClock.

October 17, 1824. Dined yesterday with Mr. Illingworth* & Doctor Chayne [*sic* for Cheyne]. Played two rubbers at whist.[.]

Arthur* still complains very frequently of his head.

October 18, 1824. A pleasant day. Elizabeth & myself walked to town.

Gual* & myself have had no communications lately, either on the slave convention or on the subject of the Claims.[94] It is time to jog him a little. This Evening Miss Johnson & Donna Molina* waited on us.

October 19, 1824. A Beautiful Morng. This is the anniversary of our departure from Caracas for this place as well as of the Capture of [Lord] Cornwallis.[95] I do not think that any journey has been lately undertaken & performed in Europe or America, where there was no peril of life from armies or robbers, which was more highly calculated to create care & concern than that. I had a family. There was no possibility of proceeding except on mules or on foot. The road was more than a thousand miles long. None of us could speak the

94. See above, July 18, 1824, and August 26, 1824, for previous mention of the claims question.
95. The British forces at Yorktown capitulated on October 18, 1781, and on October 19 almost 8,000 men laid down their arms.

language. There was a known difficulty in procuring mules. It was not known that we [were in danger] from robbers. We knew we should be[ware of] pilferers. The road was represented as one of the worst in the world. The accomodations were scant & came from precarious hospitality. The paramos[96] exposed us to much inconvenience & some peril.

I rode out with Elizabeth* & Arthur.* We are still uneasy about Arthur's* situation. He complains frequently of the head ache & his bowels have been disordered for several months.

Many months ago I had thought of writing something (may be a book) on this Country. I then thought of it only as amusement or as a means of adding some thing to my character. I have abandoned the notion for several months. But this [sic for then] I thought of it again with as much a view to *profit* as any thing else. It has occurred to me that in London possibly the manuscript might be disposed of for as much as would defray my Expenses to that Country.[97] I have written this day a page or two[.]

I recd. letters from [Beaufort T.] Watts* the new Secy. of legation at Carracas[.]

October 20, 1824. Cold ugly morning[.]

October 22, 1824. It has not rained for 3 or 4 days[.] Arthur still unwell[.]

This day & yesterday I walked to the City. Called on Capt. Quartel* the Dutch Comm[issione]r & on [Mariano de] Rivero* the Chief of the School of Mineralogy.

October 23, 1824. No rain for several days. Yesterday evening [Christian L.] Manhardt,* M[anuel] St. Maria [sic for Santamaría]* & his son from S[an]t[a] Marta took coffee with us.

From the papers of the UStates & from what I think men

---

96. The high and cold areas through which they passed.
97. Anderson's association with Colonel J. P. Hamilton, who was writing a book about his travels in Colombia, may have stimulated such thinking.

will do, I think that if [John Quincy] Adams is elected P. &
[John C.] Calhoun not V. P. that the latter will be the Secy.
of State to the former—notwithstanding [that] the late restlessness of C[alhoun] & his precocious desire of being P. must
have displeased A[dams.] I think that Adams* will be elected
ultimately.

October 27, 1824. Rain almost every day. Yesterday evening
[Christian] Manhardt* [&] St. Maria [*sic* for Santamaría]*
drank coffee with[.]

Gual* yesterday gave me assurance that he wd. soon be
ready to settle the claims[.]⁹⁸ He again mentioned the subject
of the Slave trade & said that he wd. write to me a letter
desiring me to present a proje[c]t—& said moreover that he
would sign a convention such as had been assented to by the
Senate of the U. S. with England.⁹⁹

He again adverted to the Great American Confederation
& the proposed meeting of [the] Congress at Panama. [He]
Said that Mr. [José María de] Salazar* had been directed to
broach the subject & give an invitation to the U. S. to send a
deputy if [he] had reason to believe that it would be accept-
able.

October 28, 1824. A good day. Yesterday Eveng. Betsy, Elizabeth, & myself walked to Antonio St. Maria's [*sic* for Santa-
maría].* We found him engaged with his game cocks & his
wife who was too sick to be sitting up on the bed, playing
cards with a lady.

[James] Henderson,* [Capt.] Quartel* & [Doctor Mariano de] Rivero* visited me in the[ir] Court dresses[.] [They]
Have just been to wait on the V. Presdt. this (St Simons)
day.

---

98. See above, July 18, 1824, August 26, 1824, and October 18, 1824.
99. Gual may have meant Article X of the Treaty of Ghent. This article
simply stated that since the United States and Britain found the traffic
in slaves to be against the principles of humanity and justice, both countries "shall use their best endeavors" to accomplish its abolition. However,
an Anglo-American Slave Trade Convention of a more formal nature was
signed on March 13, 1824, and this is probably the one Gual mentioned.
See also below, December 10, 1824.

October 30, 1824. Yesterday was a fine day & so is this morning. Yesterday I was writing my chapter on "the population & Slavery of Colombia."

November 1, 1824. Rain yesterday & today. [James] Henderson* & [Christian] Manhardt & [Mariano de] Rivero [visited] me today.

On Saturday I received a letter from Gual soliciting farther [*sic* for further] communication on the subject of suppressing the slave trade[.]

[Christian] Manhardt & [James] Henderson were here. B. Alcazar* [came] in the Evening.

November 3, 1824. Gual promises a speedy adjustment of the claims.

Mrs. English paid a morning visit. Betsy & myself rode to Mr. [James] Henderson. I fear that his second daughter cannot live long.

We are uneasy about Arthur. Poor fellow, he is occasionally much better, but his bowels have not been quite well for a long time.

November 4, 1824. Arthur* is very unwell. This is the anniversary of that horrible day [of Arthur] St. Clair's defeat.[100]

This day I send Gual a *proje[c]t* of a convention on the Slave trade[.]

November 5, 1824. I think Arthur is better but he is not permanently relieved. Little Nancy* is also unwell.

November 6, 1824. Arthur* is much better. A fine morning. We have been thinking a little of going down to Cartha-

---

100. In 1789-1790 Governor Arthur St. Clair was ordered by President Washington to lead an expedition to punish the Indians and bring peace to the settlements along the Ohio River. St. Clair, leading 2,000 men, began the expedition in October, 1791. After erecting Fort Hamilton, above Cincinnati, and Fort Jefferson, near Greenville, St. Clair moved to a point on the Wabash near the present Ohio-Indiana line. There, on November 4, 1791, his force was attacked by Indians in a daybreak raid. Almost 1,000 of St. Clair's troops were killed or wounded, and the rest straggled back to Cincinnati.

gena[101] this fall—on account of the children & Betsy & it will be on our way home—tho I shall have to return.

The 2 Santa Marias [*sic* for Santamarías] & R[ivero?] & [Christian] Manhardt took chocolate with us yesterday Eveng. Much rain & hail this evening[.]

November 7, 1824. We are anxiously expecting the Caracas mail now due two days. These are some of the vexations of a new Country where the mails are not yet regulated in a proper manner.

November 9, 1824. Betsy & Elizabeth took [walks] in town visiting different ladies[.] No mail from Caracas or Carthagena. Both due. Very vexatious.

November 10, 1824. This Evg. Betsy & myself set off to go to the Church at St. Guadaloupe—but we went only about ½ way. The evening was fine, but it was too steep to ride & she could not walk[.]

November 11, 1824. A fine morng. again. The mail came to day. Nothing from Kentucky[.]
November 12, 1824. Mr. [James] Hendersons* daughter died this day at 7 oClock[.]

November 13, 1824. A delightful morning. Arthur, thank God, is better. We still think of going towards Carthagena.

November 14, 1824. Sunday. Yesterday Eveng. [we] went to Suacha on our way to the famous Salto of Tequendama.[102] The company was composed of Mr. M[anuel] & R[aymundo] Santamaría, [Christian] Manhardt, Betsy, Elizabeth, Arthur, & myself, Spencer [Hite*][103] & another Servant. We carried a bed & some blankets, a Turkey, Chickens, some pork, rum & wine. We slept at Suacha, in the morning took some chocolate & went on to the falls, staid about 2

---

101. See Map 3, p. 133.
102. See Map 3, p. 133, for the route taken to the Salto. A painting of the falls may be seen in Duane, *op. cit.*, p. 490.
103. See above, June 22, 1823, n. 6.

hours & retd. to Suacha about 12 o/clock. Ate & set off home on our return at 2½ [*sic* for 2:30 pm.] & arrived all well but a little tired at Sunset. The weather was good. The fall has been often described accurately. The perpendicular fall is 600 ft—the body of water considerable. The rain bows appear in quick succession. The mist is sometimes like rain & fertilizes the Country around for miles. We had only a view from above & on the side. To see it from below would require you to go several miles around & then you wd. not come near unless with great difficulty. [Christian] Manhardt,* a preacher publickly sometimes & always privately, got pretty drunk out of *chicha*[104]—very much to the diversion of Santa Maria [*sic* for Santamaría]. Elizabeth rode alone on a mule—& Arthur occasionally before all the gentleman.

The appearance around Suacha is very poor. There is not a shrub for several miles until you reach the influence of the vapour of the fall. Then every thing denotes extraordinary fertility.

November 16, 1824. Yesterday a pleasant day[.] I went to the city & bought some trunks[.] To Santa Marias [*sic* for Santamaría's] & [Christian] Manhardt took coffee[.]

November 17, 1824. Dry weather yet[.] Arthur is better[.] Betsy, Elizabeth & myself went to see Mrs English & Elizabeth went to Mr. [Juan P.] Ayala's.*

November 19, 1824. Dry weather yet. It is said here to be very unusual to have ten days without rain at this season.

Gual* promises me to close the business of the claims in a few days.

Arthur* is much better. He and myself rode to town yesterday[.]

Yesterday & this day the mails from Caracas & Carthagena came in. Nothing from the US. Larz [Anderson]* is on the Magdalena[.]

---

104. A fermented beverage usually made from maize or pineapple.

November 21, 1824. Such has been the delay of Larz['] arrival & of course his return to Washington will be so much postponed that I fear I shall not receive letters in answer to mine of soliciting *leave* to go home, by the first of May, the day I desire to leave this place.

My inclination to go in the Spring & see the US. is great. But I have not yet determined that it is most proper to resign the Mission, and office wh. yields a sum of wh. you can save a part & where saving is necessary, should be abandoned with great caution. Still it is important that Elizabeth* shd. return for the purpose of going to school.

Waited on the V. President.

November 22, 1824. Fine rain again.

M[anuel] St. Maria [*sic* for Santamaría] took breakfast with us.

November 27, 1824. [Manuel] Santa Maria [*sic* for Santamaría] has been trimming trees all day. Doctor & Mrs. Gual came to see us this Evening. In a conversation with Gual he evinced very strong feelings of hatred towards the Spaniards. He wd. not admit that their emigration to this Country even in families should be admitted.

The Constitutionalists in Spain have done more to alienate the feelings of the people here than the Royalists. Their pertinacity in refusing to recognize the Separation & Independence of this Country while they had the ascendency made a very deep impression & is the cause of the present law excluding all Spaniards.[105]

November 29, 1824. This day we recd. letters from G[eorge] C. G[wathmey]* We rejoice to hear that our friends in K[entucky] are well up to the 12 Sept. The worst of the sea-

---

105. During the Napoleonic wars representatives from Cádiz and other commercial towns framed the liberal Constitution of 1812. Ferdinand VII, who resumed the throne of Spain in 1814, soon suspended the Constitution, but in 1820 the revolutionists or constitutionalists pressed him under threat of violence to reinstate the Constitution of 1812. In 1823, however, a French army crossed the Pyrenees and restored the authority of the King.

son has past. This letter also tells me that an Ex[ecution] has been levied on my property as Security for my father. This [is] vexatious & mortifying & may produce injury to me. No loss is sustained yet & I believe none will be eventually sustd. by me. But my conduct in [a] like case w[oul]d[,] & I rejoice to think it, be the same again, my father has been to me too affectionate, too indulgent, too devoted to all his children for me to hesitate to incur any responsibility wh[ich] w[oul]d not ruin my own family. This issue in this case is one to which I feared things were approaching.[106]

Gual to day gave me in return a translation of my pro-je[c]t of a Slave convention[.] He wants time on the *Claims.*

November 30, 1824. The intimation in the London Courrier [*sic* for *Courier*] that Colombia may not soon be recognized has given a good deal of disgust here. If it were not for the power of England her conduct wd. produce lasting dislike but she is here reg[arde]d so powerful & feared so much that she can do any thing & still be recd. with open arms.

December 1, 1824. This the 14th anniversary of my marriage. It produces emotions something like those which take place on the reoccurrence of a birth day. I have certainly had many happy days during that time, but I have had also much un-happiness; I have seen four children die. I have suffered uneasiness from debt, but it seems almost impious to con-sider *that* an unhappiness, when others so much greater strike a father's heart from the death of his children. My children are in Heaven, but, Oh, God, it is the most terrible [thing for a father] to see his children die—and I believe that the suffering of a mother is greater.

December 2, 1824. This morng. I had a conference with Gual*, urging him again to settle the claims.

---

106. Letters written by Colonel Anderson to his son-in-law, John Logan, and others, indicate in 1824-1825 that he was being pressed for money. See Anderson Papers, Filson Club, Louisville, Kentucky.

December 3, 1824. [León] Galindo* came to see me. [I] can get no money from [Ferdinand] Sirawkowski [Sirakowski].[107]
[I] recd. a letter from Gual desiring a conference on the subject of the Slave trade convention[.]

December 4, 1824. Last night & this day very unwell.

December 5, 1824. I am better. A fine Sunday[.] Doctor Gual & lady were with us last evening. He still wants delay on the claims—not for himself I believe as he is truly ashamed, as he says, of asking more delay, but the VP. [Santander]* is creating difficulties.[108]

Betsy & myself have been talking about ret[urnin]g to this Country even if we go home next year. This shows that peoples notions of what they are to do _next_ year are worth very little. I shall return with great reluctance. Nothing but the necessity of saving a little money could induce me.

December 6, 1824. A gloomy Monday Morng. [The] Congress of the US. [opens today.] The delay of Larz [Anderson]* in getting here begins to give me some uneasiness about his returning to Washington with the treaty. There has been seldom a more vexatious & expensive trip than he has had.

December 9, 1824. I have been all day busily engaged in writing the Slave trade Convention, which it was agreed last night should be signed tomorrow.

December 10, 1824. This is the anniversary of my arrival in Bogota. It is also the anniversary of Mr. Tho[mas] Bullitts* death.

This has been a year of not much enjoyment. I believe that all the [foreigners here] consider it something that [we have] to submit to. This indeed is the way we all regard our

---

107. See above, April 22, 1824, and June 22, 1824.
108. See above, March 8, 1824, for an indication of the length of these negotiations on the claims.

residence here. It may have the effect (it is by no means certain) of adding to my goal or political character.[109]

This Evening Gual* & myself have signed a Convention for the suppression of the African Slave trade. It is a copy of the Convention signed last year in London, with two exceptions which I consider unimportant.[110]

This day also I recd. many letters from our friends in K. Y. Thank God they are well—but the people of the State are running wild under the guidance of the Arch Demagogue [John] Rowan* & the subaltern demagogues who act their parts. I fear that R[owan]* has already recd. his reward in an election to the US. Senate which has been the object of all his schemes & apostacies.[111]

December 11, 1824. I have been all this day poring over the Newspapers from the UStates.

December 15, 1824. Such is the delay of Larz [Anderson]* that I fear I shall have to go to Honda to meet him.[112] It is very unpleasant to me & no doubt it will be to him to come so far to see us & turn back in 3 days from the time of his joining us[,] but every days delay involves a doubt whether he could get back in time with the treaty.

Arthur* is not well.

109. This reflected Anderson's hope to free himself from debt and either to return to a seat in Congress or to obtain a political appointment in Europe.

110. The British Convention referred to by Anderson was signed on March 13, 1824, and Secretary of State Adams expected no trouble in securing its approval in the Senate. He was too optimistic, for politicians who wished to eliminate Adams as a presidential candidate and those who feared that the suppression of the slave trade by the United States and Britain would "turn to a concert for the abolition of slavery" defeated the treaty by attaching so many qualifying amendments to it that Canning of Great Britain could not accept it. In this atmosphere Anderson's treaty did not have a chance. The rejection of these treaties, writes Samuel Flagg Bemis, *op. cit.,* p. 435, showed that the "slavery question had again entered American politics through the narrow treaty door of the Senate and was making rude headway. . . . Not until 1862 after the Southern States had seceded, could the United States make a treaty for the suppression of the Slave trade."

111. Anderson was correct; Rowan had been elected to the Senate.

112. This town on the Magdalena river is located on Map 3, p. 133.

December 18, 1824. Arthur has not been well for several days. Betsy is unwell and Elizabeth* has a sore throat.

For two or three days I have been copying the Slave trade convention & preparing letters to J[ohn] Q[uincy] A[dams] in anticipation of the arrival & departure of Larz [Anderson.]*

[Manuel?] St. Maria [*sic* for Santamaría]* & Son have not visited us for more than a Week[.]

On Sunday Elizabeth* & myself went to see Mr. [Johann B.] Elbers* & his bride & to see the procession pass his house. The [illegible] & the Saints were as usual dressed as fine as modern belles & beaux & [illegible].

The V. P. has put off the consideration of the claims till the meeting of Congress in spite of me.

I cannot avoid expecting Larz [Anderson]* this day or to-morrow.

December 23, 1824. This day about 4 oCl Larz came. Of course we had much talk about people & things in Jefferson [County, Kentucky].

December 24, 1824. Betsy was taken ill last night & has suffd. much with pain[.]

December 25, 1824. Betsy was very unwell.

Larz [Anderson]* & myself visited the V. Pres., [José María del] Castillo [y Rada]* & Mrs. English.*

December 29, 1824. This morng. Larz left us with the Conventions for the US.[,] his baggage having gone yesterday. His stay with us was short, rendered so by his great delay in reaching us.

On the day before yesterday he went to the Salto [of Tequendama].[113] I shall of course be uneasy until I hear of his safe arrival in the US. as the time is so short that with a little bad luck in getting a passage or bad management he might not reach Washington until Congress has re-cessed[.]

---

113. See above, November 14, 1824, for Anderson's description of a trip to the Falls.

I have written J. Q. Adams soliciting leave to visit the US. this Spring.[114]

Betsy is still very unwell. She has suffd. greatly with something like the dysentery.

On the 19 of this month I recd. the Secretarys (Adams) instructions about the late captures made on the principle that our flag does not protect Spanish property. I have been preparing a letter for some days. I am directd. to remonstrate ag[ains]t the commission & conduct of Capt. Chase an American citizen who made the captures.[115]

December 30, 1824. Betsy I think better, certainly in less pain[.]

By Larz [Anderson]* I have sent an a/c vs the US for $2000[,] the amt. of the Secretarys salary for one year—the services having been performed by me entirely. I am not assured in getting it—but I do know that cases involving the same principle have been paid.

December 31, 1824. At 3 oC. this morng. Betsy had a son. Only a few hours previously had we any intimation what would be the event. She is yet very sick. Except when I thought that some of my children were dying, it was one of the most unhappy nights I ever passed. The birth is premature by five weeks. She is in a critical state I fear. I thank God that she is so far living. No one was with her but Doctor [R. N.] Cheyne* & Mary.[116]

January 19, 1825. Since I made the last note, my sufferings have been great indeed. My Betsy, my beloved, my virtuous, my amiable wife left me for Heaven on the 9th of this month

---

114. In a letter to Secretary Adams on December 27, 1824, Anderson explained that "circumstances in relation to my domestic affairs . . . render a return to the United States for a short time, very important to me."

115. In late September, 1824, a Colombian privateer, *General Santander,* arrived in Norfolk with a crew of 250 men. The ship was formerly commanded by Captain Chase, who was then apparently still on board. The *Santander,* together with another Colombian privateer, then sailed to New York where the crews of the privateers captured, or at least prevented the departure of, a Spanish vessel then in the harbor.

116. Anderson's slave.

about 6 oc in the morning. Her sufferings had been beyond any thing I ever saw. Her God has received her. What was her offence I do not know. I have thought a thousand times, what offence can she have committed to deserve such punishment from her maker. But the ways of God [are] inscrutable. I can not search the motive or the cause. [I] do not arraign them—but the more I think the more I am lost. Never was there a more loving, kind, wife, mother & woman. Fourteen years & 40 days I lived with her. She has left me three children out of 8. The last infant was dead when I made the last note in this book on the 31 [December] but I did not then know it.

Oh God have mercy on me & my children. My Betsy does not require my prayers. May she look down on me, Guide me in my path & direct her children. Whatever may happen I can never forget her.

My present intention is to go in a few weeks with my children to the UStates—to leave them there & return for a short time to this Country.

My return is of course uncertain as I go without the leave [of] the Government. With my present feeling I cannot have much apprehension about the course the Government may take. Such have been and now the real afflictions of my heart, that I cannot much fear any political event or misfortune. They are too light to affect me much.[117]

January 21, 1825. An extraordinary season of dry weather. I do not recollect any rain for six weeks until the day before yesterday there was a slight shower[.]

Col: [Beaufort T.] Watts the Secty. of legation arrived on the 2d inst. He has been living with me since the 12, most of the time very sick & is now but a little better. His temper & spirit are destroyed, I know not whether by the present sickness or by the nature of his general constitution.

---

117. Anderson wrote to Adams on January 19, 1825, explaining his action in leaving without permission.

I have not been out of the house since the 30 of december. My children & my books engage as much of time & mind as I can divert from the most unhappy of all contemplations—the loss of my dear, virtuous & beloved wife[.]

The prospect of getting an eligible situation for my children is by no means satisfactory. They have many & affectionate relations, but not one I fear whose family affords in every way an eligible residence. I must do everything however that a father can do to secure the best. The situation of Elizabeth* presents the greatest difficulties. If her own feelings would permit it, I would at once place her at some good school without reference to a residence with her relations, but I fear such violence to her feelings as that would produce.

Arthur & Nancy are yet too small to regard my absence much & where there was kindness shown to them, they wd. require nothing else—but Elizabeth* requires more than kindness. She is at an age when she requires instruction, good example & judicious management.

January 23, 1825. This I believe is my fathers birth day. If living he is 74 or as the old Bible says 75. May God remember him in his old days. He has been and still is a most kind father to me.

It is Sunday. The children are at Doctor Guals. Colo: [Beaufort T.] Watts is getting better—but he has not the spirits of a man.

[Mr. Cade,] the Secretary of the British Commission broke his leg yesterday evening—driving a carriage with [James] Henderson* the consul[.]

Yesterday I heard of the death of W[illiam] D. Robinson,* he has done every thing for many years to invite [death] Eating, drinking & all kind of dissipation. He had nothing to war against death but good spirits—but all have at last sunk before that dread enemy.

January 27, 1825. Colo: [Beaufort T.] Watts is better. My children are tolerably well.

Yesterday Doctor [José Manuel] Restrepo, Colo: [John P.] Hamilton & Mr. [James] Henderson came [to] see me. Mr. R[estrepo] will send the manuscript of history to London in a few months & perhaps to the US. also.[118]

This morng. I rode out with Arthur. He is I think better.

I think I shall leave here about the 1st. March for the US. I have been yesterday & this day bundling my papers.

The Gazettes of the US state the probability that [Henry] Clay & not [William H.] Crawford will be ret[urne]d to the H[ouse of] R[epresentatives] with [John Quincy] Adams & [Andrew] Jackson. It does seem to me that J[ackson] will be elected. Until very recently I thought A[dams] wd. be elected certainly.

January 28, 1825. The intelligence of the surrender of the Viceroy of Peru [José de la Cerna] with his whole army to Genl. [Antonio José de] Sucre* commanding the combined forces of Colombia & Peru arrived to day.[119] This indeed is decisive; it must I think nearly terminate Spanish resistance in America. It is important not only here but important to the cause of free government throughout the world. Bolivar was in Lima, but with the world he will have the credit of the victory. If he now resigns his dictatorship in Peru—he will be one of the most distinguished living [men.]

January 29, 1825. This day recd. the Presidents Message. He mentions the Convention signed by me with this Country but in such a way that I can infer but little from it as to his approbation.

---

118. This was probably Restrepo's manuscript for his *Historia de la revolución de la república de Colombia* (10 vols.; Paris, 1827). Anderson often wrote of his intention to prepare a volume of "notes on Colombia" (April 22, 1824); on October 29, 1824, he wrote "a page or two" of a book; on February 11, 1826, he began the preparation of an "essay" for the *North American Review*, sent it to the editor on April 19, 1826; then he set about preparing a "digest of the commercial regulations of Colombia" for the Department of State; on May 27, 1826, he recorded that for some days he had again been preparing materials for his "half-contemplated essays on Colombia." No such work was ever completed and no portion of it preserved.

119. The Battle of Ayacucho, December 8, 1824; see June 20, 1824, n. 69.

Larz [Anderson]* has a prospect of reaching the US about this time with the original Conventions.

January 30, 1825. Another cold morning. Colo: [Beaufort T.] Watts is not so well as he was. He is the merest child I ever saw.

January 31, 1825. I walked to town this day for the first time since Christmas day. I believe that [Ferdinand] Sirawkowsky [Sirakowski]* means to pay me at last. He paid $400 to day.[120]

Eveng. 4 oC. on the Back porch Elizabeth [Anderson]* is darning her stockings. Arthur & Nancy are making book houses.

If I return to this Country, I have a great inclination to go as far South as Quito [Ecuador], to be by land & return by water or vice versa.

February 4, 1825. This day 14 years ago I well remember.[121]

My daughter Elizabeth is now darning stockings by me on the back porch at [Manuel?] Santa Maria's [*sic* for Santamaría's]*

Arthur had a high fever last night. He is very unwell.

February [nd], 1825. Arthur* is better but is not well. Colo: [Beaufort T.] Watts mends slowly.

Gual* was here yesterday Evening. He promises to do the [claims] business soon, for which I am only waiting.

Mr. [James] Henderson & all his family visited me yesterday Evening.

I have not made up definitely my mind as to the delay. [Illegible sentence.] Probably I shall finally leave it [Colombia] in October or November, 1826.

February 15, 1825. [I am awaiting the] completion of the

---

120. See above, April 22, 1824, June 22, 1824, and December 3, 1824.
121. The diary gives no clue to what Anderson remembered. Fourteen years does not go back to his marriage, although it does come close to the birth of his daughter, the first Elizabeth, in 1811.

business about the claims. I have nothing else to do before
I am ready to go.

I do not know what to do with my children when I
reach the US. I have thought of various places at wh[ich]
to send her [Elizabeth] to school. To a country school among
her friends, Lexington, Bardstown, Bethlehem, Philadelphia
—each has its advantages & disadvantages.[122] Arthur & Ann
must remain with their relations. I have thought of putting
Arthur* at his grand father's [R. C. Anderson, Sr. or Owen
Gwathmey] & Ann with her Aunt Bullitt. But all this is
subject to change.

February 16, 1825. This was the birth day of my dear [son]
Louis. I remember the day of his birth well. He & his dear
Mother are gone, forever gone. They are locked in heaven.[123]

I walked to town & [William] Bunch* & [Augustus]
Leland* returned [with] me[.]

I saw Gual* in his office and Mr [Pedro] Molina[,]* the
Minister from Guatemala—a plain old man.

The [navigation and commerce and slave trade] Treaties
are ratified by this Govt. I hope they may be by the US.
I have some apprehensions.

February 18, 1825. No rain. A warm day. This day last year
Ferdinand Bullitt* died.

Colo: W[atts]* is well. He is a more intelligent man
than I at first thought he was.

February 19, 1825. This day I recd. a letter from G[eorge]
C. G[wathmey.] All well in K. Y. up to 18 Nov. [1824]
[He] confirms the death of J[ohn] Gwathmey* in N. Orleans.
Poor man—he had an unhappy life. The last years were
most miserable—but this should not have been so, as he
preserved his honesty & character.

How different are the feelings with which I now open a

122. See below, August 4, 1825, for Anderson's decision.
123. See above, April 5, 1823, for an account of Louis' death.

letter from K[entucky] from those I had a few months ago. They then were pleasant. Now—

February 20, 1825. Sunday[.] Colo: [Watts] was sick. I am far from being well.

This Evening Gual* walked down to see me. He promises to hasten the [claims] business on wh[ich] my return to the US. depends, as much as possible.

Oh God, how different will be my return from what I expected two months ago.

February 21, 1825. My stomach is still [upset] & I feel badly[.]

I have lately seen the law giving [the Marquis de] Lafayette* $200[,ooo]—[124] [I know] that if I had been in Congress, I shd. not have had [the] firmness to vote against it, but I cannot approve it. When thousands who devoted themselves to their Country are now in straitened circumstances & many in want, I can not think it right to give one man such a sum.

February 23, 1825. Colo: [Beaufort T.] Watts* this day left us to live in the house of Doctor [Henry George] Mayne [*sic* for Maine].* He thinks probably that he will [be] better—as we live somewhat poor here[.]

February 24, 1825. Had a long conversation with Gual.* He mentioned to me a memo. of a Conference between [Manuel José] Hurtado* & Mr. [George] Canning* from which it is manifest that the British Govt. had no intention of recognizing his country soon.[125] Indeed Mr. C[anning] seemed to be anxious but on a single point [wished] to impress on the Minister of Colombia that it wd. be injudicious in this Country to make any attempt on Cuba.[126]

---

124. The sum of $200,000 was voted to Lafayette for his services during the war, and for the loss of income suffered by the Marquis during that service. Twenty-six representatives in the House voted against it, and, although the Marquis said that he might have been the twenty-seventh, he took the money.

125. Britain had actually decided to recognize the Republic on December 31, 1824. Canning was jubilant, saying that the United States would "lose most by our decision." See Parks, *op. cit.*, p. 105.

126. Canning preferred that Cuba remain in Spanish hands and there

Gual read to me his despatches to the various Colombia Mi[ssions]s ab[roa]d concerning the Congress at Panama.[127] Surely it is a design, most grand & important. He is very anxious to go himself as one of the Members or Ministers, but fears there is some difficulty in his appt.

It wd. suit me very [well] to go, if I cd. get an outfit, it wd. save me of many months of tedious delay here & show me a new Country. I shall ascertain when I return to the US. whether it be feasible.[128]

February 25, 1825. Colo: Watts came down & borrowed $500. [León] Galindo* & Leland the younger [Francis] came down to visit us.

February 27, 1825. Sunday. Last Evening we had a pleasant rain—but the earth soaked it up in a few minutes.

The children are tolerably well. Elizabeth is now looking over my shoulder wishing to know what I am writing. She is about reading this Morng.—the 9th ch[apter] of Matthew.

Elizabeth,* Arthur* & myself went to Dr [Henry George] M[aine']s* & staid an hour or two. I went for the purpose of going with & introducing Colo: Watts to the V. P. but W[atts] was sick. I went to the V. P.

March 1, 1825. Yesterday I sent to Niles Walsh of the Govt. Journal[129] a number of the Gaz[ette] of Col[ombia] con[tainin]g Gual's observations on the "American Confederacion"

---

is some evidence that he might have attacked the island had nations of the Americas gone to war against Spain. Britain's interest centered mainly on questions of commerce and investment. Britain, for example, hoped that a prosperous Cuba might supply revenues to Spain and help her pay off large loans from the British government.

127. See above, Introduction; August 12, 1824, and October 27, 1824.

128. The story of Anderson's appointment may be found in the Introduction.

129. Hezekiah Niles was editor of the *Niles Weekly Register* (Baltimore) and Robert Walsh was editor of the *National Register* (Philadelphia). The *National Government Journal and Register of Official Papers* (Peter Force, editor) was published in Washington. Since all of these papers regularly published Latin American news, it seems probable that Anderson sent materials to the three.

with [them] to draw some observations from these writers & to attract public attention to it.

I am told that the law has passed authorizing the Executive to settle the "claims." If so, I shall probably leave this [place] in ten or 15 days.

Arthur is, I fear, very unwell.

March 3, 1825. I dined with Mr. [James] Henderson's* family. Just after dinner came down galloping rapidly [Charles] Wilthew,* Ellingworth [*sic* for Illingworth],* Mrs. English &c. to tell the news that G. Britain had recognized the Independence of Colombia. I never saw the English *pride* of *Country* show itself more plainly. They seem to think that Colombia never was Independent before, but that now her prosperity & freedom were *sealed.* I came by the V. P. at [home and] saw the New[s]paper. I suppose the Intelligence is true but it is very far from the official form which these *English* gave it.

March 4, 1825. Yesterday was the last day of Mr. Monroe's* term—& this the first of some man who is entering at last on the theatre of his ambition & his long hopes. Which is the happiest man? Probably neither are very happy. I can well believe that while the liberation from cares & responsibility gives much pleasure to a man in Mr. Monroes* situation, that the consideration that *this is the last day* of his public life, that on this day he abandons a course which has been the employment of his life, gives serious & sad reflections. There is something solemn, almost awful to me & I believe to all, in the words "last time."

The children & myself are all unwell—Arthur* very much so.

March 5, 1825. This day four years ago I remember well. It was the 2d. inauguration of Mr. Monroe. It being Monday —the inauguration was postponed from the preceding day. My pecuniary fortunes were in a state most desperate.

[Beaufort T.] Watts & [Augustus] Leland* came down this Evg., Doctor Gual also. He says that he believes that [Joaquín] Mosquera* & himself will be apptd. plenipotentiaries to Panama.

March 6, 1825. Sunday. I went with Colo: Watts to introduce him to Doctor Gual. We saw Mrs. G[ual] & her Mother [Señora María Dominguez], then went to G's office who went with us to see the V. P. Thence we went to [José María del] Castillos.* He was sick.

[B.] Alcazar* & Doctor [R. N.] Chayne [*sic* for Cheyne]* came down in the evening. Elizabeth & Arthur were at Doctor G[ual]'s Mother in law's all day.

March 7, 1825. A cold disagreeable morning[.]

March 9, 1825. Yesterday & this day I walked into town. No news. No rain.

March 10, 1825. No mail yet.[130]

March 12, 1825. This day I went to Mrs. English.* She expects to marry Colo: [Patrick] Campbell* soon after his arrival.[131]

Last Evening Gual made an appt. with me to come this day & settle the claims[.]

March 12,[132] *1825.* Gual came last night. I believe we have adjusted nearly all [claims]—most of them *satisfactorily.*[133] I think I shall leave here about the 25th inst.

---

130. The mail came to Bogotá three times a month, leaving Cartagena on the 10th, 20th, and 30th of each month. The mail usually arrived in about nineteen or twenty days. It was taken from Cartagena to Barranca by mule; from Barranca to Honda in a canoe; and from Honda to Bogotá by mule.

131. Colonel Campbell, see above, July 6, 1824, had been in England.

132. Anderson may be in error here, but it is possible that his preceding entry should read March 11, 1825, and that this one is correct.

133. Two claims for damages resulting from the seizure of American ships by Colombian privateers before the recognition of the Republic were rejected by Gual and Anderson. Anderson wrote to John Quincy Adams on March 15, 1825, saying that "successful settlements" had been made on the cases of five ships. The largest claim was settled for $21,000. Various problems, among them the question of who was to receive payment for

This Eveng. Alcazar* came down to make an apology for Gual's not writing to me this day.

There is to be a great ball this Eveng. in commemoration of the recognition by Great Britain.

March 13, 1825. Sunday. Rode with Colo: Watts to visit the Guatimala [*sic* for Guatemalan] Minister, S[e]ñ[o]r [Pedro] Molina*—then to Mr. [José Felix] Restrepo's* & to Colo: Hamiltons.* Neither at home.

The children passed the day with Mrs. Gual. Passed the Evening at home alone.

March 15, 1825. This day ten years ago my daughter Elizabeth was born. Besides the happy & safe birth of my child, there were some other little circumstances that made it a happy day; I remember it well. She was born about 8 oClock P. M. in the west room upstairs at her Grandfather's [Owen Gwathmey]* on Harrods Creek.[134] On that day I attended a Jury trial in the Country. May God give her happiness through life, may he protect and guide her.

The children are gone to Mr. [James] Hendersons.* I shall go down at dinner time. I am now alone at 1 oC. Genl. [Baron Friedrick von] Eben* & Doctor [Henry George] Mayne [*sic* for Maine]* have just visited me.

We dined at Mr. Hendersons;* where there was no conversation or any thing else that could give interest to any one.

March 16, 1825. Mrs. English having sent me word that she meant to dine with me, this day, came. [Charles] Wilthew* came with her & [Beaufort T.] Watts & [Christian] Manhardt* having *fallen* in were desired to stay to dinner. Oh God, what were my feelings when sitting at [the] table, to think that my Betsy was gone—to see her seat occupied by a gentleman—to think that never more was I to see her where she had so long sat.

---

some of the oldest claims, helped to prolong final disposition of the cases until long after Anderson's death in 1826.

134. John Clark's home may be located on Map 1, p. 5

March 19, 1825. Part of yesterday & to day I have been writing to J[ohn] Q[uincy] A[dams.] I suppose [it is] my last letter (at least for the present) to him.

Yesterday I recd. the bills of Exchange for the amount of the claims.[135]

This day [Beaufort T.] Watts & myself went to Gual's. I went for the purpose of getting him to deliver a letter to [José María del] Castillo [y Rada].*

March 20, 1825. Sunday. The children have walked out and I am alone.

March 21, 1825. Dined with [Doctor Henry George] Mayne [*sic* for Maine]*—dined at 7 o. & did not get away before ten.

March 22, 1825. The news came that Colo:s [John P.] Hamilton* & [Patrick] Campbell* are app[ointe]d to negotiate a treaty between G. Britain & Colombia—& that C[ampbell] is to remain as Charge d'affaires.[136]

March 23, 1825. Gual was here early—not satisfied with the proceedings of England, says that the Colombian Minister [José Rafael Revenga]* is not rec[ognize]d in England, but that the British Ministry wish to recognize only by making a treaty, which is equivalent to saying, "make this treaty with us & you are recognized, *otherwise* not.

Colo: Watts was here today. I see that he is bent on being Chargé in my absence & no doubt in receiving the salary of one. I believe indeed he is already preparing *to draw* on the faith of it.

Saw [Henry George] Mayne [*sic* for Maine]* at his home. Rode to see [Ferdinand] Sirakowsky.*

March 24, 1825. Engaged in packing & other preparations.

---

135. See above, March 12, 1825. This was done because the Colombian government did not know exactly who was to receive the money. Anderson delivered the bills of exchange to the United States government, which could then make payment to the proper persons when they were found.

136. An account of Campbell's activities as chargé in Colombia may be traced in Rippy, *op. cit.*, pp. 178-187.

March 25, 1825. Engaged in preparing [for the trip.] My God, what terrible feelings it produces.

Introduced [Beaufort T.] Watts as Chargé des affaires. Recd. from Gual one of the most encomiastic of letters by orders of the V. Presdt.[137]

This has made me know how much less I value earthly favours than I did three months ago. Once it wd. have given me great pleasure. Now it does not [please] me.

I have taken leave of [James] Henderson & family, [John P.] Hamilton, Mrs. English, [Félix de] Restrepo, [José María del] Castillo [y Rada].

March 26, 1825. Saturday. 8 oClock—in the Morng.

I expect in a short time to leave Bogota with the children. All are now engaged in fixing the baggage.

My God, is it possible that my Betsy does not go with me.

March 27, 1825. Facatativa. We left Bogota about ten oClock & arrd. here last night.[138] Doctor Gual, [Christian] Manhardt, [Beaufort T.] Watts, [James] Henderson, [Doctor R. N.] Cheyne accompany [us] a short distance. At this village we staid at Donna [*sic* for Doña] Catalinas, where we found Colo: Esmenard [d'Esmenard].* The road [was] over a perfect plain, about 7 leagues.[139]

March 28, 1825. Villete. We came to this Village last night. It is a miserable one in a handsome valley. The first league from Facativa was in the plain, the rest a terrible road over the mountains.

March 29, 1825. Guaduas. Arrived last [night]—in this hand-

---

137. The letter, which can be found in the Colombian Despatches, National Archives, was written by Gual on May 25, 1825. Gual also sent a letter of introduction with Anderson requesting that the Intendant of Magdalena give the United States Minister whatever help he might need. This letter is in the Gual Collection, Library of Congress, and was given to the Library by Mrs. Edward L. Hicks, Jr.

138. The Colombian portion of Anderson's trip back to the United States in 1825 may be traced on Map 4, p. 195. It follows much the same route described by Duane, *op. cit.*, chap. xxxvii.

139. The league here equals about three miles.

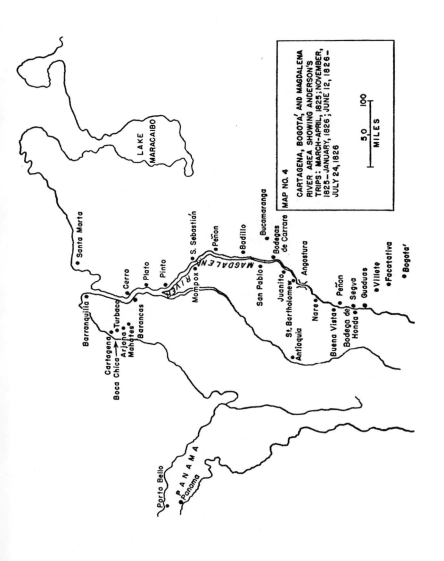

LAKE
MARACAIBO

Santa Marta

Barranquilla
Cartagena
Boca Chica → Turbaco
Arjona
Mahates
Barancas

Cerro
Plato
Pinto

Mompox
S. Sebastián
Peñon
Badillo
Bucamaranga

San Pablo
Juanito
St. Bartholomew
Antioquia

Bodegas
de Carrare

Angostura

Nare
Buena Vista
Bodega de
Honda

Peñon
Segva
Guaduas
Villete

Facatativa
Bogotá

MAGDALENA RIVER

Porto Bello
Panama
PANAMA

MAP NO. 4

CARTAGENA, BOGOTÁ, AND MAGDALENA
RIVER AREA SHOWING ANDERSON'S
TRIPS: MARCH-APRIL, 1825; NOVEMBER,
1825—JANUARY, 1826; JUNE 12, 1826—
JULY 24, 1826

50   100
MILES

some valley. The Mountains we have passed have a greater appearance of fertility than the plains.

Recd. very kindly by Colo. Acosta.* Expect to leave here the day after tomorrow. This seems to [be] a fine little valley. This place [is] 17 leagues from Bogota according to the pillars placed by the Spaniards indicating the distance.

I now wish that no one had written for me from Bogota, as from the information the Governor of Honda gives me I shall be imposed on by Mr. Aguelo—who will probably not be ready with the Boat.

March 30, 1825. Well-treated by Colo: Acosta. This day about 4 oC arrived Colo. [Patrick] Campbell, the British Com[missioner] & Charge des Affaires. It makes him almost as much of a conceited [man as William P.] Duval*[140] was when he was made Governor of Florida. Soon after him, arr [ive]d [José Rafael] Ravenga [sic]* who had been Colombian Minister in England. He is said to be man of talents, but he seems to me to be a babbler.

Honda, the port of debarkation for the Magdalena.

March 31, 1825. This day at 10 c[clock] We left Guaduas & after a terrible road of 5 leagues reached this terribly hot place at dark. Are well received by the assessor.[141]

Nothing very unpleasant has yet occurred. Indeed we have been some what fortunate so far. The assessor & the Juez politico[142] says the boat & the [boga-men][143] shall be

---

140. Duval, the Governor of Florida Territory in 1825, was not a popular executive primarily because of his opposition to state-chartered banks, his many vetoes of legislative acts, and his insistence on executive prerogative.

141. The assessor was an appointive position. In 1825 he was a law officer with mixed functions and was also deputy to the Intendant in the area.

142. Colombian provinces were divided into cantons and the political judge was an officer of this unit of government. No salary went with the job but he was occasionally given money by municipal or even national bodies.

143. The crew that poled the champans, the flat-bottomed boats used as the river became more shallow. Feats of great strength by these men were recorded. Some of them claimed to have propelled boats for seventeen hours against the tide without rest.

ready tomorrow. Whatever be the change in some respects in the political & civil freedom of this Country, the situation of the bogas is but little altered. I was told by the Alcalde[144] that the Boat wd. certainly be ready for me, as the Bogas* had been put in jail last night to have them ready. I know that this practice is common whenever the officers of Govt. travel. This place is very subject to Earthquakes & many of the inhabitants are in the habit of going every night to small cabins covered with straw. It has a ruined appearance.

We are preparing provisions for the voyage.

April 1, 1825. We staid this day in Honda. Very hot. Well entertained by the Assessor.

April 2, 1825. This day about 9oC. we left Honda & embarked at the Bodegas 1½ below, for Barancas in a long boat called a *Champan* covered with leaves very effectively to keep off the sun or rain.[145] The boat was furnished by a Mr. Andelo at a price 3 times as great as I was told was the common price. Surely there never was a place better calculated than Honda to ensure an imposition on a Stranger— for no man wd. hesitate to give to the utmost of his means to get away from this hottest of furnaces. The Boat is large & we have it all & there is a fine breeze.

April 3, 1825. Stop[p]ed last night on a handsome beach. All bathed. Every thing rather pleasant. No flies or musquetoes. No suffering from heat.

April 4, 1825. Yesterday Elizabeth was a good deal indisposed—& today she is worse with a dysentary. Last night again on the beach[*sic*] No suffering yet from the heat or otherwise.

144. Presided over municipalities, usually the lesser ones. They seldom received a salary but their reputation for corrupt practices was great. The alcalde might also be a justice of the peace with some legislative and executive functions.

145. A flat-bottomed boat, the champan might be sixty feet long, seven feet wide, and be poled by twenty boga-men. The word derived from a large tree called the *champacoda.*

April 5, 1825. The river has become gentler in its current. Near Honda there were many riffles & some snags.

I am really uneasy about Elizabeth. She suffers much. The heat is becoming greater, as we had no breeze yesterday.

This day two years [ago] we left Louisville. These anniversaries or events that produce deep recollections or make much impression, are no longer agreeable. The occurrences of the intervening time become every year more distressing. *It is to the young only that birth days & other anniversaries produce pleasure.* You will know it, my son, if you live to be old or even arrive at the middle age.

April 6, 1825. We suffer from heat. I am uneasy about Elizabeth.

The Bogas stop frequently to buy plantains,[146] which boiled with dried beef or fish is almost their only diet. We have suffered no unnecessary delay. We float day and night. Indeed there is rowing nearly half the time. We see many Caymans or alligators. They show no fierceness. I have seen two in the act of swallowing large Catfish. I do not think there is a great variety of fish in the river. I have seen only Catfish & a fish some thing like the *Buffalo* of the Ohio.[147] There are many species of parrots; and a great many water fowl of the crane kind about the river & shores. I do not think that there is a great variety of other birds. I have seen a beautiful crane of a reddish colour.

April 8, 1825. The last nights have been excessively hot. I think Elizabeth* is better. The Bogas say we shall be in Mompox early on Saturday (tomorrow). I fear they will wish to stay there to have a frolic.

But for the sickness of Elizabeth the voyage so far would not have been so unpleasant as I expected.

At 9 oC. A. M. on the Magdalena[.]

---

146. A type of banana, larger and more starchy than the ordinary variety.
147. Any of several large fish of the sucker family usually found in the Mississippi Valley area.

April 9, 1825. Elizabeth is much better for which I thank God. Last night was more pleasant than the two preceding.

The current is becoming more sluggish. It seems to be a river well calculated for Steam boat navigation up to *Nairi* [*sic* for Nare] & although there are riffles above I see nothing to prevent the navigation much higher.

For a day or two below Honda the River was bound on both sides with a range of mountains, [but] since there seems to be a perfect flat on both sides.

There are at intervals many villages on the river, but there are no settlements or plantations as on the rivers in the US. until you approach Mompox. I have seen no geese or duck like those in N. A[merica].

Arrived at Mompox at 1 oC. I am now waiting for the return of the Bogas, who say that they have gone to town for provisions.

Denis [Hite] & Arthur have gone into town. Elizabeth, Nancy, Mary the Nurse & myself are in the boat. 4 oC. A Mr. Harley & four or five young men came down to the boat; they are Cabinet Makers from New York sent for by Mr. [Manuel Antonio] Arrublas* at Bogota. Mr. Harley presented us with a few bottles of port[,] wine & porter.

Mompox is from the river the best looking town I have seen in Colombia—& there is a greater appearance of thriftiness & labour than I have seen any where else. It is a large town. The sweetest oranges I ever ate, we bought here. We left Mompox at 5 oC. & passed a rainy and thundering night.

April 10, 1825. Sunday. Stopped about day break. The Bogas are gone to a village about a mile off. They have been back with a part of the villagers, trading & drinking.

I walked on the Bank and saw wild cotton growing.

Mary[148] is sick.

12 oC. There is yet no appearance of getting off. 4 oC.

---

148. One of Anderson's three Negro slaves.

The Bogas have not yet returned, & I fear will not, this evening.

Arthur & Nancy are stripped quite naked & Elizabeth* is amusing herself with them by throwing water on, & washing them. Mary is sick or asleep. I am making these notes with a sad heart.

April 11, 1825. We waited yesterday in vain for the return of the Bogas. They did not come until this morng. Whereby we have lost one clear day.

I wished to arrive at Barancas on this night, for the purpose of writing by the mail to Bogota, which I should meet at Bara[nca]s. But now it is uncertain whether I shall arrive in one, two or three days.

This river makes me think of *not returning,* even if I make no arrangement for other employment. But when I *cool* again & feel well & a little forget what now perplexes me, it is probable that my courage will again return. This is according to my nature, & I well know, to human nature. About 12 oC. passed the mouth of the Cauca. It has there the appearance of being much the largest river, having recd. a considerable part of the Magdalena, through an outlet which takes off above Mompox, making the Country back of that town an Island. Very few habitations. This day I counted forty Caymans lying on one sand bar.

April 12, 1825. A clear hot morng. It has rained almost every night. No rain in the day.

There is not so much maize used in Colombia as I expected. The plantain & yuca[149] supply its place generally. I have seen nothing like our corn bread. The Maize is never ground in a Mill. It is beaten or bruised on a stone.

The Bogas promise me to arrive at Barancas this night.

April 13, 1825. Owing to the freshness of the breeze we did not proceed last night and arrived here at Barancas this day

---

149. A plant grown in the tropics for the edible roots which yield a nutritious starch.

at 1 oC. It is a poor place. [We were] Well treated by the Alcaldes, the one white, the other black.

April 14, 1825. Passed on to Mahates, a miserable village. 11 leagues.

April 15, 1825. Came on to Turbaco. Nothing in the aspect of the place to justify its character for agreeableness or coolness. No doubt those who have spoken of it only spoke in contrast to Carthagena. It is poor in appearance. The water we drank is brought a league from a pond. We went to the house of Genl. [Mariano] Montilla,* then vacant. We had, for going there[,] two valid reasons, 1st. the Servant said that orders had been sent to receive us & 2d. there was no other house we could get in. Of course, there was nothing to offer us but the four walls of the home. We brought our meat, eggs, chocolate, &c & paid for the bringing of the water.

April 16, 1825. Sunday. Agreed with Capt. [William] Nicholas for a passage in the Schooner Wm. Bayard for N. York.

Here I hear of the Election of J[ohn] Q[uincy] A[dams] which suprizes me & what more suprizes me is the appt. of Clay as his Secretary. I see their enemies are handling them severely. It is a strange thing. They dislike each other, I know. But it is certain that Clay's influence elected Adams. *I do suspect corruption in them,* not an express bargain, *but moral corruption.*

I hear too of the rejection of the Slave trade convention signed by me with Colombia, by the US. Senate.[150] If as I have a right to believe, the objection is to the principle, I care nothing. I can see no account of the Com[mercial] Convention. I am of course very anxious to hear the determination of the Senate on that. If it shd. also be rejected I am unfortunate indeed but I think it cannot be.

Capt. Clirtly* of the Colo[mbian] Navy & Capt. Fowler

150. See above, December 10, 1824, footnote, for a discussion of the rejection of the Slave Trade convention.

of the Brit: Navy, Mr. [Charles] Watts* the B[ritish] Consul & some other gentlemen waited on me.

April 18, 1825. Agreed with Capt. [William] Nicholas to go tomorrow at 3 oC. P.M.

Waited on Genl. [Mariano] Montilla* the Intendant & saw [Carlos] Soublette* there. Waited on Mr. Watts.

On returning this moment I find Arthur* with a fever. I pray to God it may be nothing serious.

April 20, 1825. This day we went on board the "Wm. Bayard" & went down to Boca Chica. This port & place has been well described frequently. But the poem of [James] Thompson [*sic* for Thomson]* & the Rod:[erick] Random of [Tobias] Smollett have given it a reputation for sickliness which it certainly has not merited for many years.[151]

During our stay in Carthagena we have been most hospitably received & treated by Mr. [Charles] McNeal,* his wife & daughter. He is poor & purely hospitable—an intelligent man, of easy manners, with, I apprehend, but little common sense, and he is the first native of the UStates, I ever saw, he [*sic* for who] was British in his feelings.

At his house I saw Mr. Dallas a native of Jamaica & nephew of A[lexander] J. Dallas* late of the US. & a Mr. [William] Berrien.*

I met Mr. [William] Bunch* here—and a Mr. Brush & Kinsella.[152]

The day before yesterday I waited on Gen. [Mariano] Montilla* the Intendant—a man of fine intelligent face & elegant manners.

Genl. [Carlos] Soublette* came to see me. Elizabeth

---

151. Anderson is referring to two men and two works. The first is James Thomson (1700-1748), an Englishman whose poem "Summer" discussed the South American milieu. The second reference is to Tobias Smollet (1721-1771), *The Adventures of Roderick Random* (1748). This was the first English novel to describe life on a British warship in much detail. The main character, Random, saw action in Jamaica and Cartagena.

152. All members of Bunch, Brush and Company of Bogotá, who were representatives of some of the claimants referred to earlier in the diary, see above, March 8, 1824.

[Anderson] went home with him—on the next day. Yesterday, recd. a visit from Montilla,* [José] Padilla* & others. Went to visit Mrs. Soublett & family—& Mr. [Charles] Watts, British consul.

On the 19 a Ball was given by the Carraquenians [*sic* for people of Cartagena] in honour of the declaration of Independence 19 Apl. 1810. in Venezuela.[153] Mr. [Charles] McN[eal]* & his family went.

April 21, 1825. Denis [Hite]* having not gotten on board last evening, we are obliged to call by the gate of St. Francisco [Church] & take him in. Our accomodations are unpleasant, but not more so than they are necessarily in a vessel of the size of this. There is one passenger beside my family, a Mr. Charteris[,] a Scotchman. Arthur has been sick since the day after our arrival in Carthagena[.] His fever has intervals, but he complains much of his head.

May 7, 1825. In the Atlantic ocean about 600 miles of N. York.

We shall probably have a long passage. It has been disagreeable, not from bad weather, but from sickness. Beside the sea sickness, Elizabeth & Arthur have had the ague & fever. Arthur* has had fourteen agues in as many days. At this time 10½ oC. I have hope that he will miss his ague for the first time.

May 11, 1825. Off the coast [of] N. Carolina latitude 36 in a calm. We have had disagreeable weather lately. Arthur has missed his agues for a few days.

I can yet determine nothing as to [my] return to Colombia. Indeed I cannot determine [that] until the people at Washington [do]. My own wish is made up well enough. I will not return unless prudence shall direct it.

How different are my feelings on approaching the shore

---

153. The Caracas *cabildo* forced the resignation of the Spanish captain general and assumed control, but declared its loyalty to the Spanish monarch. Actual declaration of independence did not come until July 5, 1811.

of my Country from those I once expected to feel on reaching it.

May 29, 1825. Georgetown.[154] [Visited] Genl. [Thomas S.] Jessups [*sic* for Jesup's].* On the 16—I landed at New York. I remained there nearly a week. Stayed at McIntyres, Washington Hall.

There is a wonderful improvement going on in the town. The commerce of the City is becoming very great.

It is the place for borrowing or lending. It is said that Virginia planters are going on there to borrow money on their Estates. I predict that N. Yorkers will own them all. A planter who makes only 2 pr cent cannot pay 7 for money.

I dined with a Lawyer Wyman & [Theodorus] Van Wyck* another; friends of [De Witt] Clinton.* They still think of Clintons* elevation to the presidency. I saw in N. Y. also [Lieutenant] J[ames] Monroe nephew of Presd. M. & a Major Tho[mas Lee] Smith,* Calhounites. They [Wyman and Van Wyck] are highly inflamed against the President [Adams] & prepared, as they say, to agree that Jackson shall be Presd. [phrase illegible] This is their method of avoiding Collision between Jackson and Clinton.

Came on to Ph[iladelphi]a. Remained only half a day. Saw some of the owners for the claims lately allowed by the Colombian Government.[155]

Came to Baltimore [and] remained one day. Saw Genl. [Samuel] Smith,* took tea at Mr. [John] Gills. I think Genl. Smith [is] prepared to be an admin[istration] man. Came on to Geo[rge]town. Invited & go to Genl. [Thomas S.] Jessups.* [*sic* for Jesup's] Find him approving [Henry] Clay's course & [is a] supporter of [the] admin[istration].[156] [Jesup] Suggested what I never thought of before, that Clay

---

154. Anderson came up the Potomac River to Georgetown, see Map 2, p. 67.
155. See above, March 12, 1825. These people were connected in some way with the original owners of the schooners *Liberty, Tiger, Brig America,* or *Josephine,* whose cargoes were seized by Colombian privateers before 1819.
156. Clay's "course" was to throw his influence to Adams rather than to his western rival, Andrew Jackson.

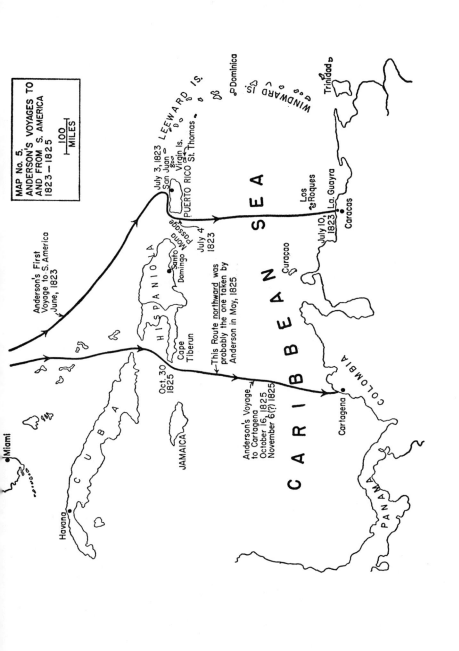

MAP No. 5,
ANDERSON'S VOYAGES TO
AND FROM S. AMERICA
1823—1825

100
MILES

Miami

Havana

CUBA

JAMAICA

HISPANIOLA

Cape
Tiberun

Santo
Domingo

Mona
Passage

Anderson's First
Voyage to S. America
June, 1823

July 4
1823

July 3, 1823   LEEWARD IS.
San Juan
Virgin Is.
PUERTO RICO   St. Thomas

WINDWARD IS.

Dominica

Trinidad

Oct. 30
1825

This Route northward was
probably the one taken by
Anderson in May, 1825

Anderson's Voyage
to Cartagena
October 16, 1825
November 6(?) 1825

CARIBBEAN   SEA

Curaçao

Los
Roques
La. Guayra
July 10,
1823
Caracas

Cartagena

COLOMBIA

PANAMA

should run as Vice P. with Adams at the next election. I do consider it a most happy notion. I believe it the only way of getting some of the Western States for Adams. I call it happy in relation to Clay. I do not & believe I cannot care much. It is most likely I should have voted for Jackson agt. Adams.

So far everything connected with my accounts are arranged to my entire satisfaction. I receive $3000 for performing duties of Secy., receive my salary during my absence from Bogota, deducting [sum illegible] for Secy [of legation Beaufort T. Watts*] as Chargé.

Friday the Presd. informed me that he had det[ermine]d to send a rep: to the Congress at Panama & invited me to take the Mission.[157] He also exp[resse]d his opinion of the importance of the Mission to Colombia at this time & of the necessity of my not being long absent. However, he did not desire that I shd. be in Colombia before October.

He also stated that Mr. Clay was inclined to have a second Com[missione]r & to appt. Mr. [Albert] Gallatin.* The Prest. himself did not seem inclined.[158] Yesterday I dined with the Presd. in family.

June 3, 1825. I have been detained here much longer than I expected. Nothing material has occurred during this week. On Monday I drank tea at Mr. [James] Barbours,* Secy. of War. On Wednesday the Secy. of Navy [Samuel Southard*] & Attorney General [William Wirt*] waited on me.

Tomorrow I set out with the children for Wheeling on our way to Kentucky.

I have sent $3650 to J[ohn] Gill to purchase USBank stock. Thank God I am out of debt. If my fathers debts are put on me it would be bad indeed, but I think it impossible that they can be imposed in a way that will hurt me.

---

157. The meeting is described by Adams in his *Memoirs*, VII, 15 ff.
158. Anderson, wrote Adams in his diary, *ibid.*, asked if "I had thought of giving him a colleague for the Congress. I said my own inclination was to have but one Minister there, the object of the meeting being to consult, deliberate, and report, rather than to contract any positive agreements."

July 1, 1825. At my fathers.

On the 4th of June I left Geo[rge]town on my way to Kentucky with my children. We passed the Cumberland road and arrived at Symmes [boarding house in] Wheeling on the 11th.[159] Three Steam boats having left there a short time before our arrival, we were detained until the 17th when we descended [the Ohio River] in the "Ohio" and arrived in Louisville on Tuesday the 21st [June]. We were met by Mrs. [Thomas] Bullitt,[160] [Lucy] Priest,* [Frances] Jones,* & [Catherine] Woolfolk,* George [Gwathmey]* & Temple G[wathmey]* & their families.[161] What I suffered I cannot tell. I met too *Mrs.* [Owen] Gwathmey.* Such a meeting can never happen to me again. That is impossible. It was the day to which I had once most fondly looked—but it was a day of wretchedness. God so ordained it, & I try to submit. The name of my Betsy has never been mentioned by one of the family.

On the next day [June 22] I came up with Mr. [Owen] Gwathmey* to see my father. He was well. My children were sick on my arrival. I returned to Louisville & remained with Mrs. [Thomas] Bullitt until the 28th when I came here [to Soldiers' Retreat]. I do not yet know what to do with the children. Elizabeth will go to school, but where I know not. I find nothing done in my fathers business. My responsibilities still continue for him—& I see no way of clearing myself soon.[162]

My friends generally are but little relieved from their pecuniary difficulties[.]

---

159. The Cumberland or National Road had been open from Cumberland to Wheeling for seven years when Anderson made the trip in 1825.

160. There are other possibilities, but Mrs. Thomas Bullitt was the sister of the late Mrs. Anderson and would likely be at the dock to meet Mr. Anderson. She also came alone, her husband having recently died. It was her son, Ferdinand, who died in Colombia and this might be still another reason for her presence.

161. Also see above, Introduction, for the Gwathmey family genealogy.

162. See above, November 29, 1824, for Anderson's earlier apprehensions regarding his father's financial status.

I intend going to Shelby[ville, Kentucky] next with the children.

I shall probably leave Kentucky in Aug[us]t for S. America & leave the US in October.

August 4, 1825. At my fathers.

This again my birthday. This day has long ceased to excite the emotions it once did.

In July I went with the children; Mrs. O[wen] Gwathmey & Mary A. Bullitt* to Shelbyville. We arrived on the day on which a public dinner was given to Mr. Clay. With him & several other gentlemen I spent the evening at Mr. [George] Woolfolks. I saw there Colo: [Charles S.] Todd.* He has settled as a farmer in Lexington. I know him too well to believe that he can be a contented one. I found my relations well except my sister Nancy. She has a strange rising in the throat. I see but little difference in the situation of my friends. They are struggling (I think) under less grievous circumstances that I left them—but not one is relieved. [John] Logan* looks badly. I fear he has suffered much unhappiness.

I went to see Mrs. Wm. Logan* & her family. Isaac [Gwathmey?] came up to see me from Oldham.[163]

While in Shelby, I suffered much from the headache for two days. I was relieved by bleeding & a dose of rhubarb & magnesia.

After remaining ten days we came down. Since that I have been alternately at Mrs. [Thomas] Bullitts & this place [Soldiers' Retreat]. One day I dined with Mr. [Henry* or Nathaniel*] Massie. O how did I think of the conversations I have had about that place.

I have determined to send Elizabeth to the Catholic school near Bardstown.[164] I hope that Eloise Bullitt* will go with her. How dreadful is the idea of leaving my mother-

---

163. See Map 2, p. 67, for location of Oldham County, northeast of Louisville.

164. See Map 2, p. 67, for location of Bardstown.

less children, far from their father. I know enough of this world to know that the care of the nearest relations does not approach the care of parents. Oh God protect my children.

My father has determined to go with me to Virginia to see his relations.[165] Mr. [Owen] Gwathmey says he will also go. How awful must by my father's feelings at seeing once more the land of his birth at the age of seventy five.

This day I came up from Louisville. An election has just terminated between the two parties called the Old & New Court.[163] From the intelligence received the old Court seems to have prevailed. If so—it will go far in redeeming the character of the State, which is low indeed among her sister states.

August 5, 1825. This day J[ohn] Logan* & his family came down from Shelby. [Allen] Latham* & Maria [Anderson] Latham* are now here. There now being present my fathers eleven children.[167]

August 21, 1825. My fathers.

Last week I went up to Nazareth near Bardstown & took Elizabeth* & Eloise Bullitt* to school. I am not satisfied with

---

165. Brothers and cousins, mostly in Albemarle and King William counties.

166. For background of this situation, see above, June 30, 1822, and March 21, 1824, footnotes. In December, 1824, the Kentucky legislature, the majority of whose members favored the laws giving relief to debtors, voted to reorganize the Kentucky Court of Appeals. A New Court, this one with four rather than three members, was established. A tug of war then ensued between the New and the Old Court, with the latter refusing to give up the papers and documents necessary for the New Court to function. The records were actually taken by force from the clerk of the Old Court in December, 1825. The problem had already been an issue in the governor's race in 1824, won by a New Court man, Joseph Desha, and from 1824-1826 the legislative contests were fought mainly between adherents of the two courts. In August, 1826, after Anderson's death, the Old Court and the Anti-Relief party elected a majority to the Kentucky Senate and House, but Governor Desha made a last attempt to uphold the New Court by declaring that fines would be levied against any Old Court members who attempted to carry on the business of the court. Guns were assigned to guard the records taken forcibly two years earlier by the New Court. The Old Court was, however, officially reinstated on January 1, 1827.

167. Richard Clough, Jr., Elizabeth Anderson Gwathmey, Maria Latham, Ann Anderson Logan, Mary Louisa Anderson, Sarah Anderson, Larz, Robert, William Marshall, Charles, and John Roy Anderson; Cecelia; deceased: Frances, Hugh Roy, Lucretia, and Matthew—16.

the appearance of the school. I shall never forget the distress of my dear child at being left—far from her father. May God bless & protect her.

Mr. O[wen] Gwathmey & Mary A. Bullitt went up with me also in company, Majors Smith & [John] Fowle[r]* of the army.

On the day before yesterday I came from Louisville. Mrs. F. Jones[168] & M[ary] A. B[ullitt] came also. Yesterday Mr. [Owen] G[wathmey] & Mrs. [Thomas] Bullitt came up. And this day my father, Mr. O[wen] Gwathmey & myself will set out—they for Virginia & I with them on my way to Colombia. What strange & awful sensations such an undertaking must give my father. I leave my children. God knows that I cannot help it.[169]

August 27, 1825. Mouth of Big Sandy [River].[170]

Arrived here this day at 2 oC. Our company consists of my father, Mr. O. G[wathmey],* Robt. A[nderson],* & myself. This day a Doctor Ayres joined us at Hoods [boarding house], Little Sandy.

We are all well. Last Saturday we left my fathers; dining at Russels, came to John Logans [in Shelbyville.] Next day, dining at [James] Hunters[,]* came to Frankfort. Next day breakfasting at Francisco's, 12 ms. Came through Lexington to Colby H. Taylor's. Next day breakfasting at Edmondson's [and] came to Mudlick. Next day breakfasting at McIntyres & dining at Power's, came to Wigglesworths, a miserable place. Next day breakfasting at Chenowiths (an old acquaintance)[171] came to Hoods. This day, a very hot one came here 22 ms. to breakfast. [John] Catlett* whom I knew in the legislature lives here.

Our trip has been pleasant enough. The weather until two days [ago] was pleasant. While riding in the carriage

---

168. Probably Frances Gwathmey Jones. See Appendix, List of Names.
169. This was the last time that Anderson saw his children.
170. Anderson's journey may be traced on Map 2, facing p. 000.
171. A relative of Mrs. James Chenowith (or Chenoweth), who lived with the Andersons at Soldiers' Retreat when Richard Clough was a boy.

with my father, I have observed a decay in his memory &
judgement beyond what I before knew or supposed.

September 4, 1825. At Lances [boarding house] 25 ms. west
of Staunton [Virginia]. We arrived here this morning. Now
waiting for breakfast. All well so far. From Catlett (as above)
we came to Brown's on the bank of the Ohio. A good house.
Next morning[,] crossing at the mouth of [the] Guyandot
[River] came to Maupin's[,] a very good house in Fays
valley—thence to Miller's[,] a very good house. Here met
young Johnson,[172] who told us of the sentence of Commodore
[David] Porter* condem[n]ing him to a suspension of six
months.[173] Next day came by the mouth of [the] Cole [*sic*
for Coal River] to Swindlers[.] There we met Colo. P.
Rootes Thompson. Came to John Andersons[,]* a relation
& Salt Maker. Salt he says could not be sold for 15 cents a
bushel—ruining the Salt Makers. The genl. price in the
Western Country is 30 cents. I recollect when the current
price was $3 to 3.50. Came next day to [blank] where he
[we] partook of a Water Melon weighing 16. [to] 26 [pounds]
—& heard of many others of upwards of 40 pds. Crossing the
Kenaoka [*sic* for Kanawha] river went to Morris at the
[Kanawha] falls. Next morning visited the falls.

October 9, 1825. New York.
    I will now put down my movements since the 4th of
Sept—the date of the last note.
    On the same day 4th we came within 8 miles of Staunton
—5th came, passing Staunton & Rock fish Gap to Yancey's

---

172. The son of Richard Mentor Johnson, see Appendix, List of Names.
173. John Quincy Adams in his *Memoirs*, VII, 17-19, reveals that Anderson "came very warm" on hearing about the Porter case and attempted
to intervene on his behalf to obtain a lighter sentence. Porter, known for
his hotheaded personality, had been in command of the West Indies'
Squadron engaged in suppressing piracy. One of Porter's Officers landed
in Fajardo, Puerto Rico, and was allegedly mistreated by the local officials.
Porter, in retaliation for the action, seized a port on the Puerto Rican
coast and obtained an apology for the act. He was, however, ordered to
the United States where he was court-martialed for acts hostile to a friendly
power. Porter resigned from the Navy in 1826 and later went to Mexico
where he commanded the Mexican navy.

[*sic* for Yancey Mills] old place. Here I had once staid with my *Betsy,* my Elizabeth,* & my *lost Louis.**

Next day [the] 6 [September]—while breakfasting at Gooch's, Mr. Croghan* came up going to Mr. Hancocks for his sister [Mrs. Thomas] Jessup.* We went on to Colo: [Charles] Divers an old friend of my fathers whom he had not seen for more than forty years. I left the Company there and went on to Charlottesville to dinner where I took the Stage—& next day the 7 [September]—got to the Steamboat near Fredericksb[ur]g [Virginia] about 9 oClock. As we in the Steamboat ascended the Potomac, Lafayette* in another passed down on his way to the Brandywine[, the] Frigate in which he is to sail to France so that I have not & shall not see him. 8th [September] arrived in Washington. There I saw at Genl. Jessup's* Aunt [Lucy Clark] Croghan* & Charles C[roghan].* To see that old women in Washington declared the changes & reverses which take place in this world. [The] 8th. 9th. 10th. [September] I passed in Washington—settling my accounts and having necessary conversations with the President [Adams] & Secretary [Clay]. [On the] 11th I took the Stage & went to Baltimore—12[.] Saw & dined with Mr. [John] Gill. Wrote to George C[roghan] & Mrs. [Thomas] Bullitt & sent my certificates of bank stock[174] to George C[roghan].* In the evening in the Steam Boat came towards Philadelphia. Arrived at 12 oC. Saw Ed[ward] Coles* Governor of Illinois.

I understood since that Mr. Hugh Nelson[,]* Minister to Spain[,] was also in the City that night; just arrived & on his way home. September 13, 1825. Came to N. York. Staid all night at the City Hotel, but being able to get only one third of a room in the third story I next day 14th went to the Washington Hall—a very indifferent house. Here I staid until the 20th.

Saw Wm. H. Neilson of Louisville & dined with him at the house of his brother. There being no vessel in which I

---

174. Purchased through Mr. John Gill, see above, June 3, 1825.

could get a passage for Carthagena, on the 20th [September]
I went to Albany with the design of going a little into the
Interior & probably of going to Boston by land. However,
when I arrived at Albany I was a little unwell. The day was
cold, cloudy & damp & I determined to come back. This
I did & arrived at New York [September] 22 at day light.
Feeling better, on that evening I took the boat for Providence. Arrived there at dark on the 23d [September] & next
day went in the Stage to Boston for dinner. Here I remained
until Saturday the first of October.

The weather while there was generally unpleasant. Dined
with Mr. [Daniel] Webster* on the last of Sept.; was at
the house of Mr. [George] Ticknor.* Saw [Josiah] Quincy,*
[Harrison Gray] Otis,* [Israel] Thorndike,* [Eli W.] Blake.*
On the 30 with Mr. [William] Bunch* whom I knew in S.
America, I went to Quincy to visit the Presidents, Father
& Son [John Adams* and John Quincy Adams*]. The day
was delightful & the ride fine. The old man [John Adams]
will be 90 years of age the 30 of this month. His face looks
full & his intellect strong—but his eyes, legs & hands have
failed him.

On 1st October [a] fine day I went to Salem & according
to the invitation of Mr. [Nathaniel] Sillsbee* went to his
home & staid until Monday 3d [October]. By him & his
family I was treated with every kindness. I saw at his house
Mr. [Joseph] Peabody (for whom I had recovered about
$45,000 from the Colombian Government),[175] Mr. [William]
Pickman,* [John Seeley] Stone* & some others.

On Sunday 2d [October] went to meeting with Mr.
S[ilsbee]'s* family. This is the first sermon I have heard
delivered since May 1823 at Baltimore.

Saw Judge [Joseph] Story.* [October] 3d—Waited on
Timothy Pickering.* He is 80 years of age & perfectly
healthy. I do not doubt from what I have seen & heard

---

175. For settlement of the claims' cases, see above, March 12, 1825.

that there are many more cases of longevity in the New England States than in the Southern or South Western [states].

October 3, 1825. Returned to Boston. Found an invitation from Mrs. [James] Lloyd*—& drank tea with her—a kind of levee I suppose. [On the] 4th was invited to dine with the Manufacturing Society of Waltham. It rained all day & I could not go. The President [J. Q. Adams] took lodging at the Exchange Coffee House—[176] Where I waited on him.

[October] 5th Left Boston in the Stage & came to Ashford in Connecticut. [On the] 6th Came to New Haven, passing Hartford & Middletown. Saw a part of the best cultivated district in the US. New Haven is a pretty town. There is not much evidence of Commerce but the neatness of the white mansions is very very pretty.

[October] 7th Came in the S[team] Boat to N. Y. [On October] 8 upon enquiry expect to sail this week.

Called on Mrs. [William] Bunch* whom I saw with her husband in Boston & [on] Mrs. Brooke Gwathmey[.]*

[October] 9th Wrote to George C[roghan]* & Elizabeth [Anderson].* The indisposition of Elizabeth distresses me. Oh God spare & protect her.

About 4 oClock in the evening of the 9th October 1825 at the Washington Hall in New York I write this. Robert Anderson* who has come on from Virginia to go with me to Colombia is now setting [*sic*] by, writing I believe to his Sister [Maria Anderson] Latham.*

In my feelings, in my enjoyment of things around me[,] I can mark a difference; I have not enjoyed my late visit. I see nothing with any emotion, I have lost much of my curiosity. I have nothing in prospect that interests me.

R. C. Anderson, jr.

October 12, 1825. New York.

I have been getting ready since my arrival to sail for Colombia. I shall probably go in the Wm. Bayard. The

---

176. A seven-story building when it was finished in 1808, the Exchange Coffee House burned in 1818 and was rebuilt.

Bunker Hill will sail tomorrow for Carthagena—but I cannot get ready for her. I have seen here Brooke Gwathmey (son of Temple)* & his wife—daughter of Lewis[177] late of Kenawha[sic]. They are very genteel and respectable people. He has established himself here as a Merchant.

Yesterday I dined with old Mr. [Samuel] Bayard,* in company with a Sir Michael Cromer or Clere & his lady of Jamaica. He seems to me not to have much sense.

October 14, 1825. Yesterday I dined with Mr. B[rooke] Gwathmey* at Mrs. Southout's boarding house. Mr. and Mrs. [William] Bunch* board there—and also a Mr. Morton of Bourdeaux—a sensible, talkative Virginia[n] who has lived in France some twenty years. Still busily engaged in getting ready.

I understand from [José María] Salazar* the Colombian Minister that he has recd. authority to give to our Govt. a formal invitation to send Commissioners to the Congress at Panamá. I do not by any means feel assured that the Senate wd. concur with the Presdt. if he makes a nomination to them.[178]

I have recd. a commission to sign a treaty with Colombia placing the tonnage duties &c. in the ports of each nation on the footing of the native.[179]

October 15, 1825. This day I procured a small slab of Italian Marble & gave directions for this Inscription

> "In Memory
> "of Elizabeth Clark
> "wife of Richard C. Anderson.

---

177. Andrew Lewis, 1720-1781, of Kanawha, was the hero of the Battle of Point Pleasant (confluence of the Kanawha and Ohio rivers) in October, 1774. He was commissioned brigadier general, 1776; resigned from the Continental Army, 1777; and died, 1781. Brooke Gwathmey was in his early twenties. Any daughter of Andrew Lewis of Kanawha would have been at least 43 to 45 years old. Could Mrs. Gwathmey have been the grand-daughter? Inserted above "daughter" in the diary is a word that could be read "grand."

178. The debates in the Senate are described in the Introduction.

179. This was to place the United States on an equal footing with Great Britain following an Anglo-Colombian agreement in April, 1825.

"As a daughter, as a wife,
"as a mother and as a Christian,
"she was everything, which her
"parents, her husband, her children
"and her friends could wish:
"In this world she was their
"joy and solace; in Heaven their
"guardian-angel—
"She died at Bogotá on Sunday
"the ninth of January
"1825

My God, how little, little did I think on this day last year,
what would be the employment of this hour.

October 16, 1825. Sunday. This day we sailed in the Wm.
Bayard. Capt. Betts—Robt. [Anderson]* my brother and
Denis [Hite]* are with me[.]

October 28, 1825. We have had a quick but blustering passage so far. We have indeed come in a gale of wind. Robt.
& Denis have been quite sick—and I have been more so
than usual.

October 30, 1825. For the last three days we have had a
perfect calm near Tiberoon [*sic* for Tiberun] [at the] West
end of St. Domingo [*sic* for Santo Domingo].[180] It is worse
than a heavy gale. We have caught a few fish[.] It is now
Sunday the 30 of October 12 oC. clear & no wind. Cape
Tiberoon [*sic* for Tiberun] in sight[.] I fear that I discover
my health is getting worse. My bowels certainly seem to
have lost within two or three months much of their power.
Indeed there is something alarming in their sluggishness.
To fits of contrariness I have been long accustomed, but to
nothing like that which I have lately had.

October 31, 1825. Still a dead calm.

This day I had an opportunity of seeing the beauty of

---

180. See above, Map 5, p. 205, for Santo Domingo and Cape Tiberun.

the dolphin displayed in a remarkable manner. I had seen many [a note in another hand states "page missing. till 6 of Nov."]

November 6, 1825.[181]

If I am to go to Panamá I wished I had my authority here, it would save me a most troublesome & terrible journey to Bogota.[182]

I have a prospect of getting a passage in the Steam Boat in two or three weeks. Martines, the Steam Boat agent, whom I saw today says that the Boat will go from Barancas on the 25 at farthest [*sic* for latest]. I know too much of these people to believe him.

[José María del?] Real the Intendant waited on me. Robert [Anderson] & myself are to dine with him on Wednesday. Genls. [Mariano] Montilla* & [Lino de] Clemente* came to see me. They are fine looking men. Clemente a very honourable gentleman (I knew him in Caracas) has but little sense or energy I think. He is to command the naval expedition which this Government is about fitting out, against Cuba or Porto Rico I suppose.[183] It is probable that any officer may do against the Spaniards, but against an enemy of enterprize & quickness of movement there could scarcely be a worse selection of a commander than Clemente.

On this day last year [November 14, 1824] I visited the falls of Tequendama. This, like thousands of other incidents will never pass from memory. Of those who were with me, one is gone; where we all must go.

---

181. Congress—the final word of a sentence—and another complete sentence reading "It pleased me much to meet him whom I regard as an honorable, pleasant, and most sensible gentleman," have been omitted from the text by the editors because they have no meaning without the words from the missing page.

182. Anderson was in Cartagena on November 6, 1825.

183. Bolívar apparently favored action to free Cuba from Spain, and in May, 1825, he instructed Peru's representatives to the Panama Congress to work on this matter if the question arose at Panama. When Anderson was in Cartagena at the end of 1825, an expedition to Cuba and Puerto Rico was reportedly being readied at the port. Anderson wrote to Clay from Bogotá in February, 1826, saying that the Colombians disavowed any attempt to annex the islands.

November 8, 1825. I saw today Colo: [George] Woodbine,* who rendered himself quite famous about the year 1816 in Florida. He was represented as a British Agent, & instigator of the Indians to murder and plunder. There is no doubt that if Genl. Jackson had caught him that he would have been hanged as certainly as Ambrister & Arbuthnot were.

November 9, 1825. [Charles] McNeil [*sic* for McNeal]* showed me a most curious letter this day from [Harris] Fudger* the Consul at St. Martha—stating that he intended to make charges ag[ains]t Colo: [Beaufort T.] Watts[,]* chargé at Bogotá, for neglecting his business—[and] Desiring the Consul here to inform him whether he can confirm the charges in relation to this office. Speaks very frankly & disrespectfully of Watts.*

Dined this day with the Intendant [Real] and a large party. Made a Speech in answer to a toast. &&&.

November 10, 1825. An excessively hot morng.

This is the birthday of my little Annita. Oh my God protect my little children—my Elizabeth, My Arthur, my Ann.

The British Consul [Watts] called on me to introduce a Mr. Milne—who comes out here from England & is going to Bogota as a kind of Philosopher, Chemist, Astronomer &&. I understand that he thinks he has discovered the process of making Platina[184] easily malleable—& wishes to make some proposition to this Govt. on the subject.

November 11, 1825. Excessively hot.

I saw Colo: [George] Woodbine* again, who seems to be well acquainted with the Atrato [River].[185] He represents it as a fine river for navigation, more than 300 miles. Says that the road from one [of] its branches to Tupica on the Pacific is only 15 miles—with a gentle acclivity & descent.

184. Crude native platinum.
185. See above, Map 3, p. 133, for the Atrato River.

November 12, 1825. Excessively hot.

November 13, 1825. Sunday. More breeze than we have had. An English Surgeon and a German jew, I believe have joined our mess—from England—fresh.

This evening I walked around the North or sea side of the city [Cartagena]. The fortifications seem very strong. They give another proof of the millions expended by Spain to protect this country from Foreign enemies. Nothing was done to protect their dominion against the enemy from within; the enemy to [of] misrule & oppression—An enemy which here has [destroyed] her power.

I hear every day of mismanagement among the subordinate civil officers in this Country—frequently of great ignorance & more frequently of their corruption. In the sea ports and particularly among the custom house officers, I fear there is yet no morality. It would be a regeneration (which requires) more than one *generation* can make to suppose custom house immoralities & bribery could have ceased here. It is believed that there is no Spanish port in wh[ich] smuggling is not carried on with the knowledge of some of the officers—and it is feared that in many cases, where something like a judicial decision is to be given, direct bribery is indulged in.

November 14, 1825. Again very hot and without a breeze[.]

November 19, 1825. It has not been so distressingly hot for a few days past as before. A Mr. D'Epough[?] has joined our mess late from England. He is I believe a Swiss. Seems to be a sensible, free man. Also a Mr. Friend, English. He has just retd. from Bogota; where he has been an agent for an English Speculating Company. This country is filled with such Agents.

He has made a proposal for fishing, of sifting in the sands, mud or water of the Atrato [River] for gold—& the remuneration he proposed to the Government is, the making of a road "fit for Commerce" from the valley of Cauca to Buena Ventura on the Pacific.[186]

I understand that a Steam Boat is now coming out from England prepared for the business of raising the mud & sands of the Atrato & washing or sifting for the Gold. I hope to be off for Bogota on Monday[.]

The British goods daily pouring into this country are great.[187]

November 19, 1825. This night I went to a party on board the Cores given by Genl. [Lino de] Clemente,* commander of the squadron on this station. There were men & women in abundance. A fine Supper & every thing to make a Native glad—who seems to require nothing more than enough to eat & a Waltz.

November 20, 1825. I saw the Intendant [Real]—& the British Consul [Charles Watts] & family.

Genl. [Pedro] Brizeño [*sic* for Briceño] Méndez* arrived this day on his way to Panamá.[188]

November 21, 1825. Commodore [John] Daniels* who has just come from Porto Cabello[189] waited on me this morng. He is loquacious & vulgar. I expect to get off tomorrow.

The [ship] Trinimer[?] & Mr. [William] Bunch* arrived yesterday from N. York. They bring me no instructions about Panamá.

I tell you again my son never to get your friends to do what can be done by yourself. But why can I expect you, my son to follow advice which your father gives, but has not pursued himself?? It is still valuable to give it; it will I hope have some effect, if not a complete one. But this rule has been

186. See Map 3, p. 133.

187. A general statement of this rivalry between England and the United States is found in Parks, *op. cit.*, pp. 112-115.

188. Briceño Méndez was one of the Colombian representatives to the Panama Congress. Preliminary meetings between representatives of Colombia and Peru were scheduled for December, 1825.

189. See Map 3, p. 133.

very valuable to me; although (as in a late case) I have not
followed it universally, still I derive a great deal of exactness
with which my business has been done thro. life, to that rule.

November 22, 1825. Tuesday. This day we are preparing
and expect to go to Turbaco this evening.[190]

November 23, 1825. Turbaco. We came here to the house
of Doña Juana. A decent house for this Country—that is,
it is a neat clean looking negro hut, with three rooms. The
baggage on account of the bad roads, did not arrive until
11 oC. 4 leagues from Carthagena[.]

November 24, 1825. Aljons [*sic* for Arjona]. We came to
this place, only three leagues—this day through the rain &
infamous roads. This morning at Turbaco while waiting for
the mules to be brought up, the arriero, (mule driver)
came to inform us that the mules had been all embargoed for
Genl. [José] Padilla,* who had arrived last night on his
way to Bogotá. Having looked up the Intendants letter which
announced my character & reqd. all officers to render me aid,
I was compelled to go myself to the Alcalde where I found
fortunately an officer who knew me, & the mules were released. This incident gives evidence of the state of liberty
here. A private man's horses would have been impressed
for any high officer. We are here in a miserable hovel[.]

November 25, 1825. Mahates. This day—6 leagues.[191] We are
now in another hovel & Genl. [José] Padilla & Suite in a
worse [one]. There is much sickness all through this Country, the land is low, flat & now covered with water.

November 26, 1825. We arrived here [at] Barancas 11 leagues
at Sunset. The road since we left Arroyo hondo—is better
[but] all preceding, from Carthagena is infamous. The
baggage mules fell frequently & the trunks were covered
with mud.

190. A village near Cartagena, see Map 4, p. 195.
191. His trip to Bogotá may be traced on Map 4, p. 195.

Robert [Anderson] has been shooting on the way. We have seen several beautiful birds. The country generally is rich—& with clearing & tillage would produce most bountifully.

Here we have a room in the house of a Mulatto woman— that is of a free lady of Colombia but unfortunately our room is free to all the negroes in the village. We eat at quite a decent house. We are here waiting for the coming of the Steam Boat from Barranquilla & then we must wait I know not how long for its departure.

The houses here are filled with English & others going to Bogota. Mr. Senator, Genl., Commodore [José] Padilla*192 goes this morning in a champan with Commodore [John Daniel] Daniels* and others.

November 27, 1825. A Mr. Ferguson an Englishman is now sitting, no, lying on my hammock conversing with Robert [Anderson].* 11 oClock[.]

November 30, 1825. No boat has arrived yet. We wait, unfortunately without much patience.

Mr. [William] Bunch* has arrived & comes up frequently. He is full of great speculations. He is anxious to take up the loan which this Govt. is making.193 He is anxious also to supercede [Johann] Elbers* in the steam boat privilege of the Magdalena. He has purchased a large quantity of Govt. paper at a large discount. I have had some notion of dipping a little in this. It is selling for 30 cts. on the dollar. If it is funded or pd at par the speculation will be great. The same thing happened exactly in the US. but as there is some doubt and I am not in a situation to risk—I shall certainly ponder well & perhaps decline it. A great deal of money

192. Anderson's attempt at humor, referring to Padilla's various positions and activities.

193. Colombia's finances were, for a number of reasons, in a state of disorder in 1824. In that year a favorable loan was negotiated in London by the Colombian government. But in 1825 the loss of two million pesos in a London bank failure further depleted the already fast-diminishing funds in the Colombian national treasury.

has within the last two or three years been made here with very little, & sometimes with, no trouble. It would be quite convenient to me to make ten or 20,000 dols. by a turn over. It wd. give certainly what I require, some employment to a mind that requires it. There certainly never was a time in my life when I felt so little anxiety about making money.

At our eating house we have a Mr. Brizeño of Caracas & a Mr. Montoya of Carthagena.

I saw this morning a beef killed on the ground, just before the Alcalde's door. There were nine dogs & 36 buzzards around the butcher, who began to cut off & sell the pieces before he had taken the guts from the animal. This is done to prevent the bystanders, men, dogs & buzzards, from stealing the meat, which they would do, if it were cut off. This is the common mode of butchering.

Yesterday morng. while standing in our breakfast room the host & usual procession passed at the distance of 20 yards. The Curate cried out to us to kneel & then sent a soldier (such as is always in attendance) to give or enforce his order. Montoya bid the soldier to tell the padre that he commanded in the Church but not there.

This order on the part of the priest shows the exciting state of things; but the answer shows that which is approaching. It is probably the the first time that any one in this Village had been known to refuse to kneel when in sight of the host.[194]

This day twenty five years ago—I remember well. I set off to Virginia for the purpose of going to school. But tomorrow is the return of a day which can never be forgotten nor can ever be remembered now without unhappiness. I once

---

194. The Anderson brothers reacted in similar fashion to the Church in Colombia. In a letter to his sister in November, 1825, Robert Anderson wrote: "Everything in the church induced me to believe that the Roman Catholic Religion is daily becoming weaker in this country. It will give way to more simple modes of worship." Robert Anderson Papers, Library of Congress.

thought it the anniversary of joy—as it was the anniversary of that day which formed the tenderest, the dearest of connexions.

December 4, 1825. Sunday. The boat has not yet arrived[.]

Yesterday the Cabinet Maker [Mr. Harley] whom I met in April at Mompox[195] came here on his way to N. York. He has made money at Bogota.

Robt. [Anderson]* has found in his trunk the Comegin[?], a most destructive ant. It is common in all the hot lands of this Country—& will in a single night destroy a bale of goods. Mr. Montoya tells me that in Antioquia[196] when they have gotten full possession of a house, it is common to burn it, as the only mode of getting rid of them. They destroy all the wood of the house[.]

This evening some of the English have introduced races of Jack asses & also foot races. It is difficult to make the natives comprehend that the winner would receive any thing. They could not comprehend why any one should pay them for running. A purse of $10 was made up, & each successive winner recd. a dollar until it was expended. There was one race, in which Jack asses & four footmen started, one of the footmen won the money.

I have been very unwell for two or three days[.]

We sometimes amuse ourselves shooting—but it is too hot except early in the morning. We read a little; & play a little at draughts.[197]

A child died in the house this day. I could see no evidence of sorrow or mourning—even in the mother. I am at a loss to satisfactorily account for this. That the mother can quite stifle her feelings I hold to be impossible. Does her religion bid her to rejoice that the child is transfer[r]ed to Heaven? What is the cause of her apparent gaity?

---

195. See above, April 9, 1825.
196. Western part of Colombia, see Map 3, p. 133.
197. Checkers.

Brizeno is an intelligent well educated man. I have seen no one here who has so much literary accomplishment.

There are many sick in this place [Barancas]—& certainly there is every thing here to make one fear that he may be sick.

December 5, 1825. A hot morning. This day the Congress of the US. meets. They will no doubt find subjects to keep them together until May—altho I know none likely to produce much heat, except the contest with Georgia about the Creek lands & Creek Indians.[198]

December 13, 1825. We are now at St. Sebastians 2 leagues above Mompox, tak[in]g in wood.

The Steam boat arrived at Barancas on the 6. We left it on the 8th came to Plato—next day to Pinto—Next day 10th to Mompox—where we remained 11 & 12th. Mompox is one of the neatest, cleanest looking towns in Colombia—population said to be 12,000. I saw the College, a fine building built by an individual. The College owns the house, but little more.[199]

At Mompox there is one N. American with whom I dined, [R. K.] Travis [*sic* for Travers] of Baltimore. He seems to be a good natured active man but of no education. I breakfasted with [John] Lynch* an Englishman who has become naturalized.

This seems to be a noble river. I think it has much more water than the Mississippi. The water is in fine order—but is falling—and from the infamous management & delays we may well fear that the water will run away before we get up [to Peñon.]

---

198. During the 1820's the federal government decided that the Indians in Georgia and elsewhere in the south and southwest had to be moved to the west. The move was accomplished, but not without the use of force.

199. Members of religious organizations founded most of the schools that existed in Colombia during the colonial period. The College at Mompox, actually a seminary where grammar, theology, and the arts were taught to novices, was founded by the Society of Jesus sometime after 1653. Colleges were also founded at Honda, Cartagena, and Antioquía, to mention only three.

We have about thirty passengers besides servants—three ladies. The ladies occupy the Cabin. The Gent: sleep in hammocks or cots on the deck. It is very hot. The musquitoes [are] intolerably bad[.]

There is more appearance of agriculture near Mompox (above & below) on the river, than we have seen lower down.

Among the passengers are Señor Taliaferro Senator from Panamá [and] Señores Martines & Pardo members of Congress from Carthagena.

Brizeño of Caracas

Montoya merchant Carthagena

Señora Martines

Cayetano—Colombian

A Merchant of S[an]t[a] Martha[,] a creole & two ladies[,] his wife & her sister.

Colo: [George] Woodbine*—of Florida memory[;] Colo: Hamilton[,] Irishman & Colombian Consul at Baltimore[;] Doctor Mills—an English physician, chymist &c. who is going to Bogota to make some propositions to the Govt. relating to working & coining P[l]atina. He says that he has discovered the method of doing it. Hitherto [this has been] considered a desideratum in Science. [There are also] Messrs Ferguson, Tenant & Wills—three young Englishmen going to Bogota—to be book-keepers I believe.

Senor [Lazaro de] Herrara [*sic* for Herrera] of Carthagena[.]

Mr. Meade Secy to Doctor Mills.

Mr. [William] Bunch.*

Mr. Grice an English Merchant[.]

December 16, 1825. This is the anniversary of the presentation of my credentials in Bogota[.]

We have gone on badly, principally for the want of wood. The weather is very hot & the musquetoes are more numerous than below.

Yesterday I had a conversation with [George] Woodbine*

concerning the Musquetoe [*sic* for Mosquito] Shore.[200] He seems to think the grant from the Musquetoe [*sic* for Mosquito] king to [Sir Gregor] Macgregor,* good.

Woodbine* lives in St. Andres—a small Island 12 miles long on the Musquetoe [*sic* for Mosquito] shore, belonging to Colombia. There are about 900 inhabitants who speak English & are governed by English laws & customs. They are the descendants, (mixed with the aborigines) of the Buc-[c]aneers, who settled there. The other island is Providence—fine land & fine harbours—20 leagues from the Coast.

During the day we talk, play back gammon, shoot without killing, eat & drink bad water & worse wine. In the Evening [we] have had music & musquetoes.

December 24, 1825. We are going on somewhat better for the two or three last days. The day before yesterday we were at St. [*sic* for San] Pablo. I walked with the gun into the woods. Saw very large trees, rich vegetation, beautiful birds and many monkies.

A Mr. Meade a passenger yesterday took my likeness with a pencil. He has a pretty talent in that way & has taken very accurate likenesses of several of the passengers. Mine is said to be very good & I intend to send it to Elizabeth [Anderson] if I have an opportunity.

Several of the passengers & hands are sick—none dangerously so I believe. We are getting out of the regions of musquetoes. I have this morning had an opportunity of seeing in the Spanish American character, that which I had frequently observed before in them & I think in the French —most violent quarelling attended with vehement gesticulation, & verbal insults, but with no intention of striking. It seems to me that fistfighting is exhibited almost exclusively

200. The Mosquito Kingdom was on the east coast of Nicaragua and until 1892 it had a rather independent existence under British protection. It was a "state" of half-breeds, Indians, and Negroes who from the colonial era had commercial relations with nearby English pirates and woodcutters and, through them, the Governor of Jamaica. Arguments over the right of control of the area went on long after Anderson's death.

by the English & their descendants. This quarrel too, among Members of Congress & other gentlemen arose out of a quarrel between two of their servants—and each discussed the merits of the original quarrel.[201]

December 26, 1825. This day at 1 oC. Colonel Hamilton* died. He was buried a few hours afterwards on a sand bank, on the left side of the river. His attack was most violent— whether typhus or yellow fever I know not. Colo: Woodbine is better.

December 27, 1825. We are anchored in the middle of the river 6 leagues below St. Bartholomew without wood. The hands are sent ashore to cut wood & are getting some miserable rotten stuff. Our utmost hopes are to reach St. B[artholomew] tomorrow. Mr. Martines & family have left us today— also Bunch* & Montoya. They despair of getting on in the S. Boat. I think it possible that they will again join us tomorrow or the next day.

The fatal death yesterday & two or three sick cases on board has produced much alarm—particularly among the natives; even the cups and saucers used for Colo: H[amilton]* were thrown overboard.

This day is excessively hot. I do not feel quite so well as I did a few days ago.

December 28, 1825. 12 oC. at a place called St. Juanito—a house uninhabited. We have come only a league today. [We] are again getting word from the sand banks—which when gotten does not carry us, as long as we were getting it. The day is very hot. Thank God I feel very well[.]

The Captain Batis is a good natured, smart active industrious fun-loving, ugly fellow—but has no capacity for command [and] no one respects or obeys him.

The passengers have been grumbling all the way—& this

---

201. At this point a page of the diary is missing. The end of the final entry which began on the missing page reads "necessary privation. I submit to it as such. I desire it to end as such."

morning they are more clamorous than ever. An old fellow[,] Mr. Pardo[,] a Member of Congress who has been silent & chewing his cud the whole way, has now broke out vociferously. [Johann] Elbers* is to be deprived of his privilege of navigating the river &.&.&c.

Bunch & Montoya who went ahead yesterday have sent down some chickens & eggs to the sick on board—& the Agent of the boat has sent a little wood which however is not enough to carry us to St. Bartholomew.

A champan[202] which set off from St. [*sic* for San] Pablo with us is now passing us. This gives the natives a poor opinion of *Steam*—& we all have a poor opinion of the way in which steam is managed on the Magdalena.

Robert [Anderson]* still has the head ache almost every day. It is a pain in the back part of his head. [George] Woodbine, I think, is getting well fast. Our little doctor Mills who was wondrously frightened yesterday, is well today[.]

December 29, 1825. A few miles below St. Bart's stopping again for wood. Very hot. A canoe filled with wood upset with three men in it this morng. One caught hold of the wheel. One held to the canoe. The other swam until he was taken up by the long boat—nearly exhausted.

December 30, 1825. At St. Bartholomew—where we are likely to be 2 or 3 days. Bunch & Montoya have joined us again. They say there is nothing here—neither fowls, fish, eggs, or fruit—nothing but one *bull*. To all this, I would have but little objection if there was *wood*. Woodbine is nearly well.

These Villages are settled by Indians [and] sometimes a few mixed negroes. Rarely a white man is among them[.]

The Country on the river still very rich; a little more rolling than lower down.

---

202. See above, April 2, 1825, n. 145.

January 1, 1826. Sunday.

We are still lying off St. Bartholomew's. It is a dull, hot, tiresome day. Being Sunday there is no preparation going on to get wood. It is not proposed that we leave this place before Tuesday.

On one side there is a Colombian party playing cards. On the other two Englishmen playing chess; even those playing have a lazy, dirty look.

I am ruminating on the events which have occurred on the anniversaries of this day. I can remember where I was, & my occupation on most of them for the last 30 years. A quarter of a century has just closed. Great have been the revolutions of Empires within that time—and great the change in my own situation. From boyhood, I have grown to middle age. I have been a boy—a young man,—married—a father and now—

I have had the pains & the pleasures of all these situations. I have been full of hopes. It seems to me that few men at my time of life can have run their race more completely than I have. I have no great hopes to be accomplished; no particular views to answer—no intention to make much exertion to change my situation in any way. To have something in prospect is indispensable. My children & their interests must give me the necessary excitement. I shall seek business, seek employment to fill my time & my mind, but it will be sought in a tame & careless way.

The delays on this river would at some former period of life have produced great vexations. Now indeed they produce but little. I feel that it is comparatively unimportant whether I am here or in Bogota. There is nothing pleasant in prospect there—and my quick arrival there does not hasten my return at all[.]

I am very anxious to hear from my children—particularly from Elizabeth. She was not well. Oh God grant a happy year,—many happy years to my dear children, to my Elizabeth, my Arthur, my Nancy.

January 2, 1826. This day we moved half a league for wood. [The] land is very rich. The cacao [is] growing spontaneously in the forests. Its bark looks something like that of young hickory. The tree is about the size of an apple tree. We have not seen many water fowls, nor many of any kind of birds lately. There are much fewer alligators than below.

January 3, 1826. This day we moved on with wood we suppose for 2 days—that is to Nare. The Champans which left Mompox since we did are passing us.

In observing the rich luxuriance of the forests on this river & in different parts of America, we may well believe that the minds of the European discoveries were impressed with admiration. One who has seen only the sterility or at most stunted trees of many parts of Europe, might well feel & express admiration at what is presented here[.]

The weather is very hot—equal to our warmest summer weather in Kentucky. The nights are however cooler than they were below—& we have no musquetoes[.]

January 4, 1826. We are told that we shall soon pass Angostura—the narrowest & swiftest part of the river & shall arrive at Nare today. My anxiety to get up [to Bogota] has greatly lessened. It is difficult to account for it—but it is certainly so. An anxiety to get the letters I hope to receive is the only foundation of much concern about it. It is now 5 ms. before 1 oClock. One man is sleeping, five Colombians talking with mouth, hand & feet. The Doctor [Mills] is feeling an Indians pulse & looking wise. By the bye—that is the only thing he can do *wise.* One Englishman is drawing, another reading the Spanish grammar. Bunch is talking to himself—no doubt about the Colombian funds.[203] Woodbine is examining his map of the river & making pencil marks of correct[ions.] Robert [Anderson] is reading Shakespeare when he ought to be at his Spanish grammar. Two Englishmen [are] playing

203. See above, November 30, 1825, and footnote.

chess & two Irishmen draughts. Denis [Hite] (as well employed as any of them) is cleaning my shoes.

3 oC. We have passed Angostura. It is a swift place produced entirely by the current of the river being contracted into a narrow channel. All remarkably narrow places on rivers are called in Spanish "Angostura."

January 5, 1826. A few moments after the last note was made, the boat struck on a sand bar—& we have been either on sand bars or warring against a very strong current ever since. We are now on the point of an island apparently fast. Although exertions are making to get off, still the probability of sending on the passengers in boats, is talked of. Several passengers have left us & gone to Nare, ½ league to get other means of conveyance.

We are almost without provisions; entirely without any but of the coarsest kind. It has occurred to me that probably it might be well for me to be kept on very thin & coarse food for a week or two. I certainly feel best when I am in situations where my diet is of the plainest kind. The bad wine is out & so is the sugar.

January 6, 1826. Still on the bar. Exertions are making to get the boat off; but it was amusing to see how immediately the anxiety of the passengers to get the vessel off, was changed as soon as it was known, that no farther [*sic* for further] attempt wd. be made to ascend the river, even if the boat was put afloat. Damn the boat, I wish that she may never get off, was the exclamation of half a dozen.

Doctor [Henry George] Mayne [*sic* for Maine]* passed us this morning going down the river on his way to Europe —with his wife, ugly & a *slut*. I pity him—no mind or elegance of manners about her.

January 7, 1826. This morning we got afloat. I fear that it is not much to avail the passengers, as I hear nothing yet of any attempt to go on.

This day I heard of the surrender of the fort of San Juan de Ulloa to the Mexicans.[204] Then the fortress of Callao [Peru] is the only point remaining of the vast possessions in America held by Ferdinand 7th at his ascending the throne. Certainly there are not many men living, who have fewer, just grounds of pleasing reflexion than that man. There is nothing in his public or private life not calculated to make miserable a sensitive mind.

January 8, 1826. Sunday. Very hot: still in the same position. The water has unexpectedly & greatly risen. It is said we are to go up; however, as I can as yet get no other conveyance, it is not necessary for me to determine whether or not I shall leave the boat. Cutting wood.

January 10, 1826. Yesterday we moved a mile or two above Nare—& took in wood. This day we are proceeding slowly. The current is strong & the steam low on account of the badness of the wood. This determination to go on comes from the *agent,* sorely against the will of the Captain [Batis]. Yesterday I killed a Gaucharaca—a bird between a turkey & a pheasant. Pardo [the congressman from Cartagena], Taliaferro [the senator from Panama], & another Colombian with his family went on yesterday in champans.

The Young Englishmen on board are more complaining & clamourous about the bad treatment on board than any other passengers. Not a day or an hour passes that they have not some demand to make for better treatment or better accomodation.

January 13, 1826. We are proceeding very slowly. The Engine is now in very bad order. The day before yesterday we came up to a Champan which had been overset on a log. We had previously heard of the wreck & met some of the cargo floating. We stop[p]ed, righted the boat & left her.

Yesterday I killed a very beautiful bird—red breast, green

204. A small island off the coast of Vera Cruz, Mexico.

back & black wings. Also a turkey, smaller than the N[orth] A[merican] turkey.

We have had much rain in the last three days. Very little before. It is very hot to day.

We have on board "Miss Wright's travels in the US."[205] It is amusing to see how the English are nettled at her praise of the US. & unfavorable contrasts of E[uropean] thing[s] with N[orth] A[merica.] I had no idea that they would be so sore.

Doctor Mills I believe is writing a book[.] He is very weak & vain. He may compile—he can never write a book worth reading.

January 15, 1826. This is the sixth Sunday on the river. Yesterday we took in wood just below Buena Vista. Robert [Anderson]* & myself walked up to the village & got some oranges 50 for 25 cents. It is well that my health is not injured by hard living, otherwise I should suffer much here. A delicate stomach would be starved. Last night there was a violent storm of rain & lightening. We are told that we shall arrive at Peñon tomorrow. However I have lost all faith in the movements of the boat. This morning we passed a large estate owned by a negro, who owns also many slaves. He rowed after us several miles to get (by begging) a bottle of brandy—but brought to us nothing, not even an egg. He got nothing.

Bogota *January 28, 1826.* Saturday Eveng.[206]

On Monday 16 Jan: the S. Boat having stopped 2 leagues below Peñon[207] for wood, I went up in a canoe to the landing place to secure mules for the land journey. This proved

---

205. Frances Wright (1795-1852), *Views of Society and Manners In America . . . during the years 1818, 1819, and 1820* (New York, 1821).

206. A letter in the Colombian Despatches, National Archives, written by Anderson to Secretary of State Clay on January 26, 1826, noted the journey in passing—"eight weeks—an unpleasant journey."

207. See Map 4, p. 195: the Peñon referred to will be found between Buena Vista and Segva, and should not be confused with another village of the same name farther downstream, between Badillo and S. Sebastian.

to be very judicious as there were just enough for my purpose. 17th the Boat came up and all the passengers arrived anxiously enquiring for means of Conveyance to get on. Mr. Wills a young Englishman got 4 mules & set out with us at 11 ½ for Se[g]va. After passing a very bad road we arrived at a new miserable huts called "Se[g]va" at sun set. Bought a couple of fowls, got a little bad bread. Denis [Hite]* was sick all night. The next day 18th we went over many hills but a much better road to the house of Sr. Estobar [sic]; who urged us to stop, declaring that he had a house fit for "los blancos"— the white men. After dismounting we began to enquire into the supplies for supper. Have you meat? no. Fowls? no. Bread? no; eggs? no. What have you? There—pointing to some pumpkins under the table. He had nothing else. Fortunately we had brought on some bad bread & one chicken that day—and more fortunately had killed a Turkey. These were prepared. We eat [sic for ate] & slept. 19th Very early Robert [Anderson] & myself set off to Guaduas leaving the Baggage with Mr. [George] W[oodbine]* & Denis [Hite].* We arrived at Guaduas at 11. The prospect from the hills on this side [of] the Magdalena most sublime & magnificent. Met my friend [Colonel] Acosta* at Guaduas [and] took breakfast with him & leaving Robert [Anderson]* I pushed on to Villete, arrived there at 5—exchanged the Mule, got a guide & pushed on about sun set with the design of breaking the very arduous ride of next day to Bogota, by going on as far as possible. Much against the consent of the Guide, who told me several times that I was at the house I was enquiring for, I got on two leagues. At l[e]ast he cheated me out of half a mile— making me stop that much short of my intended journey. 20th Next morning very early set out & passing the worst road I ever travelled in Colombia & of course any where else I came to Facatativa at 12 oC. Not being able to get another mule, came on the same & arrived here [Bogotá] at 6 ½— more exhausted than I ever was before by a days ride.

And here I was disappointed in that, which was the cause of my making such an effort. There were no letters for me from the US. I have heard nothing from my children since 20. Sep.

I came to the house of Colo: [Beaufort T.] Watts the Secy. of legation. The same home which I occupied when I first came to Bogota. I found W[atts] at dinner with Commodore [James] Chaytor* a Virginian.²⁰⁸ I retired to rest very soon. 21st A little recovered[.] 23[d] Robert [Anderson] & Denis [Hite] arrived with the Baggage. Both sick. I have been sick. They are now up & better. Since that day I have not been well. On Wednesday I called on the V. President [Santander].* On Thursday had a conversation with [Jose Rafael] Ravenga [sic for Revenga]* the new Secy. of F[oreign] Relations on the subject of abolishing all discriminating duties.

Wrote a letter to Clay on the subject. This morning [James] Chaytor* visited me & gave me a relation of Watts' encounter with [Leandro] Miranda*—entirely to W.s credit. He is much mortified as a paragraph has gotten in the N[orth] A[merican] papers discreditably to him [Chaytor]*— put in no doubt upon the letter of [Augustus] Leland*—the only N[orth] A[merican] here—that is living here.²⁰⁹
I am very far from being well. Have only been out of the house once. The mail from Carthagena brought me nothing.

February 2, 1826. I have been unwell for several days. On Sunday with [Beaufort T.] Watts [I] returned the visits of the Secretaries & some other gentlemen. Made the arrangement with this Govt. in relation to abolishing the discrim-

---

208. Chaytor's ship, the *Santissimi Trinidad,* had been caught in privateering operations in 1822. The United States had refused to acknowledge his expatriation, see also Appendix, List of Names.

209. The article probably referred to his exit from the United States and his alleged piratical activities. Leland, as the only North American there, would know of the story.

inating duties. By the President's message[210] I understand
that he intends to nominate [two] ministers to Panama.
Clay's opinion then has prevailed ag[ains]t the Presdt. Clay
was for app[ointin]g two & making much of the thing. The
Presd. [was] for app[ointin]g one & making no noise.[211] I am
living in the old house. Have taken possession & Watts*
lives with me[.] Last evening [José R.] Ravenga [sic for
Revenga]* visited me. I understand that this Govt. is greatly
in favor of the Independence of Cuba & P. Rico.[212] He went
much into the subject & disclaims any views of attaching
them to Colombia or to Mexico.

February 3, 1826. Rode out. Visited Mr. [James] Henderson's* family, Mrs. English* & Mr. Bing [Byng]* Feel pretty
well.

February 4, 1826. Feel pretty well. Rode out along the Ala-
meda.[213] Visited [William] Bunch & Commodore Chaytor.
Impatient to get letters from my dear children. Restless
until I hear certainly whether I go to Panamá.

February 9, 1826. I have heard that my dear children were
well up to the 26 of Nov: I thank God[.]

Recd. a letter from [Secretary of State] Clay stating that
John Sergeant* of Ph[iladelphi]a & myself were to be nominated as Commissioners to Panamá.

February 11, 1826. Understanding from Watt that the Editor
of the N[orth] A[merican] Review had written to me to
send him an essay on the Constitution of Colombia—I have
this day been preparing for him the essay I wrote two years
ago, with a design possibly of publishing it in a volume with
some others on Colombia.

Invited to dine with [Johann] Elbers.* Too unwell to
go. Robert [Anderson] is in bed sick.

---

210. James D. Richardson (ed.), *A Compilation of the Messages and
Papers of the Presidents, 1789-1897* (Washington, 1896), II, 318-320.
211. See above, May 29, 1825.
212. See above, November 6, 1825, n. 183.
213. The public walk; probably in this case the park or main street.

I have great inclination to buy some of the "deuda domestica" of Colombia.[214] It is at 25 & 33 in the hundred. I think much money might be made.

February 12, 1826. Sunday. Not well.

February 14, 1826. I have been unwell for two or three days with something of a dysentary. This too is very unusual with me. Robert is still sick in bed.

I have been engaged in preparing an essay on the Colombian Constitution for the N[orth] A[merican] Review.[215]

There is a report in town that Bolivar has received from the Emperor of Brazil [Dom Pedro I] a communication urging him to take upon himself the crown of all the revolted Spanish countries. It is no doubt to the interest of the Emperor that the Republics should be suppressed as his crown & his head are in danger so long as his Empire is surrounded by them. I have no idea that Bolivar would accept the crown of any single state. The glory of refusing it would be much greater than the acceptance but it is possible that the offer of a Crown embracing all States of S[outh] A[merica] might be too magnificent for the virtue of any man to resist.[216]

This is a fine bright morning at 10 oC. I am about walking out.

February 18, 1826. I have been very unwell for several days— but very busily engaged in writing letters of business to the

---

214. For Anderson's prior interest in Colombian finance, see above, November 30, 1825.

215. Anderson's article in the *North American Review*, XXIII (1826), 314-349, is factual rather than theoretical. He compares and contrasts the Colombian Constitution with the United States Constitution. He felt that the Colombians had given too much power to the legislative branch of government, and cited Jefferson as a man who had warned of such an occurrence in the United States. The article ended with a discussion of the qualifications for holding office and for voting in the Colombian elections, and a list of the Colombian "Bill of Rights" contained in the "eighth title" of the Constitution.

216. Bolívar was having more than enough trouble in *La Gran Colombia* during this period, see Parks, *op. cit.*, pp. 117-119. In any case, Bolívar did not think it advisable to set up monarchies in the New World.

Secretary of foreign affairs [José R. Revenga]* here, & to the Secretary at home. Robert is still in bed—better. This is the mail day. To know my anxiety on such days it is necessary that a man should place himself in my situation. Nothing prevents me from buying Certificates on this Govt. which are now selling at 25 in the hundred—but my ill health. I am not able to go out. I think if no change takes place in a few days I will make a venture in that way.

February 19, 1826. Sunday. Not much better. Rode out. Wrote a letter to Mary A. Bullitt.* No news by this mail. Ten days more to wait.

February 22, 1826. For two days I have been better.

February 23, 1826. Better. Went to the race field—poor & slow sport. Spent the evening with Mrs. English at a Whist party. I played at back gammon with the hostess.

Do not feel well this morning. A very cold damp day. Have been engaged several days busily with my essay on the Constitution of Colombia.

The other day [I] bought a little of the "deuda Domestica" at 20 pr. cent. Wish to get more.

February 27, 1826. On Saturday again went to the races & again got wet. Worse sport than before. Saw a man bet 100 doubloons to 1 on the race. He won it but suffered more for half an hour than his doubloon was worth, ten times over.

Yesterday, Sunday, Robert [Anderson]* being well enough to talk, he, Watts & myself called on the V. President [Francisco Paula de Santander],* Col: [Patrick] Campbell,* Colo: Torrens,* [the] Mexican Chargé [in Bogotá], [Juan Manuel* or Félix de*] Restrepo, [José Rafael] Revenga,* & Mrs. English.* I dined with [Segismundo] Leidersdorf,* agent of the Goldschmidts the London bankers. The V. P. was there & many others. Rainy & cold for several days past[.] This day clear & cool. Robert not so well again[.]

My dear Mother[217]

Bogota *Feb: 27, 1826*

We are disappointed very often (and unfortunately it still continues) in not getting letters from Kentucky[.] Not one word from your family since we arrived in Colombia[.] Although I am never well, still I have been better since my arrival here than any of the family[.] Robert has been unwell and I am sorry to say that he is not so well today as when he wrote to you[.]

Yesterday he was disappointed in waiting on a lady as he intended by that most troublesome companion "ague." Today he is walking about, but feels, as all do, who have such a troublesome plague.

I hope to see you towards the end of this or the beginning of the next year. Give my love to my father and all the children—and believe me to be your most affectionate son

R. C. Anderson jr.

February 28, 1826.[218] Last night the Carthagena mail came in, bringing me newspaper account[s] of my nomination (with John Sergeant)* as Commissioners to Panamá and also that there was a difficulty in the Senate on the subject of the propriety of the Mission.[219]

I wish to get to Panamá 1st Because I can save some money in it—2d Because it is honourable & 3d. because I am not prepared to live here in the way which wd. be expected from me & I do not like the expense of preparing myself. But besides all this I wd. rather go than stay, if there was neither gain, honour nor saving, because by a change of place & a change of scenery, the time which I propose to *give to this Country,* would more pleasantly wear away.

This day visited Mrs. [Manuel Antonio?] Arrublas,* Mrs. [Manuel] Ibanez* & Bernadina [Ibañez],* Mrs. Domingues[,]

---

217. This letter is not contained in the original diary but has been added by the editors. It may be found in W. P. Anderson, *op. cit.,* p. 125.
218. Anderson's diary resumes with the entry for February 28, 1826.
219. For this "difficulty," see the Introduction.

mother of Mrs. [Pedro] Gual*—Mrs. [Johann] Elbers* & Mrs. English.* Half of them only [were] at home. Robert [is] in bed & Watts* sick—also in bed.

March 1, 1826. Went to see [James] Henderson[,] B[ritish] Consul Genl. & [José Rafael] Revenga.* Had a long conversation with him concerning the attempt of this Gov: & Mexico to make Cuba & P. Rico independent. I am instructed to dissuade this Govt. from the attempt on account of the fear that those Islands cannot maintain their Independence & a fear that the slaves will get possession. I do not like much my business. I think that every belligerent has a right to annoy & distress its enemy in every practicable way. Robert [Anderson] still in bed[.]

March 3, 1826. A fine day. Visited with [Beaufort T.] Watts, [and] the Peruvian Commissioners [to the Panama Congress].[220] I have felt better for five or six days[.]

March 4, 1826. Windy unpleasant day. Rode out. Commodore [James] Chaytor* dined with us. He gave a wonderful account of Tazewell[221] not only as a lawyer, but as possessed of all kind[s] of knowledge. He says that [Tazewell] knows more about a ship than any other man he ever saw, even to the name of the smallest rope[.]

March 5, 1826. Cold Sunday Morng. Am to dine with Colo: Campbell to day.

March 6, 1826. A pleasanter day than yesterday. Mrs. English gave me some of Bolivars* hair. The grey begins to show itself. Dined yesterday with Colo: Campbell—a rough & rude Scotchman.

220. Manuel Lorenzo Vidaurre and Manuel Pérez de Tudela. In May, 1826, Bolívar wrote to Tudela describing Vidaurre as a "hard worker and fine friend" but one whose interest in anything "depended on his enthusiasm and patriotism." See Vicente Lecuna (comp.) and Harold Bierck (ed.), *Selected Writings of Bolívar* (New York, 1951), II, 525.
221. This is possibly Littleton W. Tazewell (1774-1860), U. S. Senator from Virginia (1824-1832), graduate of William and Mary College (1792), commissioner on claims under the Florida Treaty. Commodore Chaytor was a Virginian.

The mail comes in a few days. May I hear once more of the health of my children & my friends[.]

March 8, 1826. Not well to day nor yesterday. Wrote to Kitty W[oolfolk]* & Mrs. Levis—Elizabeth [Anderson's] teacher.

I am very anxious about the education of my dear daughter. Nothing is more difficult than to give a girl a good education in the US.[,] not because there are not abundance of good schools but because there are not many well educated women—not enough to make a society. And it is very difficult to make a child believe that it is important to value that wh[ich] those ladies around her do not possess.

I have often thought of taking Elizabeth to Paris and leaving her there two years. In this way only can I ensure to her the ready speaking of the french language for which I am very anxious. She can also as I understand have all the other advantages there which she could at any other place. The objections, are the violence it wd. commit on my own feelings; on Elizabeth's feelings, & the distance she wd. be from my protection. May God bless my child & guide me—!

Robert* is very unwell.

March 10, 1826. The mail has not arrived.

Yesterday I am writing letters nearly all day—to Clay*— G[eorge] C. G[wathmey]*—Elizabeth & her teacher Mrs. Levis & others.

March 11, 1826. Feel much better again. A fine day. Desired by Colo: Campbell not to make any engagement for the 22d of this month, which wd. prevent me from dining with him in honour of Mrs. English's birth day[.]

Brizeño[222] was here yesterday. He is going to the US. where his sons are in school. He wants letters. He is a man of talents, but I wish he were whiter; the people in the US. will take him for a Negro[.]

---

222. This is the Brizeño that Anderson met on the trip to Bogotá (November 30, 1825), and not the Colombian government official and minister to Panama, Pedro Briceño Méndez.

Robert is very sick. I am uneasy about him. No mail yet[.]

March 14, 1826. The mail brought me no letters. I have not been well since Sunday evening. This is a cold damp day— so was yesterday.

March 15, 1826. This is my daughter Elizabeth's birth day. May God protect & bless her! This day was completed the election of the President & V. Presdt. for 4 years from the 2d Jany next. On counting the votes it was ascertained that Bolivar* (as was previously known) had a great majority & was elected by the Electors. No one had the necessary ⅔ds for V. P. Santander,* [José María del] Castillo [y Rada]* & [Pedro] Brizeño [Méndez]* were the three highest & the first was elected by the Congress at the first ballot. S. 71. C. 22. B. 5.

Colo: Campbell the British Charge told me this day, that he had received a letter from his Government desiring him to make known to this Gov. that his B[ritannic] M[ajesty] had accepted the invitation & would send a Minister to Panama. This is news and strange to me. This Govt. has never intimated the least intention of inviting any European power. I thought the Congress was to institute an American System, and to be composed solely of American representatives.[223] I think the US. will not like it; although it may have the effect of determining them to be represented there, as they may not deem it safe to be absent while G. Britain has her agent there. However it is to me so strange that I think yet there may be some mistake. It always occurred to me as possible that GB. wd. have some agent in the shape of a Consul or some other shape there. But I never supposed she was to be invited.[224]

---

223. The truth was that Bolívar had not even intended to invite the United States to the Congress. If any outside power was to be invited, Bolívar preferred it to be Great Britain, but under the prodding of Vice President Santander an approach was made to the United States.

224. The British eventually sent an observer, Edward J. Dawkins, to the Congress. Canning's instructions to Dawkins exhorted him to be watchful

March 16, 1826. This day all the English (at the request of the Chargé [Patrick Campbell])* went in a body to congratulate the V. President [Santander]* on his election. The Diplomatic Corps [was] in full dress. These people from Monarchies are well tutored in such things. They do everything for *effect* & Every vagabond Englishman in town was mustered up to increase the show.

March 17, 1826. Dined, Robert [Anderson] & myself with Mr. [James] Henderson *en famille*—to take as he says *pot luck*—and generally at his table the *luck* is bad. I saw there a Mr. Abernathy, who seems to be a man of cleverness.

March 18, 1826. The mail came in this morng. I thank God that my children are well to the 6th of January. But this day brings me the sad news of John Logan's* death. How uncertain is life! How dreadful has been the visitation of death upon our family in the last three years! I never knew a better man. He & my old father in law, [Owen Gwathmey] I have frequently thought of as the purest of men. I fear that his family is distressed by his death in many ways. I fear that his affairs are disordered.

At the last advices the Senate had not acted on the Panamá mission. The delay is vexatious to me. It keeps me in an unsettled, restless state. I believe yet the Mission will be confirmed, although the papers say the opposition to it is serious.[225]

I received a letter from my dear daughter [Elizabeth.]

---

of any attempt to put the United States "at the head of an American Confederacy as against Europe." He was also to push for recognition of familiar British maritime rules—the right of search, the refusal to recognize as national any vessel not built in the country whose flag floated above its deck, and the restriction of the carrying trade between Latin America and England to British and Latin American ships—that the United States had opposed for years. Dawkins was also to offer British mediation in arguments between Latin American states and in all discussions concerning Cuba was to take a different approach than that of the United States. It is not difficult, therefore, to understand why Anderson was apprehensive regarding Britain's appearance at the Congress.

225. See Introduction.

She says she can play one tune. My feelings are strange! but—

Little Arthur too is going to school & my little Annita is well.

March 19, 1826. I have been writing all this day, particularly to Secretary Clay on the subject of this Country & the other S. American Confederates' attacking & emancipating Cuba & Porto Rico. I think our Govt. has assumed great responsibility in urging this country to suspend its operation on Cuba under the hope that Spain can be induced to make peace. I do not believe Spain will; & then the US. is placed in a delicate posture, having induced this Gov. to suspend the "uplifted arm" as it says. The day before yesterday I recd. a note from the Secy. of foreign affairs, [José Rafael Revenga]* saying that "in deference to the US.," proceedings will be suspended in the meditated attack on Cuba until the Congress at Panamá shall determine on it. Now this is very adroit—as I know well this Govt. cannot send out an expedition for many months but they are now putting this delay upon the solicitation of the US. I think the US. has incurred a very great and unnecessary responsibility of which they will hear hereafter.

March 20, 1826. A fine clear morning. A little too cool[.]

March 22, 1826. There are processions every day—this being "semana santa."²²⁶

This evening went with Robert to a race at the Florestra. A poor thing.

March 23, 1826. A fine morning. Last evening dined with Colo: Campbell; dinner given to Mrs. English in honour of her birth day. Robert was obliged to retire from dinner sick—& [Beaufort T.] Watts* lost his *chapeau bras.*

March 24, 1826. Writing nearly all yesterday my essay on

---

226. This may have been the Festival of the Holy Patron. It began in the evening after church with fireworks and a religious procession.

the Constitution of Colombia and copying some public letters for my private use.[227]

This day went to see the procession. This being good friday, a magnificent procession was expected, but it was a miserable thing. The saints were shabby and dirty.

Yesterday Commodore [James] Chaytor* dined with us. He seems to be a man of honour & gentlemanly in his deportment—but has not much sense. This day Mr. Byng* dined with us. A man of some sense. He is the agent for Admiral [Pedro Luís] Bryon's [*sic* for Brión's]* family and told us unhesitatingly that he could get no accounts passed but by making large presents to those, who were to pass them. This I knew very well before was done by him & others.

March 25, 1826. I have got up with a cold & slight head ache.

March 26, 1826. This day one year ago I left this place for the U. States with my children. It was a mournful day, it was a terrible day to my feelings. Poor creatures[,] they were too young to feel as I did. It was also the day on which Colonel [Leonardo] Infante* was shot. He was executed at 9 oClock[,] the hour at which I left town.

Yesterday I took a long ride along on the road which goes near the mountains down the valley to the South. Most of the valley was very poor[.]

This day I have been invited by [Segismundo] Leidersdorf* to dine with & meet the V. Presdt. at dinner. I shall not go. [José Rafael] Ravenga [Revenga]* has visited me, he is a little Jesuit.

March 28, 1826. Feel tolerably well. Dined alone. [Beaufort T.] Watts & Robert [Anderson] went to the races and then dined with Byng. Robert has been better for a few days.

The mail came in today, bringing me nothing but old newspapers from the US. Indeed I expected nothing, having

---

227. See above, February 11, 1826, and February 14, 1826.

received letters so lately before. By the next mail I hope to hear from home. Certainly I shall hear the result of the Panamá affair.

March 29, 1826. Borrowed some old National Gazettes[228] from [José Rafael] Ravenga [Revenga]* & am reading them. There [are] some interesting literary pieces in them that are as good, old, as new.

Robert [Anderson]* is copying some drawings which represent the costumes of this country. They would be queer indeed in any other part of the country [*sic* for world].

March 30, 1826. Last night not well. I feel tolerably well now, 2 oClock.

I understand that [Francisco de Paula] Santander* has tendered his resignation of the Vice Presidency to Congress. This shows a strange state of feeling & opinion. It is fashionable for every body to resign in order that the resignation shall be rejected & to receive encomiums on past services.

Last night [Beaufort T.] Watts, Robert [Anderson] & myself played whist; I with the dead man. It was a dull business & we soon quit it.

April 1, 1826. This day Com[modore James] Chaytor* dined with us; played a game of whist after dinner. [Beaufort] Watts & myself rode out today[.]

Have been reading [Thomas] Moore's life of Sheridan.[229] It is very interesting. S's life presented so many incidents, that a memoir of it could not fail to be so. The account of his wife, her devotion to her husband, the manner in which she entered into all his pursuits, whether political, or literary or private affected me much. It seems to me that the life of few men could give so much interest as Sheridan; while his public reputation was of the highest kind, his social

---

228. The *National Gazette* was published in Philadelphia.
229. Thomas Moore, *Memoirs of the Life of the Rt. Hon. Richard Brinsley Sheridan* (2 vols.; New York, 1825). This is Richard Brinsley Butler Sheridan (1751-1816).

habits were of a character continually producing interesting incidents. [Charles James] Fox* was a good deal in the same way—[William] Pitt* not [at] all. He was always & every where *minister*.

April 2, 1826. Sunday. The V. Presd. receives a military treat on the plain in honour of his election & of his Saints day. He is 34 years of age.

Visited [José Manuel or Félix de] Restrepo, [Carlos] Soublette, & Mrs. [Manuel] Ibana [*sic* for Ibáñez].* Visited by Colo; [George] Woodbine,* Illingsworth,* Boardman, & Wills.

[Beaufort] Watts & Robert [Anderson] gone to ride. 3 oClock.

April 4, 1826. Bad weather. I have been better *generally* for a month past than before.

Robert* & myself drank tea with Mrs. English*—a house full of talking & impudent English.

April 5, 1826. This day three years [ago] I left Louisville to come to South America. The recollection of the day produces mourning feelings. How terrible is my situation changed!

Colo: [Brooke] Young* a gentleman who came over with me in the ship John Adams visited me. He has just come from Quito [Ecuador].

April 6, 1826. This day I finished my essay on the Constitution of Colombia. I intend soon to send it to the North American review according to the request of its Editor.[230]

April 7, 1826. A fine day. Last evening could not go [to] the race on account of the rain. These races are to be sure but for little but to pass the time till the mail comes. The arrival of the mail is the only epoch in Bogota, which serves to mark time to me. It will be in again tomorrow or the next day.

---

230. See above, February 14, 1826, and footnote.

Robert* & myself rode to day to the house surrounded by trees on the right of the road to Honda—about 1½ leagues from town. About the 25th of Feb. two years ago I rode on the same road with one with whom I shall never be again in this world!

April 8, 1826. The mail has arrived bringing me nothing from my children or friends.

The consideration of the Panamá mission was not concluded on the 24 of Feb: If nothing more comes out of it, I have the honour to be named on a mission which has excited more attention in Congress & out of it than any other ever proposed in the US. It very possibly may be the question which will first divide parties into the friends & opposers of the new administration.

April 9, 1826. Writing letters for the mail nearly all day. Robert [Anderson]* has an ague again.

April 10, 1826. This is [Beaufort T.] Watts birth-day. It seems to me that he has nearly arrived at the time that a man begins to not feel much pleasure at the return of birth-days. However he seems well pleased—and on the strength of it Byng,* Vincedon [?] & Commodore [James] Chaytor* dined with us. After dinner played a game of whist.

April 11, 1826. I am not very well & Rob[er]ts ague has returned. Rode out about 3 oC.

April 12, 1826. A cold dark day. Most unexpectedly [Ferdinand] Sirawkoski [Sirakowski]* came & paid me the remaining $100; so long due & the lingering balance of $1300. This is clear gain.[231]

April 14, 1826. Tolerably well. Nothing new. A great rain yesterday. Rode out this evening alone.

April 15, 1826. This day Robert [Anderson] has gone with Junca,* [William] Bunch* & others to the village of [blank]

---

231. Anderson's first encounter with Sirakowski is noted April 22, 1824.

a few leagues over the mountains, where there are warm baths & a warmer climate. I hope the change will break his ague.

Visited Mrs. English and had an opportunity of seeing how disgusting a pretty & sensible woman can make herself by indulging in passion. Her maid Matilda had committed some offence—and the Mistress railed & scolded until she was red & disgusting with passion. I decamped very soon.

April 16, 1826. Sunday. [Beaufort T.] Watts & myself visited the V. Presdt. [Santander] & Secretary [of Foreign Affairs José Rafael] Ravenga [Revenga].

A Mr. Azuero[,] merchant of Maracaybo[,] & Byng* dined with us.

April 17, 1826. A cool Monday morning. The mail may come in tomorrow.

April 18, 1826. Yesterday I was very unwell all day. Am a little better today. This day and yesterday very cool and disagreeable. Mr. [Harris E.] Fudger* & [Augustus] Leland* visited me. F: is the US Consul for S[an]t[a] Martha. He looks like a tight yankee[.]

I am writing to Pleasanton the auditor [in Washington] and preparing my accounts which are two quarters behind hand. The mail has just come in but I have not ascertained whether there is any thing for me[.]

April 19, 1826. Nothing for me by the mail[.] Robert is still at the Village over the mountains[.]

Have been writing until I am tired & unwell. A dark cold day. [Beaufort T.] Watts is sick—& [William] Bunch very sick[.] This day sent my essay on the Constitution of Colombia to the Editor of the North American review. I'll see how it comes out. Perhaps it may animate me to write & publish some *other* essays. Perhaps it may have the better effect of causing me to save myself any trouble in that way.[232]

---

232. See above, February 11, 1826, February 14, 1826, and March 24, 1826.

April 20, 1826. Another bad day. Damp & cold. Last evening I got wet. I am waiting to see if the weather will permit me to go to the race.

April 21, 1826. I went to the race yesterday and was polite enough to lose an ounce [*sic*]. Of course I was too wary to let a gentleman fool me, but I had not fortitude enough to escape from the designs of a lady on my purse.

April 22, 1826. Rather pleasanter than yesterday[.] I have not been well for a week.

I have been since I despatched my "essay" preparing a digest of the commercial regulations of Colombia for the State department under its instructions.

April 23, 1826. Sunday morning. Raining hard. Much rain has fallen within a week[.] Writing all day my report on Commercial regulations—except between 2 & 4 o. [when] I rode out. Had a pleasant ride.

Byng dined with us. Robert [Anderson] came while we were at dinner. He says he is better, indeed he considers himself quite well.

April 25, 1826. The Caracas mail came bringing Philadelphia news to the 4th—& Washington to 1st—of March. Nothing important. Nothing from children or friends.

April 27, 1826. Writing the digest [of Colombian commercial regulations] yet. On Monday I saw [José Rafael] Ravenga [Revenga],* who told me of the steps taken by this Govt. to effect a conciliation between Buenos Ayres & Brazil.[233]

On completion of his article, "Constitution of Colombia," Anderson began the preparation of a report (see below, April 22, 1826) on "Commercial Regulations of the Republic of Colombia" (33 pages), filed following his Despatch no. 43, May 1, 1826; Despatches, Colombia, Vol. III, National Archives.

233. The war between Buenos Ayres (the United Provinces of Rio de la Plata) and Brazil was caused by a dispute over the area later known as Uruguay. The struggle for control there had its origins in the Colonial era. In 1825, after years of intermittent argument and hostility, Buenos Ayres supported a revolution in the region, which had recently been annexed by Brazil. War broke out and went on until September, 1828, when Uruguay was formed as a buffer state.

[He] fears it may embroil the other American Republics—[and] wishes the US. to become mediators. He spoke I think very wisely. These are a very sagacious people, if they act as well as they know how they will act very wisely[.]

April 29, 1826. I am very unwell this morning. My head & stomach are greatly disordered[.]

The mail has come bringing nothing from the UStates. This is unusual. An interval of three weeks without an arrival of any vessel from the US. has been very uncommon of late.

April 30, 1826. I feel somewhat better today.

May 1, 1826. I feel better. This was a gloomy morning but warm—fine evening. I went to the races & saw some poor running. Mr. [James] Henderson* lost three races & about a thousand dollars. This makes somewhat of a hole in the quarters salary.

May 2, 1826. This Govt. has passed a law making a Contract for issuing a new currency of platina.[234] They seem to have the idea that it is judicious for a nation to have a currency which will not go out of the Country[.] Upon these subjects & indeed all subjects of political economy there is much uncertainty & contrariety of opinion, but it seems some that this notion of having a currency that can't run away is greatly behind the illumination of the present age.

May 3, 1826. I took a ride in the plain. The vegetation looks fine. The wheat is good. I never saw such an appearance of the potatoe crop either in quantity or quality. The agriculture of that part of the plain which is nearest the city has certainly improved.

May 4, 1826. More rain[.] Evening. It has rained nearly all day.

---

234. See above, November 10, 1825.

May 5, 1826. This day two years [ago] I remember well. Several gentlemen dined with me, among others Wm. D. Robinson,* Miralla* & Sylva [*sic* for Silva],* who are all dead.

I have just returned from a ride in the plain. All is mud & water.

May 6, 1826. I have not for several years looked much into ancient history. Lately I have peeped a little into, read a part of Plutarch's lives &c—and have become confirmed in what I have long suspected, that Roman & Grecian virtue & simplicity exists only in imagination & in those histories which are written long after the facts they speak of. I am satisfied that there is more virtue in the present state of Society than ever was in Greece or Rome. I can not find any historian however ancient, who lived *in the times* of *virtuous simplicity*. They all speak of it as an age *past*. When I take any period of history I find enormities too shocking for the present age. I do not mean extraordinary acts of violence, because they may occur at all times, but I refer to those only which were sustained by the public sentiment of the day. Vice and corruption show themselves now under different forms, on account of difference of manners existing between this & former ages, but the quantum is not greater, and although it might be deemed just to suppose that the aggregate of Vice was about equal in all ages. I believe that the progress of Civilization[235] in modern times has been to lessen the quantum of Vice & increase that of Virtue. If you think differently, when was the time? In the age of Cato?* Read it again if you think so. In that of Scipios?[236] Read it. Do not judge of the age by one man. Was it in the time of Aristides? Or to give you the advantage of the remotest antiquity known to profane authors, take the age of Homer. Was not the most shameless violence, licentiousness, bar-

---

235. The "x" referred readers to an Anderson footnote which was placed two lines below the mark. It read: "literature, improvement in the arts &c—& above all, the propagation of the Gospel," and was Anderson's definition of civilization.

236. Scipio, Aemilianus and Scipio, Africanus.

barity to slaves & prisoners, perfidy, corruption of morals, & superstition displayed in all those ages—greater than the public sentiment of the present day will bear. For it shd. be remembered that an age must not be estimated by single acts of vice but by those only which the general sentiment approves or sustains.

May 7, 1826. A day of almost incessant rain. During the last night there was hardly an intermission of half an hour in the rain. I have felt better for two or three days than I did on the first of the week. I have been in the house all day reading Sully's Memoirs.[237]

Robert [Anderson]* has been reading a little tract in Spanish on the geography of Colombia—and I can now hear [Beaufort T.] Watts reading aloud in a very animated tone some speech that he thinks he is delivering in Congress.

May 8, 1826. It rained all night—and is yet raining. [Charles B.] Sutherland* & an English party have just returned from visiting the Bridge of Pandi.[238] Never did a set pass through such floods of rain. They report the bridge as not worth[y] of visiting. Very probably they were not in a state of mind to appreciate justly any spectacle either natural or artificial, as they report themselves cold & wet during the whole time.

Went to see [José Rafael] Ravenga [Revenga]* in the evening. He has been sick. He was drying some books he lately received from Europe which have come wet & injured.

May 9, 1826. The mail is due this day. Such is the state of the [Magdalena] river & the roads that I fear it will not arrive puncutally.

May 10, 1826. The mail has not yet arrived. By the mail of last night I sent to the Secretary of State [Clay] a digest of the Commercial regulations of Colombia. It is not long but

---

237. *Mémoires de Maximilien de Béthune, duc de Sully* [1559-1641], *principal ministre de Henri le grand.* Londres, 1767.
238. See above, Map 3, p. 133, for the Bridge of Pandi.

was troublesome. It was necessarily collected from several different laws.

Robert [Anderson]* has not been well lately. He is strangely affected. The ague & fever have left him—but his old pain in the back of the head has returned.

May 12, 1826. Not so much rain yesterday & this day as for many before, tho it rained both days. I have been better for two or three days. I rode out this day—a fine sun & drying wind after 12 oC.

The mail arrived bringing nothing from the US. I have not heard from my children & friends in K. Y. since 12th of January[.]

The Panamá mission was not settled on the 10th of March, as I learn from straggling papers, which [José Rafael] Ravenga [Revenga]* lent me. The opposition to the present admin[istration] seems strong & very violent. Yet I think that there will be a difficulty in organizing it—that is in producing a coalition between the friends of [William H.] Crawford & [Andrew] Jackson[.]

Great stir is here now on account of the failure of Goldschmidts, the Bankers of Colombia in London. Colombian stock [is] very low. I still wish I had some spare money to buy a little.

May 14, 1826. Sunday. Yesterday I rode out. The plain is not quite so wet as it was. The atmosphere here dries the ground much sooner than in lower positions—I suppose on account of its rarity. But there are no certain indications that the rain has ceased. It rained a little this morng. & is very cloudy yet.

Byng* dined with us again the other day. He is a sensible, well behaved man, somewhat vain, which does not render him disagreeable.

This day the idea occur[r]ed to me of sending to the department of State a memoir on the situation of Colombia; something like this is embraced in my instruction. The idea has occur[r]ed to me before, in a different form. I thought of throwing my views of this Country into the shape of a long report with a view of having that report published—but my present notion is to present a short memoir & also if I think proper publish a few essays, which may embrace the same facts, with others & my speculations also.

May 15, 1826. I think the rain is ceasing. It did not rain last night, nor has it yet rained to day—but it is cold & damp.

I have occasionally for several days been reading Sully's memoirs.[239] It is an interesting & valuable book, not only as it gives an authentic history of Henry 4th[240] but as it gives *food for thinking.* I read it ten years ago.

Yesterday [James] Henderson,* Wall, [Charles B.] Sutherland* & Colo: Torrens* called on me. No news.

About an hour after writing the above, the mail from Maracybo brought me the intelligence that the Senate had approved the Panamá mission by a vote of 24 to 19. The late intelligence. . . .[241]

May 23, 1826. I have this morning been reading the President's [John Q. Adams] Message to the HR. & documents, explaining the objects of the Panamá Mission.[242] Like all his compositions it is able & elegant—but I have always thought that there was too much prettiness, or floridness as you may call it in his composition for grave state papers. He gives an instance of a man cold, almost icy in his appearance & social intercourse whose writings are marked by fervour & fire.

May 24, 1826. Robert [Anderson] & myself attempted to ride out yesterday, & got wet before we got out of town. More rain last night.

---

239. See above, May 7, 1826, and footnote.
240. Henry (IV) of Navarre.
241. A page of Anderson's diary is missing at this point. On the following page the end of a sentence begun on the missing page reads: "Newspapers to the 28th of March."
242. See James D. Richardson, *op. cit.,* II, 329-340.

My friend Colo. [Patrick] Campbell has been grievously disappointed in not getting his letters. Those that came from England by the February packet, have by mistake been sent back from Carthagena to Jamaica. This disappt. is greater as he has a sneaking notion of being sent to Panamá in some station. He is constantly expressing his wonder as to who will be the man—until every body knows that he thinks of but one man.

This Govt. is in trouble indeed as to the ways & means. The failure of Goldschmidt her banker in London has added to the perplexity by increasing her losses. Her foreign loan is down in the market to 40—& her "deuda domestica" to 20 or 25. To borrow money when her credit is so low will be indeed to hold her nose to the grind-stone.

May 25, 1826. A great "fiesta" this day. I think it exceeded any thing of the kind I have seen in Colombia. It is suggested that the officers of Government, particularly the V. Presdt. [Santander] aided in giving unusual magnificence to the procession & whole religious ceremony from a supposed necessary flattery to the Clergy. In the exterior ceremony there was surely nothing that could induce a Protestant even to conceive the idea that it was a religious rite. There was fiddling, dancing, masks, representations of cranes, cocks, & other birds of prodigious magnitude & a large turtle of 12 feet diameter. All these things were so made that they were placed over the heads of men who went through the streets, thus giving to these animals apparent motion & life. Indeed there was every thing grotesque & disgusting. But there was also a profusion of plated & gilded Saints—children representing Catholic & Indian deities & costly church furniture of gold, plate & jewelry. In the evening came on the Bull fighting & at night the fire works. All day [there was] cock fighting in the National Cock-pit.

Amused myself for an hour reading the English newspapers at [José Rafael] Ravenga's [*sic* for Revenga's].*

May 27, 1826. Yesterday Colo: [George] Woodbine,* Commodore [James] Chaytor* & Byng* dined with us. The conversation turned mostly on oysters, crabs, canvass-back ducks &&&—Things of which, the jaws & belly of[,] the Commodore declared he was well fond of.

I have been for some days again preparing materials for my half-contemplated essays on Colombia.

With delay, my anxiety to hear from my dear children increases. It is now nearly five months since I have even heard that they were living.

May 29, 1826. A troublesome alcalde lives near us & is frequently taking up the Servants for some alleged offence. I was obliged to attend & deny the jurisdiction of his court this evening, on a charge he brought against Denis [Hite]* for insulting him by *carahoing* [*sic*] at him. I brought the thing to a draw battle.

In the expectation that the Congress at Panamá may end in some way honourable to those who first suggested or promoted it, there is already a contention for the honour of the suggestion, but I believe there is no doubt that the first recorded suggestion is in a letter of Bolivar* to [Juan Martín de] Pueyrredon[,] president or Director of Buenos Ayres of the 12th of June 1818. In the year 1822 it was provided for in the treaties between Colombia and Peru & Chile. Bolivar was no doubt the author of the Idea.

A very damp cold morning with appearance of much rain.

May 30, 1826. It has rained a little only last night & very little today. Rode out towards Zipaquira.[243] Roads very bad.

No mail yet from Carthagena, altho due, yesterday[.]

Engaged in taking notes & makg. memo: from newspapers & other documents on the situation of this country.

May 31, 1826. 11 o C. No rain today—but so far a fine drying sun & wind.

---

243. See Map 3, p. 133, for location of Zipaquira.

Robert [Anderson]* was yesterday engaged in numbering some specimens of minerals & stones collected in this Country. He is today sketching some of the costumes of the natives[.]

June 1, 1826. Yesterday was a fine drying day & so is this yet. A little rain [fell] last night. Robert* & myself rode into the plain last evening[.] It was cool but dry & windy. No mail yet.

So cool is it that I have not worn less than two coats at any time since my arrival here in Jany. & frequently I am uncomfortably cold. I always wear two pairs of socks & still am compelled to rise & walk about the room every half hour to warm my feet by exercise.

A great "fiesta" again today, in which were exhibited much magnificence, gaudy show, many unintelligible ceremonies, dancing &c. The part of the show which interested me most were several birds & animals which I had not seen before. The condor, the royal buzzard, a species of spotted hare, & armadillo were among them. I witnessed the procession from the V. President's balcony, whom I seized that occasion to visit[.]

June 2, 1826. All the town is alarmed with a report that a Spanish squadron is off the Coast, and by another report which is indeed much more alarming, that Genl. [José Antonio] Páez* is in open & successful rebellion in Venezuela.[244] It would be better that the Spanish Squadron had

---

244. General José Antonio Páez (see Appendix, List of Names) was at this time the suspended general commander of the Department of Venezuela, and had been ordered to Bogotá to stand trial for acts involving the forcing of men into military service in 1825. The episode brought Federalist and Constitutional monarchial factions in Caracas and elsewhere again into argument concerning the government of the Confederation. Bolívar, then in Peru, proceeded to Bogotá to restore order. In the meantime, Páez' preparation for his trip to Bogotá was halted by a riot in Valencia on April 30, and through the efforts of an impeached and disgruntled national judge, Páez was prevailed upon to resume the office from which Congress had suspended him. Open rebellion flared in other cities, and a plea to Páez from Vice President Santander seemed to avail nothing. But as Bolívar advanced from Peru, Páez called on all Venezuelans to abandon the revolution and recognize the Liberator. The two men met on January 27,

taken already half a dozen towns than that this should be true. The report [of the Páez rebellion] does not come very straight, but from his character & disaffection of many in Venezuela it excites (& well it may) much alarm.

June 3, 1826. In the morning. I am sorry indeed to say that it rained again last night & has every appearance of continuing to rain. I am still vexed & almost distressed by the delay of the mail, which has been due five days.

This day we have heard the news (by an express from Carthagena) that the Emperor Nicholas of Russia has been assassinated,[245] that [John], the King of Portugal is dead,[246] that the Constitutionalists are making head way in Spain,[247] that France & England are on bad terms (& getting worse) with Russia[248] that a British minister has arrived in Carthagena for this Republic & a Commissioner for Panama[249]—and that Genl. [José Antonio] Páez* has proclaimed a Confederated Government in Venezuela.[250] This news burst upon us in one half-hour—and [this] one half [hour's news] is too much for a man to digest in a year & possibly more than Europe and America may digest in a dozen. The death of the King of Portugal is in no way interesting unless the Emperor [Dom] Pedro [I] of Brazil is the heir of both monarchies. It is said that there is a secret treaty by which [he] has relinquished Portl. to his younger brother Michael. If Pedro

---

1827; Páez was given the title of "Civil and Military Chief of Venezuela," and they entered Caracas together on January 10.

245. This was incorrect, as Anderson later notes, since Nicholas died in 1855 of natural causes. The rumor probably resulted from the activities of the Decembrists, a group of conspirators who attempted to stage a palace revolution after the death of Tsar Alexander I on December 25, 1825.

246. This news was correct.

247. See above, November 27, 1824.

248. The Greeks were then attempting to gain their independence from the Ottoman Empire. In 1826 Britain and France feared that Russian intervention on behalf of the Greeks might result in Russian mastery over the entire Near East. The British and French felt, therefore, that a three-power intervention might be the only way to rescue the Greeks and check the Russians.

249. The news of the arrival of a British Minister was incorrect, but the commissioner referred to was Edward Dawkins.

250. See above, June 2, 1826, especially n. 244.

attempts to hold both, I think he will certainly lose Brazil.[252] The assassination alone of the Russian Emperor is not so interesting as the reported design of that Country on Turkey &c[.][252] We do not yet know whether his death is to stop or to accelerate such a design.

Of Genl. Páez nothing is yet known beyond the above stated fact[.] Whether he means to put himself at the head of his troops or only to call on the people peaceably to effect a reform in the frame of Govt. is not known.

June 4, 1826. The mail has come this evening. No news from my dear children or friends. The newspapers give evidence of more violence in & about Congress than has existed for twelve years. Mr. Clay has been guilty of the most foolish, passionate, unadvised & almost unpardonable act of fighting a duel with Mr. [John] Randolph.*[253] Considering his age, his political situation, his views & prospects of elevation & the effect that such an act is well calculated to have on his elevation (particularly on the people of the North) I con- sider it the most outrageous act of folly I ever knew a man to commit.

The opposition to the Presidents administration seems to be violent & considerable, but to me it seems impossible that it can be well concerted or the members of it can long harmonize, the materials cannot assert [*sic*] long.

June 5, 1826. Monday morng. 10 oC. It began to rain yes-

---

251. Dom Pedro I ruled in Brazil until he was forced by Brazilian leaders to abdicate in 1831. In 1826, shortly after King John's death, Pedro began to spend large sums of money to obtain the throne of Portugal for his daughter, Maria da Gloria. Her position was, however, usurped by Pedro's brother, Dom Miguel. After Pedro left the Brazilian throne, he launched an expedition to replace Dom Miguel with Maria da Gloria, and succeeded in doing this shortly before his death in 1834.

252. See above, June 3, 1826, especially footnote.

253. John Randolph (1773-1833) was then in the United States Congress and was a violent antagonist of John Quincy Adams and Henry Clay, whom he referred to as the coalition of "Blifil and Black George." The result of this statement was the Clay-Randolph duel on April 8, 1826, on the Virginia side of the Potomac River. Neither man was wounded, although Clay's second shot pierced Randolph's coat.

terday about about 12 o.[and] has rained every [*sic*] since &
is now raining violently.

June 6, 1826. Went down to [William] Bunch's* to read his
newspapers, when returning Colo: [Patrick] Campbell*
hailed [me] & thanked me for the letter I had sent him. I
knew not until he told me that a messenger had arrived
from Carthagena bringing me despatches from the Secretary
of State [Clay]. On coming home I recd. them as old as 14
March, directing me to go to Porto Bello [Panama][254] &
there await Mr. [John] Sergeant.* The ship J. Adams took
out Colo: [John] Williams[,]* Chargé for Guatemala[,] and
has been beating up against the wind[x] so long, that I do not
doubt that Mr. S[ergeant] is on the Coast before I have heard
of his sailing from [the] US.[255] I hope that he has had sense
enough, if Mr. Clay had not, to make Carthagena the place
of meeting, instead of Panamá. It is nearly sure then (tho
not quite yet) that I go to Panamá. I am told that if unexpectedly the house of Representatives shd. not agree to the
Mission, my expenses to the coast shall be paid, this is well—
and what is better, that the Presdt. will not expect me to
return to Bogota unless I think proper.

I have heard from my dear children, though only to the
1st Feby. I thank God they were well—up to that time. I
propose going off on Tuesday.

June 7, 1826. It did not rain yesterday or to day. I am very
unwell.

June 8, 1826. I feel better—but it rained nearly all night—
and is now at 9 o. a most dark and dull and disagreeably cold
morning. Rode out on the plain[.]

254. See Map 4, p. 195.
255. Anderson's "x" might better have been placed at the end of the
sentence. Two lines below the "x" in the text Anderson placed his footnote
and wrote: "To reach Carthagena with the despatches." Given the wind
conditions going north he felt that John Sergeant would quickly arrive
in Porto Bello with the instructions for the Congress.

June 9, 1826. A better day—& [I] feel better than yesterday evening. No rain last night[.]

Waited on [José Rafael] Ravenga [Revenga]* & introduced [Beaufort T.] Watts as Chargé of the US. business at this place[.]

Robert [Anderson]* & myself got some specimans of minerals.

June 10, 1826. Had a miserable night—but have felt better today. Busy in getting ready to go off on Monday.

June 11, 1826. Sunday. Getting ready. Feel better. Paid a last visit to V. President [Santander], [José Rafael] Ravenga [Revenga], [Colonel] Torrens, [Patrick] Campbell, [James] Henderson and [Félix de or José Manuel] Restrepo. [Carlos] Soublette, Mr. [Juan P.] Ayala and others came to see me.

June 12, 1826. Monday morng. 7 oC.

A prospect of a good day. The mules have come & this day I set off for Carthagena on my way to Panama[.] I rejoice at going. I am tired of the place, my health is bad—but there are some dreadful recollections at leaving this place forever.

May God protect me and my children, and all my friends & all others. May those who are in Heaven protect & intercede for me[.]

(one mile north of Facac[at]iva)

June 13, 1826. Yesterday I set out at 10 oC. having first visited the mother of Mrs. [Pedro] Gual, & sister, Mrs. Madrid, to receive their messages for Panamá, where I expect to see Mrs. G[ual.] All this family has been kind to us.

We had a fine [section of diary torn out] & fine roads.

Colo: [Beaufort T.] Watts came [section of diary torn out] with us & is still with us [illegible phrase] to Facacativa[.] Junca;* young Leland[256] also rode with us to Fontabon. We

---

256. See Appendix, List of Names, Augustus Leland, for an identification of young Leland's father.

were joined by [Charles] Sutherland* the British Consul for Maracybo who is going down to Carthagena[,] & by others. At "Quatro esquinas" Martin & his wife returning to Carthagena came up. Came to this house & stayed all night. [On the] 14th [Beaufort T.] Watts left us yesterday morng. & retd. to Bogota. We came on to this place half a league N. of Villete.²⁵⁷ Roads good, that is dry.

June 15, 1826. Yesterday we came here ("Guaduas") & arrived at 11 oC. Found my acquaintance Colonel Acosta* well and I believe glad to see us—that is Robert [Anderson], myself, & our travelling companion [Charles] Sutherland*— *who seems to have no kind of objection to take advantage of my acquaintance on the road.* I brought my riding horse & gave him to Acosta. This I did because it was pleasing to me to acknowledge his politeness & because I did not choose to sacrifice him by sale to the advantage of some Englishman, who would be the buyer in Bogotá.

Here we met Batis the capt. of the S. Boat. This morng. [Alejandro] Vélez* the Consul Genl. for the US. & his brother came up on their way *via* Antioquia to US—& also Martin & his wife.

June 16, 1826. Bodegas below Honda. Yesterday eveng.— We left Guaduas & came to Sargento—thence this morng. to Bodegas opposite, whence Sutherland, Robert [Anderson] & *Velez,* whom we again overtook here, passed over to Honda & engaged a boat to take us to Peñon where the S. Boat lies. They retd. at 2 o. & we came down here—where we have just dined in a hovel at the invitation of Lawless a brother of Colo: L[awless] of St. Louis.

Steam Boat at Peñon—17th[.]

We arrived here at 11 oC. The Passengers have all arrived & we shall set out tomorrow. I found on board the Boat Colo: [Brooke] Young* who came with us from the

257. Anderson's stopping points on his trip to Panama may be located on Map 4, p. 195.

US. in 1823. Also Martin & his wife, Grice an Englishman, Carnaval & [blank,] members of Congress are passengers.

June 19, 1826. Yesterday morng. we set out & had a fine run, with fine water until 4 oC. when he stuck on a bar, & are now there 11 oC. AM—about a league above St. Bartholomew's. It is extremely hot & the sand flies are troublesome.

No Musquetoes yet. The time is not unpleasant, if we can rid ourselves of the apprehension of sticking here too long. We have as a passenger a Swedish Gentleman who tells me that he intends on his return to Europe to publish something on this Country, particularly on Antioquia. His name is—too hard for me to write.[258] [Things that in the past have] distressed me have now comparatively little effect. The natural effects of great & real calamities seem to be to show the folly of regarding minor incidents & have an influence which strengthens the mind against the lesser vexations—but this experience is bought at a price costly & dreadful. May my worst enemy never feel it! May God guard me against any further purchase of an experience so dreadful.

The Thermometer hanging against the middle post of the Boat, sheltered by the awning, ranges in the middle hours of the day from 90 to 98°.

June 26, 1826. We are on another sand bar. Yesterday with the exception of one hour we were on one just below St. Pablo. The weather is excessively hot. Last night we suffered severely from heat and musquetoes. The mail passed yesterday & I wrote to [J. M.] MacPherson, [US Consul] at Carthagena. Sutherland & the Swede playing whist now (as they were yesterday Sunday) vs. Grice & Young for 4, 5, & 6 doubloons a rub[ber]. *The latter are cheating, as I heard their agreement.*

June 27, 1826. At 2 o Clock P. M. The Thermometer is (in its usual position) at 103° of Farenheit. It is to be ob-

---

258. A page of the diary is missing at this point.

served however that it is protected only from the Sun by an awning of sail cloth. We are again on a sand bar and the prospects of getting off are by no means, bright. Ascending the river, the doleful cry was "ˣfalta la lena," now it is "estamosˣ barrados."259

The game of whist still goes on and the cheating continues. It has not yet had its ordinary success. What is called "luck" has as yet overwhelmed it. The steward is now setting the table and the passengers are looking anxiously to see what will be put on it, as it is currently reported among them that the last piece of meat is gone and we seem to be equally distant from every place in the world. This moment a canoe has come along side with plantains. It has raised a laugh at the idea of raising *our bellies.*

Last night we had no musquetoes. I took a bath & slept better than I have done for many nights. My general health is better [than] while I was in Bogota.

The Swede's name is Gosselman.260 He is going to Jamaica & the US. to Sweden—& seems to be going only for observation & rational instruction. He is modest & *honest* enough to admit, that he is obliged to consult economy in his travels. This is an admission that very few travellers, whom I have met, ever make. The English rarely do. There are three of them now on board, two of them I know to be scarce of money and they talk as if frugality was a thing not necessary for them at all.

June 28, 1826. 11 oC. All hope of getting off pronounced as gone—unless the river should rise, of which there is no indication. Here we are basking in the broiling sun, for the thin awning gives but little protection, and with but little to eat. Most of the passengers have gone on shore for the purpose of shooting. Although in the proper temperature I

---

259. Anderson's footnotes (x) are explained by the diarist eight lines below. The first "x" reads "the wood is out;" the second reads "we are on a bar."

260. Carl A. Gosselmann, *Reise in Colombien in deu Jahren 1825 und 1826* (2 vols.; Stockholm, 1829-1831).

am a veteran sportsman with a gun, this propensity never comes over me in the tropics.

We are waiting, without making an effort of any kind, for a boat to come and kindly take us on our journey and as more than one will be required to take us all, it will probably be some time before all of us leave the boat.

Very hot—92° at Breakfast[.]

June 29, 1826. On the sand bar, with no immediate prospects of getting off. At 2 oC. the thermometer was at 105°.

This day we have lived entirely on the fruits of Denis's [Hite]* shooting. He killed six Guadiaracas (a bird something between a turkey & a pheasant) and a pigeon[.]

June 30, 1826. Last night there was a terrible storm of rain. All on the deck were drenched with rain. The passengers have a hope that this rain will cause the river to rise. It has as yet had no effect but to check its fall. Just as the steward had informed us that the last meat was on the table, a canoe arrived with a fat, black hog.

This day I expected certainly to have been at Carthagena & on this day I intended to date my letter resigning my situation as Minister to Colombia & commencing my duties as Commissioner to Panamá.

There seemed to be a fitness in it as it is the end of quarter in my diplomatic career and also in the financial year at the treasury.

July 1, 1826. This day Martin & his wife & Carnaval left us in some canoes, despairing of getting off. This renders the situation of the remaining passengers better, as our chance of getting off in *passing* boats is increased as our numbers are diminished— (Grice & the Priest & one other Creole left us yesterday)—and the number of mouths to eat our scant supply of provision is diminished by every emigration from the Steam Boat.

July 2, 1826. Sunday. This day there was killed among other birds, a Pato *real*—a very large duck, essentially what we call the Muscovy duck.

July 3, 1826. About 10 oC. We (that is Colo. Young,* [Charles] Sutherland, Robert [Anderson], myself & our servants) left the S[team] B[oat] & embarked on a Champan which came by, destined to Mompox. The river is rising & there is a prospect of the S. B. getting off the bar, but the opp[ortunit]y of putting ourselves out of suspense is too good to lose & place ourselves on the uncertainty of a rise in the Magadalena. This day we floated very slowly.

July 4, 1826. It being a bad night we made but little progress. This, the anniversary of American Independence, on which thousands of gallons of wine will be lavishly & almost wickedly drunk or spilt, on which the richest meats & delicacies of all kinds will be consumed in wasteful abundance, I was obliged to land at 8 oC. at the Indian Village of Regidor to purchase something for breakfast. Nothing could be gotten but 3 chickens, for which I paid ½ dol. each & 3 eggs for w'h I gave 12½ cts.

This Village is situated on a *bottom* of the greatest fertility, so wide that I could not see the mountains & more than fifty miles long—where the cacoa, coffee, oranges, cocoa nuts grow spontaneously, & where coffee, sugar, indian corn, rice, indigo, pine apple either may or do grow with the slightest cultivation. Of so little avail are the gifts of Providence without the exertion of man.

It is now exactly ten oC. & we have just breakfasted heartily—having coffee, chocolate & biscuit with our fowls. We eat off a trunk & hold the breakfast in the tight & secure grasp of our fingers, which it must be admitted, execute the office with more certainty than a knife & fork could do and I am the last person in the world who shd. complain, as what is called *hard living* is probably essential to my life. *This day my Country has existed one half Century.*

July 5, 1826. This day at 4 o. PM. we arrived at Mompox. Went to [R. K.] Travers a N. American Merchant settled here. Treated very hospitably. Staid all night—[and] saw U. S. papers to the 19. May. Learn that the Emperor of Russia [Nicholas] is not murdered[261]—that Mr. [Albert] Gallatin* is appd. Minister to England instead of Mr. [Rufus] King* [who is] sick.

July 6, 1826. We left Mompox—cheated by Lynch an Englishman in getting a boat.

July 7, 1826. Passed a miserable night on account of the Musquetoes.

July 8, 1826. We arrived at this place (Barancas) last night at 8 oC. P. M. We expect to get off tomorrow morning. Here we meet again Martin & Carnaval, who passed us at Mompox. We left Gosselman* the Swede at Mompox.

I hear that the Congress at Panama was installed the 13. of June—but [I have] no news in relation to the arrival of Mr. [John] Sergeant* or any other movement on the subject in the US.

July 11, 1826. Turbaco—4 leagues from Carthagena [at] 11 oClock.

As stated yesterday evening, I detd. to stay here today. This morning Colo: Young* went on, and I have sent on Denis [Hite] with the baggage to Carthagena. Robert [An derson] & myself are here. The nights at this place are pleasant—but the days are warm; to those who come from Carthagena this place presents a treat. Still I think it as hot here as in any of the Middle states of North America.

I have just retd. from a short walk. I saw piled up in the Church many human sculls & other bones. This is a spectacle not uncommon in the churches of the Catholic Countries where the dead are negligently buried & the bodies again disintered by accident & inattention. Many Segars

---

261. See above, June 3, 1826.

[*sic* for cigars] are made in this village & are said to be very good. I have been observing a woman who seems to be very dextrous in the manufacture & who manifests as much vanity at the attention, which her skill has excited, as if it was displayed in one of the most useful & dignified occupations. All the houses here are covered with a palm thatch common in the hot lands of the Country. Asses are more generally used for riding in this providence than in any other I have seen. *Generally* in Venezuela & the neighborhood of Bogota they are used as beasts of burthen.

Most of the negroes & coloured Criles [Creoles] ride the ass by crossing the legs on his weathers, having the *seat* of the rider placed on a flat pad or saddle of palm or straw—or more frequently the rider sits between two large panniers filled with marketting or between two kegs filled with water— then extending his legs forward & crossing them below the knees.

July 12, 1826. A few minutes after I made the last note above I was taken with a fever & head ache. I immediately took some calomel pills. I feel better to day but not quite relieved. I do not know when I have felt myself under greater difficulty than this morng.

Mr. [J. M.] Macpherson the Consul at Carthagena wrote to me advising me to remain here, as that place was very sickly. Yesterday I sent on Denis [Hite]* with the baggage to get farther [*sic* for further] information as to the health of the place & also news from the US. at 11 o. P. M. He retd. bringing the information that Mr. Berrien the nephew of the Consul [Macpherson] was dead, that the town was dreadfully sickly & the advice of Doctor Byrne that no one come to it who could avoid it.

Mr. M[acpherson] also advises, indeeds exclaims against the idea of going to Chagres [Panama] in the Mail Vessel as being too small and in every way disagreeable & degrading & advises me to remain here. The temperature is pleasant here & the house is agreeable but the owner wants me off & says she is going from home tomorrow.

My instructions require me to go on. Sickness & other like causes of course afford a justification for not going, but mere uncomfortableness of the Vessel does not[.] In a state of much difficulty & indeed of some distress of mind I have detd. to take passage in the Vessel of Saturday for Chagres if my health or some other cause does not forbid it. For the purpose of making the necessary arrangements & to acquire further information, I have sent Robert [Anderson] & Denis [Hite] to Carthagena this morng. To increase the vexation, I discover on opening the desk this moment that my letter to the Consul [Macpherson] desiring him to have every thing necessary done for me is forgotten & left by Robert. I am far from being well today. I fear the medicine has not relieved me.

[The diary ends with the above entry.]

J. M. Macpherson, United States Consul, Cartagena, Colombia, to Secretary of State Henry Clay, July 26, 1826.[262]

Sir:

I have the unpleasant task to announce to you, the death of the Honble R. C. Anderson, Minister Plenipotentiary to this Republic. This melancholy event took place at half past eleven oclock on the night of the 24th of this month.

Mr. Anderson reached Carthagena from Bogota on the 14th Ins^t then suffering with fever and ague, and extremely weak and reduced. The aid of medical advice, and comfortable lodgings after a long and painful journey had an immediate and happy effect, and for three days he was free from complaints, and in some measure recovered his appetite. The fever however returned but without the chills, and his disease assumed a character, that left little hopes of his recovery. Every moment he became weaker until nature was completely exhausted.

I have to report to you Sir, that every honor and mark of

262. Department of State, Despatches, Cartagena, I.

respect was paid to his memory. He was buried yesterday at five oclock in the evening with the Ceremony observed on such occasions to a Captain General, namely a Battallion of Infantry, with Detachments of Cavalry and Artillery with three field pieces[,] music etc etc. On reaching the place of internment, and when the body was committed to the ground, three volleys were fired by the Infantry and thirteen guns by the Artillery. On this melancholy occasion I walked as chief mourner, supported by the Intendant, the Commanders in Chief of the Army and of the Navy and his Britannic Majesty's Consul.

By the death of Mr. Anderson I have lost a Superior Officer from whom I had the happiness to receive constant proofs of friendship and confidence. A few days before his arrival, my nephew Mr. Berrien died of the yellow fever. He was a young man of excellent acquirements and moral character, and had filled my official place during my absence from Carthagena with great credit to himself.

A vessel arrived this day from New York with dispatches directed to Mr. Anderson, which shall be forwarded to Bogota on the 30th Inst. She likewise brought your letter to myself dated the 20th June for which I return you my thanks.

I am happy to say that young Mr. [Robert] Anderson and Captain Wharton continue well. The former has in charge his brothers papers and effects. They will both return to the United States by a vessel to sail in about ten days.

I send this letter in duplicate by way of Jamaica.

I have the honor to be
     Sir
        Your Obde Servant
            J. M. MACPHERSON
              Consul

APPENDIXES

APPENDIX I: GENERAL CONVENTION OF PEACE, AMITY, NAVIGATION, AND COMMERCE BETWEEN THE UNITED STATES OF AMERICA AND THE REPUBLIC OF COLOMBIA, OCTOBER 3, 1824*

In the name of God Author and Legislator of the Universe The United States of America and the Republic of Colombia desiring to make lasting and firm the friendship and good understanding, which happily prevails between both nations, have resolved to fix in a manner clear, distinct, and positive the rules which shall in future be religiously observed between the one and the other by means of a treaty or General Convention of peace, friendship, Commerce and Navigation; For this most desirable object the President of the United States of America has conferred full powers on Richard Clough Anderson junior a citizen of the said States and their Minister Plenipotentiary to the said Republic and the Vice President of the Republic of Colombia charged with the Executive power on Pedro Gual Secretary of State and of Foreign Relations, who after having exchanged their said full powers in due and proper form have agreed to the following Articles

ARTICLE FIRST. There shall be a perfect, firm, and inviolable peace and sincere friendship between the United States of America and the Republic of Colombia in all the extent of their possessions and territories and between their people and Citizens respectively without distinction of persons or places

ARTICLE SECOND. The United States of America and the Republic of Colombia desiring to live in peace and harmony with all the other nations of the Earth, by means of a policy

---

* Signed at Bogotá, October 3, 1824; ratified by the United States, March 7, 1825; ratified by Colombia, March 26, 1825; ratifications exchanged at Washington, May 27, 1825; proclaimed, May 31, 1825. Hunter Miller (ed.), *Treaties and Other International Acts of the United States of America* (Washington, 1933), III, 163-185.

frank and equally friendly with all, engage mutually not to grant any particular favour to other nations in respect to commerce and navigation, which shall not immediately become common to the other party, who shall enjoy the same freely, if the concession was freely made, or on allowing the same compensation, if the Concession was conditional

ARTICLE THIRD. The citizens of the United States may frequent all the coasts and Countries of the Republic of Colombia and reside and trade there, in all sorts of produce, manufactures, and merchandise and shall pay no other or greater duties, charges, or fees whatsoever, than the most favoured nation is or shall be obliged to pay; and they shall enjoy all the rights, privileges, and exemptions in navigation and Commerce which the most favoured nation does or shall enjoy, submitting themselves nevertheless to the laws, decrees, and usages there established and to which are submitted the subjects and citizens of the most favoured nations. In like manner the Citizens of the Republic of Colombia may frequent all the coasts and countries of the United States and reside and trade there, in all sorts of produce, manufactures, and merchandise, and shall pay no other greater duties, charges, or fees whatsoever, than the most favoured nation is, or shall be obliged to pay; and they shall enjoy all the rights, privileges, and exemptions in navigation and commerce, which the most favoured nation does or shall enjoy, submitting themselves nevertheless to the laws, decrees and usages there established, and to which are submitted the subjects and Citizens of the most favoured nations

ARTICLE FOURTH. It is likewise agreed that it shall be wholly free for all merchants, Commanders of Ships, and other Citizens of both Countries to manage themselves their own business in all the ports and places subject to the jurisdiction of each other, as well with respect to the consignment and sale of their goods and merchandise, by wholesale or retail, as with respect to the loading, unloading, and sending off their Ships, they being in all these cases to be treated as Citizens of the Country in which they reside, or at least to be placed on a footing with the subjects or Citizens of the most favoured nation.

ARTICLE FIFTH. The Citizens of neither of the Contracting parties shall be liable to any Embargo, nor be detained with their Vessels, cargoes, merchandizes or effects for any military expedition, nor for any public or private purpose whatever, without allowing to those interested a sufficient indemnification.

ARTICLE SIXTH. Whenever the Citizens of either of the Contracting parties shall be forced to seek refuge or asylum in the rivers, bays, ports or dominions of the other with their Vessels, whether merchant or of War, public or private, through stress of weather, pursuit of pirates or enemies, they shall be received and treated with humanity, giving to them all favour and protection for repairing their Ships, procuring provisions, and placing themselves in a situation to continue their voyage without obstacle or hindrance of any kind

ARTICLE SEVENTH. All the ships, merchandize, and effects belonging to the citizens of one of the contracting parties, which may be captured by pirates, whether within the limits of its jurisdiction or on the high seas, and may be carried or found in the rivers, roads, bays, ports, or dominions of the other, shall be delivered up to the owners, they proving in due and proper form their rights before the Competent tribunals; it being well understood that the claim should be made within the term of one year by the parties themselves, their attorneys, or agents of the respective governments

ARTICLE EIGHTH. When any vessel belonging to the Citizens of either of the contracting parties shall be wrecked, foundered, or shall suffer any damage on the coasts, or within the dominions of the other, there shall be given to them all assistance and protection, in the same manner, which is usual and customary with the Vessels of the Nation where the damage happens, permitting them to unload the said Vessel, if necessary, of its merchandizes and effects, without exacting for it any duty, impost or contribution whatever, until they may be exported

ARTICLE NINTH. The Citizens of each of the contracting parties shall have power to dispose of their personal goods within the jurisdiction of the other, by sale, donation, testament or otherwise, and their representatives being Citizens of the other party, shall succeed to their said personal goods, whether by testament or ab intestato, and they may take possession thereof, either by themselves or others acting for them, and dispose of the same at their will, paying such dues only as the inhabitants of the Country wherein the said goods are, shall be subject to pay in like cases: And if in the case of real estate, the said heirs would be prevented from entering into the possession of the inheritance on account of their character of Aliens, there shall be granted to them, the term of three years to dispose of the same, as they may think proper and to withdraw the proceeds without molestation and exempt from all rights of detraction on the part of the government of the respective States

ARTICLE TENTH. Both the Contracting parties promise and engage formally to give their special protection to the persons and property of the Citizens of each other of all occupations, who may be in the territories subject to the jurisdiction of the one or the other, transient or dwelling therein, leaving open and free to them the Tribunals of Justice for their Judicial recourse on the same terms, which are usual and customary with the natives or Citizens of the Country in which they may be; for which they may employ in defence of their rights, such advocates, solicitors, notaries, agents and factors as they may judge proper in all their trials at law; and such citizens or agents shall have free opportunity to be present at the decisions and sentences of the tribunals, in all cases which may concern them, and likewise at the taking of all examinations and evidence which may be exhibited in the said trials

ARTICLE ELEVENTH. It is likewise agreed that the most perfect and entire security of Conscience shall be enjoyed by the citizens of both the contracting parties in the countries subject to the jurisdiction of the one and the other, without their being liable to be disturbed or molested on account of their religious belief, so long as they respect the laws and established usages of the Country. Moreover the bodies of the Citizens of one of the contracting parties, who may die in the territories of the other, shall be buried in the usual burying grounds or in other decent and suitable places, and shall be protected from violation or disturbance

ARTICLE TWELFTH. It shall be lawful for the Citizens of the United States of America and of the Republic of Colombia to sail with their Ships with all manner of liberty and security, no distinction being made who are the proprietors of the merchandizes laden thereon, from any port to the places of those who now are or hereafter shall be at enmity with either of the Contracting parties. It shall likewise be lawful for the citizens aforesaid to sail with the ships and merchandizes beforementioned and to trade with the same liberty and security from the places, ports, and havens of those who are enemies of both or either party, without any opposition or disturbance whatsoever, not only directly from the places of the enemy before mentioned to neutral places, but also from one place belonging to an enemy to another place belonging to an enemy, whether they be under the jurisdiction of one power or under several. And it is hereby stipulated that free Ships shall also give freedom to goods, and that every thing shall be deemed to be free and exempt, which shall be found on board the Ships belonging to the Citizens of either of the Contracting parties, although the whole lading or any part thereof should appertain to the enemies of either, Contraband goods being always excepted. It is also agreed in like manner that the same liberty be extended to persons who are on board a free ship, with this effect that although they be enemies to both or either party, they are not to be taken out of that free Ship, unless they are officers or soldiers and in the actual service of the enemies; Provided however and it is hereby agreed that the stipulations in this Article contained declaring that the flag shall cover the property, shall be understood as applying to those powers only, who recognized this principle, but if either of the two contracting parties shall be at war with a third and the other neutral, the flag of the neutral shall cover the property of enemies, whose governments acknowledge this principle and not of others

ARTICLE THIRTEENTH. It is likewise agreed that in the case, where the neutral flag of one of the contracting parties shall protect the property of the enemies of the other, by virtue of the above stipulation, it shall always be understood that the neutral property found on board such enemies' Vessels, shall be held and considered as enemies' property, and as such shall be liable to detention and confiscation, except such property as was put on board such vessel before the declaration of war, or even afterward, if it were done without the knowledge of it, but the contracting parties agree, that two months having elapsed after the declaration, their Citizens shall not plead ignorance thereof. On the contrary, if the flag of the neutral does not protect the enemy's property, in that case the goods and merchandizes of the neutral embarked in such enemy's ships, shall be free

ARTICLE FOURTEENTH. This liberty of Navigation and Commerce shall extend to all kinds of merchandizes excepting those only which are distinguished by the name of Contraband and under this name of Contraband or prohibited goods shall be comprehended, first, Cannons, mortars, howitzers, swivels, blunderbusses, muskets, fusees, rifles, Carbines, pistols, pikes, swords, sabres, lances, spears, halberds, and grenades, bombs, powder, matches, balls, and all other things belonging to the use of these arms; Secondly, Bucklers, helmets, breast-plates, coats of Mail, infantry belts, and clothes made up in the form and for a military use; thirdly, Cavalry-belts, and horses with their furniture; fourthly, And generally all kinds of arms and instruments of iron, steel, brass, and copper or of any other materials, manufactured, prepared, and formed expressly to make war by sea or land

ARTICLE FIFTEENTH. All other merchandizes and things not comprehended in the articles of contraband explicitly enumerated and classified as above, shall be held and considered as free, and subjects of free and lawful commerce, so that they may be carried and transported in the freest manner by both the Contracting parties even to places belonging to an enemy, excepting only those places which are at that time besieged or blocked up; And to avoid all doubt in this particular it is declared that those places only are besieged or blockaded, which are actually attacked by a belligerent force capable of preventing the entry of the neutral

ARTICLE SIXTEENTH. The articles of Contraband before enumerated and classified which may be found in a Vessel bound for any enemy's port, shall be subject to detention and confiscation, leaving free the rest of the cargo and the ship, that the owners may dispose of them as they see proper. No vessel of either of the two nations shall be detained on the high seas on account of having on board, articles of Contraband whenever the Master, Captain or Supercargo of said Vessel will deliver up the Articles of Contraband to the Captor, unless the quantity of such Articles be so great and of so large a bulk, that they cannot be received on board the Capturing Ship without great inconvenience; but in this and in all other cases of just detention, the vessel detained shall be sent to the nearest convenient, and safe port for trial and judgment according to law

ARTICLE SEVENTEENTH. And whereas it frequently happens that Vessels sail for a port or place belonging to an enemy without knowing that the same is besieged, blockaded, or invested, it is agreed that every vessel so circumstanced may be turned away from such port or place, but shall not be detained, nor shall any part of her cargo, if not Contraband, be confiscated unless after warning of such blockade or investment from the commanding officer of the blockading forces, she shall again attempt to enter, but she shall be permitted to go to any other port or place she shall think proper. Nor shall any Vessel of either, that may have entered into such port before the same was actually besieged, blockaded, or invested by the other, be restrained from quitting such place with her cargo, nor if found therein after the reduction and surrender shall such vessel or her cargo be liable to Confiscation, but they shall be restored to the owners thereof

ARTICLE EIGHTEENTH. In order to prevent all kinds of disorder in the visiting and examination of the Ships and Cargoes of both the Contracting parties on the high seas, they have agreed mutually that whenever a Vessel of War, public or private, shall meet with a neutral of the other Contracting party, the first shall remain out of Cannon shot, and may send its boat with two or three men only in order to execute the said examination of the papers concerning the ownership and Cargo of the Vessel, without causing the least extortion, violence, or ill-treatment, for which the Commanders of the said armed ships shall be responsible with their persons and property; for which purpose the Commanders of said private armed Vessels shall before receiving their commissions, give sufficient security to answer for all the damages they may Commit. And it is expressly agreed that the neutral party shall in no case be required to go on board the examining Vessel for the purpose of exhibiting her papers or for any other purpose whatever

ARTICLE NINETEENTH. To avoid all Kind of Vexation and abuse in the examination of the papers relating to the ownership of the Vessels belonging to the Citizens of the two Contracting parties, they have agreed and do agree, that in case one of them should be engaged in War, the Ships and Vessels belonging to the Citizens of the other, must be furnished with sea-letters or passports expressing the name, property, and bulk of the Ship, as also the name and place of habitation of the

Master or Commander of said Vessel, in order that it may thereby appear that the Ship really and truly belongs to the Citizens of one of the parties; they have likewise agreed that such Ships being laden, besides the said sea-letters or passports, shall also be provided with certificates containing the several particulars of the Cargo and the place whence the ship sailed, so that it may be known whether any forbidden or Contraband goods be on board the same; which Certificates shall be made out by the officers of the place whence the Ship sailed in the accustomed form; without which requisites said Vessel may be detained to be adjudged by the Competent tribunal and may be declared legal prize, unless the said defect shall be satisfied or supplied by testimony entirely equivalent

ARTICLE TWENTIETH. It is further agreed that the stipulations above expressed relative to the visiting and examination of Vessels shall apply only to those which sail without Convoy, and when said Vessels shall be under Convoy, the verbal declaration of the Commander of the Convoy on his word of honor that the Vessels under his protection belong to the Nation whose flag he carries, and when they are bound to an enemy's port, that they have no Contraband goods on board, shall be sufficient

ARTICLE TWENTY FIRST. It is further agreed that in all cases the established Courts for prize Causes in the Country, to which the prizes may be conducted, shall alone take Cognizance of them. And whenever such tribunal of either party shall pronounce judgment against any Vessel or goods or property claimed by the Citizens of the other party, the sentence or decree shall mention the reasons or motives, on which the same shall have been founded and an authenticated copy of the sentence or decree and of all the proceedings in the case shall, if demanded, be delivered to the Commander or Agent of Said Vessel, without any delay, he paying the legal fees for the same

ARTICLE TWENTY SECOND. Whenever one of the Contracting parties shall be engaged in War with another State, no Citizen of the other Contracting party shall accept a commission or letter or Marque for the purpose of assisting or cooperating hostilely with the said enemy against the said party so at War under the pain of being treated as a pirate

ARTICLE TWENTY THIRD. If by any fatality, which cannot be expected and which God forbid, the two Contracting parties should be engaged in a War with each other, they have agreed and do agree, now for then, that there shall be allowed the term of Six months to the Merchants residing on the Coasts and in the ports of each other, and the term of one year to those who dwell in the Interior to arrange their business and transport their effects wherever they please, giving to them the safe conduct necessary for it, which may serve as a sufficient protection until they arrive at the designated port. The citizens of all other occupations, who may be established in the territories or dominions of the United States and of the Republic of Colombia, shall be respected and maintained in the full enjoyment of their personal liberty and property, unless their particular Conduct shall cause them to forfeit this protection, which in consideration of humanity, the contracting parties engage to give them

ARTICLE TWENTY FOURTH. Neither the debts due from individuals of the one nation to the individuals of the other, nor shares, nor moneys which they may have in public funds nor in public or private banks, shall ever in any event of War or of National difference be sequestered or confiscated

ARTICLE TWENTY FIFTH. Both the Contracting parties being desirous of avoiding all inequality in relation to their public communications and official intercourse have agreed and do agree to grant to the envoys, Ministers and other public Agents, the same favours, immunities and exemptions, which those of the most favoured nation do or shall enjoy; it being understood that whatever favours, immunities or privileges, the United States of America or the Republic of Colombia may find it proper to give to the Ministers and public Agents of any other power, shall by the same act be extended to those of each of the Contracting parties

ARTICLE TWENTY SIXTH. To make more effectual the protection, which the United States and the Republic of Colombia shall afford in future to the navigation and Commerce of the Citizens of each other, they agree to receive and admit Consuls and Vice Consuls in all the ports open to foreign Commerce, who shall enjoy in them all the rights, prerogatives, and immunities of the Consuls and Vice Consuls of the most favoured nation, each Contracting party however remaining at liberty to except those ports and places, in which the admission and residence of such Consuls may not seem convenient.

ARTICLE TWENTY SEVENTH. In order that the Consuls and Vice Consuls of the two Contracting parties may enjoy the rights, prerogatives, and immunities which belong to them by their public Character, they shall before entering on the exercise of their functions, exhibit their Commission or patent in due form to the Government, to which they are accredited, and having obtained their Exequatur, they shall be held and considered as such by all the Authorities, Magistrates and inhabitants in the Consular district in which they reside

ARTICLE TWENTY EIGHTH. It is likewise agreed that the Consuls, their secretaries, officers and persons attached to the service of Consuls, they not being Citizens of the Country in which the Consul resides, shall be exempt from all public Service and also from all kinds of taxes, imposts, and contributions, except those which they shall be obliged to pay on account of Commerce or their property, to which the Citizens and inhabitants native and foreign of the Country in which they reside are subject, being in every thing besides, subject to the laws of the respective states. The Archives and papers of the Consulates shall be respected inviolably, and under no pretext whatever shall any Magistrate seize or in any way interfere with them

ARTICLE TWENTY NINTH. The said Consuls shall have power to require the assistance of the Authorities of the Country, for the arrest, detention, and custody of deserters from the public and private Vessels of their Country, and for that purpose, they shall address themselves to the Courts, judges, and officers competent, and shall demand the said deserters in writing, proving by an exhibition of the Registers of the Vessels, or ships roll, or other public documents, that those men were part of the said Crews; and on this demand so proved, (saving however, where the contrary is proved) the delivery shall not be refused. Such deserters when arrested shall be put at the disposal of the said Consuls, and may be put in the public prisons at the request and expense of those who reclaim them, to be sent to the ships to which they belonged or to others of the same nation. But if they be not sent back within two months, to be counted from the day of their arrest, they shall be set at liberty, and shall be no more arrested for the same cause

ARTICLE THIRTIETH. For the purpose of more effectually protecting their Commerce and navigation, the two Contracting parties do hereby agree as soon hereafter as circumstances will permit them, to form a Consular Convention, which shall declare specially the powers and immunities of the Consuls and Vice Consuls of the respective parties

ARTICLE THIRTY FIRST. The United States of America and the Republic of Colombia desiring to make as durable as Circumstances will permit, the relations which are to be established between the two parties by virtue of this Treaty or general Convention of peace, amity, Commerce and Navigation, have declared solemnly and do agree to the following points; first. The present treaty shall remain in full force and virtue for the term of twelve years, to be counted from the day of the exchange of the ratifications, in all the parts relating to commerce and navigation; and in all those parts, which relate to peace and friendship, it shall be permanently and perpetually binding on both powers; secondly. If any one or more of the Citizens of either party shall infringe any of the articles of this treaty, such citizen shall be held personally responsible for the same, and the harmony and good correspondence between the two nations, shall not be interrupted thereby, each party engaging in no way to protect the offender or sanction such violation; thirdly. If, (what indeed cannot be expected) unfortunately any of the articles contained in the present treaty, shall be violated or infringed in any other way whatever, it is expressly stipulated that neither of the contracting parties will order or authorize any acts of reprisal nor declare war against the other, on complaints of injuries or damages, until the said party considering itself offended shall first have presented to the other a statement of such injuries or damages verified by competent proof, and demanded justice and satisfaction, and the same shall have been either refused or unreasonably delayed; fourthly. Nothing in this treaty contained shall however be construed or operate contrary to former and existing public treaties with other sovereigns or States. The present treaty of peace, Amity, Commerce and Navigation shall be approved and ratified by the President of the United States of America by and with the advice and consent of the Senate thereof, and by the President of the Republic of Colombia with the consent and approbation of the Congress of the same, and the ratifications shall be exchanged in the City of Washington within eight months to be counted from the date of the signature hereof, or sooner, if possible

In faith whereof We the plenipotentiaries of the United States of America and of the Republic of Colombia have signed and sealed these presents.

Done in the city of Bogota on the third day of October in the year of our Lord one thousand eight hundred and twenty-four; in the forty ninth year of the independence of the United States of America, and the fourteenth of that of the Republic of Colombia.

[SEAL.]   Richard Clough Anderson Jr

[SEAL.]   Pedro Gual.

APPENDIX II: LIST OF NAMES WITH IDEN-
TIFICATIONS

ABBOT, JOEL, 1776-1826. Born in Fairfield, Conn.; moved to Washington, Ga., 1794; U. S. Representative, 1817-1825.

ACOSTA, COLONEL [JOSÉ MARÍA]. William Duane (*A Visit to Colombia*, p. 576) described Acosta as a man "who is at once the military commandant, the civil magistrate, the owner of the land on which the town [Guaduas, Colombia] stands, and that adjacent, and who is, by all within his jurisdiction, considered as a father, benefactor, protector and friend."

ADAIR, JOHN, 1757-1840. Born in Chester County, S.C.; moved to Ky., 1788; state representative, 1793-1795, 1798, 1800-1803; U.S. Senator, 1805-1806; Governor, 1820-1824; U.S. Representative, 1831-1833.

ADAMS, JOHN, 1735-1826. Born in Braintree, Mass.; member of First Continental Congress, 1774-1778; signed Declaration of Independence; U.S. Minister to Holland, 1780, to England, 1785-1788; Vice President of U.S., 1789-1797; President, 1797-1801.

ADAMS, JOHN QUINCY, 1767-1848. Born in Braintree, Mass.; state senator, 1802; U.S. Senator, 1803-1808; Minister to Russia, 1809-1814, to England, 1815-1817; Secretary of State, 1817-1825; President, 1825-1829; U. S. Representative, 1831-1848.

ALCAZAR, BUENAVENTURA. Secretary to Dr. Pedro Gual.

ALLAN, CHILTON, 1786-1858. Born in Albemarle County, Va.; moved to Ky.; state representative, 1811, 1815, 1822, 1830, and state senator, 1823-1827; U.S. Representative, 1831-1837.

ALLEN, CHARLES. Candidate for Ky. legislature, 1817; state senator, 1823-1827.

ALLEN, HEMAN, 1779-1852. Born in Vt.; state representative, 1812-1817; U.S. Representative, 1817-1818; U.S. Marshal for district of Vt. in 1818 and in 1822; U.S. Minister to Chile, 1823-1827.

ANDERSON, ANN CLARK, 1790-1863. Anderson's sister; married John Logan, 1808.

ANDERSON, ANN (ANNITA NANCY), 1823-1843. Daughter of Anderson; taken to Colombia when she was five months old, 1823; married John T. Gray.

ANDERSON, ARTHUR. Anderson's son. Went to Colombia as a small child; did not long survive his father.

ANDERSON, BILLY. Husband of Anderson's Aunt Cecilia Anderson (1748-1802).

ANDERSON, CECILIA, 1792-1863. Anderson's sister; never married.

ANDERSON, CHARLES, 1772-1823. Anderson's cousin; or Charles Anderson (b. 1762), his uncle.

ANDERSON, ELIZABETH, 1794-1870. Sister of Richard C. Anderson, Jr.; married Isaac Gwathmey, 1818.

ANDERSON, ELIZABETH, 1811-1814. Daughter of Anderson. Not to be confused with the second Elizabeth.

ANDERSON, ELIZABETH C., 1815-1864. Second Elizabeth, daughter of Anderson; went with father to Colombia, 1823; returned to enter private school near Bardstown, Ky., 1825; lived with Gwathmey family after father's death; married three times: (1) Anderson Miller; (2) Stephen Johnston; (3) LaFayette Flournoy of Louisville.

ANDERSON, ELIZABETH CLARK, 1767-1795. Sister of George Rogers Clark; married Colonel Richard Clough Anderson, 1787; mother of Richard C. Anderson, Jr.

ANDERSON, ELIZABETH GWATHMEY (BETSY). Daughter of Owen and Ann Clark Gwathmey; married Richard C. Anderson, Jr., 1810; died in Bogotá, 1825.

ANDERSON, JOHN. A "relation." Anderson's Aunt Mary (b. 1759) married a John Anderson.

ANDERSON, LARZ, 1803-1878. Half-brother of Richard C.; attended Harvard University; went to Colombia during Richard's service as minister; bearer of the original of the Treaty of 1824 to Washington; married twice: (1) Cynthia Ann Pope, (2) Catherine Longworth.

ANDERSON, LOUIS. Anderson's son; died July 31, 1822.

ANDERSON, MARIA, 1798-1887. Anderson's half-sister; married Allen Latham of Chillicothe, Ohio.

ANDERSON, MARY LOUISA, 1809-1868. Anderson's half-sister; twice married, to Frederick Alexander and to James Hall.

ANDERSON, MATTHEW, 1743-1805. One of several brothers of Colonel Richard C. Anderson.

ANDERSON, COLONEL RICHARD CLOUGH, 1750-1826. Father of Richard Clough, Jr.; married (1) Elizabeth Clark, 1787, sister of George Rogers Clark; and (2) Sarah Marshall, 1797.

ANDERSON, ROBERT, 1805-1871. Half-brother of Richard C.; graduate of West Point, 1825; went with Richard to Colombia, late 1825; traveling with Richard toward Panama at time of the latter's death; served under General Winfield Scott during Mexican War; in command of Fort Sumter on outbreak of the Civil War; retired from Army, 1863; died in Nice, France.

ANDERSON, SARAH MARSHALL, 1779-1854. Married Colonel Richard C. Anderson, 1797.

ANDREWS, REVEREND ROBERT. Appointed as professor of moral and intellectual philosophy at William and Mary College, 1777; one of Anderson's teachers.

ANNITA. See Anderson, Ann (Annita Nancy).

APPLEGATE, AARON or BENJAMIN, 1780-1831. Listed in the 1800 Census Report as resident of Jefferson County, Ky.

ARCHER, WILLIAM S., 1789-1855. Graduate of William and Mary College, 1806; U.S. Representative from Va., 1820-1835; U.S. Senator, 1841-1847.

ARMSTRONG, JOHN, 1755-1843. Born Pa.; left Princeton University to join the army in the American Revolution; U.S. Senator, 1800-1802, 1803-1804; Minister to France, 1804-1810; Secretary of War, 1813; blamed by many for the capture of Washington, D.C., by the British; resigned on September 27, 1814.

ARRÚBLAS, JUAN MANUEL and MANUEL ANTONIO, well-to-do merchants, owned a home in the outskirts of Bogotá, where they entertained rather elaborately. See also MONTOYA.

ARTERBURN, SAMUEL. Resident of Jefferson County, Ky., where he lived with three sons and operated a farm; owned three slaves (1810 Census).

AVENDAÑO, COLONEL FRANCISCO, 1792-1870. Born in Cumaná, Venezuela; served with Bolívar in wars for independence; held various offices in Colombia, including that of Vice Governor of Cumaná; later Minister of War under President (General) Carlos Soublette.

AVERY, CARLTON, 1779-1837. Born in N. Y.; merchant and shipowner doing business in Mexico and Colombia.

AYALA, "OLD MR." There were several Ayalas: JUAN PABLO (Colonel and General of Brigade during wars of Independence; mentioned by Bolívar in 1826 as an honorable member of his Council of Government); RAMÓN (Colonel and Governor ad interim of Province of Santa Marta, 1820); JOSÉ MARÍA (Independence soldier from Popayán).

BALLARD, BLAND, 1761-1853. Came with father to Ky.; fought beside General George Rogers Clark in Ky. Indian wars; participated in War of 1812; represented Shelby County in the Ky. legislature.

BANKS, LINN, 1784-1842. Graduate of William and Mary College, 1806; U.S. Representative from Va., 1838-1841.

BARBER, LEVI, 1777-1833. Born in Simsbury, Conn.; moved to Ohio; U.S. Representative from Ohio, 1817-1819, 1821-1823.

BARBOUR, JAMES, 1775-1842. Born in Va.; Governor of Va., 1812-1814; U.S. Senator, 1815-1825; Secretary of War, 1825-1828; Minister to Great Britain, 1828-1829.

BARBOUR, PHILIP PENDLETON, 1783-1841. Born in Orange County, Va.; U.S. Representative, 1814-1825, 1827-1830; Associate Justice of the Supreme Court, 1836-1841.

BARBOUR, RICHARD. Jefferson County, Ky., farmer; owner of thirty slaves; elected to the Kentucky House of Representatives, 1818.

BARRIGA, CAPTAIN ISIDORO, 1803-1850. Born in Bogotá in 1803; fought in the famous battles of Carabobo (1821), Ayacucho (1824), and Junín (1824), the last two putting an end to Spanish power in South America; raised to rank of Lt. Colonel in 1824; later fought in Colombian-Peruvian War in 1828-1829; appointed Brigadier-General in 1830.

BARRY, WILLIAM TAYLOR, 1784-1835. Born in Va.; entered law practice in Lexington, Ky., 1805; officer in the War of 1812; Ky. state representative, 1807, 1814; U.S. Senator, 1814-1816; state senator, 1817-1821; Postmaster General, 1829-1835; Minister to Spain in 1835; died in Liverpool, England, en route to post.

BATES, JAMES. Louisville attorney; described as a "partisan of partisans, as a Jackson Democrat [he] canvassed for the legislature in 1836 barefoot."

BATES, JOHN. Elected from Clay County, Ky., to the state senate, 1817.

BAYARD, SAMUEL, 1767-1840. Born in Philadelphia; Clerk of U.S. Supreme Court in 1791; prosecuted American claims before British Admiralty Courts under Jay Treaty of 1794; practiced law in New York, 1803-1806; retired to Princeton, N.J., where he lived until death in 1840.

BEALL, NORBORNE B. Political figure in Ky.; born in Va., 1781; came to Ky., 1802; married daughter of William Boothe and settled near Shelbyville; owned a farm operated with twenty-nine slaves.

BEECHER, PHILEMON, 1775-1839. Born in Kent, Conn.; moved to Ohio to practice law; U.S. Representative from Ohio, 1817-1821, 1823-1829.

BERRIEN, WILLIAM. Nephew of Consul John MacPherson, Cartagena; acting consul in Cartagena, late 1825; died of yellow fever, July 1826.

BETSY. Anderson's wife. See Anderson, Elizabeth Gwathmey; and Anderson's sister, *see* Gwathmey, Elizabeth Anderson.

BIBB, GEORGE M., 1776-1859. Born in Va.; moved to Ky., 1798; state representative, 1806, 1810, and 1817; U.S. Senator from Ky., 1811-1814, 1829-1835; Secretary of the Treasury, 1844-1845.

BIBB, WILLIAM W., 1780-1820. Born in Va.; moved to Ga.; state representative, 1803-1805; U.S. Representative, 1807-1813; U.S. Senator, 1813-1816; moved to Ala.; first Governor, 1817-1820.

BLACKBURN, GEORGE. Assistant professor of mathematics, William and Mary College, 1805.

BLAKE, ELI, 1795-1886. Born near Worcester, Mass.; nephew of Eli Whitney; graduated from Yale, 1816; entered employ of uncle at Whitneyville, near New Haven; after Eli Whitney's death in 1825, Blake and his brothers carried on the business.

BLEDSOE, JESSE, 1776-1836. Born in Va.; moved to Ky.; Secretary of State (Ky.), 1808; state representative, 1812; U.S. Senator, 1813-1814 (resigned); state senator, 1817-1820; moved to Miss., 1833, and Texas, 1835.

BLOOMFIELD, JOSEPH, 1753-1823. Born in Woodbridge, N.J.; Major in Revolutionary Army; Governor of N.J., 1801-1812; Brigadier General, 1812-1815; U.S. Representative, 1817-1821.

BODLEY, GENERAL THOMAS. U.S. Army, 1794-1797; Major in Ky. Volunteers, 1813.

BOLÍVAR, SIMÓN, 1783-1830. "El Liberator" of northern South America; leader of forces seeking independence from Spain, 1810-1824; President of La Gran Colombia, 1821-1828; initiator of Panama Congress, 1826; dictator, 1828-1830; died December 17, 1830.

BOOTHE, ANN GWATHMEY. Anderson's sister-in-law; married William Boothe on February 20, 1806; died October 12, 1814. *See* Introduction.

BOOTHE, WILLIAM. Farmer; married Ann Gwathmey, Anderson's sister-in-law, in 1806.

BOYER, PHILIP. According to tax lists of 1800, a resident of Jefferson County, Ky.

BRACKEN, REVEREND JOHN. Appointed professor of humanity at William and Mary College, 1792; became president of the college, 1812.

BRECKINRIDGE, JAMES D. Born in Jefferson County, Ky.; state representative, 1809-1811; U.S. Representative from Ky., 1821-1823; died in Louisville, May, 1849.

BRECKINRIDGE, JOHN, 1760-1806. Born near Staunton, Va.; moved to Lexington, Ky., 1793; state representative, 1798-1800; U.S. Senator, 1801-1805; U.S. Attorney General, 1805-1806.

BRECKINRIDGE, JOSEPH CABELL, 1788-1823. Born in Va.; practiced law in Lexington, Ky.; state representative, 1816-1818; Secretary of State of Ky., 1820.

BRICEÑO MÉNDEZ, GENERAL PEDRO, 1794-1836. Nephew and personal secretary of Bolívar; Colombian Minister of War and Marine; Colombian delegate to Panama Congress, 1826; lived in a country house near Bogotá.

BRIÓN, ADMIRAL LUÍS, 1783-1821. Born in Curaçao; inherited fortune from father; sympathizer with Colombian independence struggle; spent large sums of money outfitting Colombian vessels; commissioned and served as Admiral in Colombian Navy.

BROOKS, JOHN, 1754-1840. Served in Revolutionary War and War of 1812; lived in Louisville until his death.

BROWN, JAMES, 1776-1835. Born near Staunton, Va.; settled in Frankfort, Ky.; secretary to Governor Isaac Shelby, 1792; moved to La.; U.S. Senator, 1813-1817, 1819-1823; U.S. Minister to France, 1823-1829.

BULLITT, COLONEL ALEXANDER SCOTT, 1762-1816. Settled in Ky.

in 1783; married Mary Churchill; co-drafter of the first constitution of Ky.; first Lt. Governor of the state; Speaker of the Ky. House of Representatives.

BULLITT, CUTHBERT, 1788-1854. Born in Jefferson County, Ky.; son of Alexander Scott Bullitt; lawyer, farmer, legislator.

BULLITT, DIANA MOORE GWATHMEY. Anderson's sister-in-law; married Thomas Bullitt, 1803.

BULLITT, ELOISE, 1810-1858. Daughter of Thomas and Diana Moore Gwathmey Bullitt; attended private school near Bardstown, Ky., in 1825 with Anderson's daughter, Elizabeth; married Frederick de Kantzow in Sweden, March 9, 1840.

BULLITT, FERDINAND. Son of Thomas and Diana Moore Gwathmey Bullitt; went to Colombia as private secretary to Anderson; died there February 18, 1824.

BULLITT, MARY A. Daughter of Thomas and Diana Moore Gwathmey Bullitt.

BULLITT, MARY CHURCHILL, 1777-1817. Daughter of Armstead and Eliza Blackwell Churchill; married Colonel Alexander Scott Bullitt.

BULLITT, THOMAS, 1777-1823. Son of Cuthbert and Mary Burbridge Bullitt; married Diana Moore Gwathmey; father of Ferdinand and Eloise Bullitt.

BULLITT, WILLIAM CHRISTIAN, 1793-1877. Born at Oxmoor Farm, Louisville; son of Alexander Scott Bullitt; farmer and lawyer; candidate for state legislature, 1817; member of state constitutional convention, 1849-1850.

BUNCH, WILLIAM. Head of Messrs. Bunch, Brush, and Company, operating in Cartagena and Bogotá; handled, among other things, some of the claims of American citizens against Colombia for alleged privateering activities against U.S. shipping during the wars of independence.

BURRELL, DOCTOR JONATHAN, 1781-1850. Physician in Louisville, Ky.

BURWELL, WILLIAM A., 1780-1821. Born in Boydton, Va.; graduate of William and Mary College; private secretary to President Jefferson; U.S. Representative from Va., 1806-1821.

BYNG, MR. Agent for Admiral Pedro Luís Brión; dined with Anderson on several occasions.

CABELL, MRS. SAMUEL J. Wife of Samuel J. Cabell, 1756-1818, who served as Lt. Colonel in American Revolution and U.S. Representative from Va., 1795-1803.

CADE, JOHN. Secretary to John Potts Hamilton, British Commissioner in Bogotá during Anderson's tenure.

CALHOUN, JOHN CALDWELL, 1782-1850. Born in S.C.; state representative, 1808-1809; U.S. Representative from S.C., 1811-1817; Secretary of War, 1817-1825; Vice President of United States, 1825-1832 (resigned); U.S. Senator, 1832-1843; Secretary of State, 1844-1845; again U.S. Senator, 1845-1850.

CAMP, CAPTAIN SAMUEL. Served in the Revolutionary War; later real estate dealer and tobacco dealer in Louisville.

CAMPBELL, A. L. Owner of 40-50 acres of land west and north of Green Street, Louisville, in 1812.

CAMPBELL, JOHN W., 1782-1833. Born in Augusta County, Va.; practiced law in West Union, Ohio; state representative, 1810, 1813, 1815; U.S. Representative from Ohio, 1817-1827.

CAMPBELL, COLONEL PATRICK. One of the British commissioners sent to Colombia in 1823 to establish Anglo-Colombian commercial accord and conclude a treaty of commerce and navigation; remained after 1825 as Chargé d'Affaires. See Henderson, James; and Hamilton, John Potts.

CANNING, GEORGE, 1770-1827. British statesman; Prime Minister, 1822-1827.

CARNEAL, THOMAS, 1784-1832. Louisville attorney; served in Ky. Senate, 1821.

CASTILLO Y RADA, JOSÉ MARÍA DEL, 1776-1835. Colombian statesman and friend of Simón Bolívar; active in politics before 1820; involved in the struggle against Spain; Secretary of Treasury, 1821; later Minister of Hacienda; ran for Vice President of Gran Colombia in 1826; deputy from Cartagena at the Congress of Ocaña in 1828.

CATLETT, JOHN. Member of Ky. legislature, 1817.

CHAMBERS, BEN. One of three sons of Josiah Chambers (d. 1819); lived in Jefferson County, Ky.

CHAMBERS, JOHN, 1780-1852. Born in N.J.; moved to Ky., 1794; state representative, 1812, 1815, 1830, 1831; U.S. Representative, 1828-1829, 1835-1839; Governor of the Territory of Iowa, 1841-1846.

CHAPLINE, ABRAHAM. Member of Ky. Senate, 1816.

CHAYTOR, (COMMODORE) JAMES. Virginia; engaged in privateering operations from 1817 to the early 1820's against Spanish and other shipping; officer in the Buenos Ayres Navy; settled in Colombia after leaving the U.S. with charges of piracy pending.

CHEVES, LANGDON, 1776-1857. Born in S.C.; state representative, 1802-1810; U.S. Representative, 1810-1815; declined appointment to U.S. Senate on death of John. C. Calhoun, 1850.

CHEYNE, DOCTOR R. N. Young Scottish physician who arrived in Bogotá, 1824; became, according to contemporary accounts, a favorite of the more important families.

CHURCHILL, ARMSTEAD. Born on December 16, 1772; son of Armstead (1741-1831) and Elizabeth Blackwell Churchill. His sister, Mary (1777-1817), was wife of Colonel Alexander Scott Bullitt (1761-1816).

CHURCHILL, HENRY. Born December 10, 1768; son of Armstead and Elizabeth Blackwell Churchill; elected to the Ky. legislature, 1815.

CHURCHILL, SAMUEL. Member of Ky. Senate, representing Jefferson and Bullitt counties, 1815-1816.

CLAIBORNE, THOMAS, 1780-1856. Born in Brunswick County, Va.; moved to Tenn.; U.S. Representative from Tenn., 1817-1819.

CLARK, EDMUND M., 1762-1815. Brother of George Rogers Clark; Ensign in the Continental Line during the Revolutionary War.

CLARK, GENERAL GEORGE ROGERS, 1752-1818. Early western hero; Indian fighter; during the Revolutionary War, established headquarters in Louisville; during period covered by Anderson's diary, lived on Beargrass Creek, southeast of Louisville, with his sister, Lucy Clark, and her husband, Major William Croghan.

CLARK, JAMES, 1770-1839. Born in Bedford County, Va.; moved to Clark County, Ky., 1794; state representative, 1807 and 1808; judge of court of appeals, 1810; U.S. Representative, 1813-1816; judge of circuit court, 1817-1824; U.S. Representative, 1825-1831; Governor of Ky., 1836-1839.

CLARK, JOHN, 1726-1799. Anderson's grandfather; married Ann Rogers, 1749; father of George Rogers Clark.

CLARK, COLONEL JONATHAN, 1750-1811. Brother of George Rogers Clark; Lt. Colonel in the 8th Virginia Continental Line during the American Revolution; Anderson's uncle.

CLARK, GENERAL WILLIAM, 1770-1838. Brother of General George

Rogers Clark; Anderson's uncle; leader of the Lewis and Clark Expedition; Superintendent of Indian Affairs, St. Louis, 1807; Governor of Mo. Territory, 1813-1821; unsuccessful candidate for governorship of the new state of Mo., 1821.

CLARKE, NICHOLAS. Helped to finance bridge over Beargrass Creek, 1816-1819.

CLAY, HENRY, 1777-1852. Born in Hanover County, Va.; moved to Lexington, Ky.; state representative, 1803; U.S. Senator, 1806-1807; state representative, 1808-1809; U.S. Senator, 1810-1811; U.S. Representative, 1811-1814, 1815-1821, 1823-1825; Secretary of State, 1825-1829; U.S. Senator, 1831-1842; unsuccessful candidate for the presidency in 1824, 1832, and 1844; U.S. Senator, 1849-1852.

CLEMENTE, GENERAL LINO DE, 1767-1834. Venezuelan; Captain in Navy, 1811; General in Army; Bolívar's special envoy to U.S., 1818; Deputy to Congress of Angostura, 1819; Commandant of Cartagena, 1825.

CLINTON, DE WITT, 1769-1828. Born in Orange County, N.Y.; state senator, 1798-1800, 1806-1811; U.S. Senator, 1802-1803; Mayor of New York City, 1803-1807, 1810, 1811, 1813, 1814; Governor of N.Y., 1817-1821, 1825-1828.

CLINTON, GEORGE, 1739-1812. Born in Ulster County, N.Y.; member of Continental Congress, 1775-1777; Governor of N.Y., 1777-1795, 1801-1804; Vice President of U.S., 1805-1812.

CLIRTLY. Probably Captain Walter D. Chitty. Englishman who distinguished himself in Venezuelan naval service; mentioned in early U.S. diplomatic and consular reports.

COBB, THOMAS W., 1784-1830. Born in Columbia County, Ga.; U.S. Representative from Ga., 1817-1821, 1823-1824; U.S. Senator, 1824-1828.

COLEMAN, E. SPILLSBEE. Settled in South Frankfort, Ky., in 1806; established a tanning business.

COLES, EDWARD, 1786-1868. Born in Albemarle County, Va.; attended William and Mary College; private secretary to President James Madison, 1809-1815; moved to Ill., 1819; Governor of Ill., 1822-1824; defeated for U.S. Senate, 1824.

COLSTON, EDWARD, 1786-1852. Born in Berkeley County, Va.; state representative, 1812-1814, 1816, 1817, 1823-1826, 1833; U.S. Representative from Va., 1817-1819.

COOPER, HUGH. Born 1792; taken to Ky., 1794; served in War of 1812; became a farmer, shoemaker, potter, in Maysville.

CORNWALLIS, LORD, 1738-1805. Educated at Cambridge; Member of Parliament, 1760; British General during Revolutionary War; surrendered at Yorktown, 1781; Governor of India.

COSBY, JUDGE FORTUNATUS, 1766-1847. Born in Ga.; graduate of William and Mary College; moved to Ky. and admitted to the bar, 1797; large realty owner in Louisville, Ky.

CRAWFORD, WILLIAM HARRIS, 1772-1834. Born in Va.; moved with father to Ga., 1783; state representative, 1803-1807; U.S. Senator, 1807-1813; U.S. Minister to France, 1813-1815; Secretary of War, 1815-1816; Secretary of the Treasury, 1816-1825; defeated as the Democratic candidate for President in 1824.

CRESAP, THOMAS. Western explorer, Indian fighter, surveyor; sent by the Ohio Company to open a road westward from Will's Creek (now Cumberland, Md.), 1750; engaged in Indian wars at the Forks of the Ohio, 1774; later accused of responsibility for killing Logan, a friendly Indian chief of the Mingo tribe.

CRITTENDEN, JOHN JORDAN, 1787-1863. Born in Woodford County, Ky.; graduated from William and Mary College, 1806; aide-de-camp to Governor Isaac Shelby during War of 1812; state representative, 1811-1817; U.S. Senator, 1817-1819; state representative, 1825, 1829-1832; U.S. Senator, 1835-1841; U.S. Attorney General, 1841; U.S. Senate, 1842-1848; Governor of Ky., 1848-1850; U.S. Attorney General, 1850-1853; U.S. Senator, 1855-1861; U.S. Representative, 1861-1863.

CRITTENDEN, THOMAS T. Member, Ky. House of Representatives, 1818, from Fayette County.

CROGHAN, CHARLES. Born June 19, 1802, the son of William Croghan and Lucy Clark Croghan; brother of George Croghan; cousin of Richard C. Anderson.

CROGHAN, COLONEL GEORGE, 1791-1849. Son of William Croghan; graduated from William and Mary, 1810; aide-de-camp to William Henry Harrison during War of 1812; Captain in the regular army; commanded Fort Stephenson in northern Ohio in 1813 and defended that post on August 13 against an overwhelming force of British and Indian soldiers; promoted to Lt. Colonel; served under General Zachary Taylor in the Mexican War; died of cholera in New Orleans, 1849.

CROGHAN, JOHN. Cousin of Anderson; graduate of William and Mary, 1809; brother of George Croghan.

CROGHAN, LUCY CLARK, 1765-1838. Referred to in the diary as "Aunt" Croghan; sister of Anderson's mother, Elizabeth; married William Croghan.

CROGHAN, MAJOR WILLIAM. Emigrated from Ireland to Va., then Ky.; married sister of George Rogers Clark; soldier in the Revolutionary War; son, George (see above), was hero of Sandusky in the War of 1812; brother-in-law of Colonel Anderson and Richard Clough's uncle; died, September, 1822.

DABNEY, ISAAC. Neighbor and probably distant relative of Anderson. His uncles, Matthew, Robert, and Samuel Anderson, married Dabneys.

DABNEY, WILLIAM, 1771-1813. Distant relative of the Anderson family; married Sarah Watson of Louisa County, Va.

DALLAS, ALEXANDER J., 1759-1817. Born in Jamaica; settled in Philadelphia; became naturalized American citizen; Secretary of the Treasury, 1814-1816.

DANIELS (DANELLS), COMMODORE JOHN DANIEL, 1786-1856. Born in Baltimore; served as Captain of Armada under José Artigas in Rio de la Plata area; joined squadron of Admiral Brión, 1818; operated off La Guayra and Puerto Cabello; dispatched to U.S. (1822) to purchase vessel, which he presented as a gift to the Patriots; later given pension by Venezuela; died in Baltimore.

DAVIDSON, WILLIAM, 1778-1857. Born in Charleston, S.C.; moved to N.C.; state senator, 1813, 1815-1819, 1825; U.S. Representative from N.C., 1818-1821; state senator, 1827-1830.

DEARBORN, HENRY ALEXANDER SCAMMELL, 1783-1851. Born in Exeter, N.H.; graduate of William and Mary College, 1803; collector of customs, Boston, 1812-1829; Brigadier General in War of 1812; state representative, 1829, senator, 1830; U.S. Representative, 1831-1833; Adjutant General, Mass., 1834-1843; Mayor of Roxbury, 1847-1851.

DECATUR, STEPHEN, 1779-1820. Son of Stephen Decatur of Revolutionary War fame; reputation for being impulsive and hotheaded; involved in various duels; naval officer in command of U.S. fleet in the Mediterranean area, 1803; earned fame in the Tripolitan War; served in the War of 1812; led American naval forces against the Dey of Algiers, who was plundering American shipping; served on the Board of Navy Commissioners, 1815-1820.

DENNY, JAMES. Defeated for Ky. legislature, 1818; chosen trustee of City of Louisville, 1822.

DESHA, JOSEPH, 1768-1842. Born in Monroe County, Pa.; moved with parents to Ky., 1779; served in Indian wars under Anthony Wayne and William Henry Harrison; Ky. state representative, 1797, 1799-1802; state senator, 1803-1807; U.S. Representative, 1807-1819; Governor, 1824-1828.

DESMENARD, COLONEL. Probably Colonel Juan Bautista d'Esmenard. Frenchman; agent for the House of Powle, Herring & Company in Bogotá.

DORSEY, LEAVEN. Born on May 25, 1775; landowner in Jefferson County.

DOUGHERTY, THOMAS. Clerk of U.S. House of Representatives during the fifteenth session, December, 1817–March, 1819.

DOUGLAS, JAMES. Sent by Governor Dunmore of Va. to establish settlements in Ky. to prevent Indian depredations; died in 1774 (?) making survey along the Ky. River.

DRAKE, JOHN R., 1782-1857. Born in Pleasant Valley, N.Y.; U.S. Representative from N.Y., 1817-1819; state representative, 1834; "president" of Oswego Village, 1841-1845.

DUNMORE, LORD JOHN MURRAY, 1732-1809. Fourth Earl of Dunmore; colonial administrator in America.

DUPEY, BERRYMAN P. Member of the Kentucky House of Representatives, 1817.

DUVAL, WILLIAM P., 1784-1854. Born in Mount Comfort, Va.; moved to Ky.; U.S. Representative from Ky., 1813-1815; Governor of the Territory of Fla., 1822-1834; moved to Texas, 1848.

EATON, JOHN HENRY, 1790-1856. Born in Halifax County, N.C.; moved to Franklin, Tenn.; state representative, 1815-1816; U.S. Senator from Tenn., 1818-1829; Secretary of War, 1829-1831; Governor of the Territory of Fla., 1834-1836; Minister to Spain, 1836-1840.

EBEN, BARON FRIEDRICK VON. Hanoverian; served in British Army prior to 1820; commissioned brigadier-general by Venezuelan government, 1820.

EDWARDS, WELDON NATHANIEL, 1788-1873. Born in Gaston, N.C.;

state representative, 1814, 1815; U.S. Representative from N.C., 1816-1827; state senator, 1833-1844; president of N.C. secession convention, 1861.

ELBERS, JOHANN BERNARD. German merchant of Bogotá; held contract to supply vessels to Colombian Navy during the wars of independence; later granted monopoly of steamboat navigation on Magdalena River; imported three boats from Pittsburgh, but drafts proved too heavy for river.

ENGLISH, COLONEL JAMES T. Took part in the fighting for independence in northern South America; raised a corps in England to fight for Venezuelan cause; landed in 1819 with 2,000 troops, with rank of Colonel for himself; died of fever before the end of the year; a contemporary wrote of English: "As an officer he was destitute of energy, and experience; as a man he was generous and open hearted. All that can be said of him in reference to his conduct as commander of the British legion is, that he mistook his profession, for which indeed he was physically unfitted."

ENGLISH, MRS. JAMES T. Widow of Colonel English; her home (1823) was center of Anglo-Colombian society in Bogotá.

FERGUSON, JAMES. Trustee of the City of Louisville, 1819, 1820.

FERGUSON, DR. RICHARD. Born in Londonderry, Ireland; came to Ky., 1803, via Va.; died 1853. His son, Dr. Richard W. Ferguson, graduated from Transylvania medical school in 1830 and practiced medicine with his father until the latter's death.

FITZHUGH, DENIS. Louisville lawyer, judge, and farmer; third husband of Francis Eleanor Clark, sister of Anderson's mother, Elizabeth Clark; died in 1822.

FLEMING, WILLIAM. Member of Ky. senate, 1817.

FLOYD, GEORGE R. C., 1778-1828. Listed in the 1800 Census as a resident of Franklin County, Ky.

FLOYD, COLONEL JOHN. Delegate to the first "legislative assembly" in Ky., May, 1775; one of the first members of the Ky. "County" court; helped to mark the Wilderness Road in Ky.; killed in 1781, while riding to his home on Beargrass Creek, near Louisville.

FORNEY, DANIEL M., 1784-1847. Born in Lincoln County, N.C.; Major in the War of 1812; U.S. Representative from N.C.,

1815-1818; Commissioner to deal with the Creek Indians, 1820; state senate, 1823-1826; moved to Ala., 1834.

FORSYTH, JOHN, 1780-1841. Born in Fredericksburg, Va.; moved to Augusta, Ga.; Attorney General of Ga., 1808; U.S. Representative, 1813-1818, 1823-1827; U.S. Senator, 1818-1819, 1829-1834; U.S. Minister to Spain, 1819-1823; Governor of Ga., 1827-1829; U.S. Secretary of State, 1834-1841.

FORSYTHE, DR. SAMUEL DOUGLAS. Virginian; lived in Cúcuta and Angostura, Colombia, and Caracas, Venezuela; after 1810 carried on commission business and other enterprises; granted pension by the Venezuelan government, 1830.

FOWLER, JOHN, 1755-1840. Born in Va.; Captain in the Revolutionary War; moved to Lexington, Ky.; U.S. Representative from Ky., 1797-1807; postmaster of Lexington, 1814-1822.

FOX, CHARLES JAMES, 1749-1806. British statesman; educated at Eton, Oxford; member of House of Commons.

FUDGER, HARRIS E. U.S. Consul in Santa Marta, Colombia, 1824-1826; murdered in that city, July 13, 1826.

FUNK, JOHN. Migrated, with brothers Peter and Joseph, from Md. to Ky.; one of the first trustees of Middletown, Ky.; owner of a mill in that city.

FUNK, PETER. Born in Boonesboro, Md., August 14, 1782; migrated to Ky., where he married Harriet Hite and settled in Middletown.

GAILLARD, JOHN, 1765-1826. Born in St. Stephen's District, S.C.; state senator, 1804; U.S. Senator from S.C., 1804-1826.

GAINES, JOHN POLLARD, 1795-1857. Born in Augusta, Va.; moved to Boone County, Ky., at early age; veteran of War of 1812; represented Boone County in state legislature; Major in Mexican War; U.S. Representative from Ky., 1847-1849; Governor of Oregon Territory, 1850-1853.

GALINDO, LEÓN. Englishman born of Spanish parents; Colonel in charge of the Bogotá battalion, 1823-1826.

GALLATIN, ALBERT, 1761-1849. Born in Geneva, Switzerland; moved to Boston, then to Pa.; state representative, 1790-1792; U.S. Representative, 1795-1801; U.S. Secretary of Treasury, 1802-1814; Minister to France, 1815-1823, to England, 1826-1827.

GARARD, CASSIUS. Father of Sophia Garard, who married Anderson's brother-in-law, George Gwathmey, 1814.

GARARD, SOPHIA. Married George Gwathmey (1814), Richard Anderson's brother-in-law.

GEORGE IV OF ENGLAND, 1762-1830. Ruled, 1820-1830.

GEORGE, CAPTAIN EDWARD. Defeated by Anderson in congressional election, 1816; elected to Ky. legislature from Franklin County, 1822.

GERARDIN, L. H. Appointed Professor of Modern Languages at William and Mary College, 1803.

GOSSELMANN, CARLOS AUGUSTUS, 1801-1843. Swedish traveler and author. See Select Bibliography.

GRAY, JAMES. Resident of Jefferson County, Ky., 1810.

GRAYSON, FREDERICK W. S. Ran for Ky. legislature, 1815; appointed to New Court of Appeals, 1827; refused reappointment.

GUAL, DR. PEDRO, 1783-1862. Born in Caracas, Venezuela; served Venezuela and New Granada in various civilian and diplomatic posts, 1810-1820; Governor of Cartagena; deputy to the Constituent Congress of 1821; Minister of Foreign Affairs; negotiator of Treaty with the U.S., 1824; envoy to the Panama Congress in 1826.

GWATHMEY, ANN CLARK (MRS. OWEN) 1755-1822. Anderson's mother-in-law.

GWATHMEY, ANN. Anderson's sister-in-law; married William Boothe, 1806; died in 1814.

GWATHMEY, ANN MARKS. Married Temple Gwathmey, 1803, Anderson's brother-in-law.

GWATHMEY, BROOKE. Son of Temple and Ann Marks Gwathmey.

GWATHMEY, CATHERINE (KITTY). Anderson's sister-in-law; married George Woolfolk, 1817.

GWATHMEY, DIANA MOORE, 1792-1853. Anderson's sister-in-law; married Thomas Bullitt, 1803.

GWATHMEY, ELIZABETH ANDERSON, 1794-1870. Anderson's sister; married Isaac Gwathmey, 1818.

GWATHMEY, ELIZABETH C. See Anderson, Elizabeth Gwathmey (Anderson's wife).

GWATHMEY, FRANCES (FANNY). Anderson's sister-in-law; married Paul Skidmore, 1815; then Hezekiah Jones, 1819.

GWATHMEY, GEORGE C. Anderson's brother-in-law; married Sophia Garard, 1814.

GWATHMEY, ISAAC R. Son of Ann Clark and Owen Gwathmey; married Elizabeth Anderson, sister of Richard Clough, Jr., 1818.

GWATHMEY, JOHN. Oldest son of Owen and Ann Gwathmey; Richard C. Anderson's brother-in-law; married Ann Booth; died in New Orleans, November, 1824.

GWATHMEY, LUCY. Anderson's sister-in-law; married Peter Priest.

GWATHMEY, MARY BOOTHE, 1788-1865. Married Samuel Gwathmey, 1807.

GWATHMEY, OWEN, 1735-1830. Anderson's father-in-law; married Ann Clark, 1773.

GWATHMEY, SAMUEL. Anderson's brother-in-law; married Mary Boothe, 1807.

GWATHMEY, SOPHIA GARARD. Married George C. Gwathmey, 1814, Richard C. Anderson's brother-in-law.

GWATHMEY, SYDNEY. A brother of Owen Gwathmey.

GWATHMEY, TEMPLE. A son of Owen and Ann Gwathmey; Anderson's brother-in-law; married Ann Marks, 1803.

HALL, JUDGE JAMES. Second husband of Mary Louisa Anderson.

HALL, WILLARD, 1780-1875. Born in Westford, Mass.; moved to Del.; secretary of state of Del., 1811-1814; U.S. Representative, 1817-1821; state senator, 1822; U.S. district court judge for Del., 1823-1871.

HAMILTON, COLONEL JOHN POTTS. One of the British commissioners to Colombia, 1823-1825, with instructions to establish close Anglo-Colombian commercial relations, but avoid commitment on recognition of new nation; author: *Travels Through the Interior Provinces of Columbia*, 2 vols., London, 1827. (See Campbell, Col. Patrick; and Henderson, James.)

HARBOLT, LEONARD, 1749-1829. Lived in Louisville, Ky., with a family of ten children; owned four slaves according to 1810 Census.

HARDIN, BENJAMIN, 1784-1852. Born in Westmoreland County, Pa.; practiced law in Ky.; state representative, 1810, 1811, 1824, and 1825; state senator, 1828-1832; U.S. Representative from Ky., 1815-1817, 1819-1823, 1833-1837; secretary of state of Ky., 1844-1847.

HARDIN, MARTIN D., 1780-1823. Born in Pa.; moved to Ky. when six years old; Ky. secretary of state, 1812-1816; state representative, 1812, 1818, 1819; U.S. Senator, 1816-1817.

HARDIN, THOMAS. One of three sons of Martin D. Hardin.

HARRISON, WILLIAM HENRY, 1773-1841. Born in Berkeley, Va.; Captain in U.S. Army during Indian wars of 1790's; Territorial Governor of Ind., 1801-1813; victor over Indians in Battle of Tippecanoe, 1811; Major General during War of 1812; U.S. Representative from Ohio, 1816-1819; U.S. Senator, 1825-1828; Minister to Colombia, 1828-1829; President of the United States, March 4–April 4, 1841.

HAWKINS, JOSEPH H. Born in Lexington, Ky.; state representative, 1810-1813; U.S. Representative, 1814-1815; moved to New Orleans, 1819; died, 1823.

HENDERSON, JAMES. One of the British Commissioners sent to Colombia, 1823, to establish Anglo-Colombian relations and draw up a treaty of navigation and commerce; later consul-general at Bogotá. (See Campbell, Col. Patrick; and Hamilton, John Potts.)

HILL, BROOKE. Owner of *Lexington Reporter* during the early 1820's; sold paper, 1824.

HINKLE, JACOB. Lived with his wife, seven children, and two slaves in the Louisville district, 1815.

HINLEY, JAMES, 1781-1833. Louisville resident.

HITE, DENIS. Sixteen-year-old Negro slave taken by Anderson to Colombia, 1823.

HITE, ELIZABETH SNEED, 1795-1831. Wife of Jacob Hite.

HITE, GEORGE. Member of one of first families to settle in Jefferson County, Ky. See also Hite, Isaac; Hite, Jacob.

HITE, ISAAC. A native of Va.; surveyor, tanner, miller; member of colony that Daniel Boone brought to Jefferson County.

HITE, JACOB, 1792-1872. Descendant of Abraham, head of one of the first families to settle in Jefferson County, Ky.; possibly the Jacob who graduated from William and Mary, 1810.

HITE, SPENCER. Forty-two-year-old Negro slave taken by Anderson to Colombia, 1823.

HOLLEY, HORACE. New England native and onetime pastor of the Unitarian South End Church in Boston; President of Transylvania University, 1818-1827.

HOLMES, URIEL, 1764-1827. Born in East Haddam, Conn.; state representative, 1803-1805; U.S. Representative, 1817-1818.

HOUGH, EDWARD, 1759-1820. Soldier in the Revolutionary War; later attorney in Chillicothe, Ohio.

HUGHES, DOCTOR I. N. Onetime head of a hospital in Louisville, where he died in 1853.

HUGHES, CAPTAIN or MAJOR JOHN. Served in the U.S. Army, Third Infantry, 1808-1809; died in Ky., October, 1848.

HUNTER, CAPTAIN JAMES. Born in Ky.; entered U.S. Army in 1811; fought at Fort Stephenson, Ohio, with George Croghan, discharged as a Captain in June, 1814; elected to Ky. senate, 1817.

HURTADO, MANUEL JOSÉ, 1784-1845. Colombian Senator and Minister to Britain, 1824.

IBÁÑEZ, BERNARDINA. The daughter of Lt. Colonel Manuel Ibáñez of the Colombian Army; described by R. Bache, *Notes Taken in Colombia in the Years 1822-1823:* "Her figure is finely rounded, and beautifully proportioned, her countenance languishing, and sprightly by turns." Bache was the victim of one of Bernadina's practical jokes when she dumped a bottle of cologne on him at a dance in Bogotá.

IBÁÑEZ, SEÑORA MANUEL. Wife of Lt. Colonel Manuel Ibáñez, Colombian Army.

ILLINGWORTH, JOHN. Joined firm of Jones, Powles, Herring and Company in Bogotá, 1824; name later added to the firm, which owned gold and silver mines in Antioquia and Margarita, Colombia.

INFANTE, COLONEL LEONARDO. Venezuelan Colonel; tried for the murder of Lt. Francisco Pérdomo in Bogotá; executed on March 26, 1825.

IRVING, WILLIAM, 1776-1821. Born in New York City; brother of Washington Irving; U.S. Representative from N.Y., 1814-1819.

ITURBIDE, AUGUSTÍN, 1783-1824. "Elected" Emperor of Mexico, May 21, 1822; resigned March 19, 1823, and went to Europe; returned in 1824 posing as a champion of Mexican nationalism; declared an outlaw; captured and executed on July 19, 1824.

JACKSON, ANDREW, 1767-1845. Both N.C. and S.C. claim his birthplace; moved to Nashville; delegate to Tennessee Constitutional Convention, 1796; U.S. Representative, 1796-1797; U.S. Senator, 1797-1798; Tenn. Supreme Court, 1798-1804; served in Creek War and victor in Battle of New Orleans (War of 1812); commander of expedition to Florida, 1817; U.S. Senator, 1823-1825; President, 1829-1837.

JEFFERSON, THOMAS, 1743-1826. Born in Old Shedwell, Va.; member of Continental Congress, 1775-1776; Chairman of

Committee drawing up Declaration of Independence; Governor of Va., 1779-1781; Minister to France, 1785-1789; Secretary of State, 1789-1793; Vice President, 1797-1801; President, 1801-1809; founder of University of Va.

JESUP, ANN CROGHAN. Daughter of William and Lucy Clark Croghan; wife of Thomas Sydney Jesup.

JESUP, THOMAS SYDNEY, 1788-1866. Born in Va.; entered army; decorated in War of 1812; appointed General, May, 1818; served eight years in Ky. senate.

JOHNSON, RICHARD MENTOR, 1781-1850. Born at Bryants Station, Ky.; state representative, 1804-1807, 1819; Colonel in the War of 1812; U.S. Representative from Ky., 1807-1819; U.S. Senator, 1819-1829; U.S. Representative, 1829-1837; Vice President of U.S., 1837-1841.

JOHNSTON, COLONEL GABRIEL I. Trustee of the City of Louisville, 1797.

JONES, FRANCES GWATHMEY SKIDMORE. Sister of Anderson's wife, Elizabeth; first married Paul Skidmore (1815), then Hezekiah Jones (1819).

JONES, HEZEKIAH. Brother-in-law of Richard Clough, Jr.; married Frances Gwathmey Skidmore, 1819; died September, 1822.

JOYES, CAPTAIN THOMAS. Member of Ky. House of Representatives, 1824, 1826.

JUNCA. French merchant in Bogotá.

KING, RUFUS, 1755-1827. Born in Scarboro, Me.; Mass. delegate to Constitutional Convention, 1787; moved to New York City, 1788; U.S. Senator from N.Y., 1789-1796; U.S. Minister to Great Britain, 1796-1803; U.S. Senator, 1813-1825; again U.S. Minister to Great Britain, 1825-1826.

KNIGHT, GEORGE. Candidate for Ky. legislature, 1817; member of state senate from Shelby County, 1821.

LAFAYETTE, MARQUIS DE MARIE JOSEPH PAUL YVES ROCH GILBERT MOTIER, 1757-1834. French general and statesman; served in America during the Revolutionary War.

LATHAM, ALLEN. Married Maria Anderson, Richard C. Anderson's half-sister.

LATHAM, MARIA ANDERSON, 1798-1886. Anderson's half-sister; married Allen Latham of Chillicothe, Ohio, 1822.

LAWRENCE, LEVIN. Lived in Middletown, Ky., with wife and three sons; worked farm with the help of nine slaves (1810 Census).

LECOMPTE, JOSEPH, 1797-1851. Born near Georgetown, Ky.; served with Kentucky Riflemen in the Battle of New Orleans; state representative, 1819, 1822, 1838, 1839, 1844; U.S. Representative from Ky., 1825-1833.

LEIDERSDORF, SEGISMUNDO. Agent for Goldschmidt's, London bankers, in Bogotá.

LEIGH, BENJAMIN W., 1781-1849. Born in Chesterfield County, Va.; graduate of William and Mary College, 1802; state representative, 1811-1813, 1830, 1831; U.S. Senator, 1834-1836.

LELAND, AUGUSTUS. Boston merchant; co-owner of merchandizing business in Santa Marta, Colombia.

LEWIS, WILLIAM J., 1766-1828. Born in Augusta County, Va.; U.S. Representative, 1817-1819.

LITCHFIELD, DR. FRANKLIN. American from Baltimore; resident of Caracas, Venezuela, after 1810; married a Venezuelan; organized a business; U.S. Consul at Puerto Cabello during Anderson's residence in Colombia.

LITTELL, WILLIAM, 1768-1824. Printer; awarded contract to publish Ky. statutes, 1805; published other volumes of state court decisions; received honorary degree from Transylvania University, 1818.

LLOYD, JAMES, 1769-1831. Born in Boston; state representative, 1800, 1801; state senator, 1804; U.S. Senator, 1808-1813, 1822-1826; moved to Philadelphia, 1826.

LOGAN (TAH-GAH-JUTE), ca. 1725-1780. Indian Chief, Mingo tribe; in western Pa. and Ohio; friendly to whites until his family was massacred in 1774; there followed succession of attacks on isolated settlers in Ohio, which brought on Lord Dunmore's War; Logan defeated at Point Pleasant, but refused to sign treaty; served with British during the Revolution. See Cresap, Thomas.

LOGAN, ANN CLARK ANDERSON, 1790-1863. Sister of Anderson; married John Logan.

LOGAN, JOHN. Second son of Benjamin Logan (ca. 1743-1802); married Anderson's sister, Ann, 1808; state representative, 1815-1818; died 1826.

LOGAN, WILLIAM, 1776-1822. Born in Harrodsburg, Ky.; the

eldest son of Benjamin Logan (*ca.* 1743-1802); delegate to the state constitutional convention, 1799; state representative, 1803-1806, 1808; U.S. Senator from Ky., 1819-1820; unsuccessful candidate for governor, 1820.

LOWNDES, WILLIAM, 1782-1822. Born in St. Bartholomew Parish, S.C.; state representative, 1806-1810; U.S. Representative, 1811-1822.

LOWRY, ROBERT K. First U.S. commercial agent to the Spanish Main; lived in La Guayra (with some absences), 1810-1825; U.S. Consul there prior to death, 1825.

LUCAS, JOHN B. C., 1758-1842. Born in France; came to Pittsburgh, 1784; state representative, 1792-1798; U.S. Representative from Pa., 1803-1805; Judge of the U.S. Court in the Northern District of La., 1805-1820.

LUCKETT, CRAVEN P. Member of Ky. House of Representatives from Jefferson County, 1821; name appears frequently in issues of the *Louisville Correspondent* (1813 and 1816), as merchant and warehouse owner in the city.

LYNCH, JOHN. Englishman; served in the Colombian Army; acting British Consul in Lima, Peru, in 1822; later established business in Mompox, Colombia, on the Magdalena River.

LYTLE, GENERAL ROBERT. Farmer and real estate developer; fought in the War of 1812; died, 1849.

MCAFEE, ROBERT P., 1784-1849. Born in Mercer County, Ky.; state representative, 1819, 1831-1832; Lt. Governor, 1820-1824; U.S. Chargé d'Affaires to Colombia, 1833-1837.

MACCONNEL, WILLIAM. Co-author: *Digest of Kentucky Statutes to 1821.*

MACDONOUGH, THOMAS, 1783-1825. Born in Del.; entered U.S. Navy, 1800; commander of fleet on Lake Champlain, winning the Battle of Plattsburg against the British, September 11, 1814.

MCGREGOR, SIR GREGOR. Scottish adventurer; arrived in Caracas, 1811; Adjutant General under Francisco de Miranda, 1812; served as General of division under Simón Bolívar in Venezuelan campaigns against Spain; repeatedly distinguished himself in battle; among filibusters who temporarily took possession of Aurelia Island (off coast of Florida) in 1817; later established himself as "His Highness, Cacique of Poyais," over a portion of the Mosquito Coast (extended from Cape Honduras to Chiriquí Lagoon) ; dynasty began and ended with him; died 1845. (See Alfred Hasbrouck, "Gregor McGregor and the Colonization of Poyais, between 1820 and 1824," *Hispanic American Historical Review,* VII (Nov., 1927) 438-459.)

McLEAN, JOHN, 1791-1830. Born near Greensboro, N.C.; moved to Ky., then to Ill.; U.S. Representative from Ill., 1818-1819; state representative, 1820, 1826, 1828; U.S. Senator, 1824-1825, 1829-1830.

McNEAL, CHARLES. Acting U.S. Consul in Cartagena, February-July, 1825; resigned because of ill health.

MACON, NATHANIEL, 1757-1837. Born in Warren County, N.C.; private in the Revolutionary War; state senator, 1780-1882, 1784, 1785; U.S. Representative, 1791-1815; U.S. Senator, 1815-1828.

MADISON, GEORGE, 1763-1816. Born in Augusta County, Va.; moved to Ky.; served in the Revolutionary War with St. Clair; auditor of public accounts, Ky.; served in War of 1812; Governor of Ky., 1816.

MADISON, JAMES, 1751-1836. Born in Port Conway, Va.; member of Continental Congress, 1780-1783; delegate to Federal Constitutional Convention, 1787; U.S. Representative, 1789-1797; Secretary of State, 1801-1809; President 1809-1817.

MADISON, REVEREND JAMES. Appointed President of William and Mary College, 1777; died in 1812; succeeded by John Brocken. The *History of the College of William and Mary* (Baltimore, 1870) states: "Notwithstanding the depressed and impoverished condition of the College at the conclusion of the Revolutionary War, it speedily survived under the guidance and teachings of Bishop Madison and his associates. . . ."

MAINE, DR. HENRY GEORGE. Born in England, 1781; Chief Surgeon to the Army of Venezuela, 1818; served in the battles of Carabobo and Santa Marta; head of Colombian Military Hospital at Bogotá, 1824; returned to England, 1826.

MANHARDT, CHRISTIAN L. Native of Germany; migrated to Pa.; naturalized American citizen; came to Maracaybo in 1824 to obtain permission to place steamboats on Lake Maracaybo; recommended by Anderson for U.S. Consul at Maracaybo.

MARDERS, NATHAN, 1772-1862. Early emigrant from Va. to Middletown, Ky.

MARSHALL, HUMPHREY, 1760-1841. Born in Orlean, Va.; Captain in Revolutionary War; purchased a lot in Lexington, Ky., 1783; state representative, 1793, 1807, 1808, 1823; U.S. Senator, 1795-1801; author of first published history of Ky.

MARSHALL, JOHN JAMES, 1785-1846. Born in Woodford County, Ky.; state representative, 1815-1816; state senator, 1820-1824; circuit court judge, 1837-1846.

MASON, JONATHAN, 1752-1831. Born in Boston; state representative, 1786-1796; state senator, 1799-1800; U.S. Senator from Mass., 1800-1803; U.S. Representative, 1817-1820.

MASSIE, HENRY, 1779-1841. Married Helen Bullitt, daughter of Alexander Scott Bullitt; family emigrated from Europe to Va. in the early 1700's, then to Ky.

MASSIE, NATHANIEL. Assistant to Colonel Richard Clough Anderson in surveying land in Kentucky for distribution to soldiers holding land warrants for services in Revolutionary War.

MAUPIN, RICHARD. Student at William and Mary College, 1803.

MAURY, REVEREND. Resident of Albemarle County, Va.; son, Francis T., was student at William and Mary College with Anderson; operated a grammar school in Albemarle.

MERCER, CARVER. Elected a trustee of City of Louisville, May, 1809.

MERIWETHER, GEORGE WOOD. Grandson of Nicholas Meriwether (1749-1828), who came to Louisville from Va. in 1784; son of Richard and Susanna Meriwether.

METCALFE, THOMAS, 1780-1855. Born in Fauquier County, Va.; moved with parents to Fayette County, Ky.; state representative, 1812-1816; U.S. Representative, 1819-1828; Governor of Ky., 1829-1833; U.S. Senator, 1848-1849.

MILLER, DR. ROBERT, 1792-1857. Born in King William County, Va.; buried on the Miller-Woodsmall farm between Middletown and Jeffersontown, Ky.

MILLER, STEPHEN DECATUR, 1787-1838. Born in Lancaster District, S.C.; U.S. Representative from S.C., 1817-1819; state senator, 1822-1828; Governor of S.C., 1828-1830; U.S. Senator, 1831-1833.

MIRALLA, JOSÉ ANTONIO. Citizen of Buenos Ayres; left Louisville on same conveyance as Anderson; proceeded to Caracas, then to Bogotá; late resident of Havana; suspected of being agent to encourage Colombia to send expedition to secure

Cuban independence; frequent caller at Anderson's home in Bogotá; died in Bogotá [Anderson's diary, May 5, 1826.]

MIRANDA, LEANDRO. Son of the famed Venezuelan independence leader, Francisco de Miranda (1756-1816); born in England; moved to Caracas and became co-editor of *El Constitutional*, 1824.

MOLINA, DONNA. See Molina, Pedro.

MOLINA, PEDRO. Guatemalan minister to Colombia during Anderson's residence in Bogotá.

MONROE, JAMES, 1758-1831. Born in Westmoreland County, Va.; member of Confederation Congress, 1783-1786; U.S. Senator, 1790-1794; Minister to France, 1794-1796; Governor of Va., 1799-1802; Minister to France, 1803, to England, 1803-1807; Secretary of State, 1811-1817; President, 1817-1825.

MONROE, LT. JAMES. Nephew of President Monroe; accompanied the President to Charleston and other southern points, April, 1819.

MONTGOMERY, GENERAL RICHARD, 1738-1775. Born in Dublin, Ireland; after short career in army, moved to New York; married sister of Robert B. Livingston; member of provincial congress, 1775; as Brigadier General, marched into Canada (and with Benedict Arnold), laid seige to Quebec; killed in the assault, December 31, 1775.

MONTILLA, GENERAL MARIANO, 1782-1851. Commander of Colombian forces; blockaded the Spanish forces in Cartagena, 1821; later Intendant of the Department of the Magdalena.

MONTOYA. There were several Montoyas: FRANCISCO (1789-1862), wealthy merchant, co-negotiator with Manuel Antonio Arrúblas for an English bank loan to Colombia in 1824; JOSÉ MANUEL (1800-1833); JOSÉ MARÍA (1757-1834); and LUÍS, who joined Juan Manuel Arrúblas in inviting Anderson to a "Comida del Campo."

MORRISON, JAMES, 1775-1823. Born in Cumberland County, Pa.; moved to Lexington, Ky., 1792; legislator, businessman; army contractor; left legacy for building of Morrison Hall, Transylvania University.

MORROW, JEREMIAH, 1771-1852. Born near Gettysburg, Pa.; moved to Ohio, 1795; U.S. Representative from Ohio, 1803-1813; U.S. Senator, 1813-1819; Governor, 1822-1826.

MOSQUERA, DON JOAQUIN, 1787-1882. Patriot-orator; Colombian minister to Peru, 1821; elected President of Colombia, May 4, 1830; soon ousted by General Rafael Urdaneta.

MUMFORD, GEORGE. Born in Rowan County, N.C.: U.S. Representative, 1817-1818; died December 31, 1818.

NELSON (no known first name). The *Louisville Correspondent*, February 12, 1816, contained a mention of Nelson, "a Negro man, 5′ 10", 19 years old," then in jail.

NELSON, HUGH, 1768-1836. Born in Yorktown, Va.; state senator, 1786-1791; U.S. Representative, 1811-1823; Minister to Spain, 1823-1825.

NELSON, JUDGE WILLIAM. Appointed Professor of Law at William and Mary College, 1804.

NESBITT, WILSON. Born in Spartanburg, S.C.; state representative, 1810-1814; U.S. Representative, 1817-1819; moved to Alabama; died May 13, 1861.

NOEL, JUDGE SILAS N. Associate judge, Kentucky circuit courts in the early nineteenth century.

O'BANNON, PRESLEY N. Elected to Ky. Senate from Logan County, 1817.

O'FALLON, BENJAMIN, 1793-1842. Born in Ky., possibly Lexington; son of Dr. James and Eleanor (Clark) O'Fallon; lived early life in St. Louis; Indian agent at Prairie de Chien, 1817, for upper Mo., 1819; Major, U.S. Army, 1819; signed 15 treaties between the U.S. and Indian tribes of upper Mo., 1825.

O'FALLON, DR. JAMES. Born in St. Louis; first husband of Frances Eleanor Clark, the sister of George Rogers Clark; father of Benjamin O'Fallon; died *ca.* 1800.

OGELSBY, SAMUEL. Elected to Kentucky House of Representatives, 1819.

ORMSBY, JUDGE STEPHEN, 1759-1844. Born in County Sligo, Ireland; lawyer in Danville, Ky., 1786; judge in circuit court, 1802-1810; U.S. Representative from Ky., 1811-1813, 1813-1817; first president of branch of U.S. Bank in Louisville, 1817.

OTIS, HARRISON GRAY, 1765-1848. Born in Boston; state representative, 1796; 1802-1804; state senator, 1805-1816; U.S. Representative from Mass., 1797-1801; U.S. Senator, 1817-1822; Mayor of Boston, 1829-1832.

OVERTON, JOHN. Member of family owning Overton's Mill on Otter Creek, near Louisville.

OWEN, JAMES, 1784-1865. Born in Bladen County, N.C.; state

representative, 1808-1811; U.S. Representative from N.C., 1817-1819.

PADILLA, GENERAL JOSÉ, 1778-1828. Born in Rio de la Honcha; acquired titles of both Commodore and General in the wars of independence; convicted for conspiring against Bolívar's regime and executed, 1828.

PÁEZ, GENERAL JOSÉ ANTONIO, 1790-1873. Born on northern edge of Venezuelan plains, 1790; earned fame as a cavalry leader during the Battle of Carabobo, June, 1821; led an abortive revolution against the government in 1826, but under pressure by Bolívar the movement was quelled and Páez was named "Civil and Military Chief of Venezuela"; President of Venezuela after the dissolution of *La Gran Colombia;* left country, 1863; died in New York, May 7, 1873.

PAGE, JOHN, 1744-1808. Born in Gloucester County, Va.; graduate of William and Mary, 1763; state representative, 1781-1783, 1785-1788, 1797, 1798, 1800, 1801; U.S. Representative from Va., 1789-1797; Governor, 1802-1805.

PATTERSON, THOMAS, 1764-1841. Born in Lancaster County, Pa.; U.S. Representative, 1817-1825.

PATTON, BENJAMIN. Served in Ky. Senate, 1817.

PICKERING, TIMOTHY, 1745-1829. Born in Salem, Mass.; Adjutant General in the Revolutionary War; Postmaster General, 1791-1795; Secretary of War, 1795; Secretary of State, 1795-1800; U.S. Senator from Mass., 1803-1811; U.S. Representative, 1813-1817.

PICKMAN, WILLIAM. Married to Caroline Silsbee, daughter of Nathaniel Silsbee; see also Silsbee, Nathaniel.

PIERSON, WALTER. Resident of Jefferson County, Ky.

PINDALL, JAMES, ca. 1783-1825. Born in Monongahela County, Va.; state senator, 1808-1812; U.S. Representative, 1817-1820.

PITT, WILLIAM, 1759-1806. British statesman; second son of William Pitt, first Earl of Chatham; educated at Cambridge; Prime Minister of England before age of 25.

POMEROY, GEORGE AND THOMAS. Owners of the first tracts of land sold in Middletown, Ky.; owned twelve acres of land on Floyd's Fork, east of Louisville.

POPE, ALEXANDER. Represented Jefferson County in Ky. House of Representatives, 1821, 1822.

POPE, JOHN, 1770-1845. Born in Prince William County, Va.; came to Ky. as a boy; state representative, 1802, 1806, 1807;

U.S. Senator, 1807-1813; state senator, 1825-1829; Governor of Ark. Territory, 1829-1835; U.S. Representative from Ky., 1837-1843.

POPE, NATHANIEL, 1784-1850. Born in Louisville, Ky.; moved to Mo., then to Ill.; delegate from the Ill. Territory to Congress, 1816-1818; U.S. judge for the District of Ill., 1818-1850.

PORTER, DAVID, 1780-1843. Born in Boston; entered Navy as midshipman; Captain in 1812; served in West Indies, War with Tripoli, and War of 1812 (South Pacific); Board of Naval Commissioners, 1815-1823; Commander of the West Indies Squadron, 1824; court-martialed and suspended for unauthorized seizure of a Puerto Rican fort; resigned from Navy, 1826; Rear Admiral, Mexican Navy, 1826-1829; U.S. Chargé d'Affaires to Turkey, 1831-1839, Minister, 1839-1843.

PORTER, PETER BUELL, 1773-1844. Born in Salisbury, Conn.; practiced law in New York; state representative, 1802 and 1828; U.S. Representative, 1809-1813, 1815-1816; Major General in the War of 1812; Secretary of War, 1828-1829.

PRATHER, THOMAS. First president, Bank of Kentucky in Louisville, 1812.

PRESTON, JOHN WILLIAM. Colonel during the Revolutionary War; moved to Louisville, 1815; died, 1821.

PRIEST, LUCY GWATHMEY. Sister of Elizabeth, Anderson's wife; married Peter Priest. See Introduction.

QUARLES, TUNSTALL, *ca.* 1770-1855. Born in King William County, Va.; moved to Ky.; state representative, 1796, 1811, 1812; U.S. Representative, 1817-1820; state representative, 1828; state senator, 1840.

QUARTEL, COLONEL H. (?) W. DE Commissioned by The Netherlands in 1824 to obtain modifications in Colombian laws relative to the trade of Curaçao.

QUERRY, CHARLES. Farmer of Jefferson County, Ky.; family of fourteen; owner of ten slaves.

QUINCY, JOSIAH, 1772-1864. Born in Boston; state senator, 1804, 1805; U.S. Representative, 1805-1813; state senator, 1813-1820; state representative, 1821, 1822; Mayor of Boston, 1823-1827; President of Harvard University, 1829-1845.

RANDOLPH, JOHN, 1773-1833. Born in Prince George County, Va.; U.S. Representative, 1799-1813, 1815-1817, 1819-1825,

1827-1829, 1833; U.S. Senator, 1825-1827; Minister to Russia, 1830.

RENNICK, GEORGE. Born in October, 1775; lived in Bardstown and Frankfort, Ky.

RESTREPO, DR. JOSÉ FÉLIX DE, 1760-1832. Colombian educator, humanitarian, and statesman; born in Medellin, Colombia, 1760; framed a bill designed to free the slaves in Colombia, 1816; President of Congress to Cúcuta (1821), which drafted Constitution of Colombia; later member of the High Court of Colombia; professor, Colegio de San Bartolomé.

RESTREPO, DR. JOSÉ MANUEL, 1781-1863. Distinguished historian; executive officer in Antioquía, 1814-1815; later Minister of Interior of *La Gran Colombia;* member of the unsuccessful peace commission to Quito (1832) to discuss boundary dispute with General Juan José Flores; author: *Historia de la revolución de la republica de Colombia,* 10 vols., Paris, 1827.

REVENGA, JOSÉ RAFAEL, 1781-1852. Agent to Washington, 1811; Secretary to Bolívar, 1815; Secretary of Hacienda; mission to Spain (1821); mission to Europe (1823) to straighten out Colombian financial affairs; succeeded Pedro Gual as Minister of Foreign Affairs.

RICE, MAJOR. Probably the son of David Rice, Presbyterian leader in early Ky. and figure in drafting of first state constitution.

RIVERO, DR. MARIANO EDUARDO DE. Born in Peru; studied in England, France, and Germany; Director of National Museum and head of school of mineralogy, Bogotá; died in Paris, 1857.

ROBERTSON, GEORGE, 1790-1874. Born in Mercer County, Ky.; U.S. Representative, 1817-1821; state representative, 1822-1827, 1848, 1851, 1852; Ky. secretary of state, 1828; justice of court of appeals of Ky., 1829-1834; professor of law at Transylvania University, 1834-1857.

ROBERTSON, THOMAS BOLLING, 1779-1828. Born near Petersburg, Va.; graduate of William and Mary; secretary of the La. Territory, 1807-1811; U.S. Representative from La., 1812-1818; Governor, 1820-1822; judge, U.S. Court for District of La., 1825-1827; returned to Petersburg, Va.

ROBINSON, WILLIAM DAVIS. American-born merchant and *bon vivant;* imprisoned in Mexico, 1816-1818, for alleged "seditious activities"; supplied muskets and naval stores for the Colombian armed services during the wars for independence; resident of Cartagena in 1823; died in Caracas, 1824.

RODNEY, CAESAR A., 1772-1824. Born in Dover, Del.; U.S. Representative from Del., 1803-1805; U.S. Attorney General, 1807-1812; state senator, 1815; U.S. Representative, 1821-1822; U.S. Senator, 1822-1823; Minister to Argentina, 1823-1824.

ROWAN, JOHN, 1773-1853. Born in York County, Pa.; moved to Louisville, Ky.; secretary of state of Ky., 1804-1806; U.S. Representative, 1807-1809; state representative, 1813-1817, 1822, 1824; U.S. Senator, 1825-1831; Minister to Two Sicilies, 1848-1850.

RUGGLES, BENJAMIN, 1783-1857. Born in Abington, Conn.; moved to Ohio; U.S. Senator, 1815-1833.

ST. CLAIR, GENERAL ARTHUR, 1734-1818. Born in Scotland; settled in Boston, 1762, then to Pa. frontier; Major General in Revolutionary War; Governor of Northwest Territory, 1789-1802.

SALAZAR, OLD MR. Father of José María de Salazar.

SALAZAR, JOSÉ MARÍA, 1785-1828. Colombian Minister to U.S., 1823-1827.

SANDERS, LEWIS. Born in Va., August 9, 1781; Lexington, Ky., businessman, stock raiser; early industrialist; died, 1861.

SANFORD, NATHAN, 1777-1838. Born on Long Island, N.Y.; U.S. attorney for the district of N.Y., 1803-1816; state representative, 1810, 1811; state senator, 1812-1815; U.S. Senator, 1815-1821, 1826-1831; chancellor of N.Y., 1823-1826.

SANTAMARÍA. Two Santamaría brothers, ANTONIO and MANUEL, figure prominently in the diary. Both owned nearby quintas, which they offered gratis for Anderson's use. He lived at one for a season, with Manuel taking most of his meals with him. Except when Antonio or Manuel is used, it appears impossible to determine which is intended. The R[AYMUNDO] Santamaría (1795-1868) was an Independence soldier, who later settled in Bogotá.

SANTANDER, FRANCISCO DE PAULA, 1792-1840. Colombian soldier, statesman, Vice President, President; characterized by Bolívar as "the man of laws"; shared honors with Bolívar for victory in Battle of Carabobo (1819); as Vice President under President Bolívar, practically governed Gran Colombia, 1821-1827; broke with Bolívar and departed for exile in

Europe; elected President of New Granada, 1832, and returned home via U.S.

SCOTT, JOHN, 1785-1861. Born in Hanover County, Va.; moved to Ind., then to Mo. Territory; delegate from Mo., 1816-1817, 1817-1821; 1821-1827.

SEBASTIAN, BENJAMIN, *ca.* 1745-1834. Born, possibly in Fairfax County, Va., in early years, a clergyman; moved to Jefferson County, Ky., c. 1784; involved in the Aaron Burr Conspiracy.

SERGEANT, JOHN, 1779-1852. Born in Philadelphia; state representative, 1808-1810; U.S. Representative, 1815-1823, 1827-1829, 1837-1841; appointed envoy to the ill-fated Panama Congress, 1826—never arrived.

SEYBERT, ADAM, 1773-1825. Born in Philadelphia; studied in Europe; U.S. Representative from Pa., 1809-1815, 1817-1819; author of scholarly articles in fields of chemistry and mineralogy; died in Paris.

SHAW, ROBERT. Va. farmer; moved to Ky., 1800; died, 1827.

SHELBY, GOVERNOR ISAAC. Born in Md., 1750; Governor of Ky., 1812-1816; during term of office took personal command of a division of state militia.

SHREVE, HENRY MILLER, 1785-1854. Steamboat inventor and captain; owner of warehouse in Portland, now part of Louisville; voyage of his "Washington" from New Orleans in 25 days created a sensation.

SILSBEE, NATHANIEL, 1773-1850. Born in Salem, Mass.; seaman and merchant; U.S. Representative from Mass., 1817-1821; state representative, 1821; state senator, 1823-1825; U.S. Senator, 1826-1835.

SILVA. Two prominent Silvas: General JOSÉ LAURENCIO, hero of battles of Carabobo (1821), Ayacucho and Junín (1824), one of the executors of Bolívar's last will and testament (1830); Commander RUDICENDO, allegedly involved in conspiracy against Bolívar in 1828. The diary (May 5, 1826) states, however, that Anderson's friend Silva had died during the previous two years. There were also Colonel JOSÉ REMIGIO Silva, who was involved in the Independence struggle in Peru, and MANUEL ANTONIO Silva. Exact identification appears to be impossible.

SIRAKOWSKI, COLONEL FERDINAND. Polish descent; Chief of Squadron under Bolívar during war for independence; Captain of Guard in Bogotá, 1822; promoted to Lt. Colonel; assigned task of inspecting and testing equipment and munitions purchased for Colombian army.

SKIDMORE, FRANCES (FANNY) GWATHMEY. Anderson's sister-in-law; married Paul Skidmore (1815) and Hezekiah Jones (1819).

SKIDMORE, PAUL. Married Frances Gwathmey; owner of the first iron foundry in Louisville, established in 1811; sold to Joshua Headington, then to David Prentice; factory employed 60 workers and made, among other things, steam engines; died, 1818.

SLAUGHTER, GABRIEL. Born December 12, 1767, Culpepper County, Va.; moved to Mercer County, Ky.; state representative, 1801-1808; Lt. Governor, 1808; commander of regiment at Battle of New Orleans; again Lt. Governor, 1816; on the death of Governor George Madison, became Lt. Governor and Acting Governor, 1816-1820.

SMITH, SAMUEL, 1752-1839. Born in Carlisle, Pa.; moved to Baltimore, 1759; Lt. Col. in Revolutionary War; state representative, 1790-1792; U.S. Representative from Md., 1793-1803, 1816-1822; U.S. Senator, 1803-1815, 1822-1833; Mayor of Baltimore, 1837.

SMITH, THOMAS LEE. Major in War of 1812; resigned July 27, 1815; died, 1872.

SMITH, WILLIAM, 1762-1840. Born in N.C.: migrated to Charleston, S.C.; U.S. Representative from S.C., 1797-1799; state senator, 1802-1808; U.S. Senator, 1816-1823, 1826-1831; state representative, 1824-1826; moved to La., 1831, to Ala., 1833; Ala. state representative, 1835-1839.

SNEED, ACHILLES. Clerk, Ky. Court of Appeals, 1814-1820; forced to turn over records to the New Court, created by legislative act.

SOUBLETTE, GENERAL CARLOS. Venezuelan soldier during the wars for independence; held various positions in the government of La Gran Colombia, including Governor of Cartagena and Intendant General of Venezuela; died in 1870.

SOUTHARD, SAMUEL LEWIS, 1787-1842. Born in Somerset County, N.J.; state representative, 1815; U.S. Senator, 1821-1823; Secretary of Navy, 1823-1829; Governor of N.J., 1832-1833; U.S. Senator, 1833-1842.

SPEED, THOMAS, 1768-1842. Born in Charlotte County, Va.; moved to Ky., 1782; Major in War of 1812; U.S. Representative from Ky., 1817-1819; state representative, 1821, 1822, 1840; connected, wrote one Kentuckian, "with most of the events which form the history of Kentucky in the first half of the 19th century."

STANDIFORD, DAVID. Listed in the 1800 Census reports as a resident of Shelby County, Ky.

STOKES, MONTFORT, 1762-1842. Born in Lunenburg County, Va.; served in Continental Navy during the Revolutionary War; settled in N.C. after war; assistant clerk of the state senate, 1786-1790; U.S. Senator, 1816-1823; state senator, 1826-1829; state representative, 1829-1830; Governor of N.C., 1830-1832.

STONE, JOHN SEELEY, 1795-1882. Born in West Stockbridge, Mass.; graduate of Union College; entered theological seminary; rector of various churches after graduation, 1824.

STOPFORD, COLONEL EDWARD. Came to Colombia in 1819 in the British battalion commanded by Colonel James T. English; remained in Colombia, except for trips back to England; founded the newspaper, *El Colombiano*, 1823, published in English and Spanish.

STORY, JOSEPH, 1779-1845. Born in Marblehead, Mass.; state representative, 1805-1807, 1811; U.S. Representative, 1808-1809; Justice of U.S. Supreme Court, 1811-1845; author of numerous works on the law.

SUCRE, ANTONIO JOSÉ DE, 1795-1830. "Grand Marshal of Ayacucho"; victories in Battles of Pichincha (1822), Junín (1824), Ayacucho (1824) forced the Spanish to withdraw their forces from Peru and Charcas (Spanish colonies were free); president of Constitutional Convention in Bogotá, 1830; assassinated en route from Bogotá to Quito, June 4, 1830.

SUTHERLAND, CHARLES B. British Consul at Maracaybo during Anderson's residence in Bogotá.

TAIT, CHARLES, 1768-1835. Born in Hanover County, Va.; moved to Ga., 1783; lawyer-professor, 1789-1803; judge of a Ga. circuit court, 1803-1809; U.S. Senator, 1809-1819; U.S. district judge in Ala., 1820-1826.

TAYLOR, MAJOR EDMUND HAINES. Entered the army, February 1793; honorably discharged, 1800; operated a ferry at Jeffersonville, Ky.

TAYLOR, HARRISON. Surveyor; emigrated to Ky. in the latter part of the eighteenth century.

TAYLOR, REUBEN. Farmer of Jefferson County, Ky.; owned thirty slaves, according to the 1810 Census.

TAYLOR, GENERAL RICHARD, 1744-1829. Father of President Zachary Taylor; moved to Ky., 1785; owned 10,000 acres in seven Ky. counties, plus valuable lots in Louisville; 700-acre farm on Beargrass Creek located about three miles from the Anderson home, Soldiers' Retreat.

TAYLOR, RICHARD, 1770-1830. Came to Frankfort from Winchester, Va., *ca.* 1800.

TAYLOR, THOMPSON. Elected to the Ky. House of Representatives in 1802 and 1805; listed in the 1810 Census Report as a resident of Jefferson County.

TAYLOR, ZACHARY, 1784-1850. President of the United States, 1849-1850; born in Orange County, Va.; entered the Army, 1808; Major, 1812; Colonel, 1832; commander of U.S. forces in northern Mexico during Mexican War; elected President, 1848; died July 9, 1850.

TERRELL, WILLIAM, 1778-1855. Born in Fairfax County, Va.; moved with parents to Ga.; state representative, 1810-1813; U.S. Representative, 1817-1821.

THOMSON, JAMES, 1700-1748. English poet and author; not to be confused with James Thomson, who traveled in Latin America in this period. See Select Bibliography.

THORNDIKE, ISRAEL, 1755-1832. Born in Beverly, Mass.; fought in the American Revolution; leader in finance and public affairs; carried on extensive business with the Orient; home was a social and business center; elected thirteen times to Mass. legislature.

THRUSTON, J. BUCKNER, 1764-1845. Born in Gloucester County, Va.; moved to Lexington, Ky.; judge in Ky. courts, 1791, 1802, 1803; U.S. Senator, 1805-1809; judge of U.S. Circuit Court for District of Columbia, 1809-1845.

TICKNOR, GEORGE, 1791-1871. Born in Boston; professor at Harvard, 1817-1835; authority on Spanish literature; close friend of Edward Everett, editor of *North American Review*.

TODD, CHARLES S., 1791-1871. Born in Danville, Va.; graduate of William and Mary, 1809; moved to Lexington, Ky., to practice law; state representative, 1817, 1818; married daughter of Governor Isaac Shelby, 1816; "Confidential Agent" to Colombia, 1820-1823; later a farmer, editor of the *Cincinnati Republican;* Minister to Russia, 1841-1846; died at Baton Rouge, La.

TODD, THOMAS, 1765-1826. Born in Va.; moved to Ky.; Chief Justice of Ky., 1792-1806; 1807, Associate Justice of U.S. Supreme Court for the new circuit composed of Ky., Tenn., and Ohio.

TOMLINSON, JESSE. Owner of one of the oldest tavern-hotels in U.S., 14 miles from the Youghiogheny River in Pa.; visited by Anderson en route to Washington.

TOMPKINS, DR. BENJAMIN, HENRY, and WILLIAM. Brothers; all lived in Louisville; nephews of Anderson's stepmother, Sarah Marshall Anderson. The diary is not always clear on which one is intended.

TOMPKINS, DANIEL D., 1774-1825. Born in Westchester County, N.Y.; state representative, 1803; Governor, 1807-1817; Vice President of U.S., 1817-1825.

TORRENS, COLONEL JOSÉ ANASTASIO. The Mexican chargé in Bogotá, 1825-1826.

TRIMBLE, DAVID, 1782-1842. Born in Frederick County, Va.; moved to Mount Sterling, Ky.; quartermaster during War of 1812; U.S. Representative from Ky., 1817-1827.

TUCKER, HENRY ST. GEORGE, 1780-1848. Born in Williamsburg, Va., graduate of William and Mary College, 1798; Captain in War of 1812; U.S. Representative, 1815-1819; president of Va. court of appeals, 1831-1841; professor of law at University of Va., 1841-1845; author of Tucker's Commentaries.

TYLER, EDWARD. Trustee, City of Louisville, 1819-1820.

UMAÑA, CARLOS DE, 1780-1851. Intendant of Bogotá, 1823-1825.

URDANETA, GENERAL RAFAEL, 1789-1845. General during Venezuelan independence struggle; later Senator, Minister of State, Minister to Spain, and Minister to France; died in Paris, 1845.

VAN WYCK, THEODORUS. Attorney in Sullivan County, N.Y.

VÉLEZ, ALEJANDRO, 1794-1841. Colombian Consul General and chargé ad interim in Washington.

VON HUMBOLDT, ALEXANDER, 1769-1859. German naturalist, traveler, and author.

VOORHIES, PETER G. Banker and large property holder in Frankfort, Ky.

WALKER, LUCY HILL. The daughter of Thomas Walker (1715-1794), who was a doctor, soldier, explorer, and merchant, and who married widow of Nicholas Meriwether; owned 11,000 acres in Albemarle County, Va.

WALLACE, WILLIAM BROWN. A friend of Anderson's father; born at "Ellersbee," Virginia, July 26, 1757; died at Lawrenceburg, Ky., of cholera, 1833.

WARD, DAVID. Resident of Jefferson County, Ky.; owner of farm worked by 163 slaves.

WARFIELD, DR. ELISHA. There was a Dr. Elisha Warfield on the medical school faculty of Transylvania University, ca. 1800-1806; died, 1817.

WATTS, BEAUFORT T., ca. 1790-1869. Born in South Carolina; Secretary of American Legation, Bogotá, 1824-1826, Chargé, 1826-1828; Secretary of Legation, St. Petersburg, Russia, 1828-1829; private secretary and adviser to S.C. governors, 1834-1861.

WATTS, CHARLES. British Consul at Cartagena, Colombia, 1825.

WEBSTER, DANIEL, 1782-1852. Born at Salisbury (now Franklin), N.H.; U.S. Representative from N.H., 1813-1817; moved to Boston, 1816; U.S. Representative from Mass., 1823-1827; U.S. Senator, 1827-1841; U.S. Secretary of State, 1841-1843; U.S. Senator, 1845-1850.

WEISEGER, DANIEL. Clerk of Franklin County, 1803; opened tavern in Frankfort, 1806; President of the Bank of the Commonwealth, 1826; died in Frankfort, February 22, 1829.

WELLS, GENERAL SAMUEL. Active in the American Revolution and in early Ky. politics; owned Wells' Station, three and one-half miles northwest of Shelbyville, Ky.; died, 1828.

WELLS, YELVERTON P. Farmer in Jefferson County; owned, according to the 1810 Census Report, four slaves.

WELSH, JOHN. Native of Pennsylvania; came to Kentucky, 1790; successful farmer and influential politician.

WHITE, DAVID, 1785-1834. Born in Ky.; candidate for legislature, 1817; U.S. Representative, 1823-1825; state representative, 1826.

WHITE, LEE. Member of the Kentucky House of Representatives from Jefferson County, 1816 and 1821.

WILLIAMS, JOHN, 1778-1837. Born in Surry County, N.C.; lawyer in Knoxville, Tenn., 1803; Colonel in War of 1812; U.S. Senator from Tenn., 1815-1823; U.S. Chargé d'Affaires to

Central American Federation, 1825-1826; state senator, 1827-1828.

WILLIAMS, THOMAS H., 1780-1840. Born in N.C.; Acting Governor of Territory of Miss., 1806, 1809; collector of customs at the port of New Orleans, 1810; delegate to Miss. state constitutional convention; U.S. Senator from Miss., 1817-1829.

WILTHEW, CAPTAIN CHARLES. Englishman; arrived in Colombia, 1818; Adjutant General and Chief of Staff, British Battalion commanded by General José Antonio Páez; aide-de-camp of Vice President Santander.

WIRT, WILLIAM. 1772-1834. Born in Bladensburg, Md.; moved to Va.; counsel for the government at the Aaron Burr trial; served in the Va. House of Delegates; U.S. Attorney General, 1817-1829.

WITHERS, JOHN. Served in Ky. House of Representatives, 1812-1814.

WOODBINE, COLONEL GEORGE. Signed himself as "on His Britannic Majesty's service in Florida"; one of alleged instigators of Seminole Indian attacks that led to General Andrew Jackson's Florida Campaign, 1818; lived (1825) on San Andres, a small island off the Mosquito Coast; encountered by Anderson in Cartagena, on boat up Magdalena River, and in Bogotá; new interests included Atrato River (later considered a possible isthmian canal route), and Gregor McGregor's attempt to establish himself as ruler of Poyais; appointed "General, Knight of the Green Cross, and Vice-Caciqui" of Poyais. See McGregor, Sir Gregor.

WOOLFOLK, CATHERINE GWATHMEY. Anderson's sister-in-law; married George Woolfolk, 1817.

WOOLFOLK, GEORGE. Married Catherine Gwathmey, Anderson's sister-in-law, 1817; served in Ky. House of Representatives, 1822-1828.

WOOLFOLK, WILLIAM. Farmer in Jefferson County; brother of George Woolfolk.

YOUNG, COLONEL BROOKE. Englishman; served in the British battalion commanded by José Antonio Páez, 1819-1820; sailed for Venezuela on same boat as Anderson on his first trip to his post, 1823, and on his last trip down the Magdalena River, 1826.

SELECT BIBLIOGRAPHY ON RICHARD CLOUGH ANDERSON, *Jr.*, HIS FAMILY, AND HIS TIMES

Unpublished Material

Anderson-Latham Papers, Filson Club, Louisville, Ky.

Don Pedro Gual Correspondence (17 Letters), Library of Congress.

Henry Clay Papers, Library of Congress.

John Jordan Crittenden Papers, Library of Congress.

Kitty Anderson, "A Historical House and Its Famous People." Courtesy of Alexander F. Anderson.

Robert Anderson Papers, Library of Congress.

Rogers' Index of Kentucky Names, Filson Club, Louisville, Ky.

National Archives, Washington, D.C. Despatches from U.S. Ministers, Colombia, 1823-1826.

National Archives, Washington, D.C. Consular Letters, Colombia (Cartagena, La Guayra, Maracaibo, Porto Cabello, Santa Marta), 1823-1826.

Public Documents

Kentucky, General Assembly, House of Representatives. *Journal, 1815-1822.* Frankfort, 1815-1822.

Manning, William R. (ed.). *Diplomatic Correspondence of the United States Concerning the Independence of the Latin-American Nations.* 3 vols. New York, 1925.

Richardson, James D. (ed.). *A Compilation of the Messages and Papers of the Presidents, 1789-1897.* Vols. I and II. Washington, D.C., 1896.

International American Conference, 1st, Washington, D.C., 1889-1890. *Reports of Committees and Discussions Thereon . . . ,* Volume IV, Historical Appendix, *The Congress of 1826, at Panama, and Subsequent Movements Toward a Conference of American Nations.* Washington, D.C., 1890.

United States. *Census, 1810, Jefferson County Census, 1810.* Washington, D.C., 1934.

United States. *The Public Statutes at Large of the United States of America.* Vol. III. Boston, 1846.

United States, Congress. *Annals of Congress (Debates and Proceedings in the Congress of the United States).* Vols. XXXI-XLV. Washington, D.C., 1854-1856.

United States, Congress. *Biographical Directory of the American Congress, 1774-1949.* Washington, D.C., 1950.

United States, Congress. *The Register of Debates in Congress.* Vols. I and II. Washington, D.C., 1825-1826.

United States, Senate. *The Executive Proceedings of the Senate of the United States on the Subject of the Mission to the Congress at Panama, together with Messages and Documents Relating Thereto.* Washington, D.C., 1826.

Newspapers

Louisville Correspondent. 1813-1816.

Louisville Morning Post and Commercial Advertiser. 1822.

Kentucky Reporter (Lexington). 1814-1816.

National Gazette. Philadelphia, 1825.

National Government Journal and Register of Official Papers. Washington, D.C., 1825.

Daily National Intelligencer. Washington, D.C., 1917-1918; 1823-1826.

National Journal. Washington, D.C., 1823-1826.

Niles Weekly Register. Philadelphia, 1817-1818; 1824-1825.

Books and Periodicals

Adams, Charles Francis (ed.). *Memoirs of John Quincy Adams, Comprising Portions of his Diary from 1795 to 1848.* 12 vols. Philadelphia, 1874-1877.

Allen, James Lane. *The Bluegrass Region of Kentucky.* New York, 1892.

Anderson, Edward L. *The Andersons of Gold Mine, Hanover County, Virginia.* Cincinnati, 1913.

———. *Soldier and Pioneer: Biographical Sketch of Lt. Colonel Richard C. Anderson, 1750-1826.* New York, 1879.

Anderson, Isabel (ed.). *Larz Anderson [1866-1937]: Letters and Journals of a Diplomat.* New York, 1940.

Anderson, Richard C., Jr. "Constitution of Colombia," *North American Review*, III (1826), 314-349.

Anderson, Thomas McArthur. *A Monograph of the Anderson, Clark, Marshall and McArthur Connection*. N.p., [190?].

Anderson, William Pope. *Anderson Family Records*. Cincinnati, 1936.

An Officer of the Colombian Navy. *Recollections of a Service of Three Years during the Wars of Extermination in the Republics of Venezuela and Colombia*. 2 vols. London, 1828.

Appleton's Cyclopaedia of American Biography, ed. James G. Wilson and John Fiske. New York, 1888.

Ardery, Julia H. *Kentucky Records*. . . . Lexington, Ky., 1926.

Bache, Captain Richard. *Notes on Colombia taken in the Years 1822-23*. Philadelphia, 1827.

Baralt, Rafael María and Ramón Díaz. *Resumen de la historia de Venezuela*. 2 vols. Paris, 1841.

Bassett, John Spencer. *The Life of Andrew Jackson*. 2 vols. New York, 1911.

Bell, Annie Burns. *Record of Early Kentucky Marriages, 1785 to 1851 Inclusive*. . . . Frankfort, Ky., 1931.

Bemis, Samuel F. *John Quincy Adams and the Foundations of American Foreign Policy*. New York, 1949.

Bierck, Harold. *Vida pública de Don Pedro Gual*. Caracas, Venezuela, 1947.

Biographical Encyclopedia of the Commonwealth of Kentucky. Chicago-Philadelphia, 1896.

Brant, Irving. *James Madison*. 4 vols. Indianapolis, 1941-1961.

Capers, Gerald M. *John C. Calhoun—Opportunist: A Reappraisal*. Gainesville, Fla., 1960.

Clark, Don Elbert. *The West in American History*. New York, 1937.

Clark, Thomas D. *A History of Kentucky*. New York, 1937.

Cleaves, Freeman. *Old Tippecanoe: William Henry Harrison and His Time*. New York, 1939.

Clift, G. Glen. *Governors of Kentucky, 1792-1942*. Cynthiana, Ky., 1942.

Cochrane, Captain Charles S. *Journal of a Residence and Travels in Colombia during the years 1823 and 1824*. 2 vols. London, 1825.

Coit, Margaret L. *John C. Calhoun: American Portrait*. Boston, 1950.

Cooke, Mary Frances. *Story of Early Louisville*. Louisville, Ky., 1931.

Cresson, William P. *James Monroe*. Chapel Hill, N.C., 1946.

Dictionary of American Biography, ed. Allen Johnson. 20 vols. New York, 1928-1931.

Dictionary of National Biography. 21 vols. London, 1937-1938.

Duane, Colonel William. *A Visit to Colombia in the Years 1822 and 1823*. Philadelphia, 1826.

Ducoudray-Holstein, H. *Memoirs of Simon Bolívar.* . . . London, 1830.

Dunbar, Seymour. *A History of Travel in America.* . . . 4 vols. Indianapolis, 1915.

Earle, Alice M. *Stage-Coach and Tavern Days*. New York, 1900.

Enciclopedia Universal Ilustrada: Europea-Americana, ed. S. E. Calpe, 70 vols. Madrid, 1930.

Ford, Worthington (ed.). *Writings of John Quincy Adams*. 7 vols. New York, 1917.

Gardiner, C. Harvey (ed.). *Mexico, 1825-1828: The Journal and Correspondence of Edward Thornton Tayloe*. Chapel Hill, N.C., 1959.

Goebel, Dorothy B. *William Henry Harrison*. (Indiana Historical Collection, Vol. XLV). Indianapolis, 1926.

Gosselmann, Carl A. *Reise in Colombien in den Jahren 1825 und 1826*. 2 vols. Stockholm, 1829-1831.

Green, Philip Jackson. *The Public Life of William Harris Crawford*. Chicago, 1938.

Green, Thomas Marshall. *Historic Families of Kentucky*. Cincinnati, 1889.

Hall, Basil. *Extracts from a Journal Written on the Coasts of Chile, Peru, and Mexico in the Years 1820, 1821, 1822*. Philadelphia, 1824.

Hall, Francis. *Colombia: Its Present State*. Philadelphia, 1825.

———. *Letters Written from Colombia during a Journey from Caracas to Bogotá, and Thence to Santa Marta, in 1823*. London, 1824.

———. *Notes on Colombia Taken in the Years 1822-23, with an Itinerary of the Route from Caracas to Bogotá*. London, 1827.

Hamersly, Thomas H. S. (comp.). *Complete Army and Navy Register of the United States of America from 1776 to 1887*. New York, 1888.

Hamilton, Colonel J. P. *Travels Through the Interior Provinces of Colombia.* 2 vols. London, 1827.

Hamilton, Holman. *Zachary Taylor: Soldier of the Republic.* New York, 1941.

Hanson, Earl Parker. *Puerto Rico: Land of Wonders.* New York, 1960.

Hasbrouck, Alfred. *Foreign Legionaires in the Liberation of Spanish South America.* New York, 1928.

———. "Gregor McGregor and the Colonization of Poyais, Between 1820 and 1824," *Hispanic American Historical Review,* VII (Nov., 1927) , 438-459.

Hawkshaw, Sir John. *Reminiscences of South America: From Two and Half Years Residence in Venezuela.* London, 1838.

Henao, Jesus María and Gerardo Arrubla. *History of Colombia,* ed. J. Fred Rippy. Chapel Hill, N.C., 1938.

Ibañez, Pedro M. *Crónicas de Bogotá.* (Biblioteca de Historia Nacional) . 3 vols. Bogotá, 1913-1917.

James, Marquis. *Andrew Jackson: The Border Captain.* Indianapolis, 1938.

Jennings, Kathleen. *Louisville's First Families.* Louisville, Ky., 1920.

Jillson, Willard Rouse. *Kentucky Tavern: A Sketch of an Old Roadside Inn, Its Proprietor, William Owen, and His Family, 1787-1907.* Frankfort, Ky., 1943.

———. *Old Kentucky Entries and Deeds.* Louisville, Ky., 1926.

———. *Pioneer Kentucky.* Frankfort, Ky., 1934.

Johnson, Lewis F. *The History of Franklin County, Kentucky.* Frankfort, Ky., 1912.

Kerr, Judge Charles (ed.). *History of Kentucky,* by William Elsey Connelley and E. M. Coulter. 5 vols. Chicago-New York, 1922.

Kincaid, Robert Lee. *The Wilderness Road.* Indianapolis-New York, 1947.

King, Junie Estelle Stewart. *Abstracts of Early Kentucky Wills and Inventories.* Beverly Hills, Calif., 1933.

Koebel, W. H. *British Exploits in South America.* New York, 1917.

Lecuna, Vicente (ed.). *Cartas del Libertador.* 10 vols. Caracas, 1929-1930.

———. (ed.). *Crónicas razonada de las guerras de Bolívar.* 3 vols. New York, 1950.

———. (comp.) , and Harold Bierck (ed.) . *Selected Writings of Bolivar.* 2 vols. New York, 1951.

Levin, H. (ed.) . *Lawyers and Lawmakers of Kentucky.* Chicago, 1897.

Martin, Michael. *The New Dictionary of American History.* New York, 1952.

Mayo, Bernard. *Henry Clay: Spokesman of the New West.* Boston, 1937.

McAfee, John J. *Kentucky Politicians.* Louisville, Ky., 1886.

McElroy, Robert M. *Kentucky in the Nation's History.* New York, 1909.

McMurtrie, Henry. *Sketches of Louisville and Its Environs.* Louisville, Ky., 1819.

Mollien, G. *Travels in the Republic of Colombia in the Years 1822 and 1823.* London, 1824.

Morris, Richard B. *Encyclopedia of American History.* New York, 1953.

Mulhall, Michael G. *The English in South America.* Buenos Aires, 1878.

National Cyclopaedia of American Biography. Vols. I-XX. New York, 1898-1943.

Parks, E. Taylor. *Colombia and the United States, 1765-1934.* Durham, N.C., 1935.

Pitman, Robert Birks. *A Succinct View and Analysis of Authentic Information Extant in Original Works, on the Practicability of Joining the Atlantic and Pacific Oceans, by a Ship Canal Across the Isthmus of America.* London, 1825.

Posada, Eduardo. *Bibliografía Bogotana.* 2 vols. Bogotá, 1917-1925.

Restrepo, José Manuel. *Historia de la revolución de la república de Colombia.* 10 vols. Paris, 1827.

Riebel, Raymond. *Louisville Panorama: A Visual History of Louisville.* Louisville, Ky., 1954.

Riegel, Robert E. *America Moves West.* New York, 1956.

Rippy, J. Fred. *Rivalry of the United States and Great Britain over Latin America, 1808-1830.* Baltimore, 1929.

Robinson, Lee Lamar. *Kentucky in Washington . . . 1792-1928.* Louisville, Ky., 1928.

Robinson, William D. *A Cursory View of Spanish America, Particularly the Neighbouring Vice-Royalties of Mexico and New Granada.* Georgetown, D.C., 1815.

Smith, William Townsend. *A Complete Index to the Names of*

Persons, Places, and Subjects Mentioned in Littell's Laws of Kentucky. Lexington, Ky., 1931.

Steuart, J. *Bogotá in 1836-1837; Being a Narrative of an Expedition to the Capital of New Granada and a Residence There of Eleven Months.* New York, 1838.

Stevenson, W. B. *A Historical and Descriptive Narrative of Twenty Years in South America.* 3 vols. London, 1825.

Stickler, A. M. *The Critical Court Struggle in Kentucky, 1819-1829.* Bloomington, Ind., 1929.

Thomson, James. *Letters on the Moral and Religious State of South America, Written during a Residence of Nearly Seven Years in Buenos Aires, Chile, Peru, and Colombia.* London, 1827.

Van Deusen, Glyndon G. *The Life of Henry Clay.* Boston, 1937.

Virkus, Frederick A. (ed.). *The Abridged Compendium of American Genealogy.* . . . Chicago, 1925.

Walker, Alexander. *Colombia.* 2 vols. London, 1822.

The History of the College of William and Mary from Its Foundation, 1693, to 1870. Baltimore, 1870.

Willis, George L. *History of Shelby County, Kentucky.* Louisville, Ky., 1929.

Wiltse, Charles M. *John C. Calhoun, Nationalist, 1782-1828.* Indianapolis-New York, 1944.

INDEX